THE CRADLE SONG

To Sister Winifred
    from
Mr. and Mrs. John A. Crone
        of
    Astoria, Long Island.

G. MARTINEZ SIERRA

THE CRADLE SONG

And Other Plays

BY

(G. MARTINEZ SIERRA)

Martinez, Sierra Gregorio

IN ENGLISH VERSIONS WITH AN
INTRODUCTION BY

JOHN GARRETT UNDERHILL

NEW YORK
E. P. DUTTON & CO., INC.

First published ....April, 1923
Reissued with introduction.......February, 1929

This special one-volume edition made for
the Catholic Book Club, March, 1929.

1082

CONTENTS

	PAGE
INTRODUCTION	vii
THE CRADLE SONG	5
(*Canción de Cuna*)	
THE LOVER	77
(*El Enamorado*)	
LOVE MAGIC	95
(*Hechizo de Amor*)	
POOR JOHN	119
(*El Pobrecito Juan*)	
MADAME PEPITA	153

*Translated in collaboration with
May Heywood Broun*

INTRODUCTION

Gregorio Martínez Sierra was born at Madrid March 6, 1881, María de la O Lejárraga at San Millán de la Cogolla, a mountain village in the fertile wine-growing district of the Rioja, one year previously. They were married in 1899. Gregorio Martínez Sierra is not only a name but a penname, and the works which have appeared under it are the result of a collaboration that began even before marriage and has continued through all their books and plays ever since.

Precocious in talent, Gregorio attended the University of Madrid where he came to grief in history, doubtless, as he says, because of a settled aversion to battles. His affinity for formal study was slight. María, however, early associated herself with the educational system and was already established as a teacher in the public normal schools. Together they soon abandoned all thought of academic preferment and turned to literature as a career.

At seventeen, with the manuscript of his first book, *El poema del trabajo* ("The Song of Labor"), he presented himself to Jacinto Benavente, who furnished an introduction and arranged its publication which took place in 1898. Two series of prose poems, or pastels, as they were called in that day, followed, besides a collection of short stories, *Cuentos breves,* issued independently and attributed to María. In 1900 a novelette, *Almas ausentes* was awarded the prize in a contest conducted by the *Biblioteca Mignon.* This and other tales of the sort, subsequently appearing separately, have been reprinted in three volumes, *Abril melancólico* ("Melancholy April"), *El diablo se ríe* ("The Devil

Laughs"), and *La selva muda* ("The Silent Wood"). The most notable work in the shorter form, however, is contained in *Sol de la tarde,* or "Declining Sun," which established their reputation beyond cavil in 1904. To the same year belongs the first of two novels, "The Humble Truth," while a second and more popular venture in the field of fiction, "Peace" (*Tú eres la paz*), was composed two years later.

In the beginning an intellectual by temperament and a word-painter by inclination, Martínez Sierra may be characterized as an impressionist, well-versed in the procedure of the modern French schools. Perhaps the principal personal influence of his formative period was that of the poet Juan Ramón Jiménez, with whom he kept bachelor hall at Madrid. Other associations of these days were likewise predominantly literary, and leaders of the modern movement such as Antonio and Manuel Machado and the Catalan, Santiago Rusiñol, painter of gardens, proved themselves kindred spirits. Under their friendly stimulus, he published a volume of verse, *La casa de la primavera,* a chance excursion into an alien domain, as well as a prose poem upon "Hamlet in the Person of Sarah Bernhardt." With these works his "Dream Theatre" may be coupled, a quartet of symbolic, mystical dialogues with pronounced Maeterlinckian tendencies.

The first decade of the productivity of Martínez Sierra suggests little of the theatre. It was quietistic in feeling, essentially contemplative, a communion with idyllic and elegiac poets. Yet through these days another influence had been active, although less conspicuously, which in the end was to prove decisive. In the year immediately following the publication of "The Song of Labor," the Art Theatre was founded at Madrid by Benavente. The coöperation of the more promising of the younger generation was enlisted, among whom was Martínez Sierra, who played the rôle of Manuel in support of Benavente in the latter's comedy

"A Long Farewell" at the opening performance. The ensuing months were months of intimate association with a remarkable mind. "As I listened to him talk, the fundamental laws of the modern theatre were revealed to me, and I have profited by his instruction unceasingly." So, properly, Martínez Sierra had already served an apprenticeship in the theatre before he began to write plays. His début as a playwright was delayed for ten years, and was then made in collaboration with Rusiñol, with whom he composed a comedy entitled *Vida y dulzura,* presented at the Teatro de la Comedia, Madrid, in 1907. This was followed by *Aucells de pas,* also in collaboration with Rusiñol, produced in Catalan at Barcelona in 1908, and, after a further interval of two years, by *Cors de dona,* in Catalan by the same hands. Meanwhile, during the spring of 1909, Martínez Sierra attained his first independent success with the comedy in two acts, *La sombra del padre,* presented at the Lara Theatre, one of the favorite houses of the capital. *El ama de la casa,* ("The Mistress of the House,") was acted at the same theatre in 1910, and in 1911 he achieved a definitive and permanent triumph with the production of "The Cradle Song," (*Canción de cuna*). A companion piece *Los pastores,* ("The Two Shepherds"), was brought out in 1913, also at the Lara. As Martínez Sierra's non-dramatic prose becomes most nicely expressive, most pictorial and most imaginative in *Sol de la tarde,* his comedy attains perfection in these beautiful idyls of the religious life. Radiant with the bland charm and luminosity of the Andalusian sketches of the Quinteros, these comedies possess, nevertheless, a quality which is distinctive and personal, at once richer and humanly more significant than the work of any competitors in the *genre.* No other plays convey so convincingly, or with equal grace, the implications of environment as it interprets itself in terms of character, not symbolically nor in any didactic way, but directly and visually so that the ambient becomes the protagonist rather than the individual, and the spirit of the *milieu* is felt to express more clearly than words the fundamentals which condition its life.

"The Cradle Song" has been translated into many languages, and has been played and imitated widely throughout the civilized world. Ten years after the Madrid premiere Augustin Duncan hazarded four special matinees in English at the Times Square Theatre, New York, beginning in February, 1921, without, however, attracting support. A play in two acts was held to be revolutionary by the consensus of experts, and was thought to fall wholly without the purlieus of drama. During the same season a slighter piece, "The Romantic Young Lady" (*Sueño de una noche de agosto*), reached the London stage with Dennis Eadie, achieving a *succès d'estime*. The publication of the plays in translation fortunately attracted general attention, and it was not long before the wisdom of the pioneers had been justified. On November 2, 1926, "The Cradle Song" reappeared at the Fortune Theatre, London, with Miss Gillian Scaife, to be later transferred to the Little Theatre, where it completed a run of 109 performances, while Miss Eva LeGallienne brought her singularly fine and sensitive interpretation to the Civic Repertory Theatre, New York, during the following January, where it has been repeated 125 times. A special company headed by Miss Mary Shaw later travelled throughout the United States. Productions at the Playhouses of Oxford and Liverpool and the Abbey Theatre, Dublin, also deserve mention. Meanwhile "The Romantic Young Lady" was revived at the Neighborhood Playhouse, New York, with Miss Mary Ellis, "The Lover" presented at the Fortune Theatre and on tour through England and Scotland, and "Madame Pepita" at the Playhouse, Oxford and the Festival Theatre, Cambridge. "Love Magic," the first piece by Sierra to be acted in English (Waldorf-Astoria, New York, March 1918), "Poor John", "The Two Shepherds" and "Wife to a Famous Man" are all familiar in the little theatres of Great Britain and

America. Finally, during the fall of 1927, Miss Scaife and Mr. Eadie brought "The Kingdom of God" to the Strand Theatre, and the same play, staged and directed by Miss Ethel Barrymore, was recently chosen to inaugurate the new Ethel Barrymore Theatre in this city in December, 1928.

Martínez Sierra has now written some forty-six original plays which have been acted, in addition to the three composed in collaboration with Rusiñol. He has translated and adapted forty-seven plays, chiefly from the French, English and Catalan, besides making occasional excursions into German. Perhaps the most important translation is a five-volume edition of Maeterlinck. His non-dramatic works occupy thirty-two volumes to which six others of translations must be added. In the intervals of composition, he established and edited *Helios,* a short-lived literary periodical, and founded and directed the *Biblioteca Renacimiento,* one of the most prosperous and progressive publishing houses of the capital. He has also edited a library for the world's classics in translation, and more recently has established a publishing house of his own, the *Biblioteca Estrella.* In 1916 he assumed the management of the Teatro Eslava, Madrid, installing there a stock company, the *Compañía Lírico-Dramática Gregorio Martínez Sierra,* for the presentation of the modern repertory, prominently featuring his own plays. Whether from the point of view of acting or of *mise en scène,* this company must be accounted one of the most complete and satisfying in the peninsula. A Parisian engagement was undertaken successfully in 1925, and the company has since twice visited America, appearing first in a repertory of eighteen plays upon a tour extending from Buenos Aires to New York, terminating at the Forrest Theatre in May 1927. An admirably printed and illustrated selection of monographs, *Un teatro de arte en España,* records the story of Sierra's tenancy of the Eslava and renders adequate tribute to Catalina Bárcena, the gifted and versatile actress around whom from the beginning the company has been built.

An artist who is subjected continually to the distractions of business, sacrifices with his leisure opportunity for detachment. Already, previous to the production of *Los pastores,* Martínez Sierra had manifested a tendency to approximate the main currents of the modern popular theatre. An improviser of unusual facility, he composed the slightest of musical comedies in *Margot* and *La Tirana;* a charming light opera libretto, *Las golondrinas* ("The Swallows"), based upon an earlier play, *Aucells de pas;* grand opera libretto in *La llama,* and the scenario of a dancing suite with music by Manuel de Falla for the gypsy *bailarina* Pastora Imperio. He remade old comedies, reworked juvenilia, republished forgotten stories, and dramatised his novel *Tú eres la paz* as *Madrigal.* He contrived pantomime. The lesser plays of this miscellaneous epoch become an epitome of the activities of the contemporary Madrid stage, broadened, however, by a thorough cosmopolitanism. They are eclectic, light-hearted, persistently gay, and, upon the more serious side, progressive documents considered from the sociological point of view. As he has grown older, Martínez Sierra has come to be interested not so much in the picturesque, in the life which is about to pass, as it lies inert in the present with all the remoteness of objective art, as he is in the future with its promise of the amelioration of the life which he formerly portrayed. He is an apostle of the new order, which is to be assured in his conception through the dissemination of a wider and more complete knowledge, a more truly international culture and sympathy, a keener social consciousness, and, more precisely and immediately, through the promotion of certain reforms. The more significant of the recent comedies, "The Kingdom of God" and *Esperanza nuestra* ("The Hope That is Ours") are indicative of this development. Although by no means didactic, they are purely social in genesis and in trend. Even his *Don Juan de España,* a re-embodiment of the traditional libertine celebrated by Tirso de Molina and by Zorrilla, is a Don Juan redeemed. Yet Sierra remains essentially a man of the theatre. As a social thinker, his ideas are general, by no chance controversial, rising little beyond a broad humanitarianism, temperately and engagingly expressed. "Letters to the Women of Spain," "Feminism, Femininity and the Spanish Spirit," and "The Modern Woman," all volumes of frankly confessed propaganda, are more effective because they persuade rather than provoke, avoiding partisan commitments or advocacies of any sort. They are quite as dispassionately impersonal as the plays. In these maturer works, as in those of Linares Rivas and Benavente, the modern movement, which during the earlier years of the century had been predominantly intellectual and aesthetic, turns toward the practical and political sphere, and fixes its attention upon results. It is the completion of the cycle which began in 1898.

Thirty years have slipped by since the publication of "The Song of Labor." Martínez Sierra is no longer a young man of promise. Soon he will be counted among the elders whose art has matured and attained its full extension, consolidated and ripened by experience. It is now possible to appraise his accomplishment and to determine with relative certainty his contribution to the contemporary theatre.

In this task, the secrets of a collaboration as intimate as it has been enduring, must of necessity be respected. We have no work avowedly solely by Martínez Sierra. Only one has been acknowledged by his wife as her own. Obviously, the letters and lectures in promotion of feminism are at least in great part by a feminine hand. Beyond question she is responsible for the major share of translation. An increasing proportion of the later output, also, may safely be attributed to her, more especially the collaborations with the poet Marquina and the actor Sassone, carried on during the absence of the Sierra troupe in America. Then "The Cradle Song" is a reminiscence of María's youth in Carabanchel, a town in which her father was convent doctor and where her sister took the veil, the Sister Joanna of the Cross of the play. Her intervention here has been confessed publicly. Yet these facts, though conceded, shed no light upon the basic problem, and provide no data for the identification of individual styles. A study of the earlier poems and stories might seem, indeed, to indicate that the elaboration and the subsequent simplification of the style are predominantly to be credited to Gregorio, while the bulk of actual composition—and to an increasing extent with the passing years—has been done by María.

Like the Quinteros, Sierra is primarily an optimist, a child of the sun. This is fundamental in his theatre and has not escaped the attention of the Spanish humorists:

"Glory to God in the highest,
    On earth peace, good will toward men!
    All's well with the world, says Martínez Sierra,
    And then says it again."

He is not, however, an optimist by virtue of high spirits or uncommon enthusiasms, or because he has found life pleasant and easy, but through his sensitiveness. It is an optimism that is partly aesthetic, partly emotional. His sympathies have led him to hope. He has faith in the human equation, trust in men rather than in measures. The law he esteems very little in face of the gentle wisdom whose increment is sure with the years. Social progress is individual progress and individual progress is spiritual progress whose conquests are recorded first in the heart. This, of course, is no new doctrine, but it is the core of Martínez Sierra's philosophy and the main-spring of his art. In so far as the Church is a liberating and humanizing force he is a Christian, but he is a dissenter from all creeds and doctrines which restrict and inhibit the upward march of man.

Curiously enough, as a playwright, Sierra, for all his tenderness, has little concern with the individual. This is the source of his calm. One of the most sensitive of men, he is also one of the most detached. His drama is expository, chiefly for the reason that the inception of his plays is invariably generic and abstract. They are illustrative each of some general axiom or principle, whether human or social. He is no apostle of personal causes. Every man must be suffered, none the less, to shape his own career—"Live Your Own Life." The old virtues are destined to make way before the advance of the new—"The Two Shepherds." Sometimes, again, he has paused to probe some universal passion or emotion, devotion as in "The Lover", or, as in "The Cradle Song", to echo the cry of the eternal mother instinct which has been stifled and denied. Sometimes, as in "Fragile Rosina", in a sportive mood, he is content to parade mere temperament or an idle trait. Plays like "The Cradle Song" and "The Kingdom of God" are eloquent too, above the plane of feeling, of a social scheme, a new, a better life. The course of the story is the setting forth of the idea, the impelling emotion in all its significant phases, now by direct statement, now through contrast, but, in whatever way it may be effected, the content is plainly implicit in the theme from the beginning to become evident in detail as the action proceeds. For this reason the volitional element, in so far as it passes beyond mere childish caprice, is almost wholly lacking. Sierra draws no villains, creates no supermen, heroically imposing their wills, inherits no complexes, and cherishes small love for the tricks of display. His taste is unfailingly nice. Mystery, however veiled, he abhors, complication of plot, all thrill of situation. He even flees those internal crises of character which are so absorbing to the great dramatists, through whose struggles personality is built up and self-mastery won. These savor always of violence and conflict, no matter how subjective or subtle they may be. They are drama of action, and Sierra's drama is static drama. He is content to sacrifice movement to visual quality, excitement to charm.

Although indubitably theatre of ideas, characteristically and fundamentally this is emotional theatre. It is live and warm. Naturally the spectacular ardors which have been associated time out of mind with the so-called emotional play have been discarded. Yet there is no more skilful purveyor of tears. The feeling is always direct, the presentation transparently clear. The playwright displays the intuitive grace of simple truth. The spectator sees and is persuaded without argument at sight. Life is depicted as a process of adjustment, a pervading harmony which influences the characters and tempers them to its key, so that they are never suffered to become intellectualized. This is the most extraordinary of Sierra's gifts. His men and women remain spontaneously human, unchilled by the ideas in which they have previously been conceived. Standing by themselves, it is true, they betray a tendency to pale and grow thin, because, like the action, they have been born of the theme, and acquire substance and vitality only as they fit into the general plan and merge themselves with the incidents and scenes which reflect their life history. It is an art compact of simplicities, so delicate and frail that it can exist authentically only at propitious moments. Every element must concur in the perfection of the whole. Absolute unity is indispensable. Character must synchronize with theme, dialogue with action, situation with background, until each at last becomes articulate in the other, through every shade of feeling and the concord of smiles and tears. Otherwise the spell is shattered and ceases to be. Comedy and pathos join as one. Sierra's art is a blending of the more tractable emotions, of technical elements and all the ingredients which go to make up a play, that is so complete as not to stop short of interpenetration. To achieve less for him means failure. In the rehearsal of memory, the people of the plays do not recur to the mind, nor the stories, nor any fragments nor striking features, but the atmosphere, the feeling, the impression of the ensembles. The plays live as emotion, pictures.

When posterity comes to assess the fame of Martínez Sierra, the non-dramatic works, despite their undoubted merits, beyond peradventure will be set to one side. Time will ignore, also, as it has already done in large measure, the purely theatrical, occasional pieces contrived to meet the needs of aspiring actors or to tide over the exigencies of importunate companies, including specifically his own. There will remain a body of plays, considerable in bulk, and notable, at least superficially, in variety. A surprising amount of the best work must be assigned to the plays in one-act. Few have wrought more happily in miniature, or have qualified more instinctively in the lesser *genre*. The briefer pieces are without exception deft and tenuous, by their very nature peculiarly congenial to a temperament that is shy and retiring and a method that is tactful and restrained. Sierra's success has been unquestioned in this field. In two acts, he has shown equal facility, profiting in addition by the superior dignity and weight which are corollaries of the larger scale. "The Cradle Song" is Martínez Sierra, the epitome of his virtues and the confutation of his detractors, while into this group fall also the major number of his more serious efforts often, perhaps, only by limitation of subject inferior to those better known. In drama of greater extension and presumably more profound import, prolonged through three or more acts, he has been less impressive. The expository method here becomes treacherous, for either the play or the audience in the end is obliged to move. Confronted by this dilemma, Sierra falls back upon episode, and takes refuge in devices which temporize to sustain the interest, and at best are purely conventional. The most noteworthy of the longer plays such as "The Kingdom of God", are in consequence properly sequences of one-act units, carefully assembled and held together by a common subject or related, it may be, by a single character which runs its course through them all. Still they preserve unity of atmosphere, still they plead unobtrusively their causes and retain the freshness of their visual appeal, but the problem at full length is more complex, position and juxtaposition of incident are not so potent nor so suggestive, while even the most skilfully graduated emotion proves unable except in the rarest instances to dispense with progressive action and a continuous story artfully unrolled. These are multiple dramas, spoken pageants. They are chronicles of the modern stage.

In the history of the theatre, only two names, Ramón de la Cruz and Quiñones de Benavente, both countrymen of Sierra's, have lived as creators of one-act plays. Sierra's title to fame has a broader basis. He has produced the popular masterpiece of the two-act style, already secure as an international classic. He has written also more perfectly than his contemporaries the Spanish realistic comedy of atmosphere, that gently sentimental, placid communion with patience and peace whose quiet falls like a benediction upon a restless world.

JOHN GARRETT UNDERHILL.

THE CRADLE SONG

COMEDY IN TWO ACTS
WITH AN
INTERLUDE IN VERSE

TEATRO LARA, MADRID
1911
TIMES SQUARE THEATRE, NEW YORK
1921

FORTUNE THEATRE, LONDON
1926

CIVIC REPERTORY THEATRE, NEW YORK
1927

TO JACINTO BENAVENTE

CHARACTERS

SISTER JOANNA OF THE CROSS, *18 years of age.*

TERESA, *aged 18.*

THE PRIORESS, *aged 40.*

THE VICARESS, *aged 40.*

THE MISTRESS OF NOVICES, *aged 36.*

SISTER MARCELLA, *aged 19.*

SISTER MARÍA JESÚS, *aged 19.*

SISTER SAGRARIO, *aged 18.*

SISTER INEZ, *aged 50.*

SISTER TORNERA, *aged 30.*

THE DOCTOR, *aged 60.*

ANTONIO, *aged 25.*

THE POET.

A COUNTRYMAN.

Also a Lay Sister, Two Monitors, and several other Nuns,
as desired.

ACT I

*A room opening upon the cloister of a Convent of Enclosed
Dominican Nuns. The walls are tinted soberly; the floor
is tiled. Three arches at the rear. In the right wall a
large door with a wicket in it, leading to a passage communicating with the exterior. A grilled peephole for looking out. Above the door a bell which may be rung from
the street. Beside the door an opening containing a re-
volving box, or wheel, on which objects may be placed and
passed in from the outside without the recipient's being
seen, or a view of the interior disclosed. Not far from
this wheel, a pine table stands against one of the piers of
the cloister. Ancient paintings relieve the walls. Through
the arches the cloister garden may be seen, with a well in
the middle; also a number of fruit trees, some greenery and
a few rose bushes. Beneath the arches, potted flowers—
roses, carnations, sweet basil, herb Louisa and balsam apple
—together with a number of wooden benches and rush-
seated chairs, and three arm chairs.*

As the curtain rises THE PRIORESS *is discovered seated in
the largest of the arm chairs, and* THE MISTRESS OF
NOVICES *and* THE VICARESS *in the smaller ones, the former
on the right, the latter on the left, well to the front. The
other* NUNS *are grouped about them, seated also. The
novices,* SISTER MARCELLA, SISTER JOANNA OF THE CROSS,
SISTER MARÍA JESÚS *and* SISTER SAGRARIO *stand somewhat to the right,* SISTER JOANNA OF THE CROSS *occupy-
ing the centre of the stage. The* LAY SISTER *and* SISTER
TORNERA *remain standing by the table at the rear.*

*It is broad day light. The scene is one of cheerfulness
and animation.*

SISTER SAGRARIO. Yes, do! Do! Do let her read them!

5

SISTER MARCELLA. Yes, do Mother! Do say yes!

PRIORESS. Very well. You may read them then, since you have written them.

SISTER JOANNA OF THE CROSS. I am very much ashamed.

MISTRESS OF NOVICES. These are the temptations of self-love, my child.

VICARESS. And the first sin in the world was pride.

SISTER JOANNA OF THE CROSS. They are very bad. I know you will all laugh at me.

VICARESS. In that way we shall mortify your vanity.

MISTRESS OF NOVICES. Besides, since we are not at school here, all that our Mother will consider in them will be the intention.

PRIORESS. Begin. And do not be afraid.

SISTER JOANNA OF THE CROSS. [*Reciting.*] To our Beloved Mother on the day of her Blessed Saint—her birthday:

> Most reverend Mother,
> On this happy day
> Your daughters unite
> For your welfare to pray.
> We are the sheep
> Who under your care
> Are seeking out Heaven—
> The path that leads there.
> On one side the roses,
> On the other the thorn,
> On the top of the mountain
> Jesus of Mary born.
> To Jesus we pray
> Long years for your life,
> And of the Virgin María
> Freedom from strife;
> And may the years vie
> In good with each other,
> In holiness and joy,
> Our dearly-loved Mother!

[*The nuns applaud and all speak at once.*]

SOME. Good! Very good!

OTHERS. Oh, how pretty!

SISTER TORNERA. They are like the Jewels of the Virgin!

SISTER INEZ. [*Depreciatively.*] She has copied them out of a book.

SISTER JOANNA OF THE CROSS. [*Carried away by her triumph.*] Long live our Mother!

ALL. [*Enthusiastically.*] Long live our Mother!

PRIORESS. Come, you must not flatter me, my children. The verses are very pretty. Many thanks, my daughter. I did not know that we had a poet in the house. You must copy them out for me on a piece of paper, so that I may have them to read.

SISTER JOANNA OF THE CROSS. They are copied already, reverend Mother. If your Reverence will be pleased to accept them . . .

[*She offers her a roll of parchment, tied elaborately with blue ribbons. The verses are written on the parchment and embellished with a border of flowers, doves and hearts, all of which have been painted by hand.*]

PRIORESS. [*Taking and unrolling the parchment.*] Bless me! What clear writing and what a beautiful border! Can you paint too?

SISTER JOANNA OF THE CROSS. No, reverend Mother. Sister María Jesús copied out the verses, and Sister Sagrario painted the border. Sister Marcella tied the bows.

SISTER MARCELLA. So it is a remembrance from all the novices.

PRIORESS. And all the while I knew nothing about it! The children have learned how to dissimulate very skilfully.

SISTER JOANNA OF THE CROSS. We had permission from

Mother Anna St. Francis. She gave us the ribbon and the parchment.

PRIORESS. No wonder, then. So the Mother Mistress of Novices knows also how to keep secrets?

MISTRESS OF NOVICES. Once . . . Only for to-day. . .

SISTER JOANNA OF THE CROSS. Today you must forgive everything.

PRIORESS. [*Smiling.*] The fault is not a grave one.

VICARESS. [*Acridly.*] Not unless it leads them to pride themselves upon their accomplishments. The blessed mother Santa Teresa de Jesús never permitted her daughters to do fancy work. Evil combats us where we least expect it, and ostentation is not becoming in a heart which has vowed itself to poverty and humility.

MISTRESS OF NOVICES. Glory be to God, Mother Vicaress, but why must your Reverence always be looking for five feet on the cat?

[SISTER MARCELLA *laughs flagrantly.*]

VICARESS. That laugh was most inopportune.

SISTER MARCELLA. [*Pretending repentance, but still continuing to laugh in spite of herself.*] I beg your pardon, your Reverence, I didn't mean it. This sister has such temptations to laugh, and she can't help it.

VICARESS. Biting your tongue would help it.

SISTER MARCELLA. Don't you believe it, your Reverence. No indeed it wouldn't!

PRIORESS. [*Thinking it best to intervene.*] Come, you must not answer back, my daughter. Today I wish to punish nobody.

VICARESS. [*Muttering.*] Nor today, nor never!

PRIORESS. [*Aroused.*] What does your Reverence mean by that, Mother Vicaress?

VICARESS. [*Very meekly.*] What we all know, reverend Mother—that the patience of your Reverence is inexhaustible.

PRIORESS. Surely your Reverence is not sorry that it is so?

VICARESS. [*Belligerently.*] Not upon my account, no. For by the grace of God I am able to fulfil my obligation and accommodate myself to the letter and spirit of our holy rule. But there are those who are otherwise, who, encouraged by leniency, may stumble and even fall . . .

PRIORESS. Has your Reverence anything definite in mind to say? If so, say it.

VICARESS. I have noticed for some time—and the Lord will absolve me of malice—that these "temptations to laugh" of which Sister Marcella speaks, have been abounding in this community; and these, taken with other manifestations of self-indulgence, not any less effervescent, are signs of a certain relaxation of virtue and deportment.

PRIORESS. I hardly think we need trouble ourselves upon that account. Providence has been pleased of late to bring into our fold some tender lambs, and perhaps they do frisk a little sometimes in the pastures of the Lord. But the poor children mean no harm. Am I right in your opinion, Mother Mistress of Novices?

MISTRESS OF NOVICES. You are always right in my opinion, reverend Mother. *Gaudeamus autem in Domino!*

VICARESS. Your Reverences of course know what you are doing. I have complied with my obligation.

> [*The bell rings at the entrance.* SISTER TORNERA, *who is an active little old woman, goes up to the grille and looks through it, after first having made a reverence to the* PRIORESS.]

SISTER TORNERA. *Ave Maria Purissima!*

A VOICE. [*Outside, hoarse and rough.*] Conceived without sin. Is it permitted to speak with the Mother Abbess?

SISTER TORNERA. Say what you have need of, brother.

VOICE. Then here's a present for her from my lady, the

mayor's wife, who wishes her happiness, and sends her
this present, and she's sorry she can't come herself to tell
her; but she can't, and you know the reason . . . [*The*
PRIORESS *sighs, lifting up her eyes to heaven, and the others
do the same, all sighing in unison.*] And even if she could
on that account, she couldn't do it, because she's sick in
bed, and you know the reason . . .

SISTER TORNERA. God's will be done! Can the poor
woman get no rest? Tell her that we will send her a jar of
ointment in the name of the blessed Saint Clara, and say
that these poor sisters never forget her in their prayers.
They pray every day that the Lord will send her comfort.
[*She turns the wheel by the grille, and a basket appears,
neatly covered with a white cloth.*] Ah!—and the reverend Mother thanks her for this remembrance. And may
God be with you, brother. [*Approaching the others with
the basket, which she has taken from the wheel.*] Poor
lady! What tribulations our Lord sends into this world
upon the cross of matrimony!

PRIORESS. And to her more than anybody. Such a
submissive creature, and married to a perfect prodigal!

MISTRESS OF NOVICES. Now that we are on the subject, your Reverences, and have the pot by the handle, so
to speak, do your Reverences know that the blasphemies
of that man have completely turned his head? You heard
the bells of the parish church ringing at noon yesterday?
Well, that was because the mayor ordered them to be
rung, because in the election at Madrid yesterday the re-
publicans had the majority.

ALL. God bless us! God bless us!

VICARESS. Did the priest give his consent to that?

SISTER INEZ. The priest is another sheep of the same
color—he belongs to the same flock, may the Lord forgive me if I lack charity! Didn't your Reverences hear
the sacrilege he committed upon our poor chaplain, who is
holier than God's bread? Well, he told him that he was

more liberal than the mayor, and that the next thing he knew, when he least expected it, he was going to sing the introitus to the mass to the music of the Hymn of Riego!

PRIORESS. Stop! Enough! It is not right to repeat such blasphemies.

MISTRESS OF NOVICES. Yes, calumnies invented by unbelievers, the evil-minded . . .

SISTER INEZ. No such thing! Didn't Father Calixtus tell me himself while he was dressing for mass this morning? We'll have to put a new strip pretty soon down the middle of his chasuble.

PRIORESS. What? Again?

SISTER INEZ. Yes. It's all worn out; it looks terribly. Poor Father Calixtus is so eloquent! Pounding on his chest all the time, he simply tears the silk to pieces.

VICARESS. God's will be done, the man is a saint!

PRIORESS. And all this while we have been forgetting the present from the mayor's wife. Bring it nearer, Sister.

SISTER SAGRARIO. Mercy! What a big basket!

SISTER TORNERA. It's very light, though.

SISTER INEZ. Ha! It's easy to see what sister has a sweet tooth!

SISTER MARÍA JESÚS. As if she didn't like sweets!
    [*Aside.*]

SISTER MARCELLA. Now, Sister Inez, what did we see you doing this morning? You know we caught you licking the cake pan yourself.

SISTER INEZ. I? Licking the pan? Your Sister licking the pan? Oh, what a slander! *Jesús!*

PRIORESS. Come, you must not be displeased, Sister Inez; for it was said only in pleasantry. Ah, Sister Marcella! Sister Marcella! Do have a little more circumspection and beg your Sister's pardon.

SISTER MARCELLA. [*Kneeling before* SISTER INEZ.] Pardon me, Sister, as may God pardon you, and give me your hand to kiss as a penance for having offended you.

PRIORESS. That is the way my children should behave, humbly and with contrition. Sister Inez, give Sister Marcella your hand to kiss, since she begs it of you so humbly.

SISTER MARCELLA. [*Spitefully, after kissing her hand.*] *Ay!* But what a smell of vanilla you have on your fingers, Sister! Goody! We're going to have cookies for lunch. [*The others laugh.*]

SISTER INEZ. [*Irritated, almost in tears.*] Vanilla? God-a-mercy! Vanilla! Look at me! Do my fingers smell of vanilla?

PRIORESS. [*Imposing silence.*] Surely the devil must be in you, Sister Marcella, and may God forgive you for it! Go and kneel in the corner there with your face to the wall, and make the cross with your arms while you repeat a greater station. May the Lord forgive you for it!

SISTER MARCELLA. Willingly, reverend Mother.

SISTER INEZ. [*Rubbing her hands under her scapular.*] Too bad! Too bad! *Ay! Ay! Ay!*

SISTER MARCELLA. [*Aside.*] Old box of bones!
  [*She goes and kneels in the corner, right, but keeps smiling and turning her head while she lets herself sink back on her heels, as if not taking the penance too seriously.*]

PRIORESS. You may uncover the basket now, Sister. Let us see what is in it.

SISTER TORNERA. With your permission, reverend Mother. Why! It's a cage!

SISTER SAGRARIO. With a canary in it!

ALL. A canary! A canary! Why, so it is! Let me see! How lovely!

MISTRESS OF NOVICES. Isn't it pretty?

SISTER MARÍA JESÚS. The dear! Isn't it cunning, though?

SISTER JOANNA OF THE CROSS. It looks as if it were made of silk.

SISTER INEZ. I wonder if it can sing?

PRIORESS. Of course it can sing. The mayor's wife would never send us a canary that couldn't sing.

SISTER SAGRARIO. What a beautiful cage! Why, there's a scroll on the front!

MISTRESS OF NOVICES. That isn't a scroll. It has letters on it.

SISTER MARÍA JESÚS. Why, so it has! Look and see what they say.

MISTRESS OF NOVICES. "The Convent of Dominican Nuns!"

SISTER INEZ. [*Laughing.*] I'd call that a pretty airy convent!

VICARESS. The good woman is holier than God's bread.

PRIORESS. She could not have sent me anything that would have pleased me better. I have always been anxious to have a canary.

SISTER INEZ. The Carmelite Sisters have two lovely canaries, and they say last year on Holy Thursday they hung them in the door of the tomb they have in the church for Easter, and it was like a miracle to hear them sing.

MISTRESS OF NOVICES. Then if ours sings, we can hang him in the church this year, and take the music box away.

PRIORESS. No, for the music box is a present from the chaplain, and he would rightly be offended. We will have the box and the canary there together, and when we wind up the box, it will encourage the bird to sing.

SISTER JOANNA OF THE CROSS. Oh, look at him now —he's taking his bath!

SISTER SAGRARIO. See how he jumps.

PRIORESS. What wonders God performs!

VICARESS. And yet there are misguided creatures who pretend that the world made itself!

SISTER INEZ. Sister Marcella stuck her tongue out at me.

SISTER MARCELLA. Oh, reverend Mother! I did nothing of the kind!

VICARESS. How nothing of the kind? Didn't I see it with my own eyes? And I was struck dumb!

SISTER MARCELLA. I said nothing of the kind . . . as . . . as that I had stuck my tongue out at Sister Inez. I stuck it out because there was a fly on the end of my nose, and since I had my arms out making the cross, I had to frighten him away with something.

SISTER JOANNA OF THE CROSS. Reverend Mother, since this is your Saint's day, won't you please excuse Sister Marcella this time?

SISTER MARÍA JESÚS. Yes, reverend Mother! I am sure she won't do anything that's wrong again.

PRIORESS. Sister Inez is the one who has been offended, and she is the only one who has the right to request her pardon.

NOVICES. She does! She does! You do, don't you, Sister Inez?

SISTER INEZ. [*With a wry face.*] Your Reverence will pardon her when your Reverence thinks best.

PRIORESS. Then come here, my erring daughter.—She knows that I pardon her because of the day, and so as not to spoil the pleasure of her sisters.

SISTER MARCELLA. May God reward you, reverend Mother!

PRIORESS. And set your veil straight, for this is the Lord's house, and it looks as if you were going on an excursion.—And now to your cells, every one. (*To the* NOVICES.) What are you whispering about?

SISTER SAGRARIO. We were not whispering, Mother . . . We wanted to ask you something.

SISTER MARÍA JESÚS. And we are afraid to do it.

PRIORESS. Is it as bad as that?

SISTER MARÍA JESÚS. No, it isn't bad. But——

SISTER JOANNA OF THE CROSS. Your Reverence might think so.

PRIORESS. I might? I am not so evil-minded.

SISTER SAGRARIO. I . . . I . . . Our Mother Mistress will tell you.

MISTRESS OF NOVICES. They mean me.—Do you want me to?

NOVICES. Yes! Yes! Do!

MISTRESS OF NOVICES. With God's help I will try. Though I don't know for certain, I think what they want is for your Reverence to give them permission to talk a little, while they are waiting for the beginning of the *fiesta*. Am I right?

NOVICES. Yes! Yes! You are! Do, Mother, do!

SISTER MARCELLA. Long live our Mother!

PRIORESS. Silence! Silence! What? Haven't they had talking enough to-day after the dispensation I allowed them this morning?

VICARESS. The appetite always grows by what it feeds on. It is an unruly monster, and woe to her who gives it rein. If they came under my authority, I would not give them opportunity to make a single slip, for the holy Apostle Saint James has said and well said: "He who saith that he hath not offended by his tongue, lies."

SISTER MARCELLA. Ah, Sister Crucifixion! Don't spoil this holiday for our Mother.

VICARESS. Spoil it, eh? Who pays any attention to what I say in this house?

PRIORESS. Will you promise not to whisper nor offend the Lord with foolish talk?

NOVICES. We promise.

PRIORESS. Then you may talk as much as you like until the hour for prayers.

NOVICES. Thanks, thanks! [*The bell rings at the entrance twice.*]

SISTER TORNERA. Two rings! The doctor!

PRIORESS. Cover your faces. [*The nuns lower their veils over their faces.*] And pass out through the cloister. [*The nuns begin to file out slowly and disappear through the cloister.*]

SISTER SAGRARIO. [*Approaching the* PRIORESS.] This Sister has a felon, reverend Mother.

PRIORESS. Remain then—and you too, Sister María Jesús. [*To* SISTER TORNERA.] Open, Sister. [THE PRIORESS, SISTER TORNERA, SISTER SAGRARIO *and* SISTER MARÍA JESÚS *remain.* SISTER TORNERA *unchains, unbolts and opens the door. The* DOCTOR *enters. He is about sixty years of age.*]

SISTER TORNERA. *Ave Maria Purissima!*

DOCTOR. Conceived without sin. [*He comes in.*] Good morning, Sister.

SISTER TORNERA. Good morning, Doctor.

DOCTOR. Well, what progress are we making in holiness today?

SISTER TORNERA. [*Laughing.*] Ho, ho, Doctor!

DOCTOR. Enough! Enough! No doubt, no doubt! [*Discovering the* PRIORESS.] Congratulations, Mother.

PRIORESS. What? A heretic, and yet you remember the days of the saints?

DOCTOR. You are the saint, Mother; you are the saint.

PRIORESS. Ah! You must not scandalize me before my novices.

DOCTOR. Novices? Where, where? I said so when I came in. I smell fresh meat.

PRIORESS. Don José! Don José!

DOCTOR. But I say no more. Come! To work! To work! . . . What is the trouble with these white lambs?

SISTER SAGRARIO. Your handmaid has a felon, Doctor.

DOCTOR. Eh? On the hand? And such a lovely hand! Well, we shall have to lance it, Sister.

SISTER SAGRARIO. [*Alarmed.*] What? Not now?

DOCTOR. No, tomorrow, Sister. Tomorrow, unless it yields first to a poultice and five *Pater nosters*. Remember, not one less!

SISTER SAGRARIO. [*In perfect earnest.*] No, Doctor.

DOCTOR. And this other one, eh?

PRIORESS. Ah, Doctor! She has been giving me a great deal of worry. She falls asleep in the choir; she sighs continually without being able to assign any reason; she cries over nothing whatever; she has no appetite for anything but salads . . .

DOCTOR. How old are you?

SISTER MARÍA JESÚS. Eighteen.

DOCTOR. How long have you been in this holy house?

SISTER MARÍA JESÚS. Two years and a half.

DOCTOR. And how many more do you remain before you come to profession?

SISTER MARÍA JESÚS. Two and a half more, if the Lord should be pleased to grant this unworthy novice grace to become his bride.

DOCTOR. Let me see the face.

PRIORESS. Lift your veil. [SISTER MARÍA JESÚS *lifts her veil.*]

DOCTOR. Hm! The Lord has not bad taste. A little pale, but well rounded, well rounded.

SISTER TORNERA. Don José! But who ever heard of such a doctor?

DOCTOR. So, we have melancholy then, a constant disposition to sigh, combined with loss of appetite—well, there is nothing else for it, Sister: a cold bath every morning and afterwards a few minutes' exercise in the garden.

SISTER TORNERA. [*Somewhat scandalized.*] Exercise? Don José!

DOCTOR. Unless we write at once home to her mother to hurry and fetch her and find us a good husband for her.

Sister María Jesús. Oh, Don José! But this Sister has taken her vows to the Church!

Doctor. Well, in that case cold water. There is nothing else for it. For melancholy at eighteen, matrimony or cold water.

Sister Sagrario. [*Summoning her courage.*] You always talk so much about it, Doctor, why don't you get married yourself?

Doctor. Because I am sixty, daughter; and it is fifteen years since I have felt melancholy. Besides, whom do you expect me to marry when all the pretty girls go into convents?

Prioress. Doctor, doctor! This conversation will become displeasing to me.

Doctor. Is this all the walking infirmary?

Sister Tornera. Yes, Doctor.

Doctor. And the invalid? How is she?

Sister Tornera. She is the same to-day, Doctor. Poor Sister Maria of Consolation hasn't closed her eyes all night! Don't you remember? Yesterday she said she felt as if she had a viper gnawing at her vitals? Well, today she has a frog in her throat.

Doctor. Goodness gracious! Come, let me see, let me see. What a continual war the devil does wage against these poor sisters!—Long life, Mother, and happy days!

Prioress. Long life to you, Doctor. [*To* Sister Tornera.] Go with him, Sister, and meanwhile these children will take care of the gate. [Sister Tornera *takes a bell from the table and, her veil covering her face, precedes the* Doctor *through the cloister, ringing solemnly in warning. They disappear.*] I must repair to the choir; I fear that today I have fallen behind in devotion and prayer.

Sister María Jesús. Will your Reverence give us permission to call the others?

PRIORESS. Yes, call them; but be careful that you commit no frivolity. [*The* PRIORESS *goes out.*]

SISTER MARÍA JESÚS. [*Approaching one of the arches of the cloister.*] Sister Marcella! Sister Joanna of the Cross! Pst! Come out! We are watching the grille and we have permission to talk.

[SISTER MARCELLA *and* SISTER JOANNA OF THE CROSS *re-enter.*]

SISTER SAGRARIO. What shall we talk about?

SISTER JOANNA OF THE CROSS. Let Sister Marcella tell us a story.

SISTER MARCELLA. Yes, so that you'll all be shocked.

SISTER MARÍA JESÚS. *Ay!* We are not such hypocrites as that, Sister.

SISTER MARCELLA. Or so that Sister Sagrario can run and tell on us to the Mother Mistress.

SISTER SAGRARIO. Oh, thank you, Sister!

SISTER MARCELLA. It wouldn't be the first time either.

SISTER SAGRARIO. You needn't mind me, Sisters. I am going to sit here in the corner and work, and you can talk about whatever you please. I shan't hear you.

[*She takes a pair of pincers, some beads and a piece of wire out of her pocket, and sitting down in a corner, begins to string a rosary.*]

SISTER JOANNA OF THE CROSS. Oh, come on, Sister! Don't be foolish. [*They all surround her, and finally she allows herself to be persuaded, after many expressions of protest, like a small child who says "I won't play."*]

SISTER SAGRARIO. Why! If they haven't forgotten the canary!

SISTER MARCELLA. Poor thing! How do you like to be left in this nest of silly women, little fellow? Let's open the cage.

SISTER MARÍA JESÚS. What for?

SISTER MARCELLA.   So that he can fly away, silly, if he wants to.

SISTER SAGRARIO.   No, no!

SISTER MARÍA JESÚS.   Our Mother wouldn't like that.

SISTER MARCELLA.   He would like it, though. Come on! [*She opens the door of the cage.*] Fly out, sweetheart! Fly away, the world is yours. You are free!

SISTER JOANNA OF THE CROSS.   He doesn't fly out.

SISTER MARÍA JESÚS.   He doesn't budge.

SISTER MARCELLA.   Stupid, don't you see what a bright, sunny day it is?

SISTER JOANNA OF THE CROSS.   They say canaries are born in cages and, see, now he doesn't care to fly away.

SISTER MARÍA JESÚS.   He'd rather stay shut up all his life like us nuns.

SISTER MARCELLA.   Then you're a great fool, birdie. [*She shuts the door of the cage.*] God made the air for wings and He made wings to fly with. While he might be soaring away above the clouds, he is satisfied to stay here all day shut up in his cage, hopping between two sticks and a leaf of lettuce! What sense is there in a bird? *Ay,* Mother! And what wouldn't I give to be a bird!

SISTER JOANNA OF THE CROSS.   Yes! What wouldn't you give to be a bird?

SISTER MARÍA JESÚS.   They say that the swallows fly away every year over the ocean, and nobody knows where they go.

SISTER SAGRARIO.   I often dream that I am flying in the night time—that is not flying, but floating—just floating in the air without wings.

SISTER SAGRARIO.   I often dream that I am running fast—oh so fast!—and that I am skipping down stairs, without ever touching my feet to the ground, or to the stairs.

SISTER SAGRARIO.   Isn't it nice, though? And how disappointed you are when you wake up and find out after all that it isn't so, that it was only a dream!

SISTER MARCELLA.   I have dreamed that dream so many times, that now when I wake up, I hardly know whether it is the truth or a dream.

SISTER JOANNA OF THE CROSS.   What do you suppose it is that makes you dream the same dream so many times?

SISTER MARCELLA.   I don't know, unless it is because it is the things you want to do, and you can't, and so you do them in dreams.

SISTER MARÍA JESÚS.   What nice things you want to do!

SISTER SAGRARIO.   But then what good would it be if you could do them?   For instance, if we had wings like birds, where would we fly?

SISTER MARCELLA.   I?   I would fly to the end of the world!

SISTER MARÍA JESÚS.   I?   To the Holy Land, to Mount Calvary!

SISTER JOANNA OF THE CROSS.   I would fly to Bethlehem and to the garden of Nazareth, where the Virgin lived with the child.

SISTER SAGRARIO.   How do you know that there is a garden at Nazareth?

SISTER JOANNA OF THE CROSS.   Of course there's a garden there, with a brook running by it.   The song says so:

> "The Virgin washed his garments
>   And hung them on the rose.
> The little angels sing
>   And the water onward flows" . . .

[*Simply.*]   There was a garden, too, by our house in the village, with a big rosebush on the border of a brook that ran by it; and I used to kneel beside the brook, and sing

that song while I washed my baby brother's clothes, for
there were seven of us children, and I was the oldest.
[*Feelingly.*] And that's what I miss most! [*Drying her
eyes with her hands.*] *Ay,* Mother! And I always cry
when I think of that baby boy! But it isn't right, I know
. . . He loved me more than he did mother, and the
day that they took me away to the Convent, and I left
home, he cried—he cried so that he nearly broke his little
baby heart!

SISTER MARCELLA. I have a brother and a sister, but
they are both older than I am. My sister married two
years ago, and now she has a baby. [*With an air of importance.*] She brought him here once to show me.

SISTER JOANNA OF THE CROSS. [*Interrupting her,
greatly interested.*] I remember. He stuck his little hand
in through the grille and your sister kissed it. Did you
ever think how soft babies' hands are? Whenever I take
communion I try to think I am receiving our Lord as a
little child, and I take and press him like this to my heart,
and then it seems to me that he is so little and so helpless
that he can't refuse me anything. And then I think that
he is crying, and I pray to the Virgin to come and help
me quiet him. And if I wasn't ashamed, because I know
you would all laugh at me, I'd croon to him then, and
rock him to sleep, and sing him baby songs.

[*The bell rings by the grille.*]

SISTER SAGRARIO. The bell! I wonder who it is?

SISTER JOANNA OF THE CROSS. Better ask. That's
why they left us here.

SISTER MARÍA JESÚS. Who'll do it? I won't. I'm
afraid.

SISTER SAGRARIO. So am I.

SISTER MARCELLA. You're not usually so bashful, I must
say. I'll ask, though I was the last to enter the house.
[*Going up to the grille, she says in a timid voice:*] *Ave
Maria purissima!* [*A moment's silence.*] No one answers.

SISTER JOANNA OF THE CROSS. Try again. Say it louder.

SISTER MARCELLA. [*Raising her voice.*] *Ave Maria purissima!*

SISTER SAGRARIO. Nothing this time, either.

SISTER MARÍA JESÚS. [*Summoning her courage, in a high-pitched voice.*] *Ave Maria purissima!*

  [*Another silence. The Novices look at each other in surprise.*]

SISTER MARCELLA. It is very strange.

SISTER MARÍA JESÚS. It must be spirits.

SISTER SAGRARIO. Oh, I'm afraid!

SISTER JOANNA OF THE CROSS. Nonsense! It's some little boy who has rung the bell on his way home from school, so as to be funny.

SISTER MARÍA JESÚS. Peep through the hole and see if anybody is there.

SISTER MARCELLA. [*Stooping down to look.*] No, nobody. But it looks as if there was something on the wheel. Yes . . .

SISTER JOANNA OF THE CROSS. Let me see! Yes . . . Can't you turn it? [*She turns the wheel, and a second basket appears, carefully covered with a white cloth like the first.*] A basket!

SISTER SAGRARIO. Another present for our Mother.

SISTER MARÍA JESÚS. Of course it is! And here's a paper tied fast to it.

SISTER JOANNA OF THE CROSS. [*Reading, but without unfolding the paper.*] "For the Mother Prioress."

SISTER SAGRARIO. Didn't I tell you?

SISTER MARCELLA. Somebody wants to give her a surprise.

SISTER JOANNA OF THE CROSS. I wonder if it's Don Calixtus, the chaplain?

SISTER MARCELLA. Of course it is, child!

SISTER MARÍA JESÚS. Or maybe it's the Doctor.

SISTER JOANNA OF THE CROSS. No. He was just here and he didn't say anything about it.

SISTER SAGRARIO. All the same it might be from him. Maybe he wants to keep it a secret.

SISTER MARÍA JESÚS. Let's take it off the wheel.

SISTER MARCELLA. [*Lifting and carrying it to the table.*] We'd better put it here by the canary. My! But it's heavy!

SISTER SAGRARIO. I wonder what it is?

SISTER MARCELLA. Lets lift the corner and see.

SISTER MARÍA JESÚS. No, for curiosity is a sin.

SISTER MARCELLA. What of it? Come on! Let's do it. Who will ever know? [*She lifts the corner of the cloth a little and starts back quickly with a sharp cry.*] *Ay!!*

SISTER JOANNA OF THE CROSS. [*Hurrying to look.*] *Jesús!*

SISTER MARÍA JESÚS. *Ave Maria!* [*Looking too.*]

SISTER SAGRARIO. [*Following.*] God bless us!

[*The Convent is aroused at the cry of Sister Marcella. Presently* THE PRIORESS, THE VICARESS, THE MISTRESS OF NOVICES *and the other* NUNS *enter from different directions.*]

PRIORESS. What is the matter? Who called out?

VICARESS. Who gave that shout?

MISTRESS OF NOVICES. Is anything wrong? [*The four Novices, trembling, stand with their backs to the basket, their bodies hiding it completely.*]

VICARESS. It is easy to see it was Sister Marcella.

PRIORESS. What has happened? Speak! Why are you all standing in a row like statutes?

MISTRESS OF NOVICES. Has anything happened to you?

SISTER JOANNA OF THE CROSS. No, reverend Mother, not to us; but——

SISTER MARÍA JESÚS. No, reverend Mother; it's . . .

SISTER MARCELLA. Someone rang the bell by the wheel . . . and we looked . . . and there was nobody

there . . . and they left a basket . . . this basket . . . and
. . . and your sister had the curiosity to undo it . . .

VICARESS. Naturally, you couldn't do otherwise.

SISTER MARCELLA. And it's . . .

PRIORESS. Well? What is it?

SISTER MARCELLA. It's . . . I . . . I think it would
be better for your Reverence to look yourself.

PRIORESS. By all means! Let me see. [*She goes up
to the basket and uncovers it.*] *Ave Maria!* [*In a hoarse
whisper.*] A baby!

ALL. [*Variously affected.*] A baby? [*The* VICARESS,
horrified, crosses herself.]

PRIORESS. [*Falling back.*] Your Reverences may see
for yourselves. [*The* NUNS *hurry up to the basket and surround it.*]

VICARESS. *Ave Maria!* How can such an insignifi-
cant object be so pink?

MISTRESS OF NOVICES. It's asleep.

SISTER JOANNA OF THE CROSS. See it open its little
hands!

SISTER MARÍA JESÚS. Why! It has hair under the
edge of its cap!

SISTER SAGRARIO. It is like an angel!

VICARESS. A pretty angel for the Lord to send us.

SISTER JOANNA OF THE CROSS. [*As if she had been
personally offended.*] *Ay,* Mother Vicaress! You mustn't
say that.

PRIORESS. [*Tenderly.*] Where do you come from, little
one?

VICARESS. From some nice place, you may be sure.

PRIORESS. Who can tell, Mother? There is so much
poverty in the world, so much distress.

VICARESS. There is so much vice, reverend Mother.

MISTRESS OF NOVICES. You say that there was nobody
at the grille?

SISTER MARCELLA. Nobody; no, Mother. The bell
rang; we answered . . . but there was nobody there.

SISTER SAGRARIO. [*Picking up the paper which has fallen on the floor.*] Here is a paper which came with it.

PRIORESS. [*Taking the paper.*] "For the Mother Prioress."

VICARESS. An appropriate present for your Reverence.

PRIORESS. Yes, it is a letter.

[*She unfolds the paper and begins to read.*]

"Reverend Mother:

Forgive the liberty which a poor woman takes, trusting in your Grace's charity, of leaving at the grille this new-born babe. I, my lady, am one of those they call women of the street, and I assure you I am sorry for it; but this is the world, and you can't turn your back on it, and it costs as much to go down as it does to go up, and that is what I am writing to tell you, my lady. The truth is this little girl hasn't any father, that is to say it is the same as if she didn't have any, and I—who am her mother —I leave her here, although it costs me something to leave her; for although one is what one is, one isn't all bad, and I love her as much as any mother loves her baby, though she is the best lady in the land. But all the same, though she came into this world without being wanted by anyone, she doesn't deserve to be the daughter of the woman she is, above all, my lady, of her father, and I don't want her to have to blush for having been born the way she was, nor for having the mother she has, and to tell it to me to my face, and I pray you by everything you hold dear, my lady, that you will protect her and keep her with you in this holy house, and you won't send her to some orphanage or asylum, for I was brought up there myself, and I know what happens in them, although the sisters are kind—yes, they are—and have pity. And some day, when she grows up and she asks for her mother, you must tell her that the devil has carried her away, and I ask your pardon, for I must never show myself to her, nor see her again, nor give you any care nor trouble, so you can do this good work in peace, if you will do it, for I implore you again,

my lady, that you will do it for the memory of your own
dear mother, and God will reward you, and she will live
in peace, and grow up as God wills, for what the eyes have
not seen the heart cannot understand, my lady."

VICARESS. Bless us! *Ave Maria!*

MISTRESS OF NOVICES. Poor woman!

SISTER JOANNA OF THE CROSS. Baby dear! Darling
baby!

VICARESS. What pretty mothers the Lord selects for his
children!

PRIORESS. God moves in his own ways, Sister. God
moves in his own ways.

SISTER INEZ. Is that all the letter says?

PRIORESS. What more could it say?

    [THE DOCTOR *and* SISTER TORNERA *have re-entered
    during the reading.*]

DOCTOR. Exactly. What more could it say?

PRIORESS. What do you think, Don José?

DOCTOR. I think that somebody has made you a very
handsome present.

PRIORESS. But what are we going to do with it? Because I . . . this poor woman . . . she has put this poor
creature into our hands, and I would protect her willingly,
as she asks, and keep her here with us . . .

NOVICES. Yes, yes, Mother! Do! Do!

MISTRESS OF NOVICES. Silence!

PRIORESS. But I don't know if we can . . . that is, if
it is right, if it is according to law . . . for, when we
enter this holy rule, we renounce all our rights . . . and to
adopt a child legally . . . I don't know whether it can be
done. How does it seem to you?

DOCTOR. I agree with you. Legally, you have no right
to maternity.

VICARESS. And even if we had, would it be proper for
our children to be the offspring of ignominy and sin?

PRIORESS. I would not raise that question, reverend
Mother, for the child is not responsible for the sin in which

she was born, and her mother, in renouncing her mother-
hood, has bitterly paid the penalty.

VICARESS. Yes, it didn't cost her much to renounce it.

PRIORESS. Do we know, Mother? Do we know?

VICARESS. We can guess. It is easy enough to go
scattering children about the world if all you have to do
is leave them to be picked up afterwards by the first person who happens along.

DOCTOR. How easy it is might be a matter for discussion. There are aspects of it which are not so easy.

SISTER SAGRARIO. Oh! She's opened her mouth!

SISTER JOANNA OF THE CROSS. The little angel is
hungry.

SISTER MARÍA JESÚS. She's sucking her thumb!

SISTER JOANNA OF THE CROSS. Make her take her
thumb out of her mouth. She'll swallow too much and
then she'll have a pain.

SISTER SAGRARIO. Don't suck your fingers, baby.

SISTER JOANNA OF THE CROSS. Isn't she good, though?
You stop her playing, and she doesn't cry.

PRIORESS. There is another thing we must consider.
What are we to do for a nurse?

SISTER JOANNA OF THE CROSS. The gardener's wife
has a little boy she is nursing now.

PRIORESS. In that case I hardly think she would care
to be responsible for two.

SISTER JOANNA OF THE CROSS. But it won't be any
trouble—she's so tiny! Besides, we can help her out with
cow's milk and a little pap. The milk will keep on the
ice and we can clear it with a dash of tea.

DOCTOR. It is easy to see Sister Joanna of the Cross
has had experience with children.

SISTER JOANNA OF THE CROSS. Your handmaid has six
little brothers and sisters. Ah, reverend Mother! Give
her to me to take care of and then you will see how strong
she'll grow up.

VICARESS. Nothing else was needed to complete the

demoralization of the Novices. You can see for yourselves how naturally they take to this dissipation.

PRIORESS.   I want you to tell me frankly what you think
—all of you.   [All speak at once.]

MISTRESS OF NOVICES.   Your Sister thinks, reverend
Mother . . .

SISTER TORNERA.   Your handmaid . . .

SISTER INEZ.   It seems to me . . .

PRIORESS.   [Smiling.]   But one at a time.

SISTER TORNERA.   It is an angel which the Lord has
sent us, and your Sister thinks that we ought to receive her
like an angel, with open arms.

MISTRESS OF NOVICES.   Of course we ought. Suppose,
your Reverences, it hadn't been a little girl, but . . . I
don't know—some poor animal, a dog, a cat, or a dove,
like the one which flew in here two years ago and fell
wounded in the garden trying to get away from those
butchers at the pigeon-traps. Wouldn't we have taken
it in? Wouldn't we have cared for it? And wouldn't
it have lived happy forever afterward in its cage? And
how can we do less for a creature with a soul than for a
bird?

SISTER TORNERA.   We must have charity.

VICARESS.   I am glad the Mother Mistress of Novices
has brought up the incident of that bird, for it will absolve
me from bringing it up, as it might seem, with some malice.
It was against my advice that that creature was received
into this house, and afterward we had good reason to regret it, with this one saying "Yes, I caught him!" and that
one, "No, I took care of him!" and another "He opens
his beak whenever I pass by!" and another, "See him flap
his wings! He does it at me!"—vanities, sophistries, de-
ceits all of them, snares of the devil continually! And if
all this fuss was about a bird, what will happen to us with
a child in the house? This one will have to dress it, that
one will have to wash it, another will be boasting, "It is
looking at me!" another that it's at her that it googles

most . / . There is Sister Joanna of the Cross making
faces at it already!

SISTER JOANNA OF THE CROSS. What did your Reverence say?

VICARESS. Dissipation and more dissipation! Your
Reverences should remember that when we passed behind these bars, we renounced forever all personal, all
selfish affection.

MISTRESS OF NOVICES. Is it selfish to give a poor foundling a little love?

VICARESS. It is for us. Our God is a jealous God.
The Scriptures tell us so.

MISTRESS OF NOVICES. Bless us! Mercy me!

VICARESS. And this quite apart from other infractions
of our order which such indulgence must involve. For
example, your Reverences—and I among the first—take no
account of the fact that at this very moment we are trans-
gressing our rule. We are conversing with our faces unveiled in the presence of a man.

PRIORESS. That is true.

DOCTOR. Ladies, as far as I am concerned—Take no
account of me. . . .

PRIORESS. No, Doctor, you are of no account. I beg
your pardon, Don José; I hardly know what I am saying.—Your Reverence is right. Cover yourselves—that
is, it makes no difference . . . The harm has been
done . . . only once. . . . But comply with your con-
sciences . . . [*The* VICARESS *covers her face. The others,
hesitating, wait for the* PRIORESS, *who makes a movement
to do so, but then desists. The* VICARESS, *when she is
covered, cannot see that she has become the victim of the
rest.*] But where were we? I confess that my heart
prompts me to keep the child.

VICARESS. The Doctor already has told us that we have
no right to maternity.

MISTRESS OF NOVICES. But the child is God's child,
and she is returning to her father's mansion.

VICARESS. God has other mansions for his abandoned children.

SISTER JOANNA OF THE CROSS. Don't send her to the asylum!

SISTER SAGRARIO. No!

PRIORESS. Her mother entreats us.

VICARESS. Her mother is not her mother. She has abandoned her.

PRIORESS. She has not abandoned her. She has entrusted her to others who seemed worthier to undertake her keeping.

VICARESS. Unholy egotism!

MISTRESS OF NOVICES. Christian heroism!

VICARESS. So? We are coining phrases, are we? Is this a convent, or an illustrated weekly?

MISTRESS OF NOVICES. Life is hard to some people, and thorny.

VICARESS. Yes, and into the details of it, it is not becoming for us to go, since by the grace of God we have been relieved from the temptations and the frailties of the world.

MISTRESS OF NOVICES. All the more, then, we ought to have compassion on those who have fallen and are down.

VICARESS. Compassion? Mush and sentiment!

MISTRESS OF NOVICES. The veil of charity!

PRIORESS. Silence! And let us not begin by rending it, irritating ourselves and aggravating each other.—Don José, I suppose this birth will have to be reported?

DOCTOR. It will, madam. To the Register.

SISTER JOANNA OF THE CROSS. But then they will take her away?

DOCTOR. If nobody wants her. But if you have made up your minds you would like to keep her, I think I can propose a solution.

PRIORESS. A solution that is legal?

DOCTOR. Perfectly. Thanks be to God I am a single man. But, although I am not a saint, yet I cannot take to myself the credit of having augmented the population of this country by so much as a single soul. I have not a penny, that is true, but like everybody else, I have a couple of family names. They are at the service of this little stranger, if they will be of use to her. She will have no father and no mother—I cannot help that—but she will have an honorable name.

PRIORESS. Do you mean to say?——

DOCTOR. That I am willing to adopt her; exactly—and to entrust her to your care, because my own house . . . The fact is the hands of Doña Cecilia are a little rough for handling these tiny Dresden dolls, and perhaps I might prove a bit testy myself. The neighbors all say that the air grows blue if my coat rubs against me as I walk down the street.

[*All laugh.*]

DOCTOR. Besides I am sure Sister Crucifixion is better equipped for the robing of saints.

VICARESS Doctor, God help us both!

DOCTOR. Is it agreed?

PRIORESS. God reward you for it! Yes, in spite of everything. We shall notify the Superior immediately. It is not necessary that the child should live in the cloister. She can remain with the gardener's wife until she has grown older, and enter here later when she has the discretion to do so. She has been entrusted to our hands, and it is our duty to take care of her—a duty of conscience.

DOCTOR. If I cannot be of further service, I will go. And I will speak to the Register.

PRIORESS. As you go, be so kind as to ask the gardener's wife to come in. We must see if she will take charge of the child and nurse her. And tell her also to bring with her some of her little boy's clothes.

SISTER JOANNA OF THE CROSS. Yes, for we shall have to make a change immediately.

SISTER SAGRARIO. We shall?

VICARESS. Not a change, but a beginning.

DOCTOR. Good afternoon, ladies.

ALL. Good afternoon, Don José. [*The* DOCTOR *goes out.*]

     [*A pause.*]

PRIORESS. Sisters, may God pardon us if we have acted in this with aught but the greatest purity of motive. I hope and pray that His grace will absolve us of offense, nor find us guilty of having loved too much one of His poor children. The child shall be brought up in the shadow of this house, for we may say that her guardian angel has delivered her at the door. From this hour forth we are all charged with the salvation of her soul. The Lord has entrusted to us an angel and we must return to Him a saint. Watch and pray.

ALL. Watch and pray. We will, reverend Mother.

PRIORESS. And now bring her to me, Sister Joanna of the Cross, for as yet it can scarcely be said that I have seen her. [*Looking at the child.*] Lamb of God! Sleeping as quietly in her basket as if it were a cradle of pure gold! What is it that children see when they are asleep that brings to their faces an expression of such peace?

SISTER JOANNA OF THE CROSS. They see God and the Virgin Mary.

SISTER MARÍA JESÚS. Maybe the angel who watches over them whispers in their ears and tells them about heaven.

PRIORESS. Who can say? But it is a comfort to the soul to see a child asleep.

SISTER MARÍA JESÚS. It makes you want to be a saint, reverend Mother.

SISTER SAGRARIO. Will your Reverence grant me permission to give her a kiss?

SISTER MARÍA JESÚS. Oh, no! For it hasn't been baptized yet, and it is a sin to kiss a heathen!

PRIORESS. She is right. We must send for the Chaplain and have her baptized immediately.

MISTRESS OF NOVICES. What shall we call her?

SISTER INEZ. Teresa, after our beloved Mother.

SISTER TORNERA. María of the Miracles.

SISTER SAGRARIO. Bienvenida. [*A large bell rings outside.*]

PRIORESS. The summons to the choir! We can decide later. Let us go. [*The* NUNS *file out slowly, looking at the child as they go.*] Remain with her, Sister Joanna of the Cross—you understand children; and wait for the coming of the gardener's wife. Follow the devotions from where you are, and do not let your attention falter.

[*All the* NUNS *go out, except* SISTER JOANNA OF THE CROSS, *who bends over the basket; then sinks on her knees beside it. The choir is heard within, led by a single* NUN *in solo, the responses being made in chorus, in which* SISTER JOANNA OF THE CROSS *joins. While the* NUN *is leading,* SISTER JOANNA OF THE CROSS *talks and plays with the child; then she makes her responses with the others.*]

VOICE WITHIN. *In nomine Patri et Filio et Spiritui Sancto.* [SISTER JOANNA OF THE CROSS *crosses herself and says with the other* NUNS:]

VOICES WITHIN AND SISTER JOANNA OF THE CROSS. *Amen!*

SISTER JOANNA OF THE CROSS. [*To the child.*] Pretty one! Pretty one!

VOICE WITHIN. *Deus in adjutorium meum intende.*

VOICES WITHIN AND SISTER JOANNA OF THE CROSS. *Domine ad adjuvandum me festina.*

SISTER JOANNA OF THE CROSS. [*To the child.*] Do you love me, sweetheart? Do you love me?

VOICE WITHIN. *Gloria Patri et Filio et Spiritui Sancto.*

VOICES WITHIN IN CHORUS. *Sicut erat in principio et nunc et semper et insecula seculorum. Amen! Allelulia!*

[*But this time* SISTER JOANNA OF THE CROSS *makes no response. Instead she bends over the basket, embracing the child passionately, oblivious of all else, and says*:]

SISTER JOANNA OF THE CROSS.   Little one!   Little one! Whom do you love?

CURTAIN

INTERLUDE

SPOKEN BY THE POET

You came tonight to listen to a play;
Instead into a convent you made way.
Singular hardihood! Almost profanation!
What will a poet not do to create sensation?
Pardon, good nuns, him who disturbs the rest
And troubles the serene quietude of your nest,
Kindling amid the shades of this chaste bower
The flame of love you have renounced and flower.
Nay! Do not frown because I have said love,
For you must know, chaste brides of God above,
That which you have deemed charity and pity,
The act of mercy, clemency for the pretty,
Unfriended foundling fate has brought along,
Yearning of adoption and the cradle song,
No other is than love's fire, divine and human
Passion ever brooding in the heart of woman.

Ah, love of woman, by whose power we live,
Offend so often—but to see forgive!
Whence do you draw your grace but from above?
Whence simply? Simply from maternal love!
Yes, we are children, woman, in your arms;
Your heart is bread, you soothe our wild alarms,
Like children give us the honey of your breast,
In a cradle always your lover sinks to rest
Although he prostitutes our grovelling flesh.
Mother if lover, mother if sister too,
Mother by pure essence, day long and night through,
Mother if you laugh, or if with us you cry,

36

In the core of being, in fibre and in mesh,
Every woman carries, so God has willed on high,
A baby in her bosom, sleeping eternally!

So being women, you are lovers, nuns;
Despite the ceintured diamond which runs
Across your virgin shields, showing in your lives
How to be mothers without being wives.
And in this child of all, you have poured all
The honey of your souls, and blended all
The fire of the sun, all fragrance and all light,
The first sweet morning kiss, the last good-night,
Till all her being tenderness exhales,
Her heart the home of love and nightingales.
A hundred times a woman but no saint.
The nuns pray in the choir; outside her plaint
A song; her prayer, gay rippling laughter.
Mass and the May morning slip by, she running after
Or dreaming in the garden. The roses smell
So sweetly! No child this for the hermits' cell.
She loves Heaven, but in good company;
And before the altar of the Virgin see
Her with a boy, ruddier than the candle's flame,
Who calls her "Sister," the nuns "Aunt" for name.
A smiling, bashful boy, who soon will grow
To be a strong man, learn to give a blow
And take one, conquer worlds and redress wrong,
Justice in his heart, and on his lips a song!
Sometimes she takes the cat up, calls it "Dear!"
The nuns cross themselves, religiously severe.
"The child is mad," they say. Ah! No such thing!
With her into the convent entered Spring.

This then the simple story. The poet would
Have told it day by day, if well he could,
In shining glory. But the task were vain.
The glory of our daily lives is plain.

For life builds up itself in such a way,
The water runs so clear, so bright the day,
That time is lulled to sleep within these walls.
An age or moment? Which passes? Who recalls?
The wheel turns round, but no one notes the turn.
What matter if the sisters' locks that burn
With gold, in time to silvery gray have paled?
Their hoods conceal it. And the pinks have failed
In the cheeks, and the lilies on the brow.
There are no mirrors. The sisters then as now
May walk in the garden, believe it still is May.

Among these hours which softly slip away,
This timeless time, we shyly pause at that
In which there is most warmth, the concordat
Of youth and incense, breaking of the spring.
The years have passed, the child is ripening.
The curtain rises on a soul in flower,
And a love chapter claims us for an hour.
It is quiet afternoon, quiet breeding;
The nuns are sewing and their sister reading:

CHAPTER II

Parlor of a Convent.

At the rear, a grille with a double row of bars. A curtain of dark woolen cloth hangs over the grille and intercepts the view of the outer parlor, to which visitors are admitted. This is without decoration, and may be brightly illuminated at the proper moment from the garden. A number of oil paintings of saints hang upon the walls—all of them very old and showing black stains. With them a carved crucifix or large black wooden cross. A small window furnished with heavy curtains, which, when drawn, shut off the light completely, is cut in the wall of the inner parlor on either side of the grille, high up toward the ceiling. A pine table, a carved arm chair, two other arm chairs, smaller chairs and benches, together with all the materials necessary for sewing.

THE PRIORESS, THE MISTRESS OF NOVICES, SISTERS INEZ and TORNERA, SISTER SAGRARIO, SISTER JOANNA OF THE CROSS, SISTER MARCELLA, SISTER MARÍA JESÚS and the other NUNS are discovered upon the rise of the curtain. Only THE VICARESS is absent. All are seated, sewing, with the exception of SISTER MARÍA JESÚS, who stands in the centre, to the left of THE PRIORESS'S chair, reading. A bride's trousseau is spread out upon the table and chairs. It is embroidered elaborately, trimmed with lace and tied with blue silk ribbons. A new trunk stands against the wall on the right, the trays being distributed about the benches and upon the floor.

Eighteen years have passed. It must be remembered that the NUNS have changed in appearance, and those who were novices have now professed and have exchanged the white for the black veil.

39

SISTER MARÍA JESÚS. [*Reading and intoning.*] "The Treasury of Patience, the Meditations of an Afflicted Soul in the presence of its God."

SISTER MARCELLA. [*Sighing.*] *Ay!*

SISTER MARÍA JESÚS. [*Reading.*] "First Meditation: The Sorrows of an Unhappy Spirit, Submerged in a Sea of Woe."

[*Outside,* TERESA'S *voice is heard, singing gaily.*]

TERESA.   "Come singing and bringing
        Flowers from the field,
        Flowers from the field,
    Sweet gardens, to Mary.
        Flowers you must yield
    For Love's sanctuary!"

[*The reader stops, and, smiling, glances in the direction of the window through which the voice is heard. The other* NUNS *smile also, complacently.*]

PRIORESS. [*With affected severity.*] The child interrupts us continually.

SISTER INEZ.   And a day like to-day!

SISTER JOANNA OF THE CROSS. [*Sympathetically.*] She sings like a lark.

MISTRESS OF NOVICES. [*Indulgently.*] She is so young!

SISTER MARCELLA.   *Ay,* Mother!

PRIORESS.   Continue reading, Sister María Jesús.

SISTER MARÍA JESÚS. [*Reading.*] "The Sorrows of an Unhappy Spirit, Submerged in a Sea of Woe. My God, O my God, save me, for every moment I die! Overwhelmed, I sink in the midst of this terrible storm. Every moment I am buffeted and borne down. I am sucked into the uttermost depths, and there is no health in me!"

TERESA. [*Singing.*]
    "From the glory of your brightness,
        Radiantly sweet,
    O, let me stoop and bend me
        To kiss your feet!

> Let me stoop and bend me
>   To kiss your feet!"
>
> [*Again the reader stops. The* NUNS *smile again.*]

PRIORESS.   Sister Sagrario, will you step out into the garden and ask the child not to sing? We are reading.

> [SISTER SAGRARIO *goes out, right, after making the customary reverence.*]

Continue, Sister, continue.

SISTER MARÍA JESÚS.   [*Reading.*]   "There is no health in me.   I cannot support myself; I cannot resist the shock of the horrible onrushing waves."

TERESA.   [*Singing.*]

> "You too were happy, Mary,
>   Happy in his love,
> Flowers of love and springtime
>   That bloom above!"
>
> [*The song is broken off suddenly, as if the* NUN *had arrived and commanded* TERESA *to stop. A moment later, there is a sound of light laughter.*]

PRIORESS.   It cannot be helped.   [*Smiling.*]   The child was born happy and she will die so.   [*To the reader.*]   Continue.

SISTER MARCELLA.   *Ay,* Lady of Sorrows!

PRIORESS.   But Sister Marcella, my daughter, why do you sigh like this?   Are you unwell?

SISTER MARCELLA.   No, reverend Mother.   But your daughter has temptations to melancholy.

PRIORESS.   The Lord protect and keep you.   You know how it displeases me to see the shadow of melancholy enter this house.

SISTER MARCELLA.   [*Making a reverence.*]   *Ay,* reverend Mother, pardon me and assign me some penance if I sin, but your daughter cannot help it.

PRIORESS.   Who was thinking of sin?   Go out into the garden and take a little sunshine, daughter; that is what you need.

SISTER MARCELLA.   *Ay,* reverend Mother, you don't

know what you say! For when your daughter sees the
flowers in the garden, and the blue sky so bright above
them, and the sun so beautiful overhead, the temptation
comes upon her then to sigh more than ever. *Ay!*

PRIORESS. If that is the case, return to your seat and
let us pray that it may cease. But do not let me hear
you sigh again, for I do not wish to send you to the prison
to brighten your spirit with solitude and confinement.

SISTER MARCELLA. As your Reverence desires. [*Returning to her seat.*] *Ay,* my soul! [THE PRIORESS *raises
her eyes to heaven in resignation.*]

A NUN. *Ay,* Blessed Virgin!

ANOTHER. *Ay, Jesús!*

PRIORESS. [*Somewhat ruffled.*] What? Is this an
epidemic? Nothing is wanting now but that we should begin to sigh in chorus. Remember, it is with gladness and
thanksgiving that the Lord is to be served *"in hymnis et
canticis,"* for the second of the fruits of the Spirit is joy and
there is none higher but love, from which it springs. [*A
Pause.* SISTER MARÍA JESÚS *reopens the book, and without waiting for the signal from the* PRIORESS, *resumes reading.*]

SISTER MARÍA JESÚS. [*Reading.*] "I cannot resist the
shock of the horrible onrushing waves. They break over
me unceasingly; irresistibly they bear me down."

PRIORESS. Close the book, Sister María Jesús, for the
blessed father who wrote it, alas, he too was of a melancholy
turn of mind! [SISTER MARÍA JESÚS *closes the book, makes
a reverence and sits down to sew.* THE MOTHER VICARESS
*appears in the door on the left, accompanied solemnly by
two other nuns.*]

VICARESS. [*Greatly agitated.*] *Ave Maria Purissima!*

PRIORESS. Conceived without sin.

VICARESS. Have I permission, reverend Mother?

PRIORESS. Enter and speak. [*Looking at her.*] If I
am not mistaken, your Reverence is greatly disturbed.

VICARESS. You are not mistaken, reverend Mother. No, and I dare affirm it is not for a slight reason. Your Reverence will be judge if this is the time and place to confront with a charge of *ipso facto* a member of this community.

PRIORESS. Speak, if the knowledge of the fault in public will not in itself constitute a scandal and a cause of offense.

VICARESS. In the opinion of your handmaid all cause of scandal will be avoided by looking the offense straight in the face.

PRIORESS. Speak then.

VICARESS. [*Making a profound inclination.*] I obey. Reverend Mother, while making the round of my inspection of the cells with these two monitors, as your Reverence has been pleased to command . . . [*The two* MONITORS each make a reverence.] And coming to the cell of Sister Marcella . . . [*All the* NUNS *look at* SISTER MARCELLA, *who lowers her eyes.*] I found under the mattress of the bed—in itself a suspicious circumstance and sufficient to constitute a sin—an object which should never be found in the hands of a religious, an object which, to say nothing of the sin against the rule of holy poverty which the private possession and concealment of any property whatever must presuppose, is by its very nature a root of perdition and an origin and source of evil.

PRIORESS. Conclude, Mother, in God's name! For you keep us in suspense. What is this object?

VICARESS. Disclose it, sister. [*To one of the* MONITORS.]

> [*The* MONITOR *makes a reverence, and draws from her sleeve a piece of glass, covered on one side with quick-silver.*]

PRIORESS. A piece of looking-glass.

VICARESS. Exactly, a piece of looking-glass! [*Horrified silence on the part of the community.*]

PRIORESS. What has Sister Marcella to say to this?

SISTER MARCELLA. [*Leaving her place and kneeling before the* PRIORESS.] Mother, I confess my guilt and I beseech your pardon.

PRIORESS. Rise. [SISTER MARCELLA *rises*.] Unhappy woman! What was the use of this piece of glass?

VICARESS. To look at herself in it, and amuse herself with the sight of her beauty, thus offending her Maker with pride and vain glory, and the exhibition of her taste.

SISTER MARCELLA. [*Humbly*.] No, reverend Mother; no!

VICARESS. Or else to dress herself up and fix herself by it, and make faces and grimaces such as they do on the streets in these days. [*The* VICARESS, *who has taken the mirror, looks at herself in it for a moment, then turns it hurriedly away*.]

SISTER MARCELLA. No, reverend Mother.

PRIORESS. For what then?

SISTER MARCELLA. For nothing, reverend Mother.

PRIORESS. What? For nothing?

SISTER MARCELLA. Your daughter means for nothing evil. On the contrary . . .

VICARESS. H'a! Now I suppose we are going to hear that it is a virtue in a religious to have a glass!

SISTER MARCELLA. No, reverend Mother, it is not a virtue. But your Reverences know already that your Sister suffers from temptations to melancholy.

VICARESS. Yes, yes . . .

SISTER MARCELLA. And when they seize upon her too strongly, they put it into her head to climb trees and run along the tops of walls, and jump over the fences in the garden, and to throw herself into the water of the fountain, and since your Sister knows that, in a religious, these . . . these . . .

VICARESS. These extravagances.

SISTER MARCELLA. Are unbecoming, your Sister catches a sunbeam in the mirror and makes it dance among the leaves and across the ceiling of her cell, and over the walls opposite, and so she consoles herself and imagines that it is a butterfly or a bird, and can go wherever it pleaseth.

VICARESS. It can, and stay there.

PRIORESS. For this fault, Sister Marcella . . . [SISTER MARCELLA *kneels.*] which, without being a grave one, yet is more than a little, considered according to the constitution of our rule, I assign you this penance. Tonight, before you retire, you are to repeat four times in your cell the psalm *"Quam dilecta."* Rise, and return to your seat. [SISTER MARCELLA *obeys, but before seating herself she makes a reverence before each of the* NUNS.] [*To the* VICARESS.] You may be seated. [THE VICARESS *and the two* MONITORS *seat themselves.*] [*Three light knocks on the door. It is* TERESA *who says:*]

TERESA. *Ave Maria Purissima!*

PRIORESS. Conceived without sin.

TERESA. May I come in?

PRIORESS. Come in. [TERESA *enters. She is eighteen, very pretty, very sunny and very gay, with nothing about her to suggest the mystic or the religious. She is dressed simply in gray and wears a white apron. She has a flower in her hair, which is arranged modestly, and without an excess of curls or ornament.*] Where are you coming from in such a hurry? You are all out of breath.

TERESA. [*Speaks always with the greatest simplicity, without affectation or pretense of any sort.*] From dressing the altar of the Virgin.

PRIORESS. Did that put you out of breath?

TERESA. No, Mother. It's because I wanted it to be all in white to-day, and there weren't white flowers enough in the garden, so I had to climb up and cut some branches off the acacia.

MISTRESS OF NOVICES. Did you climb a tree?

TERESA. Yes, I climbed two; there weren't enough blossoms on one.

MISTRESS OF NOVICES. *Jesús!*

VICARESS. *Ave María!*

TERESA. I wish you could see the view from the top of the big acacia! [SISTER MARCELLA'S *eyes open wide with envy.*]

VICARESS. Child, you have put yourself beyond the pale of God's mercy!

SISTER JOANNA OF THE CROSS. You might have fallen! It's too terrible to think of!

TERESA. Fallen? No, Mother. Why, I've climbed it a hundred times!

PRIORESS. Then you must not do it again.

MISTRESS OF NOVICES. [*Regretfully.*] It is too late to forbid her now.

PRIORESS. [*Sorrowfully.*] That is true.

SISTER INEZ. It is the last day she will dress the altar.

SISTER JOANNA OF THE CROSS. The very *last!*

TERESA. Ah, Mothers! You mustn't talk like this. Don't be sad.

VICARESS. No, we had better behave like you do, though it doesn't seem possible when you consider the day that it is, and you laughing and carrying on like one possessed!

PRIORESS. The Mother is right. A little more feeling to-day, daughter, a manner more subdued, would not have been out of place.

TERESA. You are right, reverend Mothers—you always are, in the holiness, which like a halo surrounds your reverend heads; but when a girl wants to laugh she wants to laugh, although, as Mother Anna St. Francis says, it may be the solemnest day of her life.

MISTRESS OF NOVICES. It is a solemn day, a very solemn day. You are leaving this house in which you have passed eighteen years, without scarcely so much as taking thought how it was you came to be here. Tomorrow, you will be your own mistress, and you will have upon your conscience the responsibilities of a wife.

VICARESS. Which believe me, are not light. Men are selfish, fickle . . .

TERESA. [*Timidly.*] Antonio is very good.

VICARESS. However good he may be, he is a man, and men are accustomed to command. They have been from the beginning of the world, and it has affected their character. And since you are very independent yourself, and like to have your own way . . .

TERESA. Yes, I have been spoiled I know; but you will see now how good I will be. It will come out all right.

SISTER JOANNA OF THE CROSS. Do you want to spoil the day for her?

TERESA. No, Mother—no; you won't spoil it, for I am very, very happy. You have all been so good to me!

VICARESS. Nonsense! No such thing.

TERESA. But it isn't nonsense. I know this is God's house, but you might have closed the doors to me, and you have flung them wide open, freely. I have lived here eighteen years and in all this time, to the very moment that I am leaving it, you have never once reminded me that I have lived here on your charity.

SISTER JOANNA OF THE CROSS. Don't say such things!

TERESA. Yes, I must say them. On your charity, on your alms—like a poor beggar and an outcast. I don't mind saying it nor thinking it, for I have been so happy here—yes, I am happy now—happier than the daughter of a king; for I love you all so much that I want to kiss even the walls and hug the trees, for even the walls and the trees have been kind to me. This has been the Convent of my Heart!

SISTER MARCELLA. It has been your home. If you had only been content always to remain in it!

PRIORESS. We must not talk like this. God moves in His own ways.

MISTRESS OF NOVICES. And in all of them His children may do His service.

VICARESS. The child was not born to be a religious. The things of the world appeal to her too strongly.

TERESA. It is true. The world appeals to me—poor me! It seems to me sometimes as if everybody loved me,

as if everything was calling to me everywhere to come. I
have been so happy in this house, and yet, all the time, I
have been thinking how great the world was, how wonderful! Whenever I have gone out into the street, how my
heart leaped! I felt as if I were going to fly, it was so
light! My brain was in a whirl. Then I was so glad to
come back again into this house, it felt so good, as if you
were all taking me up once more into your arms, as if I
had fallen to sleep in them again and was warm, folded beneath the shelter of the everlasting wings.

VICARESS. The wings of your good angel, who stood
waiting at the door—stood waiting till you came.

PRIORESS. Why should he have to wait? Her good
angel always has gone with her, and surely there never
has been a time when he has had to turn away his face.
Am I right, daughter?

TERESA. You are, Mother. [*Sincerely.*]

SISTER JOANNA OF THE CROSS. They needn't have asked
her that!

SISTER MARÍA JESÚS. [*Rising.*] Here are the bows for
the corset covers. Do you want them pinned or sewed?

SISTER INEZ. Sewed, I say.

SISTER MARÍA JESÚS. Down the middle?

MISTRESS OF NOVICES. Of course, down the middle.

SISTER MARÍA JESÚS. The reason I asked was because
in the pattern they are all fastened down the side.

MISTRESS OF NOVICES. [*Bending over to examine the
fashion plates with* SISTER INEZ *and* SISTER MARÍA
JESÚS.] Yes. Don't you see? She is right.

SISTER INEZ. That's funny! But they are pretty that
way.

MISTRESS OF NOVICES. I say it's absurd.

SISTER MARÍA JESÚS. What do you think, Mother
Crucifixion?

VICARESS. Don't ask me; I don't think. I neither
understand nor wish to understand these things—pomp

TERESA. Satisfied is too little, Mother. It does not express it. I don't deserve what you have done for me.

VICARESS. Yes, you do; you deserve it. And you might as well tell the truth as a falsehood. You have a good heart; you are a sensible girl. When you said what you did, you were thinking of your clothes; but you need have no scruples. Everything that you take away with you from this house, and more too, you have earned by your labor. That is the truth and you know it. Maybe we have taught you here how to sew and embroider, but you have worked for us in the convent, and outside of it. You owe us nothing. Besides, you had two hundred and fifty pesetas from the doctor to buy the material. Here . . . [*Producing a paper from under her scapular.*] is the account of the way they have been spent, so you can see for yourself and answer for it, since delicacy will not permit that we should be asked how it was used.

TERESA. [*Embarrassed and confused.*] What do you mean? Why, Mother Crucifixion!

VICARESS. That is all there is to it. You will find the account is correct. [TERESA *takes the paper and having folded it, puts it in her dress.*]

PRIORESS. [*To the* NUNS *who have been working.*] You may remove the table and gather up these things.

TERESA. No, Mother—let me do it. I will pick up everything. [*The* PRIORESS *makes a sign and all the* NUNS *rise and leave the room, except only herself, the* VICARESS, *the* MISTRESS OF NOVICES, *and* SISTER JOANNA OF THE CROSS.]

PRIORESS. [*To* TERESA.] What time do you go?

TERESA. My father is coming for me at five, but . . . Antonio has asked me . . . before I go . . . to say that he would like to see you all and thank you, and tell you how happy and grateful he is to you for the little girl you have brought up.

PRIORESS. We shall be very glad to see him.

VICARESS. Glad or not glad, no matter; it is our obligation. He cannot expect to carry her off like a thief in the night, and have no woman ask a question.

TERESA. I will call you when he comes. [*The* PRIORESS, *the* VICARESS *and the* MISTRESS OF NOVICES *go out.*]

> [TERESA *and* SISTER JOANNA OF THE CROSS *remain behind picking up and arranging the papers, patterns and scraps that have been left on the seats or about the floor. They say nothing but presently* TERESA *throws herself on her knees before the* NUN.]

TERESA. Sister Joanna of the Cross!

SISTER JOANNA OF THE CROSS. What do you want, my child?

TERESA. Now that we are alone, bless me while there is no one here to see—no, not one—for you are my mother, more than all the rest!

SISTER JOANNA OF THE CROSS. Get up. [TERESA *gets up.*] Don't talk like that! We are all equal in God's house.

TERESA. But in my heart you are the first. You mustn't be angry at what I say. How can I help it? Is it my fault, though I have struggled against it all my life, that I have come to love you so?

SISTER JOANNA OF THE CROSS. Yes, you have struggled. You have been wilful . . . [*Then seeking at once to excuse her.*] But it was because you were strong and well. When a child is silent and keeps to herself in a corner, it is a sign that she is sick or thinking of some evil. But you . . .

TERESA. *Ay*, Mother! Where do you suppose that I came from?

SISTER JOANNA OF THE CROSS. From Heaven, my daughter, as all of us have come.

TERESA. Do you really think that we have all come from Heaven?

SISTER JOANNA OF THE CROSS. At least you have come from Heaven to me. You say that I am your mother more than the rest; I don't know—it may be. But I know that for years you have been all my happiness and joy.

TERESA. Mother!

SISTER JOANNA OF THE CROSS. I was so glad to hear you laugh and see you run about the cloisters! It was absurd, but I always felt—not now, for you are grown-up now—but for years I always felt as if you must be I, myself, scampering and playing. For I was just your age now, a little more or less, when you came into the Convent. And it seemed to me as if I was a child again and had just begun to live. You were so little, so busy— yes, you were—but I was busy too, if you only knew, before I entered here, at home in our house in the village. I was always singing and dancing, although we were very poor. My mother went out every day to wash in the river or to do housework—she had so many children!—and I was always carrying one about in my arms. And when I entered here, as I could do, thanks to some good ladies, who collected the money for my dowry—God reward them for it—although I had a real vocation, I was sorrowful and homesick thinking of my little brothers and sisters! How I used to cry in the dark corners, and I never dared to say a word! Then the Mother told me that if my melancholy didn't leave me she would be obliged to send me home. And then you came and I forgot everything! That is why I say you came to me from Heaven. And I don't want you to think I am angry, or ashamed—or that it has ever given me a moment's pain to have loved you.

TERESA. Is that the reason that you scold me so?

SISTER JOANNA OF THE CROSS. When have I ever scolded you?

TERESA. Oh, so many times! But no matter. I always tell Antonio, Sister Joanna of the Cross is my mother. She is my mother, my real mother! So now he always calls you mother whenever he speaks of you.

SISTER JOANNA OF THE CROSS. My daughter, will you be happy with him?

TERESA. Of course! I am sure I will. He is so good,
he is so happy! He says he doesn't know where it is all
his happiness comes from, because his father, who is dead
now, was more mournful than a willow, and his mother,
poor lady, whenever anything happened to her that was
good, burst right out crying. How do you suppose it was
she ever managed to have such a boy? It must be that
sad mothers have happy children. How does it seem to
you?

SISTER JOANNA OF THE CROSS. How do I know?

TERESA. It must be that way. The first boy I have
is going to be—what is the solemnest thing in the world?
No, the first is going to be an architect, like his father; but
the second can be a missionary, and go to China if he wants
to, and convert the heathen. Just think what it would be
to have a son who was a saint! I shouldn't have to be so
humble in heaven, then, should I? I should have influence. And here you are all the time, Sister Joanna of the
Cross, praying for me and preparing miracles. So you see
I have a good start already.

SISTER JOANNA OF THE CROSS. How you do love to
talk!

TERESA. Isn't it foolish, Mother? Don't I? Listen!
When you were little didn't you ever want to be a boy?
I did. I used to cry because I thought then that I could
have been anything I wanted to be—this, that, I didn't
care what it was—Captain-General, Archbishop, yes, Pope,
even! Or something else. It used to make me mad to
think that because I was a girl I couldn't even be an
acolyte. But now, since—well, since I love Antonio, and
he loves me, I don't care; it doesn't make any difference
any more, because if I am poor and know nothing, he is
wise and strong; and if I am foolish and of no account,
he is, oh, of so much worth! And if I have to stay behind at
home and hide myself in the corner, he can go out into
the world and mount, oh, so high—wherever a man can
go—and instead of making me envious, it makes me so

happy! Ah, Sister Joanna of the Cross, when she truly loves a man, how humble it makes a girl!

SISTER JOANNA OF THE CROSS. Do you really love him so?

TERESA. More than life itself! And that is all too little. Maybe it's a sin, but I can tell you. Do you believe that we will meet in Heaven the persons we have loved on earth? Because if I don't meet him there and I can't go on loving him always just the same as I do now, no, more than I do now . . .

SISTER JOANNA OF THE CROSS. [Interrupting.] Hush! Peace! You mustn't say such things. It is a sin.

TERESA. Ay, sister Joanna of the Cross! How sweet it is to be in love!

SISTER JOANNA OF THE CROSS. But he . . . he . . . Does he love you too, so much?

TERESA. Yes, he loves me. How much, I don't know; but it doesn't make any matter. What makes me happy is that I love him. You needn't think that sometimes— very seldom though—I haven't been afraid that perhaps some day he might stop loving me. It used to make me sad. But if I had ever thought that some day I could stop loving him . . . No, it would be better to die first; for then, what would be the good of life?

SISTER JOANNA OF THE CROSS. Ah, my child! To continue in God's love!

TERESA. Do you know how I would like to spend my life? All of it? Sitting on the ground at his feet, looking up into his eyes, just listening to him talk. You don't know how he can talk. He knows everything—everything that there is to know in the world, and he tells you such things! The things that you always have known yourself, in your heart, and you couldn't find out how to say them. Even when he doesn't say anything, if he should be speaking some language which you didn't understand, it is wonderful . . . his voice . . . I don't know how to explain it, but it is his voice—a voice that seems as if it had been talking to you ever since the day you were born! You don't hear it only with your ears, but with your whole body. It's like the air which you see and breathe and taste, and which smells so sweetly in the garden beneath the tree of paradise. Ah, Mother! The first day that he said to me "Teresa"—you see what a simple thing it was, my name, Teresa—why, it seemed to me as if nobody ever had called me by my name before, as if I never had heard it, and when he went away, I ran up and down the street saying to myself "Teresa, Teresa, Teresa!" under my breath, without knowing what I was doing, as if I walked on air!

SISTER JOANNA OF THE CROSS.   You frighten me, my child.

TERESA.   Do I? Why?

SISTER JOANNA OF THE CROSS.   Because you love him so.   For earthly love . . . I mean . . . it seems to me it is like a flower, that we find by the side of the road—a little brightness that God grants us to help us pass through life, for we are weak and frail; a drop of honey spread upon our bread each day, which we should receive gladly, but with trembling, and keeping our hearts whole, daughter, for it will surely pass away.

TERESA.   It cannot pass away!

SISTER JOANNA OF THE CROSS.   It may; and then what will be left to your soul, if you have set your all on this delight, and it has passed away?

TERESA.   [Humbly.]   You mustn't be angry with me, Mother. No! Look at me! It isn't wrong, I know. Loving him, I . . . he is so good, he is so good . . . and good, it cannot pass away!

SISTER JOANNA OF THE CROSS.   Is he a good Christian?

TERESA.   He is good, Sister.

SISTER JOANNA OF THE CROSS.   But does he fear God?

TERESA.   One day he said to me: "I love you because you know how to pray." Don't you see? And another time: "I feel a devotion toward you as toward some holy

thing." He! Devotion! To me! And whenever I think
of that, it seems to me as if I was just growing better, as
if all at once I was capable of everything there was to do
or suffer in the world—so as to have him always feel that
way!

SISTER JOANNA OF THE CROSS. I hear some one in the
parlor. Draw the curtains.

[TERESA, *pulling the cord, draws the curtains over
the windows, shutting off the light. The fore part of
the stage remains in shadow, but the outer parlor is
brightly illuminated. ANTONIO has entered and may
be seen through the crack where the curtains join.
He is twenty-five years of age, well-built, manly and
sensitive of feature. He remains alone and his footsteps may be heard on the boards as he paces nervously
up and down.*]

TERESA. [*In a low voice, going up to the* NUN.]
Yes. It is he.

SISTER JOANNA OF THE CROSS. [*Seizing her hand.*]
Ah! How tall he is!

TERESA. Yes, he is tall. Doesn't he look splendidly
though?

SISTER JOANNA OF THE CROSS. Yes, he does. Has he
golden hair?

TERESA. No, it's the light; his hair is dark brown, and
his eyes are between violet and blue. It's too bad you
can't see them. They are so beautiful! When he talks,
they sparkle.

SISTER JOANNA OF THE CROSS. How old is he?

TERESA. Just twenty-five.

[ANTONIO *crosses from one side to the other, and
continues to pace back and forth.*]

SISTER JOANNA OF THE CROSS. He seems to be of a
very active disposition.

TERESA. That is because he is impatient. Shall I speak
to him and tell him you are here?

SISTER JOANNA OF THE CROSS. [*Falling back.*] No!

TERESA. Why not? He loves you dearly. [*In a low voice, going up to the grille.*] Good afternoon, Antonio.

ANTONIO. [*Looking about from one side to the other.*] Teresa? Where are you?

TERESA. [*Laughing.*] Here, boy, here; behind the grille. It is easy to see you are not accustomed to calling on nuns.

ANTONIO. Can't you run back the curtain?

TERESA. No, because I am not alone. Can't you guess who is with me? My mother.

ANTONIO. Sister Joanna of the Cross?

TERESA. [*To the* NUN, *delighted because he has guessed it.*] There! Do you see? [*To* ANTONIO.] Sister Joanna of the Cross—exactly. We have been watching you through the grille, and she says that she thinks you are a very handsome young man.

SISTER JOANNA OF THE CROSS. Goodness gracious! You mustn't pay any attention to what she says.

TERESA. Don't be angry, Mother. I think so myself.

ANTONIO. You never told me that before.

TERESA. That is because in here, where you can't see me, I'm not so embarrassed to tell you. Listen! We have to send in word now that you are here; but I want you to tell my mother something first, for if you stand there like a blockhead without opening your mouth, I am going to be very much ashamed, after all the time I have spent in singing your praises.

ANTONIO. What do you want me to tell her?

TERESA. What you have in your heart.

ANTONIO. But I don't know whether it is proper to tell it to a religious, although it is in my heart, for I love her dearly.

TERESA. Ah! I tell her that a million times a day.

ANTONIO. Then let us tell her together two million; because I must say to you, Madam, that it is impossible to know Teresa and not to love you.

TERESA. What a treasure is this mother of mine!

SISTER JOANNA OF THE CROSS. For shame, my child!
[*Blushing, to* ANTONIO.] I also have a great affection for
you, sir, for this child has been teaching me to love you.
She is a little blind perhaps, and trusting, for that is natural. She knows nothing of the world, and we—how
were we to teach her? And now you are going to take her
far away; but don't take her heart away from us, sir, and
break ours, when we let her hand go.

ANTONIO. Madam, I swear to you now that I shall
always kneel in reverence before the tenderness and virtue
which you have planted in her soul.

TERESA. I told you that he was very good, Mother.

SISTER JOANNA OF THE CROSS. May God make you
both very happy. And may God remain with you, for
his handmaid must go now and seek the Mother.

ANTONIO. But you are coming back?

SISTER JOANNA OF THE CROSS. With the sisters . . .
Yes, I think so. Good-bye. I have been so happy to know
you.

[SISTER JOANNA OF THE CROSS *goes out, greatly
moved.* TERESA *remains standing by the grille until
the* NUN *has disappeared, without speaking a word.*]

ANTONIO. Now you can draw back the curtain.

TERESA. Yes, a little. [*She runs back the curtain a
little way.*] But it won't do you any good, because you
won't be able to see me. Do you really like my mother?
Do you really? Why are you so silent? What are you
thinking about?

ANTONIO. I don't know; it is very strange. Since I
have come into this room, since I have heard your mother
speak, and have heard you, behind this grille, without
knowing for certain where you were in the dark, I have
been almost afraid to love you. But ah—how I do love
you!

TERESA. I like that better.

ANTONIO. Teresa!

TERESA. What is it?

ANTONIO. Will you never forget, will you carry with you always wherever you go, this peace and this calm?

TERESA. With you, Antonio?

ANTONIO. Yes, into the world, beyond these walls; for in the world we make so much useless noise. And you—I see it now—you are the mistress of peace and of calm.

TERESA. [*Laughing.*] I the mistress of calm? As if I hadn't been a little flyaway all my life, without an idea in my head! Mother Crucifixion says that since I was passed in on the wheel there hasn't been one moment in this house of what the rules call "profound calm." I know I don't talk much when I am with you—we have been together such a little while, and it has been all too short to listen to you; but you will see when I grow bolder and am not afraid. You will have to put cotton in your ears then. Ah, Antonio! Only think, we are going to have all our lives to be together and listen to each other talk and tell each other things—that is, all our lives for you to tell me things, because I . . . you will find out soon enough. Tell me really, truly, Antonio: aren't you going to be awfully ashamed to have such an ignorant wife?

ANTONIO. Ignorant or learned?

TERESA. I? Learned? In what?

ANTONIO. In a science which I did not know, and which you have taught to me.

TERESA. You are joking.

ANTONIO. I am in earnest. Until I met you, I knew nothing; I did not even know myself.

TERESA. Pshaw!

ANTONIO. You mustn't laugh. Did it ever seem to you, Teresa, that our soul was like a palace?

TERESA. Of course it is! It is like a castle. Santa Teresa says so: The soul is like a castle—the interior of a castle, all made of one diamond above and below. And it has seven courts, and in the last is stored a great treasure . . .

ANTONIO. Then in the innermost chamber of my soul

was stored the love I have for you, and if you had not come and opened the door yourself, and helped me to find it, I should have passed all my life in ignorance, without knowing anything was there.

TERESA. Don't repeat such heresies!

ANTONIO. Is it a heresy—the love I bear for you? No, it is a religion—the only one for me! My girl! Seven courts, you say? Then with a great effort I had passed into the first and I was running here and there aimlessly, and you don't know what horrible things I found —everywhere I stumbled on. They were my own traits. I was cold, selfish, proud, without trust or faith, without other ambitions than material desires—to pass through life easily and well, to be the first in my own petty world, incapable of sacrifice, of abnegation, of compassion, of disinterested love.

TERESA. No! No! You were no such thing.

ANTONIO. But I lived as if I were! What difference did it make? But then one day I heard your voice, and summoned by you, I again searched through the castle, and in the other courts I began to find—ah! under how many cobwebs, all covered-up with dust—humility and devotion, warmth of heart, pity and faith in so many holy things. And then I found my honor, self-respect and sympathy with my fellow man, in which we live, Teresa, for without it nothing else is life, and I began to be a man when I first loved you. For in these things you are the master, and I have learned them all from you!

TERESA. Hush! They are coming.

[TERESA *falls back from the grille, after first drawing the curtains again. The* NUNS *in single file enter silently, the youngest first, followed at last by the* MISTRESS OF NOVICES, *the* VICARESS *and the* PRIORESS. *The* PRIORESS *seats herself in the arm-chair at the left of the grille; the* VICARESS *and the* MISTRESS OF NOVICES *in two other chairs at the right. The remaining* NUNS *stand or are seated round about.* TERESA *supports herself with her hand*

on the back of the PRIORESS'S *chair.* SISTER JOANNA OF
THE CROSS *approaches her and takes her by the other hand.
There is absolute silence as the* NUNS *enter and find their
places. They look at each other with expectant attention,
and some nod and smile among themselves. When they
are seated, there follows an interval of further silence.*]

PRIORESS. *Ave Maria Purissima!* [ANTONIO, *somewhat embarrassed, and endeavoring vainly to penetrate the
darkness behind the grille, does not answer. The* PRIORESS,
*after waiting a moment, turns her head and smiles indul-
gently at the community.*] Good afternoon, young man.

ANTONIO. Good afternoon, Madam—or Madams—for
behind the mystery of this screen, it is impossible for me
to see whether I am speaking with one or with many.
[*The* NUNS *smile quietly and discreetly.*]

PRIORESS. [*In a low voice.*] Run back the curtain,
Sister Inez. [*The Sister runs back the curtain.*] You
are speaking with the entire community, which takes great
pleasure in knowing you.

ANTONIO. Ladies, the pleasure and the honor are mine,
and they are much greater than you will be ready to
imagine.

SISTER INEZ. Bless us! But isn't he a polite and
polished talker?

SISTER TORNERA. Keep still! I want to hear what
he has to say.

ANTONIO. For a long time I have desired greatly to
visit you. Teresa knows it, and she must have told it
to you.

PRIORESS. That is true. She has indeed. And we
have greatly appreciated your desire.

ANTONIO. But the first time I was in this place it was
Advent and the second it was Lent; and both times Teresa
informed me that it was impossible for me to see you.

VICARESS. Clearly. In seasons of penitence we receive
no visitors.

ANTONIO. But now it is May and past Easter time.

MISTRESS OF NOVICES.   How well acquainted he is with
the calendar!   Surely you must be very devout, sir.

ANTONIO.   I am, Madam—very; but chiefly in the worship of certain saints who as yet are not on the altars.

SISTER INEZ.   What a nice compliment!   Saints, did
he say?   [*Laughing.*]   He *is* a polished talker.

ANTONIO.   Ladies, after a hundred years they will be
lighting candles to you, and invoking you in prayers, and
in gratitude they will be bringing you thank offerings of
crutches and wooden legs.

SISTER TORNERA.   [*Laughing.*]   Does he think we are
going to be the patrons of rheumatism?

MISTRESS OF NOVICES.   After a hundred years?   You
are giving us a century of Purgatory.

ANTONIO.   No, Madam, by all that is holy!   I am
giving you a century of life, and entrance thereafter directly
into the choir of seraphim.

PRIORESS.   I fear you speak frivolously, Señor Don
Antonio.

ANTONIO.   Madam, I was never more earnest in my life.
Whenever I think of death, you have no idea of the peace
which enters my soul.   I remember how many saintly white
hands will be stretched down to me to help me into Paradise
—for I suppose that you will be able to exercise a little influence on behalf of one of the family.

SISTER SAGRARIO.   [*Laughing.*]   One of the family?

VICARESS.   Certainly.   We are all God's children.

ANTONIO.   But I shall be so in a double sense; first,
in my own birthright, and then as your son-in-law, who are
his brides.

VICARESS.   Ah!   It is not meet to jest about holy things.

ANTONIO.   Madam, you are right.   And you will pardon me all the inconsequences which I have said, for I
swear to you that they have been nothing but nervousness
and fear.

MISTRESS OF NOVICES.   You are not afraid of us?

ANTONIO.   I am, Madam, very—because of the respect

and admiration in which I hold you all. I came here more
disturbed than I ever have been before in my whole life.
I do not know whether I should thank you, or whether
I should beg your pardon.

PRIORESS. Beg our pardon?

ANTONIO. Yes, because I fear that I am not worthy
of the treasure which you are entrusting to me.

PRIORESS. We know already through the doctor that
you are an honorable young man.

MISTRESS OF NOVICES. And the love which our daughter
bears you is our guarantee. Surely the Lord would not
permit His child, brought up in His fear, to throw herself
away upon an evil man.

ANTONIO. I am not evil, no; but I am a man, and you,
ladies, with all the great piety of your souls, have been
nurturing a flower for the skies. When I first knew her,
my heart whispered to me that I had met a saint. She
was a miracle. When I first dared to speak to her, there
came over me a fear and a trembling that were out of the
course of nature; and when I told her that I loved her, my
heart stopped, and bade me to fall on my knees, and now
that I have come here to beg my happiness of you, I don't
know what I can promise you in token of my gratitude, nor
how I can give you thanks enough for the great honor which
you do me.

VICARESS. It may be you are speaking more truly than
you think, Señor Don Antonio.

MISTRESS OF NOVICES. Why, Mother!

VICARESS. No, let me speak. For he has said well.
The girl is not one of those worldly creatures who take
to their husbands a great store of physical beauty. That
is certain. You cannot call her ugly, but it is the most that
can be said. Nor does she bring with her any dower.
She is poorer than the poor. But she carries in her heart
a treasure, the only one which we have been able to give
her, which is more priceless than silver or gold, and that is
the fear of God. For this, sir, you must be answerable to

us, and we ask you your word now, that you will always respect it in her and in her children, if you should have any, if it should be God's holy will.

ANTONIO. Teresa shall always be the absolute mistress of her conscience and of my house, and my children shall ever be that which she desires. I pledge my word.

PRIORESS. You will never have reason to regret it, for she is a good and prudent girl.

VICARESS. And not hypocritical, for, although, as you have said, we have nurtured her for the skies, we have never permitted ourselves to believe that she was to reach them through the cloister.

SISTER MARÍA JESÚS. Do you mean to take her very far away?

ANTONIO. Yes, Madam. That is to say, there is no longer in the world either far or near. We sail next week. I am going to America as the resident director of a firm of architects.

PRIORESS. Yes, we know already.

ANTONIO. That is the reason for this haste. I do not wish to go alone.

SISTER TORNERA. Aren't you afraid the child will be seasick? They say you do get a terrible shaking-up upon the sea.

SISTER MARÍA JESÚS. You must promise us to take good care of her.

SISTER INEZ. If she gets overheated never let her drink cold water. She is very pig-headed about that.

SISTER MARCELLA. But you mustn't forget that she is accustomed to cold baths.

SISTER INEZ. If she takes cold or gets a cough, make her drink a glass of hot milk with a teaspoonful of hot rum in it, with plenty of sugar, for that's the only thing that will make her sweat.

TERESA. I think perhaps I had better attend to these matters myself, Sister.

SISTER INEZ. Yes, you'd be a pretty one to attend to

them! Don't you mind what she says, Señor Don Antonio, for she is spoiled utterly. If you don't give her medicines and force the spoon down her throat, she might be dying for all you'd know, but she'd never ask for them herself.

PRIORESS. We had better not confuse him with too many recommendations. Surely he knows the more important precautions already.

ANTONIO. [*Smiling.*] Perhaps it would be better if you wrote them out for me on a piece of paper.

SISTER TORNERA. A good idea! [*Laughing.*] If we began where does he think we'd leave off?

SISTER SAGRARIO. How many days will you be on the ship?

ANTONIO. Two weeks.

SISTER MARCELLA. Mercy! What an age! Suppose there should be a storm?

MISTRESS OF NOVICES. It will be at least two weeks more before we can get letters back.

ANTONIO. We will telegraph when we arrive and we will send you a message from the middle of the ocean, so that you will hear from us the same day.

SISTER INEZ. Mother of God! Can they send messages now from the middle of the ocean? How do the words come?

TERESA. Flying through the air, like birds.

SISTER INEZ. What will men invent next? When your handmaid was in the world, they came by a wire, and yet it seemed the work of the devil.

ANTONIO. I should not advise you, Madam, to believe that the devil is ever very far away from these inventions.

SISTER INEZ. Whether he is or not, when the telegram comes it will be safest to sprinkle it with holy water.

PRIORESS. Ah, Sister Inez, you are so simple! Don't you see that the young man is only joking?

VICARESS. It is five o'clock—the hour we were to expect your father.

ANTONIO. I do not wish to molest you further.

PRIORESS. You do not molest us, but we must close the parlor at five.

ANTONIO. You will pardon me if I commit a terrible breach of etiquette, but I should like to ask you one favor before I go.

PRIORESS. If it is in our power to grant . . .

ANTONIO. Although, as it seems, you have run back a curtain, yet the mystery of this screen still remains a mystery to me, a poor sinner, inscrutable as before; and I should be sorry to go away without having seen you face to face. Is it too much to ask?

PRIORESS. For us this is a day of giving. Draw back the curtains, Teresa. [TERESA *draws back the curtain from one window, a* NUN *that from the other, lighting up the room.*]

ANTONIO. [*Bowing.*] Ladies! . . .

VICARESS. Well? How does the vision appear to you?

ANTONIO. I shall never forget it as long as I live.

PRIORESS. Then may God go with you, and may you live a thousand years. [*Taking* TERESA *by the hand.*] Here is her hand. See, we give her to you with a great love, and may you make her happy.

ANTONIO. I answer for her happiness with my life.

PRIORESS. And may God go with you.

MISTRESS OF NOVICES. Teresa will give you from us two scapularies, the remembrances of a nun. They are not worth anything, but they have lain beside the reliquary of our father, the blessed Saint Dominic. Keep them in memory of this day.

ANTONIO. I shall treasure them, ladies, from this hour. And I pray you, remember me always in your prayers.

VICARESS. And upon your part do not forget to pray with them from time to time, for although it lies within the province of everyone to help our souls along the way to heaven, yet we must take the first steps ourselves. And may God go with you.

ALL. God go with you.

ANTONIO. Ladies! . . . [*He retires and disappears.
A* NUN *draws the curtain over the grille. Then a moment's silence. Some of the* NUNS *sigh and say:*]

NUNS. Ah, Lord! Good Lord! May it be God's
holy will! [*The bell by the door rings twice.*]

VICARESS. I thought so—your father.

[TERESA *stands in the midst of the group of* NUNS,
*bewildered, looking from one to the other, greatly
moved.* SISTER TORNERA *goes to open the door.*]

PRIORESS. Ask him to come in.

[*The* DOCTOR *enters on the arm of* SISTER TORNERA.
He is now very old, but neither decrepit nor cast down.]

DOCTOR. Good afternoon, ladies; good afternoon,
daughter.

TERESA. [*Kissing his hand.*] Good afternoon, father.

DOCTOR. The whole assembly—the parting, eh? Well,
did you see the young man? [*The* NUNS *do not answer.*]
A fine fellow, isn't he? He is waiting outside. We have
an hour in the coach before we arrive at the station, so
you had better get ready now, daughter. [TERESA *goes
out with* SISTER JOANNA OF THE CROSS.] Ah! The
trunk? Good! Carry it to the door. The boys outside
will take care of it. [*Two* NUNS *lift the trunk and carry
it out by the door on the right.*] There, that is done.
[*He seats himself in the* PRIORESS'S *chair.*] Well, how are
we to-day?

PRIORESS. You see, Doctor.

MISTRESS OF NOVICES. Who would ever have believed
it eighteen years ago?

DOCTOR. Eighteen years? We are growing old, Mother.
We are growing old.

PRIORESS. That is not the worst of it.

SISTER INEZ. How old are you now, Doctor?

DOCTOR. Seventy-eight, Sister.

SISTER INEZ. No one would ever think it.

DOCTOR. [*Attempting a witticism so as to cheer up the*
NUNS.] That is because I am preserved in sanctity, like

a fly in thick syrup. [*But none of the* NUNS *laugh.*]
A little mournful to-day, eh?

SISTER MARCELLA. What else did you expect?

SISTER SAGRARIO. She is not even going to be married
in our chapel.

DOCTOR. No, his mother is old and sick, and naturally
she wants him to be with her, so they must be married
in her house.

PRIORESS. Naturally. Poor woman! [*A pause.*]

MISTRESS OF NOVICES. She is going so far away!

DOCTOR. But she will come back, Mother. She will
come back.

PRIORESS. She knows nothing of the world.

DOCTOR. There is no cause to be alarmed. He is an
honorable man.

VICARESS. Yes, he seems to be one. [TERESA *and*
SISTER JOANNA OF THE CROSS *re-enter. It is plain that they
have both been crying.* TERESA, *wearing a mantilla, and
with her coat on, carries a shawl over her arm for use as a
wrap on the voyage. She stops in the middle of the room
and stands still, not daring to say good-bye.*]

DOCTOR. Well? Are we ready now?

TERESA. Yes . . . Now . . .

DOCTOR. Then say good-bye. It is late. We must be
going, daughter.

PRIORESS. Yes, you must not delay.

TERESA. [*Throwing herself on her knees before the*
PRIORESS *and kissing her scapular.*] Mother!

PRIORESS. Rise, my daughter, rise.

TERESA. Bless me, Mother! Bless me!

PRIORESS. May God bless you; so. Rise. [*As* TERESA
rises, the NUN *embraces her.*]

TERESA. Mother! I don't know what to say to you
. . . I don't know how to leave you . . . but you must
forgive me all the wrong I have ever done in all these
years. I have been foolish, wilful. I have made so much
trouble for you all. You must forgive me. I would like

to do something great, something splendid for you all.
But—but may God reward you! May God reward you!
God reward you! [*She bursts into tears.*]

PRIORESS. My daughter, come! You must not cry.
You must not allow yourself to be afflicted so.

TERESA. I am not afflicted, Mother; but . . . it's . . .
Mother, I can never forget you! You must pray for me,
pray for me! And you must never forget me!

PRIORESS. Ah, no, my child! Never! We will pray
God to help you, and to be with you, and you must pray
to Him for guidance and for counsel always, whenever
you are troubled or perplexed in anything. For the liberty which they enjoy in the world is like a sword in the
hands of a child, and life at best is hard, and bitter often-
times.

MISTRESS OF NOVICES. Be thankful that your heart is
well steeled to resist all the temptations that may come.
Is it not, my daughter?

TERESA. It is, Mother.

PRIORESS. Will you promise always to be reverent and
good?

TERESA. Yes! Yes, Mother!

VICARESS. Remember that your obligation is greater
than that of others, because you have come forth from
God's own house.

TERESA. Yes! Yes, Mother!

PRIORESS. Remember all the blessings He has showered
upon you from the cradle; remember that your whole life
has been as a miracle, that you have lived here as few have
ever lived, that you have been brought up as few have ever
been brought up, like the Holy Virgin herself, in the very
temple of the Lord.

MISTRESS OF NOVICES. As He was to the Evangelist,
so God has been to you a father and a mother, more than
to any other living thing.

PRIORESS. Remember that you are the rose of His
garden and the grain of incense upon His altar.

TERESA. Yes! Mother, yes! I will! . . . I will remember all . . . all . . . all . . .

MISTRESS OF NOVICES. And do not forget each day to
make an examination of your soul.

TERESA. No, Mother.

SISTER JOANNA OF THE CROSS. And write often.

TERESA. Yes, Mother.

DOCTOR. It is time to go, Teresa.

TERESA. [*Throwing herself suddenly into his arms.*]
Oh, father! Promise me never to leave them! Never
abandon them!

DOCTOR. Child of my heart! Ah, may they never
abandon me!—for this is my house. For more than forty
years I have been coming here day by day, hour by hour,
and now there is nobody within these walls who is older
than I. I have no children. I have had my loves—yes,
a moment's flame—but it was so long ago! I have forgotten them. And these Sisters, who have been mothers
to you, have been daughters to me; and now, when I
come, they no longer even cover their faces before me. Why
should they? It seems to me as if I had seen them born.
And in this house [*Greatly moved.*] I should like to die, so
that they might close my eyes, and say a prayer for me
when life itself has closed!

MISTRESS OF NOVICES. Who is thinking of dying,
Doctor?

PRIORESS. It is time to go.

TERESA. [*Looking from one to the other.*] Aren't
you going to embrace me? [*The* NUNS, *after hesitating and glancing a moment doubtfully at the* MOTHER
PRIORESS, *embrace* TERESA *in turn, in perfect silence.
Only* SISTER JOANNA OF THE CROSS, *taking her into her
arms, says:*]

SISTER JOANNA OF THE CROSS. My child!

PRIORESS. May you find what you seek in the world,
daughter, for so we hope and so we pray to God. But
if it should not be so, remember, this is your Convent.

Teresa. Thanks . . . thanks . . . [*Sobbing.*]

Doctor. Come, daughter, come . . . [*The* Doctor *and* Teresa *go to the door, but* Teresa *turns when she reaches the threshold and embraces* Sister Joanna of the Cross, *passionately. Then she disappears.* Sister Joanna of the Cross *rests her head against the grille, her back to the others, and weeps silently. A pause. The bells of the coach are heard outside as it drives away.*]

Mistress of Novices. They are going now. [*The chapel bell rings summoning the* Nuns *to choir.*]

Prioress. The summons to the choir.

Mistress of Novices. Come, Sisters! Let us go there.

[*All make ready to go out sadly. The* Vicaress, *sensing the situation, to her mind demoralizing, feels it to be her duty to provide a remedy. She, too, is greatly moved, but making a supreme effort to control herself, says in a voice which she in vain endeavors to make appear calm, but which is choked in utterance by tears:*]

Vicaress. One moment. I have observed of late . . . that some . . . in the prayer . . . have not been marking sufficiently the pauses in the middle of the lines, while on the other hand, they drag out the last words interminably. Be careful of this, for your Reverences know that the beauty of the office lies in rightly marking the pauses, and in avoiding undue emphasis on the end of the phrase. Let us go there. [*The* Nuns *file out slowly.* Sister Joanna of the Cross, *unnoticed, remains alone. With a cry, she falls upon her knees beside an empty chair.*]

Curtain

THE LOVER

COMEDY IN ONE ACT

TEATRO DE LÁ COMEDIA, MADRID
1913

ARTS LEAGUE OF SERVICE, MANCHESTER
1924

FORTUNE THEATRE, LONDON
1926

CHARACTERS

The Queen.
The Lover.
The Lady in Waiting.

THE LOVER

Salon in a Royal Palace. Although of extreme richness, the furnishings preserve an atmosphere of simplicity.

The stage is empty when the curtain rises. Loud shouts and cries are heard outside, as if an accident were taking place. Then various noises follow, clamor and confusion. After a moment THE QUEEN *enters, followed by* THE LADY IN WAITING.

THE QUEEN *is a beautiful woman, gowned in faultless taste. She is about forty years of age. Her hair is very dark, except for a solitary white lock which appears almost directly above the middle of her forehead; but this she does not attempt to conceal by any artifice. She enters in full regalia, as if attired for some court ceremony. From her shoulders hangs the royal mantle.*

THE LADY IN WAITING *is about sixty years of age, rather nobly plain. She also is in full court dress.*

THE QUEEN. [*As she leaves* THE LADY IN WAITING, *who attempts to support her.*] No, let me be, I am not hurt. . . . It is nothing.

LADY IN WAITING. Has Your Majesty suffered no injury?

THE QUEEN. None, I assure you.

LADY IN WAITING. But the shock, the fright—be seated, Your Majesty. [*She assists her to remove the Court Mantle.*] Your Majesty must rest. At least drink a glass of water.

THE QUEEN. [*Seating herself in an arm-chair.*] You may bring the water, but I will have nothing in it. Let it be pure as God made it.

> [THE LADY IN WAITING *brings the water from a table which stands near by.*]

77

LADY IN WAITING. But, Your Majesty, it is cold; Your Majesty is overheated—

THE QUEEN. Give me the glass. [*She takes it from the* LADY IN WAITING.] You are trembling all over.

LADY IN WAITING. Ah, Your Majesty, you have no idea how frightened I was, how frightened we all were, when the horses reared in the traces! Your Majesty can imagine . . . the overturn, the coach shattered into pieces, Your Majesty thrown upon the ground!

THE QUEEN. [*Smiling.*] Fortunately there was somebody waiting to receive me. How fortunate that that man [*Laughing.*]—my knight-errant—was so near!

LADY IN WAITING. [*Displeased.*] Certainly, Your Majesty.

THE QUEEN. [*Looking at her for a moment, then laughing.*] We shall have to award him the Grand Cross. Are you frowning?

LADY IN WAITING. Your Majesty!

THE QUEEN. But what is the matter? What is on your mind?

LADY IN WAITING. Your Majesty, that man was unmannerly and impertinent. Your Majesty will not be displeased, but his deportment was horribly incorrect. To catch Your Majesty in his arms without permission!

THE QUEEN. Yes, if he had allowed me to break my neck, his conduct would have been more correct. In that case he would not have committed a breach of etiquette. No, indeed! It is not every day that a woman, even if she is a queen, is in peril of her life, and has the experience of being saved from death in a gallant's arms.

LADY IN WAITING. Your Majesty amuses herself.

THE QUEEN. Perhaps I do, but not unkindly. Poor fellow! However, you may malign him as much as you like.

LADY IN WAITING. Your Majesty, I do not malign him when I suggest that it is incorrect and impertinent for this person to follow Your Majesty wherever you go.

THE QUEEN. [*Laughing.*] Like my shadow!

Lady in Waiting. Like a rude, ill-bred fellow who is ignorant of decency and of the requirements of etiquette. Your Majesty never leaves the Palace but that he is standing on the pavement opposite. You cannot go to church, or to the theatre, or visit the parks, or attend any public ceremony but that he is there in the front row, yes, or nearer than the front row, as he was to-day.

The Queen. Fortunately for me.

Lady in Waiting. Your Majesty, loyal vassals were not wanting to fly to Your Majesty's assistance.

The Queen. [*Gently.*] Yes, so I saw when the horses reared. Half a dozen dukes began to run, but what with etiquette which kept them at a safe distance and rheumatism which would not permit them to run, my royal person was in grave danger. [*Laughing.*] Indeed, if it had not been for him—

Lady in Waiting. Skulking in a bramble bush, like a lover in comic opera!

The Queen. Love is no respecter of hiding places. It is foolish to laugh at hidden lovers, even in comic opera. Besides, what you say was a bramble bush appeared to me to be a laurel, and men take as naturally to laurels nowadays as they did in the time of Petrarch. Some of the leaves have even clung to my robe. [*Picking off two or three.*] Almost enough to weave a crown for my lover.

Lady in Waiting. Your Majesty surely does not imply that that man is in love?

The Queen. Why not? Don't you think so?

Lady in Waiting. He is utterly deficient, lacking. How do we know? Perhaps he may be . . .

The Queen. An anarchist? But how stupid! In the twenty years he has followed me, he never yet has found an opportunity . . .

Lady in Waiting. [*Horrified.*] Your Majesty!

The Queen. [*Laughing.*] Of showing disrespect.

Lady in Waiting. Does Your Majesty consider that this extraordinary persecution shows no disrespect?

THE QUEEN. But what has become of him? Where is he?

LADY IN WAITING. He has been detained.

THE QUEEN. Where? For what reason?

LADY IN WAITING. For having introduced himself without permission into the Palace Gardens.

THE QUEEN. To save the life of his Queen! The end justifies the means.

LADY IN WAITING. Your Majesty, he could scarcely have been advised beforehand that Your Majesty's coach was to be overturned, and at that particular spot in the Palace Gardens.

THE QUEEN. Then you do not believe in presentiments?

LADY IN WAITING. Your Majesty, I am too old for such things.

THE QUEEN. [*With a note of melancholy in her voice.*] So am I—for such things.

LADY IN WAITING. Your Majesty!

THE QUEEN. No, we both know how old I am, and so does the world. Decreeing her age is not one of the prerogatives of a queen. [*Taking up a hand-glass, she gazes into it attentively.*] Horrible, is it not?

LADY IN WAITING. Your Majesty is marvellously young.

THE QUEEN. Even so, marvels do not last long. Whenever I look into the mirror I am aghast at the wrinkles which I shall find there very soon. I know, too, where they will come. [*Indicating her eyes and mouth.*] They show already when I laugh. Ah, when she is twenty, how carelessly a woman laughs! [*Putting down the mirror.*] When I laugh, I cover my face with my fan. When I am forty, I shall have all the Palace mirrors broken. [*She recites simply.*]

"When forty winters shall besiege thy brow"

You recall Shakespeare's sonnet?—

"When forty winters shall besiege thy brow
And dig deep trenches in thy beauty's field,
Thy youth's proud livery, so gazed-on now,
Will be a tatter'd weed, of small worth held;
Then being ask'd where all thy beauty lies,
Where all the treasure of thy lusty days,
To say, within thy own deep-sunken eyes,
Were an ill-eating shame and thriftless praise.
How much more praise deserved thy beauty's use,
If thou couldst answer 'This fair child of mine
Shall sum my count and make my old excuse,'
Proving his beauty by succession thine!
This were to be new made when thou art old,
And feel thy blood warm when thou feel'st it cold."

[*Sighing.*]   I have never had a child!

LADY IN WAITING. Your Majesty! [*Affectionately but disapprovingly.*] Your Majesty has no right to consider such a thing.

THE QUEEN. No, of course not. Ah! [*Smiling again.*] Do you suppose he could be a poet?

LADY IN WAITING. Why a poet?

THE QUEEN. Why not? In any case we shall soon know.

LADY IN WAITING. We shall? How?

THE QUEEN. I shall ask, and learn his answer.

LADY IN WAITING. Surely Your Majesty does not intend—

THE QUEEN. To receive him? Precisely.

LADY IN WAITING. But Your Majesty, he is nobody.

THE QUEEN. In that case we shall become acquainted more easily. I shall offer him my thanks.

LADY IN WAITING. Your Majesty's Government will thank him officially.

THE QUEEN. But he has saved me personally, and I shall thank him personally. I will receive him now.

LADY IN WAITING. Your Majesty!

THE QUEEN. If there is nothing else that you wish to suggest . . .

LADY IN WAITING. Unless Your Majesty has changed her mind?

THE QUEEN. No, do not be alarmed. There is nothing to fear.— Ah! And I will receive him alone.

LADY IN WAITING. As Your Majesty commands. [*She goes out.*]

     [THE QUEEN *again takes the mirror and gazes into it fixedly. With a woman's instinct, she rearranges her hair; then laughs at herself and lays the mirror down again.*]

THE QUEEN.

"When forty winters shall besiege thy brow" . . .

     [THE LADY IN WAITING *and* THE LOVER *appear in the doorway. He is forty years of age, neither well nor badly dressed. He wears a black sack suit, his beard is pointed, his hair somewhat long and slightly touched with gray. He comes forward greatly agitated.* THE LADY IN WAITING *retires.*]

THE LOVER. Your Majesty!

THE QUEEN. No, come in.

THE LOVER. [*Advancing a step, then making a reverence.*] Your Majesty!

THE QUEEN. Come nearer.

THE LOVER. Your Majesty!

THE QUEEN. I have sent for you to offer my thanks.

THE LOVER. I do not deserve them. Your Majesty will command.

THE QUEEN. It was a happy chance that brought you into the garden.

THE LOVER. Yes, Your Majesty, yes.

THE QUEEN. And I am deeply grateful to you.

THE LOVER. No, Your Majesty, no.

THE QUEEN. But I am. Indeed I am!

THE LOVER. Your Majesty will decide.

THE QUEEN. But how is it that you were able to gain admission to the Gardens?

THE LOVER. Very simply.

THE QUEEN. In spite of my guards?

THE LOVER. Your Majesty, it was not the fault of your guards. I climbed the wall at the rear by the plane trees, out of sight of the guards.

THE QUEEN. In broad daylight?

THE LOVER. No, Your Majesty, last night. Your Majesty must not be alarmed—

THE QUEEN. But the wall is very high there. You might have injured yourself.

THE LOVER. No, Your Majesty, I am used to it.

THE QUEEN. Used to it?

THE LOVER. Yes, Your Majesty, on Saturdays. The factory shuts down over Sunday, so I am not obliged to work. I have plenty of time; I can sleep where I like.

THE QUEEN. Do you spend the night in the open air, in the garden?

THE LOVER. It is very pleasant in the summer time.

THE QUEEN. Do you mean that in winter?—

THE LOVER. Just the same; yes, Your Majesty. [*She makes a gesture of astonishment.*] Only when it freezes, I go into the house with the orang-outang. Your Majesty keeps him now on the further side of the parterre. Don't be alarmed, Your Majesty; we are great friends. He is very fond of tarts and roast chestnuts, so you see there is no danger.

THE QUEEN. Great Heaven! Is it possible? Are you in your right mind?

THE LOVER. Yes, Your Majesty.

THE QUEEN. But, my good man, what is the object of exposing yourself in mid-winter in this fashion, in such singular company?

THE LOVER. Your Majesty . . . really . . . I don't know whether or not I ought to tell you.

THE QUEEN. But you must!

THE LOVER. Your Majesty, every night before you retire, and when you get up in the morning, Your Majesty
comes out upon the terrace before your apartments. In
the evening, you look up at the stars; in the morning, you
feed the white doves.

THE QUEEN. Yes, I do, poor things! I like to toss
them a few handfuls of corn.

THE LOVER. [*Interrupting.*] Indian corn.

THE QUEEN. How do you know?

THE LOVER. The wind usually carries some grains off
the terrace.

THE QUEEN. Do you pick them up?

THE LOVER. Yes, Your Majesty, when I can, which
is not often. The paths are swept every morning, so when
night comes, they are no longer there.

THE QUEEN. What? Do you keep them?

THE LOVER. Yes, Your Majesty. I have a collection
of souvenirs:—the grains of corn; a feather from Your
Majesty's hat, which blew out one day while you were
driving; a piece of fur from one of Your Majesty's boas,
which you wore at the last Carnival—it caught in the rail-
ing as Your Majesty left the stand; a coin Your Majesty
threw from your coach to a little beggar boy in the street;
a tortoise-shell hairpin which fell into the garden one morning
along with the corn; a pair of gloves; two of Your Majesty's
slippers—I purchased them from a maid of one of the
Ladies of the Wardrobe—and I don't know what else!
You see, it is a little museum. An Englishman offered me
a thousand pounds sterling for it.

THE QUEEN. [*Interested.*] What did you do?

THE LOVER. Your Majesty, the heart is not for sale.

THE QUEEN. You must be rich.

THE LOVER. No, Your Majesty, I was—that is to say,
rich enough; I made a good living. But now, I am poor.

THE QUEEN. Have you lost your money?

THE LOVER. Yes, Your Majesty. But we will not
speak of that; it is of no interest to Your Majesty.

THE QUEEN. But it is. It interests me very much. May I ask . . . ?

THE LOVER. How I lost my money? Yes, Your Majesty, it is not a secret. Even if it were, since it is Your Majesty . . . I spent it upon railway tickets, sea-voyages, rooms in hotels. Your Majesty is such a great traveller!

THE QUEEN. Were you following me? [*He nods his head in assent.*] But this is incredible.

THE LOVER. No, Your Majesty, no. Travelling is very expensive. As long as Your Majesty remained in Europe, it was not so bad; but when you made a voyage to India and another to the Fair at Chicago, and immediately after, a pilgrimage to the Holy Land—

THE QUEEN. Did you follow me even as far as India?

THE LOVER. Yes, Your Majesty. Your Majesty will remember that the voyage was undertaken on account of your health. Your Majesty may not know it, but the doctors agreed that it was a question of life and death. It was necessary for you to have a change of climate. Thanks be to God, Your Majesty recovered, but you might have died on the journey. Your Majesty will understand that under the circumstances it was impossible for me to remain in Europe.

THE QUEEN. Impossible!

THE LOVER. [*Ingenuously.*] Absolutely.

THE QUEEN. But I cannot consent to have you spend your fortune like this.

THE LOVER. Your Majesty, do not give it another thought. It was not exactly a gold mine. A few thousands, that was all—the factory which I had the honor to mention to Your Majesty: "The Unrivalled, Makers of Butter and Cheese"—purveyers to Your Majesty, yes, indeed! It was mine, now it belongs to another. That is all.

THE QUEEN. But you . . . ?

THE LOVER. I am assistant bookkeeper now; I check up the accounts.

THE QUEEN. That must pay you very little.

THE LOVER. Pshaw! Nothing to speak of. It is a humble position. Believe me, Your Majesty, I am capable of much more than that. If not proprietor, I might still have been manager, or foreman at least, only—

THE QUEEN. Only?

THE LOVER. Only . . . Your Majesty will not be displeased, but I must keep my time free. The fact is . . . well, I have taken this position because it gives me a living and—[*Looking down at his clothes*]—and enough to appear respectable, because it requires only two hours a day, from half past nine until half past eleven in the morning, precisely the hours at which Your Majesty confers with your Ministers. Your Majesty will understand . . .

THE QUEEN. [*Laughing.*] Certainly! At that same hour we are both at the office.

THE LOVER. No, no, Your Majesty! Your Majesty misinterprets my meaning. I never presumed to think . . . the fact is . . . well, between those hours my mind is more free; I am able to work without distraction, to apply myself. I am sure that Your Majesty is not upon the streets.

THE QUEEN. How long do you expect to continue this life?

THE LOVER. As long as I am able, Your Majesty, and Your Majesty does not prevent. Your Majesty is not offended at what I have said?

THE QUEEN. Offended? No! But . . . you must be very unhappy.

THE LOVER. No, Your Majesty, very happy. *Very* happy! That is, not as happy as I was, because now, when Your Majesty leaves Court, I am not always able to travel. Rascally coin! But, fortunately, now Your Majesty travels less. It will not do to ask too much of fortune. Your Majesty, after what happened this morning, I . . . I am

repaid for everything which I have suffered in the world.
Your Majesty cannot imagine how happy it makes me that
. . . that is, Your Majesty cannot imagine how glad I am
that this incident . . . although I would have given my
life to have prevented it . . . I mean . . . Your Majesty
understands what I mean.

THE QUEEN. Yes, yes, I do. Do not distress yourself.
I, too, am glad that it was you—

THE LOVER. Your Majesty!

THE QUEEN. Because . . . I have noticed your
face for so many years, I have seen you for so long a
time.

THE LOVER. Your Majesty has noticed me?

THE QUEEN. Naturally.

THE LOVER. Probably Your Majesty thought that I
was a photographer for one of the illustrated papers?

THE QUEEN. I thought that you were a poet.

THE LOVER. No, Your Majesty! No! Never!

THE QUEEN. Have you never written verses?

THE LOVER. [*Disappointed.*] Does Your Majesty
like verses?

THE QUEEN. Yes, I am very fond of them.

THE LOVER. Goodness gracious! No, Your Majesty,
no! Never! Never! [*Brightening.*] But I know by heart
almost all the verses which have been published about Your
Majesty—birthday verses, verses celebrating your victories,
your works of charity, and so on, and so on. There are
so many of them! Your Majesty of course knows them,
too?

THE QUEEN. Not those verses. [*Smiling.*]

THE LOVER. God bless us!

THE QUEEN. But you must not be troubled. One may
be a poet, and yet not write verses.

THE LOVER. Does Your Majesty think so?

THE QUEEN. Certainly, we may write poetry or we may
live it. [*Deeply affected.*] And devotion and self-denial,
illusion and dreaming, the sacrifice of one's life to an ideal,

an impossibility—these things are also true poetry, great poetry, are they not?

THE LOVER. [*Not understanding.*] No doubt, Your Majesty, no doubt. Of course, since Your Majesty says so.

THE QUEEN. And you are a great poet of life.

THE LOVER. Your Majesty says so.

THE QUEEN. And I—because you are—in memory of this day, of this event, which also is an extraordinary one in my life—I am going to give you a present to add to that collection which you tell me of, and I hardly know—because of your delicacy, your sacrifices, really—will you accept this remembrance from me? [*She offers him a jewel which she wears upon her breast.*]

THE LOVER. No, no, Your Majesty! No! By no means! Really. Not that jewel! No, no!

THE QUEEN. But why not?

THE LOVER. Because a jewel is—a jewel. That is, it has value—in itself; and—no, Your Majesty! No, no!

THE QUEEN. I did not wish to give offense.

THE LOVER. No, Your Majesty, no! It is not that. It is . . . the way I feel. A caprice! If your Majesty would deign to give me some reminder, something personal, perhaps, of no value.

THE QUEEN. As you wish.

THE LOVER. If you would let me have that mirror, Your Majesty, after looking into it, once. [THE QUEEN *looks into the mirror and then hands it to the Lover.*] There . . . Your Majesty! Thanks! Your Majesty will permit me to kiss your hand? [*He kisses it.*] Thanks, thanks, Your Majesty! Believe me, Your Majesty— [*Deeply moved.*] This is the happiest day of my life.

THE QUEEN. I, too, am greatly obliged to you, and I wish to ask you a favor. If at any time you desire anything, anything which it is within my power to grant, you will do me a great kindness by coming to me.

THE LOVER. [*Hesitating, wishing to ask something.*] Your Majesty!

THE QUEEN. Now . . . Tell me truly, is there nothing that you wish?

THE LOVER. Your Majesty! Since Your Majesty has been so kind . . . If Your Majesty would exert your influence with the Minister of the Interior to have him grant me a pass over the railways of the Kingdom.

THE QUEEN. You shall have it this very day. Is there nothing else? What is your name?

THE LOVER. Matthew, Your Majesty. Matthew Brown, Your Majesty's humble servant.

THE QUEEN. [*Repeating the words so as to fix them in her memory.*] Matthew Brown. You shall have it this afternoon. Now, you may retire. [*She strikes a small silver bell.*] And many thanks yet again. [*To the* LADY IN WAITING, *who enters.*] Let this gentleman be escorted to his home, and a note be made of his address. [*She bows, dismissing him.*]

THE LOVER. Your Majesty! . . . [*Bowing very low, he is about to disappear, but as he reaches the door, he turns and says:*] It need not be first class. [*Goes out.*]

THE QUEEN. [*Disturbed, pacing up and down the room, without knowing whether to laugh or to cry:*] Matthew Brown! Matthew Brown! [*To* THE LADY IN WAITING, *who re-enters.*] Has he gone?

LADY IN WAITING. Yes, Your Majesty. But Your Majesty is unwell! Has this man given offense? He has been impertinent—

THE QUEEN. No! No! On the contrary. Poor fellow!

LADY IN WAITING. Was he a poet?

THE QUEEN. A poet? No. That is—yes, in his way. Imagine—but how can you imagine? My God! This poor man has given his life for me, for to him his cheese factory was his life. Four centuries ago he would have

fought under my banners, he would have conquered a kingdom for my sake, he would have discovered a new world
and have laid it at my feet, and now—now, to see me
feed corn to the doves, he sleeps in a cage with the orang-
outang! And his name is Matthew Brown—Matthew
Brown, the Lover! The poet was right:—We have been
born too late into a world which has grown too old!

CURTAIN·

LOVE MAGIC

COMEDY IN ONE ACT AND TWO SCENES

SALÓN NACIONAL, MADRID
1908

WALDORF-ASTORIA, NEW YORK
1918

CHARACTERS

THE PROLOGUE.
PIERROT.
COLUMBINE, *Pierrot's Wife*.
PIERRETTE, *Maid and Confidant of Columbine*.
POLICHINELLE, *An Old Magician*.
HARLEQUIN.
A LITTLE GIRL.

LOVE MAGIC

THE PROLOGUE. Rum-a-tum-tum! Ladies and gentlemen! Although I am a marionette, I am the Prologue.
And invested with so high a dignity, permit me to announce
the subject of the comedy which is about to be presented,
and to address you in eulogy of the personages who are
to appear in it. Ladies and gentlemen! Inevitably it
treats of love. Love! Love! I wish, ladies and gentlemen, I were a poet at this moment so that I might present
to you in a nosegay of the sweetest smelling syllables a pane-
gyric of that dear misfortune, that delightful pain, that
fatal passion, that enchantment, that irresistible effluence
of the stars, that fierce consuming of the soul, that death-
dealing microbe—or whatever it is that you may decide
this delicious inquietude to be, which, through all the centuries, men and women have agreed to call love. You
would listen amazed, if I were such a poet, to the crackling
and scintillation of my metaphors; you would admire and
marvel at the unstable, shifting winds, the soft, unfolding
flowers, the broad expanse of heaven, the silver fountains,
the caverns, the eagles, the sun rays and the moonbeams,
and all the twinkling stars which I should make dance
before you upon the rope of my imagination to embellish
my discourse. You would twiddle your thumbs with delight, ladies and gentlemen, listening to my discourse, if
I were a poet; but I have already told you that I am not
one; I am only a marionette and the Prologue. I see you
smile. Smile, then, but don't disdain me. To be these
two things at one and the same time one must amount to
something. Marionette! I see you laugh. Joy sparkles
in all your eyes. Do you suppose that it is a small thing
to have a name the very mention of which is enough to

make people laugh? And do you suppose it is nothing, when you have it, to be able to live up to it throughout the ages and to uphold such a reputation with a dignity which, after all, is purely ridiculous? And we have upheld it, yes we have, ladies and gentlemen, splendidly, like kings and princes. Our little bodies are our witnesses. To win applause they disjoint themselves, twist and turn and bend backward, throw off their arms and heads into the air, or lose a leg in a high prance to get it back again in a pirouette. See! We palpitate from head to foot, every inch of us, as if our bodies were all hearts. And yet, ladies and gentlemen, beyond a doubt we have no hearts. What should we need of them when we vibrate and fly from one thing to another so continuously without them?

A LITTLE GIRL. But, Mr. Prologue, how can marionettes love if they have no hearts?

THE PROLOGUE. I did not say that they could love, my dear young lady.

LITTLE GIRL. Didn't you say, Mr. Prologue, that your comedy was about love?

PROLOGUE. That is exactly it. It is about love, but it is a comedy.

LITTLE GIRL. Oh!

PROLOGUE. But do not be sad, beautiful black eyes, for our comedy will be incomparably played. All the love in the world could never discover lover's sighs anywhere which would be like those of Columbine.

LITTLE GIRL. Good! Good! Are you going to tell us about Columbine?

PROLOGUE. Why not? Know then that she is white, but not pale, because in each of her cheeks every instant a rose is about to be born. She has painted her lips with the red of poppies, and one day when she sat down to dream, looking out over a meadow, two violets sprang up and jumped into her eyes. Since then nobody has been able to tell whether her glances were fragrance or light, and out of this sweet confusion, as out of all beautiful confusions, a harmony springs, which we call music. And so the look of Columbine is a song. Merely listening to her sing and hearing her laugh, men have gone mad. So her mind is like a wonderful bird-cage, filled with nightingales, which, like all captive nightingales, feed upon hearts —upon her heart. That is why Columbine is unfaithful to Pierrot, sometimes—to feed her heart. For Pierrot, who is a marionette and a puppet as she is, refuses her the heart's meat on which, as I have told you, the nightingales feed.

LITTLE GIRL. Good! Good! Now tell us about Pierrot.

PROLOGUE. What shall I tell you about Pierrot? His mind is like a sunbeam which has fallen into a globe of crystal and clear water, and all the colors are there in it, except one, which is constancy. You see today he imagines he is a philosopher, but out of his philosophy roses spring, so that our comedy which begins with a sigh, ends with an embrace, or, rather, with two embraces, because Harlequin, after he has sung his song so earnestly, and to such utter disdain, consoles himself for love by loving, and for the kisses which he cannot get, by those the girls will give. For this is the proper way all love songs should end. Try and sing them, gentlemen, you will always find some ear that is willing to hear. And you, beautiful ladies, listen to the song of love while it is floating in the air and catch it on the wing, for you will find that it is tame and it thrives in captivity. Ask Pierrette if the kisses have not turned to honey which she has taken in when they had lost their way and had nowhere else to go. Now, ladies and gentlemen, I can only add that wisdom is about to appear upon the stage of our farce, but the triumph of folly will oblige him soon to break his wand. [*The curtain rises.*] The comedy begins. This is the garden—I forgot to tell you that the stage represents a garden. Open your ears, for the fountain begins to play, open your eyes for the roses are bursting into bloom.

[*The* PROLOGUE *retires.*]

SCENE I

In PIERROT'S *garden. There is an arbor with rustic benches at the right. It is spring. Trees and bushes droop their boughs, laden heavily with flowers, perfuming all the air. The breezes sing with the voices of birds, and the sky smiles bright with sunshine.*

COLUMBINE, *seated within the arbor, whose foliage conceals her almost completely, seems wrapped in melancholy thought.* PIERROT *walks up and down at the rear, musing, and gazing contemplatively from the sky to the ground and from the ground to the sky, lingering lovingly before the flowering trees and talking to the flowers.*

PIERROT. [*Declaiming.*] O Nature! Mother without beginning and without ending, beyond the touch of time! What can I do to merit all thy gifts? Roses of fire! How can I ever hope to know the mystery which is flaming at your hearts? Lilies! How can I penetrate the secrets of your petals of white snow? Thanks, thanks, O Beauty, thanks, for thou hast rent thy veil before mine eyes! And in comtemplation of thy treasures I must end my life.

COLUMBINE. Ah! Woe is me!

PIERROT. [*Disappearing, lost in the depths of the garden.*] Thanks, thanks, a thousand thanks! I value my vision and my poet's dreams above all the splendors and above all the loves of earth and heaven.

COLUMBINE. Ah! Woe is me!

[PIERRETTE *enters, accompanied by* POLICHINELLE.]

PIERRETTE. Enter, Signor Polichinelle, quickly; for now Signor Pierrot is wrapped in his meditations. He will not discover that you are here. Enter . . .

POLICHINELLE. Did you say that your mistress had sent for me?

PIERRETTE. Oh, how eagerly, Signor Mage! Could I but make you understand how wretched the poor child has been! Does it not pierce the very soul to look at her? She spends all the day and the night-time sighing, she is fading away so fast. That divine form of hers is not what it once was, alas!

POLICHINELLE. Alas!

PIERRETTE. How oblivious men are to such things, Signor Mage!

POLICHINELLE. Not all men.

PIERRETTE. My lady is like the driven snows of heaven to her spouse. [*Turning toward the back with a menacing gesture.*] Ah, Signor Pierrot! Signor Pierrot!

POLICHINELLE. Hush! I think Columbine has discovered us.

COLUMBINE. [*Coming out of the arbor and advancing in tears toward* POLICHINELLE.] Ah, Signor Magician! How impatiently I have awaited your arrival!

POLICHINELLE. [*Bowing.*] Signora Columbine!

COLUMBINE. Bring chairs, Pierrette.—Ah! Woe is me!

POLICHINELLE. Do not sigh, lady.

COLUMBINE. I am so unhappy!

POLICHINELLE. I congratulate you—

COLUMBINE. Upon being unhappy?

POLICHINELLE. No; upon finding that your beauty has not faded so fast as I had been led to suppose. Of course, I had heard from Pierrette—

PIERRETTE. [*Returning with the chairs.*] What do you know about such things, you old dotard? Nonsense! I suppose a woman's beauty is like an article of religion in your eyes—there is no more to it than seeing and believing.

COLUMBINE.   Leave us, Pierrette!

PIERRETTE.   [*Before retiring, she looks toward the rear, where it is to be supposed that she sees* PIERROT.] There he is now. Look at him!—bending over the roses, and, I dare say, composing verses in their praise. I would hand him a bunch of roses if he had the honor to be my spouse! Ah, Signor Pierrot! Unhappiest of men! Don't you know that you are not the only poet in the world; that there are others who compose as beautiful verses as you do, and to better purpose? . . . [*The notes of a cithern are heard in the distance.*] Didn't I tell you? It is the good Harlequin.

HARLEQUIN.   [*Singing.*]

> White roses are her forehead,
> The waving grain her hair,
> The stars her eyes;
> Alabaster pure her shoulder,
> And the beauties that enfold her
> The starry skies.
>
> Who would not be of the roses,
> Or the grain that is her hair?
> Her starry eyes?
> Or her neck of alabaster,
> Serf and slave where she is master—
> Her deep heart's sighs?

[*The words are heard afar off, linked with a haunting melody.* PIERRETTE *listens, entranced, emphasizing them with gestures of approval.* COLUMBINE *rises indignantly, the first stanza scarcely concluded, and presently addresses* PIERRETTE.]

COLUMBINE.   Pierrette!

PIERRETTE. Lady!

COLUMBINE. Didn't I command you to send that impertinent fellow away? His music is displeasing to my ear.

PIERRETTE. In compliance with your command, I shut the gate in his face, and the body of your lover remains outside in the alley, sore distressed. But his spirit—woe is me!—is an immaterial thing, and who can deprive Signor Harlequin of the consolation of sending it after you wherever you may be, on the wings of his songs?

COLUMBINE. Go and tell him that he offends me with his music.

PIERRETTE. I would not be too severe with him, if I were you. What harm can it do just to hear?

COLUMBINE. [*Indignantly.*] Pierrette!

PIERRETTE. [*As she turns to go.*] All, all are blindly in love with the impossible: my lady with her husband, Harlequin with my lady, and with me, nobody—which, alas, is only too possible!

[COLUMBINE *sinks again into her chair and sighs wearily.*]

POLICHINELLE. [*Greatly perplexed.*] But will you be kind enough to explain to me what the matter is? What is the meaning of these tears, these songs of Harlequin's, this inexplicable discontent upon the part of your maid? Why all this mystery? I am distracted—I shall go out of my head.

COLUMBINE. Ah, Signor Polichinelle, love is the most mysterious thing in the world!

POLICHINELLE. I should be sorry to have you think so. Love is a natural function; it is simple, perfectly simple. The difficulty is that we complicate it with spiritual distinctions. Ah! That is where the trouble begins. Nature is never willing to have man improve upon her processes.

COLUMBINE. The fact is—

POLICHINELLE. That is precisely the fact.

COLUMBINE. The fact is that my husband does not love me.

POLICHINELLE. What do you say? What is that? Pierrot is deceiving you?

COLUMBINE. He is not even deceiving me. Oh, if only once he would deceive me! Then, at least, I might be thankful that he had had the grace to consider me, to make some effort to preserve my ideals.

POLICHINELLE. But your rival?

COLUMBINE. My rival, Signor Mage, is Nature. [POLICHINELLE *is dumbfounded*.] Yes, Pierrot is a poet —the more miserable he! He adores the carmine in the roses, but he disdains it upon my lips. He worships the azure of the overarching sky, but he cannot see it in the teardrop which glistens in my eye. He drinks sweet perfumes on the breezes, but he will not quaff them from the zephyrs which are wafted from my mouth. . . . Ah! Woe is me! Woe is me!

POLICHINELLE. Pierrot a poet? You are right. Poetry in marriage is entirely out of place. It is an intruder, an interloper, like anything else which we do not expect. But these songs of Harlequin's?

COLUMBINE. They are another complication, Signor Mage. My misfortune, thanks to the little pains which my husband takes to deceive me, has become known to all men, and Harlequin has had the audacity to presume to console me for it. He wishes me to follow the old adage which says that "Love is cured by love," he . . .

POLICHINELLE. What is it that he wishes you to do?

COLUMBINE. Have no fear, I shall not follow his advice.

POLICHINELLE. You are right. For this notion that love can be cured by love is sheer nonsense. Believe me, there is no cure for anything on earth, outside of science. You can trust me for that, Signora. I am a wise old man.

COLUMBINE. That is the reason I have sent for you.

POLICHINELLE. You have done well, my daughter. [*He meditates.*] You say that your husband has deserted you, he has abandoned and is tired of you, he writes verses —all of these are bad signs, very bad. However, fortunately—

COLUMBINE. Is there no remedy?

POLICHINELLE. One—one which is well-nigh infallible. [*He draws a crystal phial from the recesses of his robe.*] Take this phial. In it has been brewed a philter, compounded by magic art out of the essence of your tears.

COLUMBINE. But what shall I do with this philter?

POLICHINELLE. Whenever Pierrot is pensive and absorbed, wrapt in his poetic ecstasy, let fall but one drop from this phial, and poesy—adieu!

COLUMBINE. I do not understand.

POLINCHINELLE. Listen. For example, you say that Pierrot is enraptured with the azure of the skies. Spill but one drop, let fall but one tear, and the sky will be covered with thick clouds in his sight.

COLUMBINE. I understand.

POLICHINELLE. So, little by little, hour by hour, he will become disenchanted with all natural beauty, and he will turn again to yours.

COLUMBINE. Which also is natural, believe me, Signor Mage.

POLICHINELLE. I believe you—ah, too well! Adieu!

COLUMBINE. How can I ever thank you?

POLICHINELLE. Do not thank me too much, or your gratitude will overcome my wisdom, and lay it prostrate in the dust. Signora! . . .

   [*He bows and retires.*]

COLUMBINE. I am saved. [*Calling.*] Pierrette! Pierrette! [PIERRETTE *enters.*] Come and rejoice with me.

PIERRETTE. [*Disappointed.*] Do you mean—that is to say—Has the Sage found a remedy? Then—

[*Endeavoring to conceal a note which she is carrying in her hand.*]

COLUMBINE. What is that? What paper are you trying to conceal? [*She seizes it.*] A letter from Harlequin! Is this the way that you obey my commands?

PIERRETTE. I gave your message to Signor Harlequin, and he was cast down into the uttermost depths when he heard that his song had given you pain; and so, to prove that he intended no offense, he has written out the verses on this piece of paper, which he begged me to put into your hands; but if you do not wish it—

COLUMBINE. No, no, let me see. Surely I ought to read what they are. It is my duty to make an example of him—a horrible example! [*She runs her eye over the paper.*] Words and phrases of fire, fire shall put out your fire!

PIERRETTE. My lord!—my lady.

COLUMBINE. Spirit of God, aid me now!

[PIERROT *enters. He carries a bunch of purple roses in his hand. As he advances, he gazes lovingly from flower to flower, and begins meditatively to recite the verses which he has composed in their praise.*]
PIERROT.

> Purple petals, rich in hue,
> God has shed his blood for you—

[COLUMBINE *lets the first drop fall from the phial.*]
PIERROT. [*Crying out.*] Ay!
COLUMBINE. [*Running up to him.*] What is the matter?

PIERROT. A thorn pierced my hand.

COLUMBINE. My love, leave the roses, for they are full of thorns. [*She takes the flowers from* PIERROT'S *hands and dashes them violently upon the ground. They leave a purple trail behind them as they pass through the air, and then fall, their stems bare.* PIERROT *watches them fall and*

sighs heavily. COLUMBINE *flings herself into his arms.*]
What are you thinking of? What is on your mind?
Don't you know that my love is a flower that can never
be stripped bare?

SCENE II

PIERROT'S *garden in autumn. There are no more flowers in it—only a few pallid roses and some hardy chrysanthemums. At the back glows the red of the setting sun. Above, little white clouds are driven fitfully across the sky, while at intervals gusts of wind shake the trees and scatter the dry leaves upon the ground, or rustle them about in restless golden whorls.*

COLUMBINE *and* POLICHINELLE *are seated in the garden.* COLUMBINE *is even more melancholy than in the first scene.*

POLICHINELLE. But it is clearly impossible! Do you say that my remedy produced no effect?

COLUMBINE. A most marvelous effect.

POLICHINELLE. Frankly, then, I do not understand.

COLUMBINE. The remedy was worse than the disease. Pierrot has ceased to be a poet, but he has become a philosopher.

POLICHINELLE. A philosopher?

COLUMBINE. Yes, so much the more miserable he! Your philter was too efficacious. For days now there has been no sky without clouds for Pierrot, no rose without a thorn, no pleasure without loathing and disgust. Even the perfume of the flowers gives him pain, so that I, too, have almost begun to pity him.

POLICHINELLE. But have you manifested your pity with tenderness and affection?

COLUMBINE. As affectionately as I was able; but alas! when my husband, disillusioned with the perfidies and imperfections of Nature, turned to hate and despise them, he took it into his head that my beauty, also, was a natural

106

thing, and it has been impossible to disabuse him of it. You can imagine the consequence. My lips seem to him like roses, my eyes like the sea or the sky, my hair like the sunbeams; and not only that, but Pierrot has discovered in various parts of my person all the blots, scars, stains, blemishes, tempests and storm-clouds that afflict the universe or offend the sense of beauty. I am worse off than I was before, Signor Mage. [*A pause ensues.*] Have you no new remedy to prescribe for this new evil?

POLICHINELLE. It will be difficult, Signora Columbine. It seems that the spirit of your husband is obdurate to love. If you could only learn to forget, to resign yourself—

COLUMBINE. Is that all your boasted science can do? Know then that I do not wish to resign myself; I wish to love. I am looking for a cure, not for consolation.

POLICHINELLE. Do not be angry with me, lady. The problem is stubborn and involved. But I shall study it in my laboratory, and I swear to you that I will never emerge from it so long as I shall live, unless I have found an infallible medicine. [*He goes out.*]

COLUMBINE. Science and wisdom hear!

[PIERRETTE *enters*.]

PIERRETTE. Wisdom? I should like to know what wisdom has got to do with love? What does that old impostor know about it anyway? At his age!

COLUMBINE. Age is a guarantee of knowledge.

PIERRETTE. Not to me. It may be in some things, but in affairs of the heart practice makes more perfect than learning. In love, experience is the key which opens hearts; if it is not used, it rusts. And I do not need to ask you how long it must be since Signor Polichinelle has used his key.

COLUMBINE. Will you always destroy my illusions, Pierrette?

PIERRETTE. Yes, because one reality is worth a thousand illusions. Signor Harlequin—

COLUMBINE. Do not talk to me about Harlequin!

PIERRETTE. Signor Harlequin is a reality. Believe me, my lady, there is no illusion about him. I know, and I can answer for it. Besides, you must be convinced by this time that all the drugs of the sorcerers are of no avail to win back the heart of Signor Pierrot.

COLUMBINE. Alas! So I am. Woe is me!

PIERRETTE. So that you will never find a remedy through the aid of science?

COLUMBINE. I fear it.

PIERRETTE. Leave it to me, then, and let me put my plan into execution.

COLUMBINE. What plan? What is it that you wish to do?

PIERRETTE. You will soon see. Without any other science than experience, which I have picked up on my way through the world, I shall save you. The first thing to do is to receive Harlequin.

COLUMBINE. Pierrette!

PIERRETTE. Though it be only to undeceive him. One angry word from your lips would have a thousand times more effect than a thousand sermons from mine, which, to tell the truth,—were not made for sermons.—But in any case, he is here.

[HARLEQUIN *enters and throws himself at* COLUMBINE'S *feet.*]

HARLEQUIN. Queen of my soul, sun of my spirit, magnet and pole of my desire!

COLUMBINE. What is this? Rise!—Pierrette, is this the way that you obey my commands?

PIERRETTE. Pardon, lady, but it is too much for you to expect me to stand forever between the fire and the wall. You don't know to what dangers I have been exposed, contending continually against the ardors of Signor Harlequin!

HARLEQUIN. My lady, in turn I beseech you to pardon

Pierrette. It was not her negligence, but my audacity, which caused this wrong, if wrong it be.

Columbine. How?

Harlequin. Does the heart overwhelmed in darkness sin because it desires the light?

Columbine. Desire is one thing, performance is another.

Harlequin. Columbine, in the minds of lovers desire is performance. The desires of Love are mandates, peremptory as the laws of life!

Columbine. You blaspheme, Signor Harlequin. Certainly, to love like this is a crime.

Harlequin. What matter so long as it is love? Do not shrink and draw away from me! Move closer, lady. At least listen to my tale of woe. Grant me this solace—

Columbine. Will you promise to go away then immediately, if I do?

Harlequin. If you ask me to.

Columbine. And will you promise never to come back?

Harlequin. If you are not convinced by my arguments.

Columbine. You may talk.

Harlequin. Thanks.

[*He kisses her hand.*]

Columbine. I said talk.

Harlequin. My lady, that was the irrepressible cry of my soul.

Columbine. You have a soul that has been most rudely brought up.

Pierrette. [*To* Columbine.] Good! Lead him on.

Harlequin. Pardon, lady, for my soul and for me. We have both hungered through so many ages for a sight of this glory, that now when we find ourselves in your presence, my soul and I, face to face, it is small wonder that

we forget our ill-fortune, and become boys again, and throw
to the winds all sense of proper restraint.

COLUMBINE. Which my dignity cannot excuse, Signor
Harlequin.

HARLEQUIN. But your love and your sympathy ought
to excuse it.

COLUMBINE. Do you presume to talk to me of ought?

HARLEQUIN. Ought there not to be many oughts between you and me, Columbine, oughts and never an ought
not?

COLUMBINE. Between you and me?—You?

HARLEQUIN. Yes, Columbine, me; me—and you. For
I am wretched for your sake!

COLUMBINE. It is not for my sake.

HARLEQUIN. It may not be through your fault.

COLUMBINE. I like that better.

HARLEQUIN. But it is the same to me; my misery is
the same, because I love you, Columbine, I love you, I love
you so much that when I love you all I can, I hate myself—unhappy that I am!—because I cannot love you more.
I love you, I love you, I love you!

[*Each time that he says "I love you," he kisses her
hands passionately.*]

COLUMBINE. [*Defending herself a little, but not displeased at heart.*] Not so loud, Signor Harlequin! Not
so loud—there may be an echo in the garden.

[*They wander off at the rear, pursuing the debate,
and disappear.*]

PIERRETTE. I should never have believed it possible
that the grief of my mistress would have been so difficult to
console.—Ah, me!

[*PIERROT enters. He carries a book in his hand.
He reads and meditates.*]

PIERROT. To think that even in the dewdrops—the
radiant tears of morning—there is a world of monsters, a
contending universe of pain! To know that the smiling
verdure of the fields is but the mask of foul decay, the

immortal beauty which we love, the veil and dull similitude of death!

[*He paces back and forth, absorbed in his meditations.*]

PIERRETTE. [*Approaching him, sympathetically.*] Signor Pierrot—

PIERROT. Who speaks to me? Ah! Is it you? [*Angrily.*] Why are you smiling? Why are you so happy?

PIERRETTE. Signor, life is beautiful.

PIERROT. Do you know what you bear within? A skeleton, a void, nothing! [*A pause follows.*] Where is your lady?

PIERRETTE. She was here a moment since, so wretched over your philosophy. She was in tears. But now she is consoling herself—that is to say, she has company. Signor Harlequin—

PIERROT. Harlequin?

PIERRETTE. A most extraordinary young man, proud, handsome, amorous—

PIERROT. What is that?

PIERRETTE. And an excellent poet. My lady could not possibly have chosen better company.

PIERROT. What do you say? Why do you tell me these things?

PIERRETTTE. Because they are true.

PIERROT. What makes you look at me like this?

PIERRETTE. I was counting sadly the wrinkles which philosophy has dug in your brow.

PIERROT. Tell Columbine that I wish to see her.

PIERRETTE. Do you think it will be wise to interrupt them now?

PIERROT. Is she so intent upon that visit?

PIERRETTE. Look and see. There they are . . . [PIERROT *retires and peers through the shrubbery.*] Do you see anything?

PIERROT. That Harlequin is a fool.

PIERRETTE. Oh, no, he is not! Why, all the while one is with him, he has such winning ways. [COLUMBINE *laughs.*] My lady laughs. Poor lady! It is so long since I have heard her laugh. Ah! Look!—I wondered what they were doing. That was a happy stroke of Signor Harlequin's. But what is the matter? [PIERROT *starts to run and rushes headlong off the stage like one possessed.*] Where are you going? Ah, ha, ha, ha! See him run! Ha, ha, ha! A jealous man is always ridiculous! There he is now. He is furious . . . My lady pleads for mercy. And Signor Harlequin—he effaces himself—he fades modestly out of sight . . . I am sorry for that man!

[*The sound of rude voices is heard in the garden; shortly afterward* HARLEQUIN *emerges from the trees. He comes forward with a dejected, disappointed air, and hurries rapidly across the stage.*]

PIERRETTE. [*Detaining him.*] What is the matter, Signor Harlequin? Was not my lady willing to be consoled?

HARLEQUIN. Your lady is a model of conjugal fidelity.

PIERRETTE. Who told you to go wandering in other people's gardens, exploring hearts which have masters? Better stick to the highways and the byways, Signor Rover, and to fields which are virgin.

HARLEQUIN. Do you know any?

PIERRETTE. That is a reflection upon me. What do you mean, Signor Harlequin?

HARLEQUIN. I mean any disposed to receive me?

PIERRETTE. Why, Signor Harlequin! I—What do you want me to say? I am a young and inexperienced girl, but I am sure that there must be someone—perhaps not so very far away. You know what the song says: "When least you expect it"—And I never expected it. Don't look at me like that . . .

[*A pause ensues.* PIERRETTE'S *eyes become eloquent in the silence of her lips, and pronounce a significant discourse.*]

HARLEQUIN. [*With sudden resolution.*] Could you love me, Pierrette?

PIERRETTE. Ha, ha, ha! Do you think I win my victories through other people's arms?

HARLEQUIN. Don't be cruel!

PIERRETTE. My lady is much more beautiful than I.

HARLEQUIN. Illusion! The beauty of woman is all one great store, one vast and perfect body, of which every woman is but an individual part. Your lady is beautiful, you are as beautiful as she—both different parts of the same great beauty.

PIERRETTE. But, I wonder, just what part of this great beauty that you tell me of, am I?

HARLEQUIN. From what I feel, you must be very near the heart! [*They embrace.*]

[PIERROT *and* COLUMBINE *re-enter and advance into the garden. They also are locked in an embrace, and gaze steadfastly into each other's eyes, full of happiness.*]

COLUMBINE. Swear to me that you are telling me the truth, Pierrot.

PIERROT. I swear it. The fear of losing you has revealed to me the truth that your love was the soul of my life. Your words are the most beautiful of poems, and your embraces the most enduring of philosophies.

POLICHINELLE. [*Entering precipitately with a phial in his hand.*] Signora, here is the philter, the love magic, the true, the infallible medicine!

[*All laugh gaily, and* PIERRETTE *carries her impertinence so far as to mimic the magician with many a comic grimace.* POLICHINELLE *stares at them in amazement. The phial which he carries in his hands explodes with a loud report, and the Elixir of Love is scattered upon the ground.*

PIERRETTE. It was about time to explode it.

POLICHINELLE. What is this I see?

PIERRETTE. What you see, Signor Mage, is simply this:

that science is superfluous when it comes to affairs of the heart. There all wisdom is vain, and all philters are colored water. For love is cured by love, and disdain by jealousy; so it has been since the beginning of the world, and so it will be until the world has ceased to be. Spells and conjurations are of very little use. The love that has fallen asleep through excess of good fortune is not be awakened again without the menace of another love which is more passionate, and which burns like youth's fire. That is all there is to it. My master was asleep because my lady loved him too much, and he has waked at the fear that she might cease to love him so. Don't you see?

POLICHINELLE. Hum—what I see. But—[*Pointing at* HARLEQUIN.] Wasn't this gentleman also in love?

PIERRETTE. Head over heels; you can surely see it.

POLICHINELLE. [*Protesting.*] But not with you.

PIERRETTE. Ha, ha, ha! He thought not himself, but he soon found his mistake, through my assistance—and the force of circumstances.

POLICHINELLE. Hum!

HARLEQUIN. Although I am a young man, Signor Polichinelle, and a poet, I too have my philosophy. And in the first chapter, there is this maxim: "He who refuses to console himself for the kisses which he cannot get, by those the girls will give, is mad entirely."

[*The sorcerer, scandalized, takes to his heels, covering his ears with his hands, then throwing his arms into the air, brandishing them wildly. Soft, sweet music sounds, and the two pairs of lovers begin a slow and stately dance.*]

CURTAIN

POOR JOHN

COMEDY IN ONE ACT

TEATRO LARA, MADRID
1912

PACIFIC GROVE, CALIFORNIA
1920

THEATRE, LONDON
1928

CHARACTERS

MARIANA, *aged 20*
JOHN, *aged 22*
ANTONIO, *aged 23*
MAMÁ INÉS, *aged 66*
MAMÁ PEPA, *aged 70*
DON CARLOS, *aged 48*
TWO FACTORY HANDS
TWO MAIDS

POOR JOHN

A formal garden en parterre. A number of wicker arm chairs, rocking chairs and a chaise longue, all of which are plentifully provided with cretonne cushions, are set out in the shade of a sturdy walnut tree. Two tables stand near by, one containing a tray with fruit and breakfast service, the other, boxes of candy, flowers, and a bundle of lace tied with ribbon. There are flowers also on the chaise longue.

MAMÁ PEPA *and* MAMÁ INÉS *are seated together.* MAMÁ INÉS *is sewing.* MAMÁ PEPA *has been reading, and removes her spectacles, wipes them with her handkerchief, and puts them on again.*

MAMÁ PEPA. It is going to rain this afternoon.

MAMÁ INÉS. Nothing of the sort! What makes you think it is going to rain?

MAMÁ PEPA. Don't you see that cloud coming up?

MAMÁ INÉS. Yes, it is wind.

MAMÁ PEPA. I say it is rain. My leg tells me so.

MAMÁ INÉS. Well, my arm tells me that we shall have fine weather for the rest of the week.

MAMÁ PEPA. God help us both! [*The factory whistle blows.*] There goes the whistle. The factory clock must be fast today.

MAMÁ INÉS. Nothing of the sort. How can it be fast when it was eight o'clock ten minutes ago?

MAMÁ PEPA. Did your arm tell you that?

MAMÁ INÉS. No, the sun told me. It is around on the second stone in the gallery floor already.

MARIANA. [*Speaking outside.*] Good-bye, good-bye! Thank you, thank you all so much . . . [*Laughing.*] Of course! Thanks awfully just the same. Good-bye, good-

bye! [*She enters carrying a bouquet of roses in one hand.*]
I believe they all love me. Everybody seemed so happy
as they went away. Perhaps they really do love me,
too; everything in this world cannot be put on. [*She
goes over to the table.*] Roses, lilies, carnations . . .
Gracious! And chocolates! [*Taking one.*] I must save
a few, though, for John. Poor boy, he has such a sweet
tooth—just like me! Our tastes are the same in everything. [*The old ladies cough.* MARIANA *looks up, but
pays no attention.*] Isn't it too lovely to be twenty and
have so many presents? [*The whistle blows again.*] The
second whistle! It sounds more like a ship's siren than
it does like a factory whistle. I should like to go on a long,
long voyage.

MAMÁ PEPA. Yes, and get sea-sick.

MARIANA. What of it? I should go ashore on some
islands which are nowhere on the map, and discover them,
and civilize the natives—that is, not altogether, because
then they would have to wear trousers and gloves and
top-hats. Men are never so ugly as when they are all
dressed up.

MAMÁ INÉS. You don't know what you are talking
about.

MARIANA. Mamá Pepa and Mamá Inés, you two dear
old grandmothers, I am so happy! But, oh, how I do long
to be so much happier!

MAMÁ PEPA. It would make no difference to you.

MARIANA. Yes, it would; that is, it seems to me it
would make a great deal of difference. I am happy now
because the sun shines and I am twenty, and there is nothing the matter with me, I thank God for that. Everything seems to be so simple and easy, so much a matter of
course. But happiness must be something a great deal
more—it must be more inside of you, don't you know?
It must be something awfully solemn. No, not exactly
solemn either. I mean . . . Anyway, sometimes a girl
feels so happy that she would just love to cry.

MAMÁ PEPA. Mercy on us! What is wrong with the child?

MARIANA. You will find out when the time comes—if the time ever does come.

MAMÁ INÉS. She is out of her head.

MARIANA. My two dear, old respectable grandmothers, do you really think that the time ever will come? Do you really? Or are you just perfectly certain that it will not?

MAMÁ PEPA. Think what time will come?

MARIANA. The time that every girl is longing for, without having any idea what it is?

MAMÁ INÉS. My dear, you will find out soon enough for yourself that everything in life is either unpleasant, or else it comes too late.

MARIANA. God bless us!

MAMÁ PEPA. Pay no attention to what she says; it all depends upon the point of view. When the night is darkest, God sends the morning. Don't allow yourself to brood and mope. However bad things may be, they might be worse, or else we should not be here to see them. A chicken may be light-hearted and yet have a stone in its gizzard.

MARIANA. Do you know what the factory girls say? That I ought to pray for a sweetheart every day, because it's high time for me to have one.

MAMÁ INÉS. What would you do with a sweetheart at your age?

MAMÁ PEPA. She could get married, like everybody else.

MARIANA. Of course! And then I could have lots of children. I mean to have ten at least, all boys, hard workers, strong, clever, fearless, brave, so that they can travel all over the world doing great and splendid things, and build roads and factories and houses and schools, and make laws and conduct revolutions. They will be strong as castles, every one of them. I believe that ten real men would prove the salvation of any country. [*Discovering her father,* Don Carlos, *who enters.*] Father, how many ministers have we in the Spanish cabinet?

Don Carlos. Such as they are, I believe there are eight.

Mariana. Then I shall have two over. One can be a poet and the other a philosopher. And a grateful country will erect a statue to my memory!

Don Carlos. What is all this nonsense?

Mariana. Congratulate me. This is my birthday. I am of age—I am twenty. [*Submitting to an embrace.*] Aha! Are you sorry? You seem sad. [*Sympathetically.*] I know . . . it is mother.

Mamá Pepa. Carlos, she looks more like my poor daughter every day.

Don Carlos. Yes, she does.

Mamá Inés. Nothing of the sort! She is the living image of her father.

Don Carlos. Omitting all his faults, let us hope.

Mamá Inés. There are no faults to omit. I don't say so because he is my son, but I wish you could have seen him when he was twenty-five.

Mamá Pepa. I wish you could have seen my daughter when she was eighteen.

Mariana. Well, all you have to do is to look at me. How dreadfully embarrassing it is to be such a beautiful girl!

Mamá Pepa. Thank Heaven, she is good-natured.

Mamá Inés. Yes, it is a family trait.

Mamá Pepa. Naturally.

Mariana. [*To her father.*] Do look at all my presents! The flowers are from the factory hands, the candies from the girls at the sewing-school, and the Sunday School children sent me this piece of lace. The cross is from Mamá Pepa, and the rosary from Mamá Inés, with real coral beads, so you see I have two really good grandmothers, as far as one can judge from their presents. What are you going to give me?

DON CARLOS. Whatever you like. [*Taking out his pocket-book.*]

MARIANA. No, don't give me any money; I have more than I know what to do with. We started the sewing-school to help the poor girls along, but now we are all making our fortunes. I had nothing myself, yet we can scarcely keep up with the orders. The preserves that Mamá Inés and I put up are a success, too, though we only began because it was such a pity to throw the fruit away. We have had inquiries, even, from a shop in Madrid.

DON CARLOS. Name anything you wish.

MARIANA. I would if I dared. There is one thing— yes, I am going to ask for it. Now don't you say no! Promise not to be angry. It . . . it . . . it isn't for myself, but it is just the same, you know; it's for John.

DON CARLOS. For John?

[*Both old ladies cough.* MARIANA *turns and glares at them.*]

MARIANA. Yes, it's for John . . . that is, not exactly for him either, it's for his father. Don't you see? I told you that I didn't want money, but now that I come to think of it, it is money. At least it is something very like it.

DON CARLOS. Well, is it or is it not?

MARIANA. Don't be cross. No, it isn't money. Only I want you to go surety for them so that they won't lose their house.

DON CARLOS. Do you expect me to guarantee all the old Marquis's bad debts?

MARIANA. Why, papa!

DON CARLOS. Do you realize what it means to stand sponsor for a man of that character?

MARIANA. All they have left is the house, and now they are going to lose that for a miserable trifle which they borrowed of that skinflint. John's mother is sick, too, and John is worried about her. Poor John! I know that to be responsible for them—that is, for John's father—I suppose though he can't help it; it's the way he is made. I tell you what to do. You buy the mortgage, and then they can owe the money to you. You will never put them out, so everybody will be satisfied.

Don Carlos. You have strange ideas of business.

Mariana. It isn't business, it's a birthday present. I am twenty—think of it, twenty! What wouldn't you give to be twenty again? And you are, don't you see, because I am, and whatever I am, is yours. Besides, I promise never to do it again. [*Embracing him.*] Oh, haven't I a rich and stingy father! Do say yes! Look me in the eye and say yes! Say yes!

Don Carlos. Very well, to please you. [*Smiling.*] But I don't want to hear any more about it. When John comes, send him to me, and we will talk it over; I shall have nothing to do with his father. Only I want you to understand that it is casting pearls before swine; they will be worse off by the end of the month. However, to please you—

Mariana. Thanks, thanks, oh thanks!

Don Carlos. Do not thank me, for I am doing it against my will. Enough for the present!

Mariana. Where are you going?

Don Carlos. Back to the factory.

Mariana. How you do love to see people work! Remember, be home on the stroke of twelve, because Mamá Inés has promised us all sorts of good things, and if the rice is spoiled, we shall be lost. It will be a lovely surprise, too, for poor John!

[Don Carlos *goes out.*]

Mamá Pepa. [*Scornfully.*] Poor John!

Mamá Inés. Some day we are going to get sick of poor John.

Mariana. Do you think so?

Mamá Inés. Before long we shall have him in the soup.

Mariana. Nonsense!

MAMÁ PEPA. Mamá Inés is right, my dear. I do not approve myself of a young lady of twenty keeping company with a young gentleman of twenty-two. He follows you wherever you go.

MAMÁ INÉS. I see nothing to object to in that. She and John were brought up together, almost like brother and sister. There is no harm in their going about. What I do not like is having the child take an interest in him which is improper.

MAMÁ PEPA. I see nothing improper in that. It is the duty of those who have plenty to be generous with those who have not. What I am afraid of is that she may encourage him to expect something else.

MAMÁ INÉS. Nothing of the sort. He is as modest as a mallow and as good as God's bread.

MAMÁ PEPA. He may be as good for all I know, but he is a man, and men—

MAMÁ INÉS. Do you think you can tell me anything about men, Mamá Pepa?

MAMÁ PEPA. Probably not. You know it all already.

MAMÁ INÉS. What am I to understand by that remark?

MARIANA. Come, come, don't be angry, you two dear grandmothers! What if John is good? Well, so much the better for him. What if I do love him? He loves me as much, at the very least. We have always been together, so nobody is surprised; it has become a habit. I help him whenever I can because I am rich and he is poor. Besides, everybody has somebody to look out for; you have me, and I have John. So I say God help us all! Here he comes as calm and placid as can be.

MAMÁ INÉS. If he is coming, I am going. There is plenty to be done in the kitchen, and it behooves us all to roll up our sleeves.

MAMÁ PEPA. In that case, I had better run and feed the canaries.

[MAMÁ INÉS *and* MAMÁ PEPA *go out.*]

MARIANA. [*Laughing.*] Enter the ogre. Poor John!

[JOHN *appears. He is a young man of winning personality, distinguished in manner and faultless in dress, but evidently depressed and greatly cast down.*]

JOHN. May I . . . ?

MARIANA. Come in.

JOHN. [*Advancing.*] What were you laughing at?

MARIANA. My grandmothers are jealous of you.

JOHN. Your grandmothers hate the sight of me.

MARIANA. Mamá Inés says that you are as good as God's bread.

JOHN. A polite way of intimating that a man is a fool.

MARIANA. Why do you look at me?

JOHN. You are entirely too lovely for this hour in the morning.

MARIANA. I am not as lovely as I was, for I am aging very rapidly. Don't you notice it?

JOHN. You?

MARIANA. Do you notice anything unusual in my face? Don't I seem serious? I am a year older at least than I was yesterday.

JOHN. A year older than you were yesterday?

MARIANA. Exactly. I was nineteen yesterday and I am twenty today.

JOHN. Well, I *am* a fool!

MARIANA. [*Laughing.*] I accept your congratulations.

JOHN. I am a blockhead, an idiot not to remember!

MARIANA. [*Laughs.*]

JOHN. Don't laugh. Why didn't you tell me yesterday?

MARIANA. So as to be able to remind you that you had forgotten today—as usual, of course.

JOHN. Mariana, you are not fair with me.

MARIANA. Of course not! But look at all the bonbons I have saved for you. Help yourself. Besides, I have good news. How is your mother?

JOHN. What do you expect? Her cough is worse, she is exhausted. Then, by some accident, she heard about the house, although we intended to keep it from her. So now she has something else to worry over. She says that if we are compelled to give it up, it will kill her; she will die. That is all there is about it.

MARIANA. How does your father feel?

JOHN. Father says he will shoot himself.

MARIANA. He never will.

JOHN. I know, but mother believes him. Whatever he says, she takes literally. Mariana, we have lost our home. This is not living. I don't know what I should do if it were not for you. If it were not—

MARIANA. If it were not?

JOHN. If it were not for you, *I* might be the one who shot my-self.

MARIANA. You certainly are a brave man!

JOHN. How can you expect a man to be brave when he meets with nothing in life but misfortune? Everything has gone wrong with me since the day I was born. Whatever I put my hand to fails utterly. You know it better than I do. I was brought up to be rich, and I am poor. I studied law, and I can not string three words together. A man must be strong in that profession, he must have vigor of body and mind, yet I am all out of breath if I walk up a hill; I have not the heart to crush even a fly. To save the little that remains to us after the folly of my father, I need to be unscrupulous and bold, yet my mother, God bless her, has taught me to be good, good, always good, like God's bread, as you have just heard from your grandmother.

MARIANA. [*Laughs.*]

JOHN. Yes, laugh. I have a letter which I wish you would translate into English. You can help me. It will only be time wasted, but never mind. It is to some lord who is visiting the province in search of antiques—fabulous creatures, are they not? He might stop in at our house and offer us a handful of duros for the silver which still remains in the chapel.

MARIANA. Do you mean to tell me that you would sell the chapel silver?

JOHN. Yes, and the genealogical tree that hangs in the drawing-room. I have an idea that it might be worth a few pesetas.

MARIANA. Why, it would be like selling your name!

JOHN. My name? We would sell our souls, if Satan had not abandoned the practise of buying them.

MARIANA. Hush, you heretic!

JOHN. But I weary you with my troubles.

MARIANA. No, I was only thinking what a strange thing life is. Why is it that some people always have good luck, while others are always down? Everything always turns out well with me.

JOHN. [*Earnestly.*] Because you deserve it.

MARIANA. Nobody deserves anything, because nobody chooses his disposition, or the place in life he is going to fill.

JOHN. Now you are the one who is talking heresy.

MARIANA. Then I am sorry, for it is the truth. What have I ever done to deserve anything? I have simply lived and have been happy, and that is the way I go on. I thank God again and again for all my happiness whenever I remember how good He has been to me, but most of the time I forget even that. I do not believe that I have had one sorrow since the day I was born—I mean one real sorrow, that was my own. When my mother died, I was too young. Of course, I am sorry for other people who are unhappy, but all the while I am happy myself. I have never been ill. I never had any trouble with my lessons, like most children. Nobody ever found fault with me, and whatever I do prospers. Yet all the while, I hear people complain. The times are hard, they say. So I suppose my good luck, which seems to me the most natural thing in the world, is nothing short of miraculous, and I begin to ask myself when I think it over: "Why is it, good God, why is it?"

JOHN. Accept it and do not think it over.

MARIANA. Sometimes I am terribly provoked with you.

JOHN. Why?

MARIANA. Because you are so meek. Whatever happens, you resign yourself and submit to it; you ask no questions. I believe that you walk through the world with your eyes shut, and that is why you bump your head against stone walls all the time.

JOHN. Please don't be angry with me. I cannot bear it.

[*He covers his face with his hands.*]

MARIANA. Does your head ache?

JOHN. A little.

MARIANA. [*Drawing near.*] You look pale. Have some coffee?

JOHN. No, I have drunk too much already.

MARIANA. Last night? I knew it. You sat up reading. How late was it before you went to bed?

JOHN. It was morning. Don't be angry with me. You were awake yourself.

MARIANA. I? Goodness gracious!

JOHN. There was a light burning in your room all night.

MARIANA. [*Laughing.*] Because I fell asleep so quickly that I didn't have time to put it out. What did you think? I rode to Robledo yesterday to see my cousins, and we played tennis, I don't know how long, and then we went rowing, so I was tired out when I came home. I am ashamed to tell you, but I never went to bed at all. I knelt down by the bed to say my prayers, and when I came to, it was morning. I fell asleep with the first *Pater Noster.*

JOHN. You must feel ill today.

MARIANA. Don't you believe it! My eyes were a little heavy at first, but a cold shower, and no one could ever have suspected it.

JOHN. You are a cold shower, my dear girl, from head to heels, and a draught of health, outside and inside sunshine and morning. I envy you, and how I love you!

MARIANA. How you say it! Come, we had better write that letter. You might dictate it in Spanish, although it will be a waste of time, now that I think of it. I told you that I had good news for you, and you haven't even asked me what it was. However, I remembered my own birthday, so I asked father for a present. You could never guess what he gave me—the mortgage!

JOHN. [*Not comprehending.*] The mortgage?

MARIANA. Yes, yours—your mortgage. Don't you remember? The mortgage which is held by that man who threatened to foreclose and sell your house. My father is going to pay it off, whatever it is, and then you can owe it to him, just as you did to the other man, only father won't foreclose, so you can stay on and live in the house forever. [*Greatly affected.*] And you won't have to sell the silver or the family tree either!

JOHN. Mariana!

MARIANA. Hurry and see father and you can fix everything.

JOHN. [*Choking.*] Mariana!

MARIANA. Won't your mother be happy?

JOHN. Mariana! [*Seizing both her hands.*] You are the best woman in the world. Nobody else would ever have dreamed of such a thing. Thank you, thank you! I can never thank you enough. Oh, Mariana, how it humiliates me, and how it makes me happy! Because it is charity, I know that it is charity, but blessed be the charity of your hands, of your heart, because it is yours, and blessed, too, be you yourself, a hundred thousand times! [*Passionately.*] You are my life, my soul! The only reason for my existence!

MARIANA. [*Greatly surprised.*] John!

JOHN. Yes, the only one. Didn't you know? The

only one! But of course you did. Say yes, you did, my own!

MARIANA. No, John, no.

JOHN. Yes, Mariana.

MARIANA. But, then—

JOHN. Yes, I love you, I adore you, I am mad over you, head over heels in love with you, lost irretrievably!

MARIANA. Don't say that!

JOHN. I have loved you all my life.

MARIANA. No, no!

JOHN. Didn't you know it?

MARIANA. I don't want to know it.

JOHN. Why not?

MARIANA. Because it is ridiculous—no, not exactly ridiculous, but it is a pity; I am awfully sorry.

JOHN. Do you mean that you do not love me?

MARIANA. [*Somewhat more composed.*] No. Forgive me, John. I do love you. I love you very much, very, very much more than I love my father, more than I do my grandmothers, but then—I don't love you.

JOHN. Mariana!

MARIANA. I love you more than anybody else in the world, but not like that—not like that. [*She begins to cry.*]

JOHN. Don't cry; you will break my heart. Do—do you love someone else?

MARIANA. No, nobody. Honestly, I don't love anybody.

JOHN. Then—

MARIANA. But I shall some day—I am going to love somebody.

JOHN. Whom?

MARIANA. I don't know. Whoever it is, somebody—not anybody, somebody.

JOHN. But, why not me, Mariana?

MARIANA. Because I can't. I tell you, because I love

you so. I don't want you to say that I have deceived you.

JOHN. You must have a very poor opinion of me.

MARIANA. A poor opinion of you? You are the best man in the world.

JOHN. Must you say that, too?

MARIANA. It is true.

JOHN. It only makes it worse.

MARIANA. John, John! Lift up your head. Look at me, John!

JOHN. Is it possible? Can it be?

MARIANA. Why, did you think that I—

JOHN. I don't know. When I thought of it, it did seem incredible, with this miserable luck of mine, but I felt that you were so close to me, that you were so entirely my own—or that I was yours, I don't know which—and you were so good to me, so kind, so much the woman! All the happiness I have ever known in my life until now, has sprung from you—it may have been only a little, now and then, in small things, trifles, help, advice. It was presumptuous of me, Mariana, but I am so accustomed to relying upon you, that I imagined that the treasure was all mine. Besides, I love you so—I mean I need you so. Why should you not be all goodness, Mariana, and take me like a little child into your life, like a toy that you play with, or a dog of which you are fond? But let me be yours, all yours, because I love you! If you could love me only a little, I should be satisfied.

MARIANA. A little is not enough. To be husband and wife, if that is what you mean, we should have to love each other a great deal and in a different way.

JOHN. How?

MARIANA. I love you tremendously, you and everything that is yours, because it is yours—your mother, your house, yes, and your father, or, because—well, I would give my life to help you. If anybody said anything against you, I should knock him down. To save your family, I would starve. Even your name, your title which will

be yours very soon, seem to me so noble, so dignified—
I don't know how to explain it, but I just don't want
to marry you, because—because—you must not be angry,
but I think I am cleverer than you are.

JOHN. You are a great deal cleverer than I.

MARIANA. No, I don't mean exactly cleverer; I am
quicker than you are.

JOHN. No, you are cleverer and you are braver than
I. Besides you are good and beautiful. I am nothing but
a poor devil, an unlucky fellow!

MARIANA. No, you are not. You know a great deal
more than I do. You know all about books and all about
art. You are a handsomer man than I am a woman. I
am crude. My hands are red and yours are white. Then,
you are so fastidious, you have such good taste. If it
had not been for you, I am sure that I should always
have dressed like a gay masquerader. You amount to a
great deal more than I do; there is more to you.

JOHN. Yet, although there is so much to me, I am
not your ideal.

MARIANA. No, I have no ideal. Don't think that I
am so romantic.

JOHN. Well, enough of this talk! What sort of man
do you want for a husband?

MARIANA. I don't know. Wait and see. You always
lean on me when we walk out into the country—I always
have to help you up the hills. Well, the man who is my
husband will run up the hills and carry me along in his
arms.

JOHN. I will do my best.

MARIANA. Hills are symbolic of so many things!

JOHN. Ah, me!

MARIANA. I simply cannot bear to make you unhappy
—but I suppose I must; there is no escape. I should never
dream of asking you to carry me; I feel that I was born
to take care of you. When your head aches, I always
wish it was mine. You are older than I am, but it seems

to me that you must be a great deal younger; I feel as if you were my child.

JOHN. Don't say that.

MARIANA. Why not?

JOHN. Because all this love of yours, which you say you feel, which is so great, so deep, is nothing but contempt —loathing and contempt.

MARIANA. No, it is not!

JOHN. Or pity, I don't know which is worse.

[*A brief pause.*]

MARIANA. Oh, but I am so angry!

JOHN. Why?

MARIANA. To think that another woman hasn't done this to you, and then I could have consoled you afterward!

JOHN. No, Mariana, if another woman had made me suffer as you have because I loved her as I love you, even you could not have consoled me.

MARIANA. It would have been the first time. [*Drawing nearer to him.*] Don't be foolish, John; think it over, and control yourself. You don't love me as much as you think you do. If you had really been mad over me, you would have told me so before; you could never have remained silent through all these years.

JOHN. [*Tenderly.*] Don't talk nonsense.

MARIANA. Only you didn't know where else to turn to find one misfortune more. Now you can say that you have been unlucky even in love. How could two people love each other who have lived together all their lives like brother and sister? Love must come from outside, all of a sudden, from somewhere else—what is the matter? Don't you feel well? Are you ill? John, for Heaven's sake, don't take it like this! I'll have to say yes, if you do, out of pity, and then both of us will be unhappy—yes, both! John! John!

JOHN. [*Rising.*] Never mind. It is over now. You are right, your children ought not to carry the poison of a degenerate blood in their veins, they must not be born to the curse of a decaying, a contaminated race. You splendid woman, you are right to refuse a hand that is bloodless and cold.

MARIANA. How can you talk like that?

JOHN. Enough! Leave me—yes, I mean it. Then, you can come back. Leave me alone a moment, until I can collect myself, until I can persuade myself that today is to be again like yesterday—that nothing has taken place between us.

[*She retires slowly, looking back at him as she goes. When she reaches the top of the steps, she pauses, hesitating, before entering the house.*]

MARIANA. I am so sorry! Poor John! [*Stamping her foot.*] But it is not my fault. What a pity!

[*She disappears into the house.* JOHN *remains alone, seated, attempting to compose himself. A bell rings at the garden gate, but no one answers it. After a moment, it rings again. Presently,* ANTONIO *pushes the gate open and advances into the garden. He looks about, but discovers no one.*]

ANTONIO. Goodness gracious! The house must be enchanted.

[*Falling back a little, better to look up at the façade, he collides with the chair which is occupied by* JOHN. JOHN *turns sharply in great annoyance.*]

JOHN. Eh? What is this?

ANTONIO. I beg your pardon. [*Recognizing* JOHN.] John!

JOHN. [*Staring at him for a moment in return.*] Antonio!

ANTONIO. The very man!

JOHN. What are you doing here?

ANTONIO. Come, come! Embrace me!

JOHN. But where did you drop from?

ANTONIO. From your house. Where did you think?

JOHN. From my house? I thought you were in America.

ANTONIO. So I was, but you know a man can return from America—although it seems incredible.

JOHN. But what are you doing here? Have you lost anything?

ANTONIO. Nothing to speak of, my son; my heart, that is all. And I have a presentiment that if I can find it here, I shall encounter eternal happiness as well. I stopped off to have a look at you by the way—pardon my insistence on my own affairs—I thought, perhaps, you might introduce me; I did not wish to enter paradise unannounced. Your friend is charming, my boy! And charming does not express it. She is beautiful, she is glorious, she is irresistable, she is unique! One woman among ten thousand! By the way, I don't suppose you happen to be engaged?

JOHN. Engaged? What makes you say that? Explain yourself. Don't talk like an ass.

ANTONIO. Are you always so good natured when you wake up from a nap?

JOHN. A nap?

ANTONIO. You were asleep when I came in—now don't deny it. I rang the bell, I can't say how often. Then I called, I don't know how many times. Lucky devil!

JOHN. I?

ANTONIO. Yes, to be able to sleep in immediate proximity to this marvel of the ages. But you are used to it —it is force of habit. O, Mariana, Mariana!

JOHN. What business have you with Mariana?

ANTONIO. None, unfortunately, up to the present. I am mad over her.

JOHN. Absurd!

ANTONIO. Do you suppose that all men are like you— incombustible? I saw her yesterday for the first time— now don't you laugh—and I cannot live another hour without her. How do you manage not to fall in love? You have lived near her all your life.

John. Well, perhaps that may be the reason. How can two people love each other who have lived together like brother and sister ever since they were children? Love must come from the outside, all of a sudden, from somewhere else—

Antonio. Like lightning! That's a fact. That is the way it was with me. Didn't you notice when I came in that I had been struck by it? How can a man fall in love, my boy, in twenty-four hours—no, in less—in a night, lying awake, dreaming of her? She hasn't another sweetheart, has she? Pardon the question; it interests me . . .

John. No, none, whatever, but she is going to have one.

Antonio. Who?

John. [*With exceeding ill grace, annoyed.*] How do I know?—somebody, anybody.

Antonio. Is that so? You seem to be pretty well acquainted, you are great friends, of course. What sort of person—you don't mind my asking these questions in confidence—what sort of person does she seem to prefer? If it is not too much trouble—

John. No indeed! Don't consider me, anyhow. What do you care?

Antonio. I knew you were a friend of mine.

John. As you say.

Antonio. This ideal which she has formed in her mind —does it happen to present any resemblance to me? For if it does—

John. Her ideal? Could you run up a hill with her in your arms?

Antonio. And jump over the moon with her in them, and then back again, and run up to the top a second time without stopping to take breath!

John. Well, that is just her ideal of a man. Goodbye and good luck!

[*He goes out.*]

Antonio. John! Where are you going? One mo-

ment! Wait! What shall I do without you? I must be
introduced. [*The garden gate slams, causing the bell to
ring violently.*] What is the matter with him? Is it possible that they can be engaged? No, or he would have
said so, or else have knocked me over the head. I wonder—

[MARIANA *appears at the top of the steps.*]

MARIANA. John, John! Where are you?

ANTONIO. He is not here, señorita, but I am—if I can
be of service—

MARIANA. Oh! [*She comes down the steps.*] How
do you do?

ANTONIO. Pleasant morning, isn't it? Fine! Yes, indeed!

MARIANA. Do you wish anything?

ANTONIO. Nothing. [*Continuing, as she makes a gesture of surprise.*] Nothing, now that I have seen you.

MARIANA. [*Laughing.*] Oh!

ANTONIO. Don't you believe me?

MARIANA. Naturally.

ANTONIO. But how can you take it so calmly?

MARIANA. Surely you did not expect me to be greatly
surprised?

ANTONIO. Of course not; you are accustomed to it.

MARIANA. To what?

ANTONIO. To admiration which is fervent.

MARIANA. Nobody has ever killed himself for my sake.

ANTONIO. You do not know me.

MARIANA. I remember—aren't you the man who passed
on horseback yesterday afternoon, as I was standing at my
cousin's gate?

ANTONIO. *Si, señora,* I am the man.

MARIANA. Were you on the beach afterward when we
finished playing tennis?

ANTONIO. And after that I was on the float when you
got out of the boat. Yes, indeed, I was there—at your
service.

MARIANA. You are a stranger here?

ANTONIO. No, I was born here.

MARIANA. Then why did you stop at the gate to ask me the way?

ANTONIO. I was anxious to learn whether your voice was as sweet as your face.

MARIANA. I never saw you until yesterday.

ANTONIO. I have been five years in America, and home again only two weeks.

MARIANA. 'Where did you keep yourself before you went to America?

ANTONIO. You have often seen me, although, perhaps, you may not remember it.

MARIANA. I wonder—yes. No! What is your name?

ANTONIO. Antonio Losada.

MARIANA. Are you Antonio Losada? With that moustache?

ANTONIO. Yes, indeed. America is a wonderful country for hair.

MARIANA. [*Laughing.*] But then, of course, you know John?

ANTONIO. Of course! We went to school together with the *Escolapios,* and we were suspended together at the University—that is, the first time.

MARIANA. I remember. In Roman Law?

ANTONIO. No, Canon Law.

MARIANA. But that wasn't the first time.

ANTONIO. Right again! You remember better than I do.

MARIANA. Poor John!

ANTONIO. Poor John!

MARIANA. What makes you say "Poor John"?

ANTONIO. You said it first.

MARIANA. I was not thinking. Poor John!

ANTONIO. Perhaps if you could forget him a little, and sympathize with me—

MARIANA. Oh! Are you in trouble?

ANTONIO. Terrible trouble.

MARIANA. Nobody would ever suspect it from your face.

ANTONIO. No, it is more deeply seated; there is nothing the matter with my face.

MARIANA. I hope it is not your heart.

ANTONIO. It might be, for all you know.

MARIANA. Has it pained you very long?

ANTONIO. Since the beginning of the world.

MARIANA. That is a very long time.

ANTONIO. And not one day less. When God made up his mind to create the universe, he jotted down in his note-book that I was predestined, after centuries and centuries had passed, to suffer torment because of two beautiful black eyes which I am gazing into now.

MARIANA. Very likely. Can't you ever be serious?

ANTONIO. Very. Will you marry me?

MARIANA. *Ave Maria!* God bless us! You frighten me out of my wits.

ANTONIO. Am I as unattractive as that?

MARIANA. [*Looking at him.*] No, I do not object to your looks.

ANTONIO. Thanks.

MARIANA. Thanks for what? Besides, looks are of no importance anyway.

ANTONIO. Certainly not. Would you mind telling me what is of importance?

MARIANA. Have you a cough?

ANTONIO. No, I never cough.

MARIANA. Are you subject to headaches?

ANTONIO. Yes, I had a headache once when I was a boy. Another boy cracked me on the head with a stone.

MARIANA. Oh, then you must be quarrelsome?

ANTONIO. I am; fairly so—when I can't get what I want.

MARIANA. What you want, or what you ought to get?

ANTONIO. Will you tell me the difference?

MARIANA. Don't you know?

ANTONIO. No. Neither do you.

MARIANA. I?

ANTONIO. You always get what you want; I can see it in your face.

MARIANA. Then you must be clairvoyant.

ANTONIO. Love sees at a distance; it penetrates.

MARIANA. Not at all. Love is blind.

ANTONIO. That was in the old days; but now it has been operated upon, and we have removed the cataracts.

MARIANA. Only imagine the sights that that poor boy must see!

ANTONIO. Some of them very nice, no doubt, beginning with you.

MARIANA. But where will he leave off?

ANTONIO. With you, too. After encircling the globe and seeing everything, he will come back to you.

MARIANA. After encircling the globe?

ANTONIO. What do you say? Shall we go along?

MARIANA. I warn you that he would find me an extremely disagreeable traveling companion.

ANTONIO. In what way?

MARIANA. I should expect too much of him.

ANTONIO. Expect it of me, then, and you will not be disappointed.

MARIANA. Never?

ANTONIO. Never.

MARIANA. Suppose that what I have set my heart on proves difficult to get?

ANTONIO. I will get it.

MARIANA. But suppose it does not exist?

ANTONIO. I will invent it.

MARIANA. Suppose that it costs you your life to obtain it?

ANTONIO. I shall give up my life, and then come straight back to life again, for you may be perfectly certain that I shall never leave the world as long as it contains you.

MARIANA. Not even if I marry some one else?

ANTONIO. John?

MARIANA. No, I shall never marry John, but the man who marries me must take care of him and protect him, for I shall always have him around. You are not laughing at John?

ANTONIO. By no means.

MARIANA. Because it is not safe to laugh at him. Wherever I go, he is coming along. Whatever I have, I mean to share it with him; my house shall be his house, and whenever he calls, I shall rush to his side.

ANTONIO. Yet the man complains of his fate!

MARIANA. He is a privileged person. Besides, I don't want you to be jealous. You must not be ridiculous. John is John.

ANTONIO. From this hour forth evermore. Anything else?

MARIANA. If I marry—

ANTONIO. If you marry!

MARIANA. I must have ten children, all boys.

ANTONIO. [*As a matter of course.*] Anything else?

MARIANA. I thought perhaps that might be enough.

ANTONIO. Why not add a couple of girls while we are about it, if it is not inconvenient, so that the breed of valiant women shall not become extinct?

MARIANA. Are you laughing at me?

ANTONIO. No, only I think we had better hurry. We are wasting valuable time.

MARIANA. I don't know. What are you doing?

ANTONIO. Loving you madly, passionately. I have been doing nothing else since yesterday, at eight o'clock in the morning.

MARIANA. I mean, what are you doing for a living?

ANTONIO. Why not do anything that happens along? Don't you think that with courage and a little luck, pretty nearly anything would do?

MARIANA. Yes, but—

ANTONIO. In America, my dear, I did a little of everything; I grew tobacco, I canned meat, I raised cane.

MARIANA. How perfectly dreadful! I am sure you must have thrown your money away.

ANTONIO. Dreadful? It was fine! I made lots of it.

MARIANA. You must be very rich, then.

ANTONIO. No, I enjoyed life as I went along. I shall be rich, however, when I marry you.

MARIANA. Do you plan to turn miser at my expense, when it is your duty to support me?

ANTONIO. Not miser, precisely; although we shall need to be economical if we are to provide for the boys.

MARIANA. [*Laughing.*] When do you expect to return to America?

ANTONIO. I expect to return—when, I don't know. As I shall not sail without you, perhaps I shall remain ashore.

MARIANA. I hope you don't think that I am afraid of the water?

ANTONIO. You? No, indeed! But John might be sea-sick.

MARIANA. [*Laughing.*] You are a real man. [*Holding out her hand.*]

ANTONIO. [*Kissing it.*] And you are an angel!

MARIANA. So you think now.

ANTONIO. Yes . . . I'll see you later.

[*Shouts and confusion outside.*]

VOICES. No, no! Here—not that way!

MARIANA. What has happened?

[MAMÁ INÉS *and* MAMÁ PEPA *rush in from the gallery, greatly agitated, followed by two servants.* DON CARLOS *and a group of factory hands enter simultaneously at the garden gate. They carry* JOHN *in their arms, covering him up with a poncho which*

*conceals him from view almost completely. They lay him
down upon the chaise longue, where* MARIANA *and the
other women surround him. Meanwhile the dialogue
proceeds with great rapidity, almost all speaking at the
same time.*]

DON CARLOS. This way! This way! In here. . . .

MAMÁ INÉS. John!

MAMÁ PEPA. John!

MARIANA. Why, John!

MAMÁ INÉS. God bless us! An accident?

MARIANA. John! John! Can't you speak? Look at
me! What have you done? What is the matter? Can't
you answer?

DON CARLOS. He is unconscious, my dear. He is not
able to talk.

MAMÁ INÉS. Mercy on us! A terrible calamity!

MAMÁ PEPA. He was a fine young man.

A MAID. Oh, he was lovely!

SECOND MAID. He was so handsome!

DON CARLOS. Ladies, he is not dead yet.

MAMÁ INÉS. But he is going to die.

MAMÁ PEPA. Nothing of the sort, unless his time has
come—which may be now.

FIRST MAID. He has opened his eyes.

MAMÁ INÉS. Quick! Run for a cup of hot broth.

ANTONIO. I should suggest a nip of cognac.

MAMÁ INÉS Give him a warm punch.

MARIANA. [*At the table.*] Yes, strike a match.

MAMÁ PEPA. [*To one of the maids.*] Bring some
rum.

MAMÁ INÉS. But how did it happen? Why don't you
tell us?

FIRST FACTORY HAND. It was nothing much. He was
walking up along the edge of the cliff, and he toppled over
into the sea. That's all.

SECOND FACTORY HAND. He didn't fall, I tell you; I
saw him jump.

MAMÁ PEPA and MAMÁ INÉS. God have mercy on our souls!

FIRST FACTORY HAND. I tell you I saw him topple off the edge of the cliff.

SECOND FACTORY HAND. I tell you I saw him jump. How could he fall when the track there is wide enough for a team?

FIRST FACTORY HAND. He got dizzy.

MARIANA. Yes, but who pulled him out of the water?

FIRST FACTORY HAND. Nobody, because he fell plop into Little John's boat, which was tied up there below the rock, waiting to catch lobsters.

MAMÁ PEPA. Praise God and bless His Holy Name!

MAMÁ INÉS. If he isn't drowned, then what on earth is the matter with him?

FIRST FACTORY HAND. He fell fifty feet, lady, which is plenty to give a man a bit of shock.

FIRST MAID. [*Entering.*] The punch!

MARIANA. Give it to me. [*She goes up to* JOHN *and forces the punch into his mouth.*] Drink this! Here, more, more. Do you feel very badly? [JOHN *coughs.*] He coughs—naturally, after the wetting.

JOHN. [*Faintly.*] No, I didn't get wet. The water splashed into the boat; it tipped a little when I came down, that was all. I am all right now, thanks; don't worry. Forgive me—

MAMÁ INÉS. You did give us a nice fright!

DON CARLOS. Everybody pass into the house and take something. [*To* MAMÁ PEPA.] See what you can do.

MAMÁ PEPA. Come with me.

FIRST FACTORY HAND. [*To* JOHN.] All right, son. Glad it wasn't any worse.

SECOND FACTORY HAND. Better luck next time.

[*All pass into the house except* MARIANA, ANTONIO *and* JOHN.]

MARIANA. [*In a low voice.*] Did—did you really commit suicide?

JOHN. Yes, really. And even then I had bad luck.

MARIANA. A nice way to celebrate my birthday, making it as unpleasant for me as you can!

JOHN. I am sorry, but the temptation to leave this scurvy world was too strong.

MARIANA. Promise never to do it again!

JOHN. What good would it do if I did?

ANTONIO. [*Advancing sympathetically.*] Well, well, man! What was the trouble?

MARIANA. Nothing. He was walking along the edge of the cliff, and grew dizzy.

JOHN. [*To* ANTONIO.] What! You here yet?

ANTONIO. Yes, indeed! No sooner were you out of the way, than she appeared, so I—

MARIANA. Exactly. I appeared, so he—

JOHN. Say no more! It was foreordained.

MARIANA. Yes, he dropped from the clouds, as it were.

JOHN. [*Forcing a smile.*] When—when is the happy day?

ANTONIO. Whenever she fixes the date.

MARIANA. Oh, there is no hurry.

ANTONIO. No hurry?

MARIANA. We have so much to do before we sail.

JOHN. Sail?

MARIANA. Yes, Antonio feels that we must return to America.

ANTONIO. But you are coming along.

JOHN. I?

ANTONIO. Yes. You are to be godfather to the first of our ten. We are planning to christen him John.

MARIANA. That is if, as we hope—

JOHN. No, no, never! Impossible! . . .

MARIANA. What makes you think so?

JOHN. Because if he inherits my luck with my name, the poor wretch will not be able even to drown. Besides, when things go wrong with him, I don't want to hear you saying forever: "Poor John!"

MARIANA. No, and we ought not to say it to you either. [*Moving away unconsciously.*] Poor John!

ANTONIO. Poor John!

CURTAIN

MADAME PEPITA

COMEDY IN THREE ACTS

TEATRO DE LÁ COMEDIA, MADRID
1912

THE PLAYHOUSE, OXFORD
1924

TO RICARDO LEON

CHARACTERS

MADAME PEPITA, *aged 38.*
CATALINA, *aged 17.*
GALATEA, *aged 25*
CARMEN, *aged 28.*
CRISTINA, *aged 16.*
A SEWING GIRL, *aged 20.*
DON GUILLERMO, *aged 40.*
ALBERTO, *aged 22.*
DON LUIS, *aged 55.*
AUGUSTO, *aged 25.*
ANDRÉS, *aged 30.*

ACT I

Reception salon in the establishment of MADAME PEPITA, *a fashionable dressmaker. The room is elaborately fitted out with gold furniture. upholstered in silk, but too elaborate for good taste. In the centre and at the right, small tables strewn with fashion magazines, colored plates of French and Viennese models and samples of materials such as wholesale houses supply to dressmakers. A large three panelled mirror, in front of a pier glass reaching to the floor, points to the fact that, on busy days, the salon is pressed into service as a fitting room also. One or two smart hats hang about on high stands; almost in the centre of the stage is a dress-form, on which is draped an elaborate evening gown.*

At the rise of the curtain, CARMEN, *one of* MADAME PEPITA'S *fitters, is kneeling before the form, pinning a design of flowers and foliage on the gown. She pauses every now and then to compare the result with the fashion plate which she takes from the floor at her side, in order to examine it more closely.* CRISTINA *stands near by, handing her pins from a small box, besides flowers and buds from a large carton which is placed on a chair.*

CARMEN, *a smart looking young person of the type employed in the better dressmaking establishments of Madrid, wears a black frock set off with a small white apron. Her shoes are neat and her hair and general appearance faultlessly correct.*

CRISTINA, *an apprentice, still in short skirts, is well-groomed and smart. Both girls speak with the easy sophistication of the capital, but without marked vulgarity.*

CARMEN.   Give me a pin, a rose, a bud . . . quick!

CRISTINA. You're not in any hurry, are you?

CARMEN. Well, you'll see what will happen if the Snapdragon appears upon the scene, and this dress isn't finished.

[CATALINA, *a girl of seventeen, enters, innocent and attractive in appearance. She is horribly dressed, and her hair is done frightfully. Although her clothes are well cut and of good material, her skirt is on crooked and dips down on one side, her blouse gapes where it fastens, and her apron, which is made of lace and batiste of excellent quality, is decorated with a huge ink spot. Her skirt is neither long nor short, while her hair hangs loose, except for a large bow tied where it does the least good. In moments of abstraction, she bites her nails furiously. In one hand she carries a book. Her conversation is that of a spoiled child who is aware of her importance as daughter of the head of the establishment.*]

CATALINA. [*Entering, overhearing* CARMEN'S *last words.*] See here, you needn't call my mother the Snapdragon. She has a name, like everybody else.

CARMEN. Dearie, you're a sweet ghost—you always appear when you're not wanted.

CATALINA. Whether I'm wanted or not, is none of your business.

CARMEN. Excuse me, dearie.

CATALINA. [*Walking over and seating herself in an armchair.*] You needn't excuse yourself, but be a little careful what you say; I'm here. [*Cuddling herself down into the chair like a cat.*] And I'm not as silly as you think.

[*She opens the book and begins to read to herself, evidently with great difficulty.*]

CARMEN. [*Under her breath.*] Little Miss-Know-It-All is not as silly as you think.

CATALINA. [*Turning quickly.*] See here! You

needn't call me Little-Miss-Know-It-All. I've got a name, like everybody else.

CARMEN. What you've got is a consumptive's quick ear.

CATALINA. [*Much offended.*] Consumptive yourself.

CRISTINA. [*Intervening.*] Ah, now, don't be cross. It was only a joke.

CATALINA. [*Immediately appeased.*] That's all right, but be a little careful with your jokes. My name is Catalina, I'll have you know, and my mother is not the Snapdragon, she's the Señora, the head of this establishment.

CARMEN. [*Maliciously.*] The madam.

CATALINA. No, sir, not the madam—Madame Pepita, which is very different. [*Insisting.*] Madame Pepita, Madame Pepita!

CARMEN. We heard you, dearie. [*Maliciously.*] Well, then, if Madame Pepita comes in and this trimming isn't finished, [*Emphasizing every word.*] *the head of this establishment* is going to create a disturbance that will make a hurricane seem tame.

CATALINA. And quite right, too, because you're lazy things, all of you.

CARMEN. Wise talk, eh, from the pet of the house?

CRISTINA. Why don't you turn in and help?

CATALINA. [*Scornfully.*] I? You've got cheek. [*Turning her back, she begins to read again, applying herself laboriously, pronouncing each syllable as children do when they learn.*] "The hu-man bod-y con-sists of three parts: head, trunk, and ex-trem-i-ties," [*Repeating, without looking at the book*] "The human body consists of three . . ."

> [*A bell rings at the entrance, which is at the head of the stairs.*]

CARMEN. [*To* CRISTINA.] Look and see who is coming. The doorbell rang.

CRISTINA. [*Glancing toward the door upon the right.*]
It's the boy from the silk shop.

[ALBERTO *appears in the doorway. He is a youth
of twenty-two, unusually well-educated, of good family,
whom reverses have obliged to seek employment as
clerk in "La Sultana," silk, lace and haberdashery shop.
He dresses plainly but respectably, and displays the
excessive timidity of a person who feels himself above
his position. He is delivering a number of large boxes
containing laces.*]

ALBERTO. [*Hesitating before he enters.*] May I?
With your permission . . . I beg your pardon . . . [*The
two girls do not answer, as they are busy laughing.*] Good
morning. . . .

CATALINA. [*Raising her eyes from her book, instantly
attracted by the young man. As the scene progresses, little
by little her attitude alters from sympathy to admiration.
The actress should mark the transition simply and ingenuously, as the girl's innocence does not permit her to realize
its significance.*] Good morning. Did you wish anything?

ALBERTO. [*Advancing a few steps, smiling timidly.*]
Here are the laces from "La Sultana," so that you may
select what is required.

CARMEN. Very well, you may leave them and return a
little later.

ALBERTO. [*Timidly.*] But . . . pardon me. The proprietor wishes me to bring back what you do not desire.
When all the laces are here, and ladies call at the shop,
naturally we have nothing to show.

CARMEN. Well, madame has a fitting at present; she
has no time to make selections now.

CRISTINA. The idea! You wouldn't refuse to oblige
a lady, would you, just because your employer tells you to?

ALBERTO. No, indeed! I shall retire, then, with your
permission, and return later.

[*Backing awkwardly toward the door, in his embarrassment he collides with a chair, which, in falling,*]

*carries with it a table loaded with fashion plates,
both crashing down together. Greatly disconcerted,*
ALBERTO *attempts to gather up the scattered papers,
becomes entangled, proceeds to extricate himself, finally
almost falling in his turn. The two girls burst out
laughing, while* CATALINA *rushes toward him with a
cry.*]

CATALINA. [*Hurrying to* ALBERTO.] Oh! Did you
hurt yourself?

ALBERTO. [*Smiling, in spite of his confusion, but looking askance at the two girls, who are still laughing.*] No,
señorita. Thank you very much.

CATALINA. Won't you let me get you a glass of cold
water?

ALBERTO. Oh, no, señorita! It is quite unnecessary.
  [*The girls continue to laugh.*]

CATALINA. [*Turning to the girls.*] I don't see what
you are laughing at.

CARMEN. Can't we laugh if we feel like it?

CATALINA. Not when there's nothing to laugh at.

ALBERTO. Never mind, señorita, they are laughing at
me. When a man trips, it invariably amuses the ladies.
I suppose it seems only natural.

CRISTINA. Yes, we can't teach you anything.

CATALINA. [*To* ALBERTO, *confidentially.*] They're
stupid things, both of them.

ALBERTO. [*Gratefully.*] You are an angel, señorita.

CATALINA. [*Drawing away, half shyly, half surprised.*]
Am I?

  [*During this episode, the girls have returned to their
  task of trimming the gown.* CARMEN, *kneeling on the
  floor, leans backward better to sense the effect, and
  presently makes a gesture of dissatisfaction.*]

CARMEN. This can't be right.

CRISTINA. I don't think so, either. It's too broad;
there's too much of it.

CARMEN. [*Rising and taking the sketch in her hand.*]

Well, it is exactly like the drawing, and that is awfully smart. I don't know what it is.

ALBERTO. [*Interrupting.*] Pardon me—[*Snatching the sketch from* CARMEN, *who looks up, astonished.*] The lines of this model were designed for the ideal woman, a woman with a figure built on Gothic lines. [*His self-assurance now offers a striking contrast to his former embarrassment.*]

ALL. What?

ALBERTO. [*Smiling, looking from one to the other, as if making a demonstration in mathematics.*] I mean to say that she has very long legs.

CARMEN. Say, now!

ALBERTO. I am sure of it. [*Estimating the height of the plate with his eye, and measuring it off with one finger, as painters do.*] One, two, three. . . . We have exactly eight heads.

CRISTINA. Eight heads?

ALBERTO. [*Smiling pleasantly.*] Yes, señorita, that is, in total height; and the lady for whom you are making this gown must be only— [*Glancing at the dress-form.*] Let me see. One . . . two . . . three . . . we may give her five and a half. [*With perfect assurance.*]

CRISTINA. Five and a half? Heads?

CARMEN. [*Sarcastically.*] Five and a half heads ought to seem a lot to you.

ALBERTO. [*Intensely serious.*] No, not at all. Five and a half are not nearly enough. The ideally proportioned figure has a total height of seven heads—that is the Greek type in all its purity and elegance. French and Viennese models always exaggerate somewhat, but Spanish women, particularly here in Madrid, are rather Romanesque in contour, like—like you, señorita. [*To* CRISTINA.]

CARMEN. [*Laughs.*]

CRISTINA. [*Offended.*] Like me?

ALBERTO. Don't be offended. I mean wide and thick. So, when we attempt to adapt the ideal lines of the model to the shapes which we actually see, the result is ridiculous. [*Waxing eloquent, as he studies the garment.*] Three parallel rows of trimming on a short skirt? Horrible! And the pity of it is that just as long as women neglect to study the divine mysteries of line, they will continue to go about looking as if their worst enemies had designed their clothes. It breaks a man's heart to go out for a walk and meet masterpieces of the Creator transformed into monstrosities by the sacrilegious, criminal hands of tailors and dressmakers.

CRISTINA. [*Laughs.*]

CARMEN. [*Half amused, half angry.*] What was that about tailors and dressmakers?

ALBERTO. [*Recollecting himself, his customary timidity returning as he realizes what he has said.*] Please excuse me. I wasn't thinking of you.

CATALINA. [*Who has been listening in openmouthed admiration.*] But who are you? How do you know so much?

ALBERTO. I am nobody, señorita; I amount to nothing. Only I draw a little, I sketch, and I hope to become a painter, some day. In the meantime, I am working in "La Sultana," silk, lace and haberdashery shop. I shall retire, now, with your permission, ladies. . . .

[*Goes out. A moment of astonished silence follows.*]

CARMEN. [*Laughing.*] What do you think of that?

CRISTINA. He's a scream.

CATALINA. [*Earnestly.*] I don't see what makes you call him a scream. I think he's awfully nice and attractive.

CARMEN. Ahem! Attractive and everything else. So Don Simplicity has turned your head, has he?

CATALINA. [*Almost in tears.*] I don't see what makes you call him Don Simplicity. He's got a name, like everybody else.

CARMEN. But we don't know his name.

CRISTINA. Yes, we do; it's Alberto.

CATALINA. [*To herself.*] Alberto? What a nice name! [MADAME PEPITA *is heard talking outside.*] Oh, here comes mamma!

CARMEN. [*Resuming work precipitately.*] Good-bye my wages! [*To* CRISTINA.] Give me another pin.

MADAME PEPITA. [*Outside.*] Yes, yes! I tell you, yes!

A SEWING GIRL. [*Outside.*] But, Madame—

[MADAME PEPITA *enters. She is still a fine look-ing woman. Her tailored suit is strictly in the mode, and her coiffure arranged with extreme care. She carries an elaborately trimmed sleeve in one hand, talking and gesticulating immoderately as she enters, evidently in great annoyance. At the same time, she is careful to maintain a noticeable affectation of refine-ment. The Sewing Girl follows deferentially.*]

MADAME PEPITA. There is no "but" about it. I tell you the sleeve is a botch, and a botch it is. You'll rip it this very minute, and baste it over again and say noth-ing, and if that doesn't suit you, you can go. The idea of a little monkey like you presuming to differ with me in a matter of taste!

SEWING GIRL. But I didn't say anything.

MADAME PEPITA. So much the better! Here, take your sleeve. [*Throws it at the girl, who catches it.*] The thing's a nightmare—it's about as *chic* as you are. To think I pay this girl six pesetas a week!

SEWING GIRL. [*Between her teeth, as she goes out.*] Any one who stands you ought to be paid six hundred.

CATALINA. [*Going up to* MADAME PEPITA.] Mamma, do you hear what she says? She says any one who stands you ought to be paid six hundred.

MADAME PEPITA. [*Brusquely.*] Is that your business?

CATALINA. [*Completely cowed.*] Oh!

MADAME PEPITA. [*Approaching* CARMEN *and* CRIS-

tina.] What are you doing? Wasting time—as usual? Why aren't you in the workroom?

CARMEN. We were finishing this gown for exhibition.

MADAME PEPITA. [*Examining the model through her lorgnette, which is attached to an extravagantly bejewelled chain.*] And a sweet exhibition it is!

CARMEN. Don't you like it?

MADAME PEPITA. It might do for the patron saint of your village, which is in the back country—way back, if one is to judge by the taste.

CARMEN. I was born in Madrid, the same as you.

MADAME PEPITA. Then, my dear, your taste is bad naturally.

CARMEN. It's an exact copy of the model as you ordered. Won't you look?

[*Hands her the sketch.* MADAME PEPITA *examines the gown and the model alternately through her lorgnette.*]

CATALINA. [*Breaking in, eagerly, perfectly sure of herself.*] But the model was designed for a woman built on Gothic lines.

MADAME PEPITA. [*Looking at her daughter, alarmed.*] What's that?

CATALINA. [*Positively.*] Of course! And the lady who ordered this is Romanesque.

MADAME PEPITA. What are you talking about?

CATALINA. Yes, Romanesque. She has only seven heads, and to be true to type, with perfect proportion, you must have. . . . [*Stops to think.*] Oh, a great many more—I don't know just how many; and if you put three rows of trimming on a short skirt, why, the woman who wears it will go around looking like a Greek monstrosity whose worst enemy has made her clothes. There! Just see if I'm not right. [*Breaks off suddenly.*]

MADAME PEPITA. [*Alarmed.*] Child, have you a temperature? Come here, let me see.

CATALINA. No, mamma!

CARMEN *and* CRISTINA. [*Laugh.*]

MADAME PEPITA. [*Angrily.*] What are you laughing at?

CRISTINA. [*Intimidated.*] Nothing, *Madame.*

CARMEN. We just heard all that rigmarole from the boy from "La Sultana."

MADAME PEPITA. Has the boy from "La Sultana" been here?

CARMEN. With the laces.

MADAME PEPITA. The same boy?

CARMEN. No, another one, *Madame.*

MADAME PEPITA. Did you tell him that he was no good and that the proprietor is a cheat and an extortioner?

CARMEN. [*Smiling.*] No, *Madame.*

MADAME PEPITA. You missed a fine opportunity. I'll tell him when I see him.

CATALINA. [*Aroused.*] No, don't you do it, mamma.

MADAME PEPITA. [*Brusquely.*] Is that your business?

CATALINA. [*Moving off, suppressed.*] Oh!

CARMEN. [*Pointing to the dress-form.*] What shall we do with this?

MADAME PEPITA. Take it to pieces and pin it together all over again. But not here. People will be coming soon, and the whole place is a mess. Carry it into the workroom—I'll be there in a minute. Get out of my sight!

CARMEN. [*With her tongue in her cheek.*] Yes, *Madame.* [*Picking up the form with* CRISTINA'S *help and carrying it out, muttering between her teeth as she does so.*] With the greatest of pleasure.

CATALINA. [*Approaching her mother.*] Mamma, she says "With the greatest of pleasure."

MADAME PEPITA. [*Brusquely.*] Is that your business?

CATALINA. [*Intimidated.*] Oh!

MADAME PEPITA. What are you doing here? Idling?

CATALINA. No, Mamma, I am studying.

MADAME PEPITA. Is that so? Let me see that book. Is it a novel?

CATALINA. [*Protesting.*] No, mamma, it's a book Don Guillermo lent me—don't you know? The gentleman on the floor above. It is, really—if you want to see it. [*Giving her the book.*]

MADAME PEPITA. [*Turning the pages.*] Heavens and earth! What's this? A skeleton?

CATALINA. [*As pleased as a child.*] Yes, mamma. It's a book that tells how many bones we have and how we are made, inside and out.

MADAME PEPITA. Eh?

CATALINA. [*Continuing.*] And what everything inside us is for. [*Reciting.*] "The human body consists of three parts: head, trunk"—

MADAME PEPITA. [*Interrupting, scandalized.*] Hush, hush! That's immoral! Throw the book away this minute. Such things are only for men to know. No decent woman has any occasion to study her insides.

CATALINA. [*Innocently.*] Oh, yes, mamma, she has. Don Guillermo says that women are just the ones who ought to know, so that when they grow up and become mothers, they can nurse their own children, as God intended.

MADAME PEPITA. [*Sincerely shocked.*] The man's a satyr!

CATALINA. [*Innocently.*] Oh, no, mamma, you mustn't say that! He writes articles for the papers, and he's a member of the Academy.

MADAME PEPITA. [*Softening, as if by magic.*] A member of the Academy! Who told you so?

CATALINA. The janitor's wife. She saw it on his letters, and it's on the papers, too, that come to him from the printers: Don Guillermo de Armendáriz y Ochoa, of the Royal Academy of Fine Arts, yes, mamma. Besides, he's awfully nice and awfully sweet to me, and he has his rooms all stuffed full of big pieces of stone and statues that haven't any heads, and whenever he meets me on the stairs he always stops to talk to me, and he's told me he'll lend me books so that I can learn something, because he thinks it's a great pity that I am such a big girl and such an ignoramus, and he asked why didn't you send me to school when I was little, and I told him that you didn't want me to associate with common children, and he says that it is better to be common than to be ignorant, and that's true, isn't it, mamma?

MADAME PEPITA. [*Abstracted, impressed.*] A member of the Academy?

CATALINA. [*Enthusiastically.*] Yes, mamma. And the other day he had his picture in the *Nuevo Mundo* with the King and Queen.

MADAME PEPITA. With the King?

CATALINA. Yes, mamma, at the opening of the picture exhibition; he was there to receive them and explain everything, so that they could tell which were the good pictures and which were the bad ones. You can see them all here for yourself. [*Producing a copy of the Nuevo Mundo, which is concealed among the fashion plates.*] He has medals all over, and wears a sash.

MADAME PEPITA. [*Impressed.*] Probably the Order of Carlos III, or maybe he's María Luisa. [*Mollified, gazing at the photograph.*] How attractive a man does look when he's decorated!

[*The doorbell rings, after which* CARMEN'S *voice is heard outside.*]

CARMEN. [*Outside.*] Yes, Señor Conde. Will the Conde step in? I'll tell *Madame*. [*Appearing in the doorway, and discovering* MADAME PEPITA.] Oh, here is Madame Pepita! *Madame,* the Conde de la Vega de Lezo.

MADAME PEPITA. [*Suddenly becoming sweeter than honey.*] Conde! Come in, come right in. [*Giving her daughter a hasty push.*] Go and dress yourself! Don't stand there in the middle of the room—you're a sight.

CATALINA. [*Cowed.*] Oh! [*Runs out, escaping by one door as the* CONDE *enters by the other.*]

[DON LUIS DE LARA, CONDE DE LA VEGA DE LEZO, *though but fifty-five, is in appearance much older, love, wine and other excesses having undermined his health prematurely. Nevertheless, he still affects the airs and graces of the beau, which contrast lamentably with the general decay of his person. He dresses with undue pretense to fashion, carrying himself gallantly in the grand style, although his gestures and poses are marred for the most part by his premature senility. He wabbles and totters and bends forward unexpectedly, which causes him the keenest annoyance. Kissing the girl who opens the door as he enters, he appears to be dispensing a favor. The girl receives the salute with ill-concealed disgust, wiping her face with her apron as soon as the* CONDE'S *back is turned. Then she goes out.*]

DON LUIS. My dearest Pepita!

MADAME PEPITA. I was afraid the Conde had forgotten us. It is three months since we have seen you.

DON LUIS. Oh, my dear, I have been traveling—troubles and worries without number! I have not been well.

MADAME PEPITA. The Conde has been ill?

DON LUIS. Yes, mental anguish, moral suffering; that is all. Society is in bad case, Pepita; the aristocracy has degenerated. Money is replacing blue blood nowadays, and it is prejudiced against the nobility. Poverty devours our vellum riches. We are nobodies.

MADAME PEPITA. Oh, don't say that, Conde! Money cannot purchase blue blood.

DON LUIS. [*Sighing.*] No, blue blood cannot be bought, nor sold either, for that matter.

MADAME PEPITA. Be seated, Conde.

DON LUIS. Ah, Pepita, who would believe that your dear, departed mother had lived in our house, that she had acted as maid to my departed wife?

MADAME PEPITA. [*Unduly affected.*] Your poor wife!

DON LUIS. Yes, you were born in our house, brought up under the protection of my wing. [*Looking about the room.*] But, today, you travel the road to riches, while I. . . .

MADAME PEPITA. [*Countering promptly.*] Conde, I have troubles of my own. Believe me!

DON LUIS. Come, come, don't tell me you'll ever hang for want of a couple of thousand pesetas.

MADAME PEPITA. Conde, what put that idea in your head? A dressmaker invests her entire capital in clothes. These gowns cost me a fortune, and just as soon as the style changes, nobody will look at them. Then, I have to pay wages to no end of girls, and, finally, there are the customers. They grow meaner and meaner every day. Even the actresses and the demi-mondaines, who only a little while ago never dreamed of questioning the price of anything, would you believe it—nowadays the way they scrutinize their bills is something shameful. They know what everything, down to a yard of satin, costs. Why, Conde, I had a lady here the other day, the wife of a cabinet minister—I'd rather not mention her name—who insisted upon supplying her own trimming for a court costume. Fancy! Trimming! To me! [*Greatly outraged.*] What next, I wonder? She said the lace was antique, it had a history. I thought to myself, it's antique all right. As for the history, there's plenty of that that's not so antique, in which your husband figures conspicuously.

DON LUIS. It is the way of the world, Pepita.

MADAME PEPITA. Dressmaking is not what it used to be, Conde.

DON LUIS. Come, come, you have land at Escorial, which is money assured. Everybody knows you have property.

MADAME PEPITA. What good is a little property when you haven't the money to build?

DON LUIS. Your daughter will be one of the finest matches in Spain.

MADAME PEPITA. [*Flattered.*] Oh, Conde, how can you say that?

DON LUIS. I have a soft spot in my heart for you, Pepita.

MADAME PEPITA. Thank you, Conde.

DON LUIS. You are an exceptional woman, enterprising, systematic, who has exquisite taste.

[*At each additional flattery,* MADAME PEPITA *swells with pride, blushing with excess of emotion.*] I express my admiration freely whenever I can find the opportunity.

MADAME PEPITA. I am more than grateful, Conde.

DON LUIS. Today, I have come with a purpose.

MADAME PEPITA. Conde!

DON LUIS. A lady will arrive shortly—naturally, at my suggestion—who wishes to order some clothes.

MADAME PEPITA. A relative of the Conde's?

DON LUIS. [*With a superior air.*] No, she is not of my world, socially. Rather, I should say, of the artist class. Her name is Galatea—a stage name, of course. You must have heard of her—something quite out of the ordinary—high class vaudeville, don't you know? Living pictures.

MADAME PEPITA. Oh, yes! Of course!

DON LUIS. Stunning creature! Exquisite! She has been in despair in Madrid over the problem of clothes. She can find nothing appropriate. [*With a deprecatory gesture.*] Finally, I said to her: Why not see Madame Pepita?

MADAME PEPITA. I am overwhelmed, Conde!

DON LUIS. So now she is coming to you. The difficulty is—at least, I assume it is—she treats me like a father, or even more so. Although she is fond of me, there are some subjects we never discuss. However, I am convinced that somewhere, in the background, there must be somebody who pays the bills. Tragic, is it not? But, obviously, that is not our affair.

Madame Peptia. [*Innocently.*]   Certainly not, as long as they are paid.

Don Luis.   Naturally, that is understood.   I might suggest that in fixing the price. . . .

Madame Pepita.   [*Quickly.*]   The Conde knows that my prices are not exorbitant.   As the lady is a friend of his . . .

Don Luis.   No, no, that is not it exactly.   Permit yourself, for once, the luxury of a few hundred pesetas more or less.   Suppose we say a thousand more.

> [Madame Pepita *responds with a gesture of astonishment.*]

Times are hard.   I could use seven hundred and fifty myself . . . [*Quickly.*] which you may set aside for me when the bill is paid, unless of course, you care to advance them, if it is not inconvenient.

Madame Pepita.   [*Disconcerted.*]   But, Conde—

Don Luis.   [*Affecting depression, pacing up and down the room.*]   Sad, Pepita, is it not?   Democracy has reduced us to this.   A Conde de la Vega de Lezo accepting commissions upon clothes!   Think of it!   I shed tears.

Madame Pepita.   [*Capitulating.*]   Don't feel too badly, Conde.   If there is anything I can do. . . .

Don Luis.   [*Simulating feeling.*]   Thanks, Pepita. [*Embracing her.*]   I accept it because your heart is pure gold.   But it demeans me.

Madame Pepita.   Not at all, Conde.

> [*The door bell rings.* Galatea's *voice is heard.*]

Galatea.   [*Outside.*]   Is Madame Pepita in?

Don Luis.   Here she is; I recognize her voice.   [*Transported.*]   Ah, her voice!   [*Advancing to the door.*]   This way, Galatea.   [*Hurrying forward to offer his hand.*]

> [Galatea, *a woman of twenty-five, displays an extremely smart street costume, somewhat over-elaborate, but nevertheless in good taste.   Her manners and speech are vulgar, contrasting with her appearance, and*

*indicating that she has been brought up among the least
sensitive of the lower classes.*]

GALATEA. [*To the* CONDE.] So you're here, are you?

DON LUIS. [*Obsequious and infatuated, losing all his
grand manner at once.*] Yes, I am here, as you see—
whispering naughty things about you. I am interested in
whatever you do.

GALATEA. Well, I'll have to credit you one for getting
up early, and it was cold this morning, too.

DON LUIS. I am capable of any sacrifice for your sake.

GALATEA. The sacrifice will come later, but remember
I don't count asthmatic attacks any sacrifice.

DON LUIS. Asthmatic attacks? A great joke!

GALATEA. Is this the Madame Pepita you talk so much
about?

MADAME PEPITA. Yes, indeed. At your service.

GALATEA. [*As affable with* MADAME PEPITA *as she is
abrupt with the* CONDE.] I am charmed.

MADAME PEPITA. The pleasure is mine. The Conde
informs me that you are very particular in the matter of
clothes.

GALATEA. Usually, I think clothes so commonplace.

MADAME PEPITA. I am sure that we have something
which will appeal to your tastes.

GALATEA. I suppose you're frightfully expensive?

MADAME PEPITA. Quality is always expensive. However, I do not believe that we shall differ over the price.

DON LUIS. You may have absolute confidence in Pepita.
Although not nobly born, she holds herself high.

[*Whenever the* CONDE *speaks,* GALATEA *stares at
him contemptuously, looking him over from head to
foot, but he simulates entire obliviousness.*]

MADAME PEPITA. You embarrass me, Conde. [*To*
GALATEA.] Have you any ideas, or would you prefer to
look over some of our models first, so as to see what we
have?

GALATEA. Yes, perhaps you might show me something.

MADAME PEPITA. If Madame will step into the other room. . . .

GALATEA. I am anxious to see your display.

DON LUIS. [*Unable to resist.*] Quite right. Step this way!

GALATEA. No, trot along; you're excused. Dressmakers despise nothing so much as men who hang about fitting rooms.

MADAME PEPITA. Oh, no indeed! If it is any pleasure to the Conde. . . .

GALATEA. Well, if you don't mind, I do. That settles it.

DON LUIS. [*Visibly disappointed.*] Always clever and coy!

GALATEA. Yes, it's the way I'm made.

DON LUIS. I must be off, then. I have business of my own to attend to. Does your motor happen to be at the door, by any chance?

GALATEA. What do you want of my motor?

DON LUIS. [*Smiling.*] Nothing of your motor, but I should like permission from you to ride in it, as far as my house.

GALATEA. [*After a moment's hesitation.*] Very well, if you send it right back. Mind that you don't smoke and get my cushions all smelling of tobacco, because, when I'm alone, I don't care to be reminded that there are such things as men in the world. [*Fanning the air with her handkerchief.*] Ouf!

DON LUIS. *Au revoir*, Pepita. Good-bye. By the way, attend to that little matter as soon as possible; the need is urgent.

MADAME PEPITA. I shan't forget, Conde.

[*The* CONDE *goes out.*]

GALATEA. [*As he disappears, utterly indifferent as to whether he overhears or not.*] Silly ass! Side-splitting, isn't he? And he thinks he's a sport!

MADAME PEPITA. [*Alarmed, fearing the* CONDE *may*

hear.] Oh, but the Conde is so distinguished! He is just in his prime.

GALATEA. Yes, prime for a mummy in a museum. My God, I've no use for antiques, not even when they're gold lined! Men oughtn't to be allowed after they are twenty. These hang-overs disgust me. [*Sighs.*]

> [MADAME PEPITA *lifts the curtain at the door lead-ing to the fitting room, and ushers* GALATEA *out. For a moment the stage is empty. Then the bell rings, and* CARMEN *enters with* AUGUSTO.]

> [AUGUSTO *is a young man of twenty-five, whose sole preoccupation is the care and adornment of his person. He is dressed in an ultra-fashionable, light colored morning suit, which is slightly effeminate in effect. His shirt, tie, shoes—in short all the articles of his attire—blend in a harmony of delicate hues. He sports a velour hat, whose soft, wide brim, turned up on one side and down on the other, rivals the meticulous lure of the coquette. His blond hair billows above his brow in sweeping waves, one or two of which break gracefully over his forehead. His moustache is equally exquisite, yet, in spite of his preciosity and affected speech, there is something about his person which is undeniably attractive.*]

CARMEN. [*Obsequiously.*] Do step in, Señor Viz-conde, and be seated. I will deliver the message.—My God, how sweet that man smells!

AUGUSTO. [*Deigning to accept the proffered chair, but without sitting down.*] Thanks awfully.

CARMEN. Did the Vizconde meet his father, the Conde, on the stairs?

AUGUSTO. Meet my father? No.

CARMEN. [*Seeking a pretext to prolong the conversation.*] The Conde left a moment ago. . . .

AUGUSTO. Did he? Tell Madame Pepita that I am here—that is, if she is disengaged.

CARMEN. Certainly. If the Vizconde has a moment to

spare . . . *Madame* is with a customer, an actress. Perhaps you have heard the name? Galatea.

Augusto. [*Quickly.*] Galatea? When did she arrive?

Carmen. Half an hour ago, Vizconde. She is selecting models with *Madame*.

Augusto. Let me see her at once.

Carmen. Galatea?

Augusto. No, Madame Pepita.

Carmen. Yes, Vizconde.

Augusto· Do not tell her I am here, but say it is urgent. Remember, not one word to Galatea.

Carmen. No, Vizconde. She will be with you directly.—Holy Mother! What beautiful nails! [*Goes out examining her own.*]

Augusto. [*Smiling fatuously.*] It cannot be helped. Ah, I wonder what they see?

> [*He looks at himself in the three-panelled mirror, then in the pier glass, then in a hand mirror which lies upon the table, adjusting some detail of his suit, tie or hair at each. Pulling a chain, to which a small bottle of perfume is attached, from his trousers pocket, he pours a few drops upon his handkerchief. Then, he takes a small comb from a case and deftly fluffs the waves of his hair. Then, he twists the ends of his moustache between his thumb and forefinger, makes the circuit of the mirrors again, and, finally, selecting a slender Egyptian cigarette from an incredible case, lights it with a patent lighter before sitting himself down to smoke, seated midway between the two mirrors, from which point of vantage he is able to survey himself upon all sides at once. He is interrupted in this agreeable occupation by* MADAME PEPITA, *who enters hurriedly, followed by* CARMEN.]

Madame Pepita. [*To* Carmen.] But why all this mystery? Will you tell me who wants to see me? What is the matter with you, anyhow?

AUGUSTO. [*Remaining seated, without deigning to re-move his eyes from the mirror.*] Pepita, it is I.

MADAME PEPITA. Vizconde!

[AUGUSTO *directs a killing glance at* CARMEN, *who responds with a look of admiration.*]

CARMEN. [*As she goes out.*] When he looks at you, it's divine!

AUGUSTO. [*Twirling his moustache complacently, with-out taking his eyes from the glass.*] Yes, Pepita, it is I. Don't call me Vizconde, call me what you used to when you lived with us.

MADAME PEPITA. [*Ravished.*] Oh, Señorito Augusto!

AUGUSTO. [*Still more condescendingly.*] Or just plain Augusto.

MADAME PEPITA. Señorito Augusto! The very idea!

AUGUSTO. You witnessed my entrance into the world, Pepita.

MADAME PEPITA. How long ago it seems! [*About to cry.*] Your poor mother!

AUGUSTO. [*Abstracted, still preoccupied with himself.*] Yes, my poor mother! Such is life; some die, others are born. Which is which?

MADAME PEPITA. Who knows, Vizconde?

AUGUSTO. No doubt you wonder how it is I come to be up so early?

MADAME PEPITA. The Vizconde knows he is welcome at any hour.

AUGUSTO. It may surprise you, but I have come, my dear, to ask a favor.

MADAME PEPITA. Oh, Vizconde!

AUGUSTO. Pepita, times are hard. Although my habits may be. . . . [*Lowering his eyes.*] The pace today is a trifle rapid. A man of my age with my advantages. . . . [*Gazing at himself from head to foot.*] Well, I must resign myself. [*Smiles.*] Love is expensive. And women have become so dreadfully prosaic. I am madly in love with a woman—why conceal it? You know her—Galatea?

MADAME PEPITA. Galatea? Who . . . ?

AUGUSTO. Precisely. [*Smiles.*] Who is looking over your models. Hence the need of secrecy: I do not wish her to see me. [MADAME PEPITA *moves over and closes the door.*] Thank you so much. She is a regal creature. [*Turning to admire himself again in an ecstasy of self-satisfaction.*] Although I say it myself, she has exquisite taste.

MADAME PEPITA. Well, she is certainly hard to please.

AUGUSTO. But she is crazy about me. I am sorry for the poor girl. She is in despair over the question of clothes; you know what models are in Madrid. Finally, I said to her: Why not see Madame Pepita?

MADAME PEPITA. Oh, Vizconde!

AUGUSTO. It will be worth your while—and so I dropped in myself. Money is no object in this case. When you make out the bill. . . .

MADAME PEPITA. Oh, Vizconde! Since you are to pay the bill. . . .

AUGUSTO. No, Pepita, no; not exactly. Unfortunately, I shall not pay.

MADAME PEPITA. Eh?

AUGUSTO. I adore her, she adores me, but there are complications. In fact, I suspect that somewhere, in the background, there is some despicable creature who does pay. [*Sighing.*] Some miserable old reprobate—at least so I gather from her maid, Carmelina, an adorable blonde —[*Lowering his eyes*] who conceals nothing from me.

MADAME PEPITA. [*Sincerely alarmed.*] You don't tell me . . . ?

AUGUSTO. Permit yourself a little liberty when you make out the bill—I mean as to price. [*With an endearing pat.*] And we'll split the difference. How is that?

MADAME PEPITA. But, Vizconde—

AUGUSTO. [*Growing more and more affectionate.*] Nonsense. Let the other chap do the worrying. Ah,

Pepita, you are just like my poor, dear mother. [*Becoming sentimental.*] She was fond of you.

MADAME PEPITA. [*Overcome, preparing to cry.*] Yes, your poor mother.

AUGUSTO. But enough of that! Charge her fifteen hundred pesetas.

CATALINA. [*Entering suddenly, without noticing* AUGUSTO.] Mamma, I am going out to the corner to buy some note paper. Gregoria has asked me to write to her young man.

MADAME PEPITA. What on earth is the matter with you? Don't you know how to address a gentleman?

CATALINA. [*Frightened.*] Oh!

MADAME PEPITA. Here is the Vizconde.

CATALINA. Yes . . . I didn't see him first.

MADAME PEPITA. Well, what else have you to say for yourself?

CATALINA. [*Offering her hand to* AUGUSTO, *who takes it gingerly.*] How do you do?

MADAME PEPITA. Say how do you do, Vizconde?

AUGUSTO. [*Condescendingly.*] Oh, never mind!

CATALINA. [*Firmly.*] I'm sure I don't care.

AUGUSTO. [*Insinuatingly.*] Is this . . . original young lady your daughter?

MADAME PEPITA. Yes, Vizconde, my daughter and my punishment.

AUGUSTO. Very well, then we understand each other. You needn't bother to see me out. [*Smiling.*] The girls will be waiting at the door.

 [*Retires, accompanied by* MADAME PEPITA, *who returns immediately.*]

CATALINA. [*As he disappears.*] Conceited puppy.

 [*She has changed her dress, but is still ungroomed and untidy, as before.*]

MADAME PEPITA. [*Re-entering.*] Are you still here?

CATALINA. [*Intimidated.*] I was looking for my book.

MADAME PEPITA. Haven't I told you a hundred times

not to come in when I have people here, without first dressing yourself properly?

CATALINA. [*Inspecting herself in the mirror.*] But I am dressed properly.

MADAME PEPITA. [*Surveying her from head to foot.*] For what?

CATALINA. [*With sincere conviction.*] I have on a new skirt and a clean waist.

MADAME PEPITA. And then you've taken a turn with them on in the coal bin! Come here! [*Pushing her this way and that, as she fixes her dress.*] Aren't you ashamed to be seventeen and not be able to put your skirt on straight yet?

CATALINA. Ouch! You hurt.

MADAME PEPITA. [*Still pushing her around.*] It will do you good.

CATALINA. Yes, it's fun for you.

GALATEA. [*Outside.*] It's awfully good-looking, of course . . .

MADAME PEPITA. [*Opening the door, which she closed previously.*] Get out! Somebody is coming.

CATALINA. Well, can I go, then?

MADAME PEPITA. Go to the devil, if that will do any good.

> [CATALINA *goes out on the left as* GALATEA *enters on the right. A sewing girl accompanies her, who retires immediately without speaking.*]

GALATEA. [*Sniffing the air.*] Hm! So he has been here?

MADAME PEPITA. [*Pretending not to understand.*] I beg your pardon—

GALATEA. [*Immensely pleased.*] Ha! Ha! Ha! What did he want? I can smell him.

MADAME PEPITA. I have no idea to what you refer, señora.

GALATEA. How innocent we are! I refer to that rascal, Augusto. Nobody could mistake that odor of tuberose. [*Deeply gratified.*] It would have surprised me if he hadn't come. Probably he wanted to find out whether or not I was alone. Ha, ha, ha! What did you tell him? Suppose he meets the author of his being on the stairs? Ha, ha, ha! [*Becoming serious.*] Well, I ought not to laugh, I suppose. He's been an angel to me—yes, that's a good joke, isn't it? A real angel. What in heaven's name were we talking about, anyway?

MADAME PEPITA. I hope you found something to suit?

GALATEA. Oh, yes! You have wonderful taste.

MADAME PEPITA. [*Bowing.*] Señora!

GALATEA. There's a blue gown that fairly took my breath away, and a lace negligee, somewhat low . . . do you get me? [*Sighing.*] It was fascinating. Imagine me in it!

MADAME PEPITA. Did you notice a mauve *crêpe de chine* teagown, with a jacket effect of *point d'Alençon?* It would be marvelous with your lines. Try it on, and we can mark the alterations.

GALATEA. No, thanks, I don't believe I'll try on anything to-day.

MADAME PEPITA. You won't?

GALATEA. No, I am not interested. You might make me up two or three batiste blouses, perhaps—don't you know? The cheapest things you have—what you use for chemises will do. And send me a bill for four thousand pesetas.

MADAME PEPITA. Four thousand what?

GALATEA. Half for you and half for me. My God, a woman has to live somehow!

MADAME PEPITA. Oh, the bill? But . . .

GALATEA. While you are about it, I don't suppose you'd mind sending it in duplicate?

MADAME PEPITA. In duplicate?

GALATEA. One for the old man and one for the boy. [*Noticing the horrified look on* MADAME PEPITA's *face.*] While a woman's young, she's got to provide for her old age. What are men for, anyway, except to pay bills? There are lots of women who enjoy spending money. Every time they have anything, something else takes their eye, so off they go and buy. [*Very earnestly.*] But that's not my style; I've too much sense. The old man is no good. [MADAME PEPITA *makes a gesture of dissent.*] I am merely taking him as an example—no reflections upon you. Tell me, would you put up with him for a minute if he never came across? Of course not. [*Imitating in pantomime the counting of bills.*] But the young fellow is all right. Besides, what's the use of denying it? I'm mad over him. But what does he expect? I'm not going to be the only one who loosens up. Take that from me.

MADAME PEPITA.   If you look at it in that light . . .

GALATEA.   Light nothing! Look at it as it is. Suppose now I go in for clothes? Clothes cost money— you know that; and you can't raise a cent on them afterwards to save your neck. A woman's a fool to spend money on clothes. [*Contemptuously.*] Jewels are no better. You have to pay twenty for what you can't sell for ten. Cash is safer, and land. Every penny I save goes into land.

MADAME PEPITA.   [*Impressed.*] Then you think well of real estate?

GALATEA.   Yes. The next time you run up to Paris, look out of the window as the train leaves Torrelodones. You'll see a house on the right, with a fence painted blue.

MADAME PEPITA.   With a tin summerhouse in front, with a vine on it?

GALATEA.   Lovely, isn't it? That's me.

MADAME PEPITA.   [*Enchanted.*] You?

GALATEA.   Drop off if you have time and look me over.

MADAME PEPITA.   Thanks.

GALATEA.   I'm usually there Sundays, watering my lettuce. [*A pause.*] But probably you have more important things to do, and I'm taking your time.

MADAME PEPITA. No, indeed!

GALATEA. Oh, yes, you have! I'll look you up later. Remember—two bills. Don't forget! See you later.

MADAME PEPITA. I shall hope to see you. . . .

GALATEA. I've taken an awful fancy to you—indeed, I have!

MADAME PEPITA. Charmed, to be sure.

[*Both go out. After a moment,* MADAME PEPITA *returns.*]

MADAME PEPITA. [*To herself.*] A thousand pesetas, four thousand pesetas, fifteen hundred, two bills—and all for two batiste blouses! God, at this rate I can dismiss the establishment!

[*She goes up to the table and examines the samples that* ALBERTO *has left. A noise outside. Then, the bell rings and* DON GUILLERMO *enters, supporting* CATALINA, *pale and frightened.* CRISTINA *and another girl follow immediately.*]

MADAME PEPITA. [*Alarmed, rushing up to her daughter.*] What is the matter? What has happened, Catalina?

CATALINA. [*Very much frightened.*] Nothing, mamma . . . nothing at all.

DON GUILLERMO. Don't be alarmed, señora.

MADAME PEPITA. Sir!

CATALINA. Mamma, this is Don Guillermo.

DON GUILLERMO. The young lady has turned her ankle. Perhaps you had better sit down. [*Assisting* CATALINA *to an armchair.*] As she was crossing the street, an automobile almost ran over her. Fortunately, it missed . . .

CATALINA. There wasn't any danger.

DON GUILLERMO. Naturally, she was frightened. Have you a glass of water?

MADAME PEPITA. Squeeze a lime in it.

[CRISTINA *goes out.*]

DON GUILLERMO. I should suggest an orange.

[*The* SEWING GIRL *goes out.*]

CATALINA. I'm all right now. I was frightened, that's all.

MADAME PEPITA. Mooning along as usual, were you, with your head in the clouds?

DON GUILLERMO. Don't scold her. Accidents will happen.

CATALINA. [*Insisting.*] Mamma, this is Don Guillermo, the gentleman who lives upstairs.

MADAME PEPITA. [*Brusquely.*] I heard you the first time. [*Affably, to* DON GUILLERMO.] This is a great pleasure. We are much obliged to you.

DON GUILLERMO. Not at all. I was in time to prevent a catastrophe, which somebody else would have prevented had I not been in time.

[*Meanwhile* CATALINA *has taken his hand, affectionately.*]

MADAME PEPITA. Won't you sit down?—Catalina, let go of the gentleman's hand; it embarrasses him.

[CATALINA *lets go of* DON GUILLERMO'S *hand.*]

DON GUILLERMO. [*Sympathetically.*] No, indeed. She is a little nervous. [*The* SEWING GIRL *re-enters with a glass of water, which* DON GUILLERMO *offers to* CATALINA.] Drink this.

SEWING GIRL. We had to put vinegar in it because there wasn't anything sweet in the house.

MADAME PEPITA. That will do.

CATALINA. [*Almost choking, refusing to drink.*] Yes, mamma, because Gregoria finished the orangeade yesterday, when she had that fainting fit, after she had a quarrel with her young man.

MADAME PEPITA. Gregoria a fainting fit? The kitchen cat will be having a nervous breakdown next! [*To the girl.*] Take this away and go back to your work.

[*The* SEWING GIRL *retires with the glass.*]

CATALINA. [*Aside, to* DON GUILLERMO.] Don't you go away.

MADAME PEPITA. What was that?

CATALINA. [*Timidly.*] I asked Don Guillermo not to go away.

DON GUILLERMO. But I must. However, I live only one flight up. If you need me at any time, Guillermo de Armendáriz is my name.

MADAME PEPITA. My daughter tells me that you are a very learned man.

DON GUILLERMO. [*Unimpressed.*] That depends.

MADAME PEPITA. You are a member of the Academy.

DON GUILLERMO. [*Smiling.*] I could scarcely avoid that.

MADAME PEPITA. [*Astonished.*] Avoid it?

CATALINA. He says it's a great pity that I am such an ignoramus.

DON GUILLERMO. I never said that, because you are not an ignoramus.

MADAME PEPITA. Oh, yes she is! But it's not her fault. It's mine—that is, it isn't mine, either. What could I do? I've spent my whole life working for her like a slave, trying to scrape together enough money so that she wouldn't have to go through what I've been through in this world. Tied down as I am to the worry of these miserable clothes, how was I to tend to her education? That's why she's like this, but you needn't think that it isn't a mortification to me, because when God has given you a daughter—or maybe it was the devil—you just want to have her nonplussed ultra, and it's a great grief to me that she isn't. But why am I telling all this to you, when you don't know what it is to have a child? That is, maybe you do know. Anyhow, it's none of my business. I don't mean to be inquisitive . . .

DON GUILLERMO. [*Smiling.*] No, unfortunately I do not know. I am alone in the world. When I was young, I had no time to marry, and now that I am growing old, it is too late. My books are to blame, and they console me for what I have lost, which is no more than their duty.

Since the subject has been mentioned, I wonder if you would allow me to devote a little of my time to Catalina's education?

MADAME PEPITA. Education?

DON GUILLERMO. It seems providential—we are good friends already. We have talked together, and I am fond of her. She is intelligent.

CATALINA. [*Greatly astonished.*] Am I?

DON GUILLERMO. She will learn quickly; I guarantee it.

MADAME PEPITA. You give her lessons? A member of the Academy?

CATALINA. Certainly, mamma.

DON GUILLERMO. It will be a pleasure. Then, I shall feel that my learning is actually of some use in the world. It has all been rather selfish till now. What do you say? Is it agreed?

MADAME PEPITA. [*Greatly affected.*] Ah, you have no idea how I appreciate this! [*Throwing her arms about* CATALINA, *and bursting into tears.*] My dear, you are to sit at the feet of an Academician!

DON GUILLERMO. [*Surprised.*] It hardly justifies the emotion. It is not so serious.

MADAME PEPITA. But I feel terribly, because we are dreadfully unhappy. Naturally, you would never suspect it, but since you're so fond of my daughter, I can tell you. Besides, everybody knows it, anyway. We are dreadfully unhappy, right here as we sit, because this poor child has no father. You imagine that I am a widow . . .

DON GUILLERMO. Señora, I imagine nothing of the sort.

MADAME PEPITA. [*Hastily.*] Well, I'm not, I'm married; that is, I am not married either—I mean, yes I am; but it's just the same as if I wasn't because my husband, that is, the man I thought was my husband—

DON GUILLERMO. But you owe me no explanations; I am not concerned in the affair.

MADAME PEPITA. [*Without stopping to draw breath.*]

But I want you to know, so that you won't think . . .
You see, it was this way: My parents were good, honest
people, my mother was lady's maid and my father butler
in the house of the Counts de la Vega de Lezo—you have
heard of them?—but I always had a taste for clothes, so
I went with some French women to be a dressmaker in
Buenos Aires; and when I got there I met the father of
this child. I was young and impressionable then. He
was a Russian—no doubt about that—and we got married,
church and all, but without his settling anything on me,
because it isn't done out there, and I thought he was the
manager of a printing house; but two months afterwards
he turned out to be a duke—yes, sir, a Russian duke, who,
because he was the black sheep of the family, had been
shipped off to America, and then his father died, and he
inherited, and had to go back to his own country. But
that wasn't the worst of it. The worst of it was that he
was a bigamist.

DON GUILLERMO.   A bigamist?

MADAME PEPITA.   Yes, he was married already in
Russia to a woman of his own rank, and he ran off with
her. So when this poor child came into the world, she
hadn't any father.

DON GUILLERMO.   How singularly unfortunate!

MADAME PEPITA.   But I kept right on sewing, and
when he got back to Russia, he sent me money, for it is only
fair to admit he was always a gentleman, and then I
came back to Spain, and established myself in business,
and since I've got taste, if I do say it myself, we've gotten
ahead. Besides, now and then he sent me money. But
it's a long time now since he went away, and I haven't
seen him for sixteen years, and my daughter doesn't know
him at all, and she never will, for we don't even know
whether he is alive or dead, and probably he has other
children, anyway; and here I am neither married nor single,
and not even a widow! So you see that I have plenty of
reason for being unhappy.

DON GUILLERMO. Not so much as you think. You have your health, you have your work, an income, a quiet conscience . . .

MADAME PEPITA. Yes, one thing I can say is that my conscience never troubled me.

DON GUILLERMO. What more do you ask? Love played you a trick. Pshaw! In exchange, you have a daughter, a pledge of happiness, a reason for living. You had your illusion of love for a time, but, believe me, even sadder than to have been deceived, is never to have had the opportunity. Hereafter, you must count me as one of your friends. For the present, I must bid you good-bye. You have my sympathy . . .

MADAME PEPITA. Thanks very much. If I can be of any service—

DON GUILLERMO. Perhaps later. Good-bye.

MADAME PEPITA. *Adiós.*

[DON GUILLERMO *goes out. A pause follows.*]

CARMEN. [*Entering.*] *Madame,* the salesman has come with the English samples.

MADAME PEPITA. [*Drying her eyes.*] Show him into the other room. I shall attend to his case immediately. [*To* CATALINA, *who is gazing pensively into space.*] What are you mooning about?

CATALINA. Isn't it sad not to be anybody's daughter, and not to have a father like everybody?

MADAME PEPITA. [*Taking her into her arms.*] You are *my* daughter.

CATALINA. Oh, mamma, we are dreadfully unhappy!

MADAME PEPITA. We are, my child, we are, indeed! [*Moving off a little, and placing both hands on* CATALINA'S *shoulders, while she looks her straight in the eye.*] But remember this: one thing consoles me for all our misfortunes. In my daughter's veins runs noble blood!

CURTAIN

ACT II

CATALINA *and* DON GUILLERMO *are discovered as the curtain rises.* DON GUILLERMO *paces up and down with the air of a person feeling himself thoroughly at home, while* CATALINA *writes at a small table which has been installed near one of the windows to do duty as a desk. It is littered with books and papers, all in hopeless confusion. Presently,* CATALINA *ceases writing, examining the paper on which she has been working as if looking for mistakes. After conscientious scrutiny, she blots it and lays it upon the table, turning to contemplate her inky fingers with an expression half despairing, half resigned. Upon a second inspection, she becomes even more discouraged, as the ink has not disappeared. Finally, running her fingers nervously through her hair, she rubs them upon her apron, and heaves a profound sigh.*

DON GUILLERMO. [*Turning.*] Have you finished?

CATALINA. Yes.

DON GUILLERMO. What are you doing now?

CATALINA. [*Still rubbing her fingers.*] Wiping my fingers. [*Exhibiting her hands.*] I've a little ink on them. [DON GUILLERMO *smiles.*] Writing makes me furious!

DON GUILLERMO. Why?

CATALINA. Because it gets my hands in such a state— it's the pen. I dip it into the ink, and it runs up all over the handle. I use the pen-wiper just as you tell me to, but the more I wipe, the more ink comes off.

DON GUILLERMO. Have patience. It will all come in time. [*Amused.*] The beginning is always difficult. We shall soon see how fast you get on.

CATALINA. [*Discouraged.*] But look at these letters.

The *l*'s are all crooked, and the *m*'s are all pointed. It makes me mad.

DON GUILLERMO. [*Smiling.*] Does it?

CATALINA. Because I know how things ought to be, and, then, I go and do them just the opposite, so, although I know, I don't know, and I get desperate. [*Looking at the paper.*] The *l*'s ought to be straight. Well, I try to make them straight, and they turn out crooked, so what's the use of knowing? Of course, when I'm wrong because I don't know, I'm an idiot, but when I know I'm wrong and then do it, what am I?

DON GUILLERMO. [*Patting her affectionately on the head.*] You are an intelligent young woman, who must work hard in order to overcome the first difficulties, and put what she knows to good use. That is precisely what learning means.

CATALINA. [*After a pause, looking at* DON GUILLERMO *intently.*] Don Guillermo, what use is learning, anyhow?

DON GUILLERMO. Learning teaches us to know.

CATALINA. Yes, I understand that. But what use is it?

DON GUILLERMO. [*Smiling.*] You will soon see. It is useful in many ways, which, little by little, you will discover yourself. Even if it were of no use, it would still be the most wonderful thing in the world, because it is the only thing that is satisfying in itself. When we have once peeped into the Garden of Knowledge, even at the tiniest gate, it is astounding what marvellous voyages we are able to make, and what sights we can see, without taking the trouble of leaving our chairs.

CATALINA. I suppose that's why you never notice what's on your plate at dinner, and laugh to yourself all the time, and walk out on the street without tying your shoes?

DON GUILLERMO. [*Slightly annoyed.*] What a keen little critic we are!

CATALINA. No, I don't mean anything uncomplimentary, only I can't help noticing what you do, because I

watch you all the time. You mustn't think I'm criticis-
ing. Everything you do seems right to me.

DON GUILLERMO. [*Greatly pleased.*] Yes, my dear,
I know you are sweet and good, and you are very fond of
me.

CATALINA. Yes, I am. [*Artlessly.*] Are you very
fond of me?

DON GUILLERMO. Don't you know it?

CATALINA. [*Sincerely pleased.*] Of course I do. I
may be stupid about other things, but not about that. I
know you are fond of me, because when I broke that jar
the other day in the library, you didn't say one word about
it, though it was valuable. That's how I know. I didn't
mean to.

DON GUILLERMO. You have talent, too, for psychology.

CATALINA. Now you're making fun of me.

DON GUILLERMO. I am very fond of you—fonder than
you can imagine, fonder than I could have believed possible myself. I love you better than I do art and science
put together.

CATALINA. [*After a brief silence.*] Are we going to
begin this all over again?

DON GUILLERMO. No, that will do for today.

CATALINA. I want to tell you a secret. [*Drawing near,
mysteriously.*] We're rich.

DON GUILLERMO. Who?

CATALINA. Mother and I. Who did you think?
We've inherited a million. My father died and left it in
his will. We got word yesterday, and mother has gone
to see the lawyer. Nobody knows except Don Luis; he
was here last night when word came. Mother says she
is going to retire from business, because she's sick and
tired of clothes, and we're going to Escorial to live.

DON GUILLERMO. To Escorial?

CATALINA. Yes, mamma owns property there, and she
says she's going to build houses and rent them, and keep
one, too, for us to live in, that has a big garden with a

grotto, and a fountain in the middle, besides a hot-house where we can grow camelias.

[*The bell rings.* Catalina *stops short.*]
Here she comes now.

[Madame Pepita *enters, attired in a simple tailor-made suit of grey or dark blue; also a mantilla. She is visibly flustered and out of breath.*]

Don Guillermo. Good morning.

Madame Pepita. [*About to pass without seeing him.*] Oh, excuse me! I didn't notice you. Good morning. I'm so excited I don't know whether I'm on my head or my heels. Has she told you?

Don Guillermo. Yes, indeed.

Madame Pepita. Terribly sad, isn't it? And to think of my being caught without a stitch of black to my name! No wonder they say: "Go to the Cutler's house for wooden knives." Here I am fussing about other people's clothes, and I look like a fright myself. I wonder what the notary thought when I walked in in colors on such an occasion?

Don Guillermo. Don't worry, probably he never thought at all. Sit down. It is a matter of taste.

Madame Pepita. [*Sitting down.*] Oh, dear, no! Whatever's right is right, and for my part, I always want to do the correct thing. Poor dear! Think of his remembering us at such a time!

Don Guillermo. He has done no more than his duty.

Madame Pepita. But so nicely. [*Bursting into tears.*] Ah, my dear, your father was always a gentleman! They tell me the poor man was ill for over two years, not able to move out of his chair. And all the while he was thinking of us, and we were sitting here calm and collected as could be, without suspecting the first thing about it. Oh, my daughter! [*Embracing* Catalina, *who, as befits the occasion, assumes an expression of supreme anguish.*]

Catalina. Poor mamma!

Don Guillermo. [*Removing* Catalina.] Come,

come, you must not upset your daughter. It is not right to grieve like this.

MADAME PEPITA. [*Between her sobs, artlessly.*] But I'm not grieving. I feel I can tell you, because you're so wise that you understand anyhow.

DON GUILLERMO. [*Smiling.*] In a measure.

MADAME PEPITA. And that's what makes me feel so badly, not to be able to grieve as I ought. Because you see how the man has behaved to us. And I did care for him, yes, I did! He was the apple of my eye. And when it all happened, seventeen years ago, and he left me forever, believe me, it was all I could do to go on living because of my child, and more than once, yes, more than twice, too, I had a mind to put an end to it all.

CATALINA. [*In tears also.*] Poor mamma!

MADAME PEPITA. And now he's gone and died, and they send me word about it! [*Beginning to cry again.*] Before I can cry the way I feel I ought to cry, I have to stop and try to remember how it was I was able to cry then.

DON GUILLERMO. But there is no obligation whatever upon you to cry. Even if there were, your feelings are beyond your control.

MADAME PEPITA. You are right there.

DON GUILLERMO. To compel ourselves to feel what we do not feel is hypocrisy, a fraud upon ourselves, because it mortifies our pride to realize that our feelings do not measure up to our expectations. If your feelings do not prompt you to cry, you ought not to cry. Tears, unless they are heart-felt, are injurious. They do no good to the deceased.

MADAME PEPITA. [*Exaggeratedly.*] But you don't know how I loved him!

DON GUILLERMO. Certainly I do, but your love has evaporated, like perfume which has stood in a wardrobe for years. Today you have been cleaning house; you find the bottle and it is empty. The contents are gone, they have been dissipated, they have ceased to be. You have forgotten him, so why worry? Little by little our bodies change, until, after seven years, not one atom of what we once were remains. Remember, he has been absent sixteen years. Not one vestige now remains of the flesh and blood that glowed and quivered with love for him. You are not the same woman, you are a different woman, who has had nothing whatever to do with that man.

MADAME PEPITA. [*Sentimentally.*] But the soul, Don Guillermo? What of the soul?

DON GUILLERMO. The soul may recall vaguely the emotions which the body has felt, but it cannot continue to feel them.

MADAME PEPITA. [*Very positively.*] Well, anyway, it will be safer to go into mourning.

DON GUILLERMO. And very proper, if it affords you any relief.

MADAME PEPITA. No, on account of what people will say. After all, remember I'm inheriting a million.

DON GUILLERMO. Yes, that fact deserves to be taken into consideration.

MADAME PEPITA. [*To* CATALINA.] Dear, run out and tell Carmen to cut you a blouse from the crêpe we're using for the Baroness's tea-gown. I'm too upset to think of anything for myself.

CATALINA. Yes, mamma. Don Guillermo . . .

DON GUILLERMO. I am going also. It is growing late.

CATALINA. Aren't you coming back to dinner?

DON GUILLERMO. I dined here yesterday, and day before yesterday, and Sunday, too, if my memory is correct; and this is only Wednesday.

CATALINA. Pshaw! What of it? He is coming, isn't he, mamma?

MADAME PEPITA. Of course he is. If he isn't here, I always feel as if there must be something wrong with the table.

Don Guillermo. Well, since you insist. You have my sympathy, as you know, although I believe you are to be congratulated.

Madame Pepita. I appreciate it. [*Greatly downcast.*] We must do the best we can.

Catalina. [*Going to the door with* Don Guillermo, *and taking his hand as if he were her father.*] Don't forget the meringues you promised.

Don Guillermo. I'll bring them along.

[*As* Don Guillermo *and* Catalina *go out, the door bell rings, and they come face to face with* Don Luis, *who enters. Each gentleman displays plainly his discomfiture at the presence of the other. The* Conde *turns his back, affecting indifference, while* Don Guillermo *stares him up and down in disgust, which he does not attempt to conceal. They salute each other, however, the* Conde *remaining frigidly polite, while* Don Guillermo *mutters an acknowledgment between his teeth.*]

Don Luis. Good afternoon, Señor de Armendáriz.

Don Guillermo. Good afternoon. [*Biting off the words.*]

    [*Goes out with* Catalina.]

Don Luis. [*After* Don Guillermo *has disappeared.*] Does this good man spend his entire time here?

Madame Pepita. [*Smiling.*] He is giving my daughter lessons.

Don Luis. Ah! [*Apparently to himself, but with the evident purpose of being overheard.*] Such assiduity makes me suspicious.

Madame Pepita. How so?

Don Luis. [*Significantly.*] We may take that up later. At present, more pressing business demands our attention. Have you had time to rest? Have you recovered from last night? [Madame Pepita *nods.*] Have you got the money?

Madame Pepita. Yes.

Don Luis.   Where is it?

Madame Pepita.   Why, as soon as I received it, I deposited it in the bank.   The notary went along, because I was afraid to trust myself in the street alone with so much money.

Don Luis.   Have you any of it about you now?

Madame Pepita.   No.   Why do you ask?

Don Luis.   I fear you are making a mistake.   It is a matter which involves a will.   A demand for money may be made upon you at any time, and I consider it important that you have sufficient on hand.

Madame Pepita.   I thought so, too, but it seems not. The notary says all the expenses have been paid.   My poor dear arranged for everything off there on his estate, so that I shouldn't have a thing to do but accept the money.

Don Luis.   I appreciate your situation.   By the way, do you happen to have four hundred pesetas?   [*Without allowing her time to recover.*]   As a first installment upon a purchase which it is important that you make, a magnificent opportunity—a piece of property next to your own at Escorial, which may be had for a song.   A friend of mine is in financial difficulty.

Madame Pepita.   [*Interested.*]   Is the Conde positive that it is a bargain?

Don Luis.   It is a gift!   If you miss this opportunity, you will regret it all your life, and you will miss it unless you can let me have four hundred pesetas this very day. What would I give if I had the money!

Madame Pepita.   [*Producing a brand new check book from her bag.*]   Well, I'll sign a check.   [*Seating herself at the table, she begins to make out the check.*]

Don Luis.   You certainly are in luck.   Money breeds money.   While you are about it, you might make it five hundred, so as to provide for emergencies.

Madame Pepita.   [*Rising, after writing the check.*] Here it is.

Don Luis. [*Solicitously.*] Allow me to sign the receipt.

Madame Pepita. Oh, not at all! Conde, I should be offended.

Don Luis. [*Convinced.*] As you wish. Now let me offer you a piece of advice. This confidence, which you place in me, deservedly, extend to nobody else. Be on your guard. You are rich, and the world is full of scoundrels. They will cheat you, rob you, they will swarm to your millions as flies to their honey. Pepita, if you are not careful, your generosity will be taken advantage of. I myself have abused it not a little.

Madame Pepita. Oh, don't say that, Conde!

Don Luis. Yes, Pepita, unavoidably, perhaps, but the fact remains that I have abused it. However, Providence is repaying your kindness with interest. You are rich. [*Suddenly overcome.*] God knows I rejoice with you, although this unexpected good fortune obliges me to renounce a dream—It is a subject, however, which as a gentleman, I prefer not to dwell upon.

Madame Pepita. [*Interested.*] A dream?

Don Luis. [*Loftily.*] Alas!

Madame Pepita. But to an old friend? Surely the Conde can tell me.

Don Luis. Yes, after all, why not? Now that it has become impossible, what difference does it make? Catalina and Augusto—you must have noticed how they have become attached to each other?

Madame Pepita. [*Surprised and delighted.*] The Vizconde and my daughter?

Don Luis. Then you have noticed it?

Madame Pepita. No, I hadn't noticed.

Don Luis. Pepita, you are blind. I have suspected for some time, but now I am certain. He has practically confessed, under compulsion, and it is not surprising. Your daughter is an original creature—unusual, fascinating. And

Augusto's temperament is so artistic! It was inevitable.

MADAME PEPITA. But, Conde, pardon me . . . The Vizconde . . . I thought . . . Is he the sort of man?

DON LUIS. My dear, talk; it is all put on. Disappointment will result in irregularities. Men are naturally that way, anyhow. When he realized that he had become the victim of an impossible passion, for I may say that it never occurred ·to him that I would relent—although you are worthy people, your daughter has no father. We are what we are.

MADAME PEPITA. [*Sobbing.*] Yes, we are.

DON LUIS. However, it is too late now for regrets. When I found myself confronted with a crisis, I was prepared to lay prejudice aside. Adversity has its uses. But you have inherited money.

MADAME PEPITA. Thank God!

DON LUIS. So it is out of the question. You are rich, we are poor. People would think that we were after your money. Never! Never that! Never!

MADAME PEPITA. Why, Conde!

DON LUIS. Never! I could never reconcile myself to such a thing, at least not without a bitter struggle. But my heart aches for my boy. And there is another obstacle.

MADAME PEPITA. Another?

DON LUIS. Which is a great deal more serious. What position does the gentleman on the floor above occupy in this establishment?

MADAME PEPITA. But I have already explained to the Conde that he is giving Catalina lessons.

DON LUIS. But he remains to dinner, he remains to supper, he spends all his time here . . .

MADAME PEPITA. He is devoted to my little girl.

DON LUIS. He is entirely too devoted.

MADAME PEPITA. We are awfully fond of him, Conde.

DON LUIS. That makes it worse.

MADAME PEPITA. He's so gentlemanly and refined.

DON LUIS. No doubt; that is neither here nor there.

The question is not what he is, but what you are. These visits compromise your reputation. Besides, there are too many of them. Remember, you are a young and beautiful woman.

Madame Pepita. Yes, I'm thirty-seven.

Don Luis. With a past—although it was not your fault. With a past! It is another phase which I prefer not to dwell on.

Madame Pepita. Conde!

Don Luis. Your daughter is grown, yet you persist in permitting this gentleman liberties which are extended customarily only to a husband or a father.

Madame Pepita. Oh, no! Nothing of the sort. Believe me, there must be some mistake . . .

Don Luis. Morally, I decline to sanction the situation. I had hoped that our children might unite, but you must realize that a name such as mine is peculiarly sensitive to the breath of slander. I could never tolerate such a dubious situation—not that I wish to criticise your conduct or to dictate in any way. No, do as you see fit. Nevertheless, if this gentleman continues his visits to this house, I shall be obliged to discontinue mine. Interpret it as you may, I shall retire—regretfully, Pepita, but with dignity, I shall retire.

Madame Pepita. Conde!

Don Luis. However, I must hurry to place this money in the hands of my friend. Remember, your interests are first with me. If you need advice, come to me. But as it is, I feel that I intrude. Think it over, think it over very carefully. Do not force me to say good-bye. *Au revoir!* [*Goes out.*]

> [Madame Pepita, *surprised and delighted at the prospect of her daughter's becoming a countess, remains behind completely dazed.*]

Madame Pepita. My daughter? The Vizconde? Impossible! No, it isn't either . . . Catalina! Catalina!

Catalina. [*Appearing in the door-way.*] Did you

call, mamma? [*Noticing her mother's agitation.*] Don't
you feel well?

MADAME PEPITA. Yes . . . no, I don't. Come here;
look at me. How would you like to be a countess?

CATALINA. I, a countess? Why?

MADAME PEPITA. Would you or wouldn't you? Answer me at once!

CATALINA. How can I tell?

MADAME PEPITA. Tell me the truth. Are you in love?

CATALINA. I? In love?

MADAME PEPITA. Isn't there any one you'd like to
marry? Are you engaged?

CATALINA. [*Alarmed.*] No, mamma. I'm not engaged.

MADAME PEPITA. But you like some one, don't you?
There is some one you're awfully fond of? Don't you
find him attractive?

CATALINA. No, mamma . . . not exactly attractive.
What are you talking about? Mamma, I don't love anybody.

> [*The bell rings, and* GALATEA *enters like a whirl-
> wind.*]

GALATEA. Where is she? Ah, give me a kiss! An-
other for luck. A hug, too, this time! [*To Catalina.*]
And one for you. [*Embracing mother and daughter in
turn.*] Congratulations! You don't know how delighted
I was to hear it. Think of it . . . a cold million! What?
Pesetas?

MADAME PEPITA. No, francs.

GALATEA. Exchange is at seven and a half. It may
not seem much, but when you figure it up . . . [*Considering
a moment.*] It comes to fifteen thousand duros. I wish
something like that would happen my way. You knew
what you were doing, all right, when you married a Russian. Now don't tell me it was love. I've always stuck
to the home article, Madrid is good enough for me—although I don't suppose I can teach you anything. Anyway,

I'm tickled to death that you've really got the money, because I don't suppose you'll mind so much now about the bill. I've given up hope of the old man, and his son is no better; they simply haven't got it. Not that I care about the boy . . . I'm silly over him, but the old chap ought to pay somehow. Does he think a man can make an ass of himself at his age for nothing?

MADAME PEPITA. [*To* CATALINA, *who is displaying keen interest.*] Catalina, see if the girls are ready to try on your blouse.

GALATEA. Yes, run along. Things will be coming your way pretty soon. [CATALINA *retires.*] She's a lucky girl! God remembers her while she's young; she won't have to go through what you and me have. Look out now that some young whippersnapper don't get after her money. The world's pretty rotten, and I don't know whether a woman's worse off when she has money or when she hasn't any, because what's the satisfaction of marrying a man and then sitting around watching him spend your money on somebody else?

MADAME PEPITA. [*Moistening her lips.*] There are all sorts of men.

GALATEA. And then a few. You've said it.

MADAME PEPITA. It strikes me you're a sensible woman. Why don't you break off with the Vizconde?

GALATEA. With Augusto? Never in the world!

MADAME PEPITA. You're not getting anywhere as it is, it seems to me.

GALATEA. I ought to know that better than you do.

MADAME PEPITA. I say!

GALATEA. I wouldn't give him up if I starved. I could lose everything, but I'd love him just the same. I've thought I'd leave him, sometimes, and march myself off to Paris, where a woman can do something. Out of sight, out of mind, don't you know? There's nothing in this for me. But when the time comes, I can't tear myself away.

MADAME PEPITA. It might be a good idea, though.

GALATEA. No, it simply can't be done. I'd feel as if I was committing murder. I love him more all the time, and it's a shame. Last night I started for the station—

MADAME PEPITA. Did you miss the train?

GALATEA. No, he dropped around. Do you know what I've got in this box? Neckties, to make up. Whenever I feel I can't stand him any longer, I just run out and buy him a handsome present. [*Dubiously.*] Well, I suppose somebody's got to do it.

CARMEN. [*Entering.*] *Madame,* the lady in the Calle de Lista wants you to hurry up those negligees. She says she can't wait any longer.

MADAME PEPITA. Yes, better let her have something for tonight; I'd forgotten all about her. Dear me, life is just one emergency after another!

GALATEA. Congratulations again—I am going. I hear you're retiring from business. If you're selling out cheap, tip me off. I know a good thing when I see one. But don't let me detain you . . .

[MADAME PEPITA *retires.* GALATEA, *after adjusting her hat at the mirror, is about to leave by the other door, when* AUGUSTO *enters.*]

GALATEA. [*Surprised.*] Augusto!

AUGUSTO. Galatea! Are you here?

GALATEA. I was just congratulating Madame Pepita.

AUGUSTO. What were you doing last night?

GALATEA. I was out. [*Smiling.*]

AUGUSTO. But where were you going? You left no word. I searched all Madrid; I was furious. Don't you love me any more?

GALATEA. [*Smiling.*] Search me.

AUGUSTO. Yes, but how about me?

GALATEA. I didn't get very far.

AUGUSTO. What are you doing tonight?

GALATEA. [*Coyly.*] Is it a date?

AUGUSTO. I must have a moment first with Pepita; I shan't be long. You might wait outside in the motor, and then we can go for that ring. I know you've set your heart on it—although I had planned it as a surprise.

GALATEA.   I have planned a little surprise for you, too.

AUGUSTO.   Do you mean it?

GALATEA.   [*Handing him the box of neckties.*] Promise not to look.

AUGUSTO.   [*About to open the box.*] What can it be?

GALATEA.   Wait until you are alone.

AUGUSTO.   [*Kissing her hand.*] You're an angel!

GALATEA.   So are you. Peep and see. [*Goes out.*]

AUGUSTO.   [*After a discreet, but rapid glance in the glass.*] What can it be? [*Opens the box.*] Cravats! [*Becoming sentimental.*] Although her taste may be bizarre, how she loves me! [*Kissing a cravat.*] And how I love her! [*Rising into transports.*]

> [MADAME PEPITA *enters, greatly pleased to discover* AUGUSTO.]

MADAME PEPITA.   [*Entering.*] Vizconde! . . . Oh, Vizconde!

AUGUSTO.   [*Coming to, hastily bundling up the cravats.*] Pardon me.

MADAME PEPITA.   Were you thinking?

AUGUSTO.   Thinking? I was trying not to think.

MADAME PEPITA.   [*Sympathetically.*] Vizconde!

AUGUSTO.   I am in desperate need of seven hundred pesetas. If you cannot let me have them, I shall grow violent. I know you have a million, but I do not ask upon that account. No, I should have had to have them anyway. Life has become insupportable.

MADAME PEPITA.   Oh, Vizconde!

AUGUSTO.   My heart is broken. What is the good of a heart nowadays? Nobody seems to have one. My heart will be my ruin.

MADAME PEPITA.   A tender heart is a priceless treasure.

AUGUSTO.   But so expensive! Man cannot exist without woman, woman cannot exist without money.

MADAME PEPITA.   Don't let that worry you, Vizconde.

All things come to him who waits, even when it seems impossible. If you are in trouble, come to me. I have the gift of sympathy.

AUGUSTO. So I am coming to you. Can you let me have the seven hundred at once? I am in a hurry, or I should not ask.

MADAME PEPITA. Just a moment, while I write the check.

[MADAME PEPITA *retires.* AUGUSTO *paces back and forth, admiring himself in the mirror. Presently* CATALINA *enters, approaching the table which contains the papers, without noticing* AUGUSTO. *They collide with a violent shock while he is still absorbed in the contemplation of his person in the glass.*]

CATALINA. Oh! Excuse me.

AUGUSTO. Can't you see where you are going?

CATALINA. Can't you see anything but yourself? Puppy! [*Making a face, which he sees in the mirror.*]

AUGUSTO. Let me give you a piece of advice, young lady. Don't you make faces at me.

CATALINA. If you weren't so stuck on yourself, you wouldn't have noticed it.

AUGUSTO. It wouldn't do you any harm to be a little stuck on yourself.

CATALINA. Wouldn't it?

AUGUSTO. Do you take out a license for that poodle effect with the hair?

CATALINA. When it rains, don't forget yours is gummed down and glued.

AUGUSTO. Can't you let me alone?

CATALINA. Who are you, anyway? [*Seating herself at the table, she opens a drawing book in which she proceeds to copy a map.*]

[AUGUSTO *stalks up and down without speaking. They exchange glances of mutual contempt from time to time, until the entrance of* MADAME PEPITA *with*

*the check. Highly gratified at finding them together,
she beams upon them with maternal tenderness.*]

MADAME PEPITA. [*Entering.*] The poor dears are embarrassed. What a picture they would make! [*To
AUGUSTO.*] The check, Vizconde.

AUGUSTO. Thanks. I shall never forget this—I feel
like another man with this money. I may have to go to
work to repay you, Pepita; love is a great leveler. Ah, for
love's sweet sake! I'm off. . . . [*Rushes out without paying any attention to* CATALINA.]

MADAME PEPITA. [*Deeply affected.*] For love's sweet
sake! [*Looking at her daughter.*] Poor Vizconde!

ALBERTO. [*Appearing in the doorway.*] May I come
in?

MADAME PEPITA. What is the matter with you?

ALBERTO. No, it's the proprietor, who wishes the
samples of English point, and the gold galloons; they're re-required.

MADAME PEPITA. God knows what's become of them
by this time.

ALBERTO. We need them to fill an order, just received.

MADAME PEPITA. Very well. Wait, and I'll have
them brought, if they can be found. [*Retires, leaving*
CATALINA *with* ALBERTO. *Both smile, and* CATALINA *continues her work.*]

ALBERTO. [*Slyly.*] Pleasant day, isn't it?

CATALINA. Yes, very. [*A pause, during which she continues working, while he stands a little way off without
removing his eyes from her.*] Won't you sit down?

ALBERTO. Thanks. You are very kind. [*Sits down
at the farther end of the room. Another pause.*] Are you
sketching?

CATALINA. [*Smiling timidly.*] No, I don't know how
to sketch; I'm copying a map.

ALBERTO. [*Unconscious of what he is saying.*] Ah! A
map?

CATALINA. It's the map of Europe.

[*Another pause. *CATALINA* draws busily; then stops
and sucks her pencil.*]

ALBERTO. [*Rising.*] Pardon . . . please don't suck
your pencil.

CATALINA. Eh?

ALBERTO. It may be impertinent, but it grates upon m
nerves.

CATALINA. [*Ready to cry.*] It does look horrid, doesn't
it?

ALBERTO. [*Effusively.*] No! You couldn't possibly
do anything that looked horrid, because . . . because . . .
well, of course not.

[*Another pause. *CATALINA* draws industriously
and breaks the point of the pencil.*]

CATALINA. Oh, dear, I've broken the point!

[*Taking a penknife, she hacks a fearful looking point after
great effort; then inspects it with a sigh.*]

ALBERTO. [*Impetuously, rising again.*] Pardon. That
is not the way to sharpen a pencil. This is the way.
[*Rapidly and easily making a perfect point.*] It's very
simple.

CATALINA. [*Admiringly.*] Oh, what a beautiful point!
You certainly are a handy man.

ALBERTO. That's my business.

CATALINA. Oh . . . yes! You're an artist. Do you
really paint pictures?

ALBERTO. I should like to, but I do not.

CATALINA. Why not?

ALBERTO. I am too poor. My mother is a widow.

CATALINA. [*Interrupting, charmed.*] Just like me!

ALBERTO. [*Without heeding the interruption.*] Only
I have six young brothers and sisters. Mother teaches
school in a town not far from here, and she says that only
rich people can afford to be artists, so she wants me to be
a clerk in "La Sultana," as the proprietor is my uncle.
She thinks, when he dies, he may leave the shop to me,

since he's a bachelor, and then, naturally we'll all be rich, and we can educate the other children. However, I see no indications . . . but of course that does not interest you.

CATALINA. [*Earnestly.*] Yes, it does; very much.

ALBERTO. I am twenty-two now, and all I do is to carry bundles back and forth to dressmakers and other stupid people who have not the first idea about art. Pardon me . . .

CATALINA. No, you are right. It would be a great deal better to paint pictures.

ALBERTO. [*Enraptured.*] Yes, wonderful pictures, marvellous pictures, such as nobody has ever seen before, palpitating with sunshine and light! Pictures of the sea, the sky—the deep blue Italian sky! Ah, Italy! Rome!

CATALINA. [*Ingenuously.*] Rome is here on the map.

ALBERTO. Rome is in paradise!

CATALINA. Is the sky really so blue there?

ALBERTO. So blue that it is the despair of those who worship her.

CATALINA. Really? I hadn't heard. . . . Funny, isn't it? I've marked the name in blue ink.

ALBERTO. Mark it in gold and precious stones.

CATALINA. Why don't you go if you want to? There's a railroad here, or you can take the boat, across the sea.

ALBERTO. The boat and the railroad cost money, and I have no money.

CATALINA. Oh, don't worry about that. How much do you need?—because we can ask mother for it.

ALBERTO. Mother? No! That would not be right.

CATALINA. Yes, it would. Everybody asks her. Besides, we're rich now. We've inherited a million, and it's in the bank, and all we have to do is sign a paper, and they give us all we want.

ALBERTO. You are kind and generous, but I could never accept it. Thanks just the same; I shall never forget your kindness. I am grateful, really. Could I kiss your hand?

CATALINA. [*Taken aback, hiding her hands.*]   Oh, no!

ALBERTO.   Why not?

CATALINA.   Because . . . because they're all covered with ink.

ALBERTO. [*Seizing her hands.*]   What of it?   They are lovely, they are dear and sweet, the hands of a generous woman, who understands, who sympathizes.

CATALINA. [*After a pause.*]   So you do think you will go to Rome, then, after all?

ALBERTO.   Yes, I shall; I have a plan.   I work all day, but I study at night.   I attend a life class, and when the next competition takes place, I shall enter, I shall win a prize, and then I shall go, no matter what mother says, and when I come back I shall be a great painter.   I wish you could see the marvellous pictures I shall paint in Italy.

CATALINA. [*Somewhat anxiously.*]   I suppose while you are there you will paint some lovely ladies?

ALBERTO.   Oh, naturally!

CATALINA.   Like the ones you were telling us about . . . with lines, you know, and proportions?

ALBERTO.   'When I am famous, I intend to paint your picture.

CATALINA.   My picture?

ALBERTO.   And win a prize with it.   Yes, indeed!

CATALINA.   But I . . . I . . . At least mother thinks so . . . [*Looking at herself in the mirror.*]   And she's right, too.   I haven't any proportions at all.   [*Almost reduced to tears.*]

ALBERTO.   You haven't?

CATALINA.   And I don't know how to dress or fix my hair.   [*Crying.*]   You can see for yourself.

ALBERTO. [*Greatly troubled.*]   No, no, indeed!   Not at all!   You are . . . yes, you are, señorita . . . Yes, indeed you are . . . [*Choking, almost ready to shed tears himself.*]   You, you . . . you have character!

CATALINA. [*Overcome with surprise and delight.*]   I have?

[CRISTINA *enters with two boxes of samples, without noticing* ALBERTO.]

CRISTINA. So you got rid of it, did you?

ALBERTO. [*Moving away from* CATALINA.] It?

CRISTINA. Oh, are you still sticking around? Here are your samples, and you needn't bring any more, because Madame Pepita is retiring from business.

ALBERTO. Thank you so much.

[CRISTINA *goes out.* ALBERTO *is about to resume the conversation, when* DON GUILLERMO *enters, carrying several packages, one of which, apparently, contains a bottle of champagne.* ALBERTO *bows and disappears.*]

Adiós!

[CATALINA *makes no reply.*]

DON GUILLERMO. [*Stepping to one side to allow* ALBERTO *to pass.*] *Adiós!* [*Eyeing him, curiously.*] Here are the meringues. [*Handing the package to* CATALINA, *who takes it mechanically, and remains standing with it in her hand.*] Who is the young man?

CATALINA. [*Almost choking.*] It's the boy from the silk shop.

[DON GUILLERMO *deposits the packages upon the table.*]

Don Guillermo, is painting a nice business?

DON GUILLERMO. It is more than a business. It is an art.

CATALINA. But is it nice or isn't it?

DON GUILLERMO. That depends upon how one paints. A good painter has an excellent business.

CATALINA. But a bad painter?

DON GUILLERMO. A bad painter, my dear, cannot exactly be sent to jail, but he belongs there.

CATALINA. [*Alarmed.*] Not really? Is it awfully hard to win the *prix de Rome?*

DON GUILLERMO. It will be in the next competition, as I shall be one of the judges. I am chairman of the jury.

CATALINA. [*Torn between hope and fear.*] You are?

DON GUILLERMO. Yes.. Why all this sudden interest in painting?

CATALINA. Don Guillermo, when a painter says that you have character, does, that mean that you are pretty or the opposite?

DON GUILLERMO. Neither. It means that you have something characteristic about you, something. original, distinguishing you from other people. It means that you are interesting.

CATALINA. But is it a compliment, or isn't it?

DON GUILLERMO. It is the nicest kind of a compliment.

CATALINA. One more question: Does a woman have to be a countess because she's rich?

DON GUILLERMO. [*Alarmed.*] A countess? What makes you ask that?

CATALINA. Nothing, only mother thought perhaps I'd better be one.

DON GUILLERMO. [*Exercised.*] She did? When?

CATALINA. Just now, while you were out, after talking to the Conde.

DON GUILLERMO. Never! There must be some mistake.

CATALINA. Why must there?

DON GUILLERMO. [*Greatly agitated.*] No, you don't have to be a countess. It is absurd, and I shall take care that you don't become one. Never!

CATALINA. What's the difference, anyway? Why fuss so much about it?

DON GUILLERMO. [*Striding up and down, muttering to himself.*] This is too much! Outrageous! I shall make this my business.

CATALINA. [*Timidly and affectionately.*] Why, Don Guillermo? Have I done anything wrong? Are you angry with me? [*Kissing his hand.*]

DON GUILLERMO. No, no. [*With a paternal caress.*]

I was thinking of something else. [*To himself.*] Keep cool! Be calm! [*Aloud.*] This is my business.

CATALINA. [*Affectionately, hesitating what to do.*] Before you settle down, would you like me to bring your cap and slippers?

> [MADAME PEPITA *enters. She stops short upon discovering* DON GUILLERMO.]

DON GUILLERMO. [*Pleasantly.*] Well, I am here, you see. Is dinner ready?

MADAME PEPITA. [*Disconcerted; then frigidly.*] Dinner? . . .

DON GUILLERMO. [*Handing her a small package.*] I brought you some nice iced lady-fingers, and a bottle of champagne to enliven the repast. We are fond of them, so we shall enjoy ourselves in love and good fellowship.

MADAME PEPITA. [*Visibly embarrassed.*] Yes . . .

DON GUILLERMO. [*Hands* CATALINA *the bottle.*] Put this on the ice, too. Oh, by the way, here are some potato chips *à la inglesa.* They are one thing your cook does not do to perfection. [*Handing her another package.*] Crisp them. Mind the bottle . . . [CATALINA *goes out. To* MADAME PEPITA, *making himself perfectly at home.*] Well, this house has become a vice with me, Doña Pepita. You and Catalina have taken complete possession of my heart. I never cared for a family, but now I could not get along without the illusion of family life which you supply. One of these days you will be removing me from the door with a broom.

MADAME PEPITA. [*Greatly embarrassed, steeling herself with a determined effort.*] Don Guillermo, that is exactly what I wanted to speak to you about.

DON GUILLERMO. [*Surprised.*] Eh?

MADAME PEPITA. [*Scarcely able to articulate.*] Since my daughter has left the room . . .

DON GUILLERMO. [*Becoming serious.*] What do you mean?

MADAME PEPITA. To begin with—now don't be offended, it's not as bad as that. That is, it's unpleasant, of
course, especially for me, Don Guillermo, because . . .
Well, the fact is you've been very kind to us, and all
that, and we can never thank you for what you've done
and are doing for my daughter's education. I know it
can never be paid for, not to speak of your having taken
all this trouble, seeing that she's nobody and you are who
you are, and know what you do . . . I don't say so because she's my daughter, but a princess wouldn't be a great
deal for you to be giving lessons to . . .

DON GUILLERMO. Yes, but come to the point. What
do you mean to say?

MADAME PEPITA. Well, Don Guillermo, circumstances
alter, you know, so what used to be . . . It does seem
too bad, though, doesn't it? It can't go on forever. You
know what I mean.

DON GUILLERMO. I certainly do not. Explain yourself.

MADAME PEPITA. Well, we're just two unprotected
women, and everybody's so ready to gossip about what is
none of their business, and to make things worse than
they are, so people might think . . . Especially since I
have a past, I'm sorry to say, which is nobody's business,
either. Anyhow, when people were coming to this house
because I was a dressmaker, it didn't make so much difference who they came to see, but now that I've retired,
it don't look respectable . . .   [*Swallowing hard.*]   Do
you understand me?

DON GUILLERMO. I certainly do—better than I could
wish. [MADAME PEPITA *heaves a sigh of relief.*] You
think, or somebody thinks for you, that my visits may compromise your reputation, or your daughter's?

MADAME PEPITA. Virgins and martyrs, don't be offended, Don Guillermo!

DON GUILLERMO. What hurts does not give offense.

MADAME PEPITA. But—

Don Guillermo. You wish me, then, to confine myself to giving Catalina lessons?

Madame Pepita. That won't be so easy, either, I'm afraid, now that we are moving to Escorial to live.

Don Guillermo. I have absolutely nothing to detain me in Madrid.

Madame Pepita. My daughter is grown, and she will probably marry before long, so, under the circumstances . . .

Don Guillermo. Say no more; I understood from the beginning. I merely wished to hear it stated in plain words. You want to get rid of me.

Madame Pepita. No, no indeed! We shall always be glad to see you, whenever you have time. Why not run out some Sunday for dinner?

Don Guillermo. [*After a pause.*] I see only one drawback to your plan; it won't work.

Madame Pepita. It won't?

Don Guillermo. [*With dignity and restraint.*] I shall not give up Catalina.

Madame Pepita. [*Alarmed.*] Don Guillermo!

Don Guillermo. [*Smiling.*] Don't take it so hard. As you say, it sounds worse than it is. [*Deeply moved, but assuming a satiric tone, in order to conceal his emotion.*] I have spent the forty-five years of my life so completely shut off from the world, that I have scarcely become acquainted with myself. Now that I look back, I realize that I have wasted my time. My mother was wrapped up in me, and watched over me until a few years ago, so that I never had occasion for another woman's love. I grew up a selfish old bachelor, salted down in my books. But the strange part of it is, that while I have never cared for women, I have always been fond of children, no matter how ugly or dirty they might be, as they stumbled along. I yearn to take the little dears by the hand, to teach and protect them. Love between men and women is a relation of equals, it may even imply inferiority on the part of the man. Perhaps I am proud—it is one of my failings; but I have never felt like kneeling before a woman, though I have often had a desire to hold a loving creature in my arms. [DON GUILLERMO, *in reality, has been talking to himself, his eyes fixed upon the floor, but, when he arrives at this point he suddenly becomes aware of the presence of* MADAME PEPITA, *and turns toward her.*] I beg your pardon . . .

MADAME PEPITA. [*Vastly impressed, but without understanding one word.*] Pardon me.

DON GUILLERMO. Since I have known Catalina, this desire has become concrete. She is everything to me. I could not say whether she is quick or dull; I am not sure whether she is beautiful or plain; I can not even tell you the color of her eyes; but I feel that she is my daughter, much more than she is her father's, yes more, certainly much more than she is yours.

MADAME PEPITA. But it seems to me . . .

DON GUILLERMO. Much more. You brought her into the world, but I have brought a new world to her, fresher, more striking, materially and spiritually, than the old. I have rejuvenated myself so as to bring my mind down to her level. I talk like a child so as to companion with her innocence, and I should gladly forego all the joys of this world and the next, merely for the pleasure of holding her hand while she writes.

MADAME PEPITA. Why, Don Guillermo!

DON GUILLERMO. [*Firmly.*] No, I cannot surrender the child. She requires protection which is absolutely disinterested and sincere. Perhaps you may need it, too. I know what I am doing . . . although you would be entirely within your rights if you put me into the street.

MADAME PEPITA. I shouldn't think of such a thing.

DON GUILLERMO. I should not question your decision. Your point of view is as proper as it is absurd. Legally, I have no right to paternity. My position is extra legal, yet it can be recognized and reduced to legal status; and the sooner it is done, the better for us all. Don't stare at me—I am not crazy. Desperate diseases demand desperate remedies. The pill is a bitter one, but I shall swallow it. You are a woman of courage yourself.

MADAME PEPITA. What in heaven's name are you talking about?

DON GUILLERMO. I must be accepted in this house as a husband and a father, otherwise I shall not be free to act —I shall be hampered. Why not face the facts? We must marry, and conform to the conventions of society, however inconvenient. I am willing to marry you.

MADAME PEPITA. You?

DON GUILLERMO. [*Visibly worried.*]   You, yes and I . . . if you are agreeable.

MADAME PEPITA. [*Speechless with amazement.*]   You and I?

DON GUILLERMO. You and I. Pardon my abruptness—you never occurred to me before, I mean, in the light of a wife.

MADAME PEPITA. But you knew that I had been married?

DON GUILLERMO. [*More and more disturbed.*]   Be that as it may, this would be a marriage of convenience, pure and simple.

MADAME PEPITA. Pure and simple?

DON GUILLERMO. A moral necessity; love does not enter into it. But we shall be spared embarrassment. You are rich, while I am not poor, which will be sufficient to silence evil tongues, although the opinion of others has no influence with me. I have means to support myself and to permit me to indulge in some pleasures, so money will not be lacking. If you will marry me, I offer to defray the household expenses like a good husband, while you dispose of your million in any way you think convenient. I shall not even take note of its existence. I am a famous man—my name appears in the papers. I have the entrée of the Palace, and a place of honor at all Court ceremonies, which, naturally, you will share with me. You will be entitled to a reserved seat at the functions of the Academy; the doorkeepers will bow whenever you appear. You will be the distinguished wife of an illustrious author, of an eminent critic, who is one of the glories of his country. Whenever a monument is unveiled or a cornerstone laid, you will be among those who remain for refreshments, and if photographs are taken for *La Ilustración* or *Blanco y Negro* you will be immortalized with me in the group.

MADAME PEPITA. But . . . are you in earnest?

DON GUILLERMO. [*Offended.*] Do I look like a man who would treat marriage as a joke?

MADAME PEPITA. If that is the case . . .

DON GUILLERMO. Your fondest dreams will be realised. One of my ancestors crossed the sea with Hernán Cortés, and undertook the conquest of America. He proved so adept at killing Indians that His Majesty conferred a coat of arms upon him, which I have somewhere under cobwebs at home. You are at liberty to dust it off, since you are partial to nobility, and to display it upon our note-paper, so that people can see who we are.

MADAME PEPITA. [*Deeply affected.*] Don Guillermo!

DON GUILLERMO. And on the door of our automobile too, for we shall have one. We shall get along faster, it is permissible for a man nowadays to blow his own horn. [*Greatly excited, striding to and fro, until, finally, he comes face to face with* MADAME PEPITA.] Well, what is your answer?

MADAME PEPITA. It would be very nice, of course. Protection means so much to a woman, especially when it's a celebrated man. But Catalina . . .

DON GUILLERMO. With due respect to the Slav aristocracy, Catalina will be far better off as the step-daughter of a Spanish gentleman than as the natural daughter of a Russian duke. She will be more marriageable, too, and it is no compliment to myself.

MADAME PEPITA. No, of course not. But . . . I must
say you don't seem enthusiastic.

DON GUILLERMO. I know what I am doing, and that is
enough. You are not responsible.

MADAME PEPITA. But how do you suppose that I feel?

DON GUILLERMO. My reasons are disinterested, so forgive me; I am anxious, too, to have you satisfied. I am nervous, upset . . . I appreciate what you are. Besides, I am a
gentleman, who respects the sex. I do not love you—I
shall not pretend that I do—but whatever I have is yours.
You will never regret having accepted my name. [*A
pause.*] That is, if you do accept it.

MADAME PEPITA. [*Vastly moved.*] Certainly. What
else can I do? But I wonder what my daughter will say.
I shall never have the courage to face her.

DON GUILLERMO. Leave that to me. [*At the door.*]
Catalina! Catalina!

CATALINA. [*Outside.*] I'm coming. [*A pause. DON
GUILLERMO and MADAME PEPITA wait, but CATALINA does
not appear.*]

MADAME PEPITA. [*Impatiently.*] Catalina, are you
coming or are you not?

CATALINA. [*Outside.*] Yes, I'm coming. [*After a
moment she enters, not yet quite fastened into a flamingly
audacious gown, which scarcely permits her to walk. In
the attempt, she entangles herself in the train.*] Did you
call?

MADAME PEPITA. But . . . What have you been doing?

CATALINA. Dressing.

MADAME PEPITA. What in the devil's name have you
got on?

CATALINA. It's the latest model. I picked it out myself. I'm seventeen now, and I'm no Cinderella any more.
I have lines and proportions, and it's time to show my character. [*Looking at herself in the mirror, turning half
way round and tripping over her train as she does so.*]

MADAME PEPITA. [*Staring at her, completely stupefied.*] You? In that dress? [*With sudden inspiration.*] Praise God, it's the Vizconde! A miracle of love!

CURTAIN

ACT III

Garden of a country house at Escorial, hopelessly modern and in bad taste. A fountain in the middle contains the familiar group of two children huddled together beneath an umbrella. This masterpiece is zinc, painted to look like marble. The ground is neatly sanded. At the rear, a wall separates the garden from that of the adjoining house. Morning glories cover the wall, vying in luxuriance with a number of fruit bearing vines, while, above the wall, the tops of the trees of the neighboring garden may be seen. The façade of the house is upon the left. The building is an absolutely modern, two-storied structure, boasting a flight of steps, a glass baldaquin, a balustrade decorated with urns which are too large for it, and a crystal ball which hangs from the baldaquin in such a manner as to reflect a view of the garden. Half a dozen wicker chairs are scattered about between the fountain and the house, as well as a small wicker table, on which a sewing basket reposes, also of wicker ware.

The garden extends some distance toward the right, the street gate being a little farther on.

The morning is a bright, sunny one.

When the curtain rises the stage is empty. After a moment, DON LUIS *appears above the wall, followed shortly by* AUGUSTO. *They wear light outing suits and broad-brimmed straw hats, and ascend cautiously by means of a step-ladder from the neighboring garden.* DON LUIS *carries a sharp-pointed stick in one hand.*

DON LUIS. [*To* AUGUSTO, *who has not yet appeared.*] Up, my son! You ought to be ashamed of yourself not to be able to climb a wall at twenty-five.

AUGUSTO. [*Appearing above the wall, in obvious ill*
215

humor.] I am able, but ascensions among wall flowers do not appeal to me.

Don Luis. You fail to appreciate the delights of country life. Give me air, fresh air! What a morning for filching one's neighbor's figs! [*Extending the stick toward a fig tree, whose top obtrudes between the wall and the house.*] Aha! The biggest one—it's for you. Now, my turn . . .

Augusto. [*Placing the fig on a leaf, which serves as a substitute for a plate.*] Why not ask Pepita for them? She would hand them over already picked. It would be more convenient.

Don Luis. The pleasures of the chase, my boy. [*Reciting.*]

"Flérida, sweeter far
Than fruits of neighbor's garden are!"

Augusto. [*Impatiently.*] Bah!

Don Luis. Besides, by removing Pepita's figs, we deprive that literary husband of hers of their enjoyment. He has been eying them for the past week, watching them ripen to sweeten his lunch.

Augusto. You'll lose your balance and topple over.

Don Luis. Don't worry about me. [*Drawing back a little.*] Some one is coming.

[Catalina *is heard calling in the house.*]

Catalina. Papa! Papa!

Augusto. The daughter! Down quick!

Don Luis. Never retreat under fire.

[Catalina *enters from the house and crosses the garden. She has discarded short dresses, and now wears a simple, smart morning frock instead.*]

Catalina. [*Looking about.*] Papa! He isn't here.

Don Luis. Good morning, little rosebud.

Catalina. [*Startled.*] Eh? [*Looking up at the wall.*] What are you doing up there?

Don Luis. [*Affably.*] Waiting for you.

Catalina. Me?

Don Luis. To tell you how charming you are.

Catalina. Awfully sweet, I am sure. You almost scared me to death. [*Goes off at the left.*]

Augusto. Ingratiating creature.

Don Luis. Yes. Wait until you are married.

Augusto. Still harping on that, eh?

Don Luis. I am more enthusiastic than ever.

Augusto. I could not endure the sight of her, painted and gilded.

Don Luis. You place your expectations too high. Don't be so deucedly romantic. She is pretty, and will learn to wear clothes, to develop personality. Suppose you don't love her? After all, that is not expected. Marry with your eyes open, like other people.

Augusto. But she can't endure the sight of me, either.

Don Luis. What of it? You are young and dress well—that ought to satisfy her. You are noble, besides.

Augusto. I have no money.

Don Luis. After you are married, you will have as much as your wife.

Augusto. That follows, naturally.

Don Luis. Naturally. My son, we are confronted with a crisis. We have not a penny in the world, and this Academician is insufferable. Pepita may become disillusioned at any moment, and the girl fall in love with another. We subsist as by a miracle. It is absolutely essential that you propose today—sacrifice yourself. What the devil! If I were in your place, if I were twenty-five, I should sacrifice myself with alacrity. [*Losing his balance in his excitement, he is about to tumble into the garden.*]

Augusto. Be careful or you'll fall! Climb down.

Don Luis. Perhaps it would be best. We are in no position to argue. Lend me a hand . . . Oblige me this time, and take the stick. What do you care? Steady the ladder . . . [*Disappearing.*] Marriage usually steadies a man, anyway.

[*As soon as they are out of sight,* CATALINA *and* DON GUILLERMO *are heard upon the left.*]

CATALINA. [*As she becomes audible.*] I searched through the garden for you. How did you manage to slip out?

DON GUILLERMO. [*Smiling.*] Now that you have grown to be a young lady, not to say a coquette, you spend all your time dressing. I could not wait.

CATALINA. Yes, I am a young lady. How do you like my gown?

DON GUILLERMO. Very pretty. You look well in it.

CATALINA. Do you think it's a good thing for a woman to fuss over her looks, or don't you think so?

DON GUILLERMO. If she is clean and healthy, and there is nothing false about her, I see no occasion for her to fuss.

CATALINA. [*Smoothing her hair, uneasily.*] I suppose you're going back to Madrid pretty soon, aren't you?

DON GUILLERMO. Now that the competition is over, there is nothing to take me back. Your protegé will win the prize.

CATALINA. [*Her heart in her throat.*] Honestly?

DON GUILLERMO. Yes, he is certain to be a great painter some day.

CATALINA. Then will he have to go to Rome?

DON GUILLERMO. Assuredly. How are the figs, by the way? I wonder if they are ripe yet. They hang so high that we shall have to climb the tree for them. Get me a basket.

CATALINA. [*Taking a basket from the table.*] Put some leaves in the bottom to make it look nice.

[*They retire behind the corner of the house, under the fig tree. After a brief interval,* MADAME PEPITA *enters, breathlessly, from the street, hatless, but carrying a parasol.* ANDRÉS, *a village lad, evidently impressed but lately into the family service, follows.*]

MADAME PEPITA. Ask Paco to help you unpack the crate.

ANDRÉS. Yes, señora.

MADAME PEPITA. Then you can go to the mason's and tell the head man to come here at once. Oh, and be sure you count the bags of lime and the bricks that the workmen bring very carefully, because the number they charge me for is outrageous. The way I am spending money here is something wicked.

ANDRÉS. The Conde says that he don't need any help to count bricks; he says he's managing your property himself, and he don't want me around when he counts the lime, either.

MADAME PEPITA. [*Looking about, indignant and surprised.*] But where are the benches? What have you done with the benches? Didn't you set them out?

ANDRÉS. Just as you said, but as soon as you left we took them away again, because. . . .

MADAME PEPITA. Because what?

ANDRÉS. The gentleman told us to.

MADAME PEPITA. My husband?

ANDRÉS. Your husband.

MADAME PEPITA. Why?

ANDRÉS. Because . . . because he said they were monuments of vulgarity.

MADAME PEPITA. [*With suppressed ire.*] Very well.

ANDRÉS. Is there anything else?

MADAME PEPITA. [*Venting her spleen.*] Only get out of my sight!

ANDRÉS. Excuse me. [*Goes out.*]

MADAME PEPITA. [*Pacing up and down.*] Monuments of vulgarity! Monuments of vulgarity! [*In mingled rage and despair.*]

     [DON GUILLERMO enters.]

DON GUILLERMO. Apparently we raise figs for the neighbors. We are conducting a charitable institution. [*Dis-*

covering MADAME PEPITA, *and altering his tone.*]   Hello!
I didn't see you.

MADAME   PEPITA.   [*Sweetly.*]   Why?   Is   anything
wrong?

DON GUILLERMO.   Yes, our figs are gone.   We have
lost six—six fat ones, oozing honey.

MADAME PEPITA.   The sparrows must have eaten them.

CATALINA.   [*Entering behind* DON GUILLERMO, *deeply
dejected.*]   No, mamma, it wasn't the sparrows; it was
the Conde and his son.   I saw them on the wall with a
long stick.   They said they were looking for me, which I
knew, of course, was a lie.

MADAME PEPITA.   Of course.   They are nothing if not
polite.   [*Wishing to cut short the conversation.*]

CATALINA.   I thought you ought to know, because they
are there all the time.   Yesterday, they reached through
the fence in the garden patch and stole all our raspberries,
and they threw a stone into the poultry yard day before
yesterday and frightened the chickens, so one flew over
the wall into their yard, and they never sent it back, because they ate it, if you want to know what they did with
it.

MADAME PEPITA.   How perfectly silly!   Run in and
set the table for lunch as fast as you can.   We expect company.

CATALINA.   Again?   Are they coming to lunch again
today?

MADAME PEPITA.   Why not?   Run in and do as I say.

CATALINA.   Yes, mamma.   [*Waving to* DON GUIL-
LERMO *from the top of the steps.*]   Wait for me!   I won't
be long.

DON GUILLERMO.   [*Waving back.*]   I'll be there before you.

MADAME PEPITA.   [*Going up to* DON GUILLERMO.]
Don't you like it?

DON GUILLERMO.   Certainly.

MADAME PEPITA.   Do you mind their coming to lunch?

Don Guillermo.   This is your house; invite whom you please—you are at liberty to do so.

Madame Pepita.   I should be sorry if you didn't like it, because I always feel that Don Luis and Augusto are members of the family.   However, if you object . . .

Don Guillermo.   It is a matter of complete indifference to me.

Madame Pepita.   Don Luis has some important business to talk over.   They were coming anyhow.

Don Guillermo.   Relative to the purchase of the adjoining property from one of his friends?

Madame Pepita.   [*Slightly embarrassed.*]   No, this is about some mines.   The Conde felt terribly because that investment turned out the way it did.   But this is different. It's a stock transaction.   A big company has been formed to take in everybody.   If you care to see a plan of the mine . . .

Don Guillermo.   No, thank you.

Madame Pepita.   Aren't you interested?

Don Guillermo.   No.   I have no desire to interfere in the management of your estate, nevertheless I advise you to be cautious.   Receive this gentleman with the proper warmth, only be careful to confine your expansions to the sentimental sphere, where they are not dangerous.   When he and his son install themselves as tenants, rent free, in the very first house that you build, leaving us to stand around and wait for the paint to dry on the second, I say nothing. But don't let your affections run away with your principal.   I warn you; you are heading straight for ruin in the arms of your friend.

Madame Pepita.   [*Sentimentally.*]   Everything Don Luis does seems wrong to you.

Don Guillermo.   If you are going to cry over it, I shall retire.   Lose your money and enjoy yourself.   I am willing.

Madame Pepita.   [*Verging toward tears.*]   It is awfully hard to please everybody.

Don Guillermo. You are under no obligation to please me.

Madame Pepita. [*As before.*] But I'm sure I'd like to. [*Sighing.*] That is, if such a thing is possible.

Don Guillermo. [*Surprised.*] What is the trouble now?

Madame Pepita. [*Assuming a martyred air.*] Nothing. Although . . . We had better talk of something else. [Don Guillermo *stares at her.*] You had those benches taken away that I had set out.

Don Guillermo. Oh, is that what you have against me? Yes, I did. Pardon my interference in your domestic arrangements, but for once it was too much for me. Artificial stone! Imitation trees! I cannot abide the abominations. They are . . .

Madame Pepita. [*Interrupting.*] Monuments of vulgarity! Is that it?

Don Guillermo. Worse! They are immoral.

Madame Pepita. Immoral? I cannot see how. There were no statues on them. [*Staring at him as if he were crazy.*]

Don Guillermo. What is there immoral in a statue? It's the deception of the thing.

Madame Pepita. [*Failing to understand.*] Deception?

Don Guillermo. Yes, benches which pretend to be stone and make believe to be wood, when they have never even seen a forest or a quarry—they dissemble their true nature, they are impostures. This door, which looks like mahogany when it is miserable pine, these solid marble children who at heart are hollow zinc, these bars and gratings which pass for wrought iron and are the cheapest of calamine—they are impostures, cheats, perpetual lies! In a word, they are immoral. Furthermore, they are ugly.

Madame Pepita. But if all our furniture has got to be genuine, it will cost a fortune.

Don Guillermo. Then go without; don't counterfeit.

These everlasting frauds, which deceive nobody but ourselves, create an atmosphere of deception. How do I know
that a woman who swathes her neck in cat's fur which is
dyed to look like sable, will not as easily deceive her husband if she has the opportunity?

MADAME PEPITA. Don't suggest such a thing! Suppose
somebody should hear?

[ANDRÉS *enters.*]

ANDRÉS. Señora, the crate is unpacked. Do you want
us to bring it in, or what shall we do with it?

MADAME PEPITA. Yes, bring it here. [ANDRÉS *retires.*
MADAME PEPITA *turns to* DON GUILLERMO.] I'm so glad
it came, just when we were talking about art. You'll like
this when you see it.

[ANDRÉS *and a second youth enter. Between them,
they carry a life-sized figure of a hideous negro, seated
in a chair, smoking a cigarette.*]

ANDRÉS. Where shall we put it?

MADAME PEPITA. [*Ecstatically.*] Set it there.

[*The boys set the negro carefully upon the ground.*]

DON GUILLERMO. [*Clasping his head with his hands.*]
Merciful Powers!

MADAME PEPITA. [*Delighted.*] Do you like it? [*Discouraged.*] You don't like that, either! [*Sinking into a
chair and beginning to cry.*]

DON GUILLERMO. But, Pepita! Don't cry, please! It's
not worth it, really.

ANDRÉS. Shall we leave it there, Señora?

MADAME PEPITA. I don't know. Anywhere. Throw
it down the well!

DON GUILLERMO. No, stand it in the hall. It was
intended for the hall, was it not?

MADAME PEPITA. [*Through her tears.*] Yes, for the
hall.

DON GUILLERMO. Put it where it belongs. [*The boys
mount the steps and stagger into the house.*] Don't feel so
badly. [*Relenting.*] It's too awful! If you like it, I am

satisfied; only don't cry. I must go to the city—on business—I may have time yet to run to the station and catch the express. Forgive me . . . Catalina! What has become of Catalina?

CATALINA. [*Appearing at the window.*] Did you call?

DON GUILLERMO. What do you say to a stroll to the station?

CATALINA. I'll be ready in a minute; I've finished the table. Wait under the pine tree.

DON GUILLERMO. Bring your hat along. It's growing pretty hot.

> [DON GUILLERMO *withdraws;* CATALINA *waves to him from the window. As soon as he has disappeared, her mother calls her.*]

MADAME PEPITA. Catalina!

CATALINA. Yes, mamma.

MADAME PEPITA. Come here; I want to speak to you.
> [CATALINA *leaves the window, descends the steps, and goes up to her mother.*]

CATALINA. What is it?

MADAME PEPITA. Sit down.

CATALINA. What is the matter with you? You're all excited.

MADAME PEPITA. No, my dear; I have been discussing art with your father.

CATALINA. I knew it was something awful.

MADAME PEPITA. Sometimes, my dear, a woman does feel sentimental.

CATALINA. [*Impressed.*] Yes, mamma.

MADAME PEPITA. And, my dear, it is my duty to warn you. We have invited to lunch—

CATALINA. The Conde and his son.

MADAME PEPITA. But I didn't tell you that they're not coming merely for lunch.

CATALINA. Aren't they? What else do they want?

MADAME PEPITA. They, or rather we, expect you and

Augusto to arrive at an understanding. We are anxious to have it settled.

CATALINA. Settled?

MADAME PEPITA. Yes, your engagement.

CATALINA. My engagement?

MADAME PEPITA. Don't be silly. You know what I mean, though you're so coy about it. Augusto—I mean the Vizconde—is willing to marry you. It's an honor.

CATALINA. No!

MADAME PEPITA. Yes. He has consented.

CATALINA. Never!

MADAME PEPITA. Never?

CATALINA. I don't love him.

MADAME PEPITA. How do you know whether you love him or not, when you've never been in love? You will find out after you're married.

CATALINA. I shall never love him.

MADAME PEPITA. I don't see why. He is young and handsome, and dresses well.

CATALINA. He frizzles his moustache with an iron.

MADAME PEPITA. To make it curl.

CATALINA. A man's moustache oughtn't to curl unless it curls naturally. It must be geniune. Truth is more important than anything else in the world.

MADAME PEPITA. You, too!

CATALINA. Yes, me too, mamma.

MADAME PEPITA. [*Rising nervously.*] This a pretty state of affairs. [*Seizing* CATALINA *and shaking her, greatly incensed.*] Catalina, this is shocking nonsense, the chatter of a silly little parrot! You are going to marry Augusto because it's the best thing you can do. Besides, he's a fine fellow, and he's crazy about you. You'll be a countess, then, which has been the dream of my life. I only wish I was in your place. He is good enough for you, anyway, considering who you are.

CATALINA. I'm my father's daughter—Don Guillermo's daughter, remember that.

MADAME PEPITA. Don't you come that on me.

CATALINA. But, mamma, he loves me and he is kind to me, and I love him. If you insist on my marrying, I'll run and tell him, and he'll protect me, and you'll find out then whether or not I marry.

MADAME PEPITA. You'll marry because I tell you to— and be very careful how you say I will and I won't to me. You silly girl, do you know what you are doing? Making faces at your happiness! I suppose you've got some snip of a prince tucked away up your sleeve?

CATALINA. No, I haven't got any prince there, and you needn't think you can work off any Vizcondes on me, either.

MADAME PEPITA. Wait! You forget you're unmarried. What good is an unmarried woman, anyhow? That's the reason she's unmarried. Your happiness is at stake, and some day you'll thank me for it. A mother's duty is to protect her children.

CATALINA. Yes, and so is father's! I'm going to tell father.

MADAME PEPITA. Oh, let up on father!

CATALINA. Let up on father?

MADAME PEPITA. Yes, your mother is talking now, and your mother comes before everybody else in the world. It would be nice, wouldn't it, if a man who has known you only two or three weeks . . .

CATALINA. I won't have you talk like that about father! [*Beginning to cry.*] You don't love him!

MADAME PEPITA. [*Loftily.*] Whether I love him or not, is none of your business.

[DON LUIS *and* AUGUSTO *appear at the left.*]

DON LUIS. Do we intrude?

MADAME PEPITA. [*Composing herself.*] Oh, no! Come in! Come right in! [*To* CATALINA.] You stay here with me.

CATALINA. But father?

MADAME PEPITA. To hell with father! Send word out you're engaged.

Don Luis. We anticipate, perhaps, but I am impatient to conclude that transaction.

Madame Pepita. Ah, yes! About the mines?

Don Luis. Yes. [*Glancing significantly toward* Augusto *and* Catalina.] About the mines. We might look over the plans in the house, where it will be more convenient.

Madame Pepita. No doubt something of the sort would be best.

Don Luis. Meanwhile the young people may enjoy themselves in the garden—until luncheon.

Madame Pepita. Yes, it will not be ready for a long time.

Catalina. [*Pulling at her mother's skirts.*] No, mamma.

Madame Pepita. Don't be so damm Gothic! [*To the* Conde.] After you.

Don Luis. Precede me.

> [*They mount the steps and disappear into the house, closing the door behind them.* Augusto *and* Catalina *remain alone. They look at each other, but say nothing. After an interminable silence,* Augusto *ventures a remark as gracefully as the state of his feelings will allow.*]

Augusto. Would you care to take a little walk?

Catalina. You don't call it walking, do you, in the garden?

Augusto. I do.

Catalina. I do not.

Augusto. You do not?

Catalina. Walking is climbing mountains, and scrambling over rocks, and crashing through the underbrush. I adore walking.

Augusto. I do not.

Catalina. Oh! Don't you like mountains?

Augusto. When I hunt.

Catalina. Do you like to hunt?

Augusto. I do.

Catalina. I do not.

Augusto. You do not?

Catalina. It's silly for a grown man to spend all day killing poor little animals, who have never done him any harm. It would do you a great deal more good to stay home and read a book.

Augusto. Do you like to read books?

Catalina. Very much. Do you?

Augusto. I do not.

Catalina. [*Aggressively.*] Well, what do you like?

Augusto. I like horses and dogs.

Catalina. Oh, I thinks dogs are disgusting! They jump all over you, and upset things, and eat everything there is in the house. Besides, they have fleas. I would rather have a canary; it's pretty and it sings.

Augusto. You don't call that singing—shrilling because it is shut up in a cage? I hate anything that's in a cage. Canaries are in the same class with yellow novels and romantic girls.

Catalina. [*Delighted.*] Don't you like romantic girls?

Augusto. I don't like any kind of girls.

Catalina. [*Enchanted.*] You do not?

Augusto. I like women who have spirit and nerve, blood and fire, who know something, and are not ashamed to show it. They may laugh at a man, and have no use for him twenty-three hours out of the twenty-four, but in the one hour that they do, they make him live, or they take his life away. I forgot I was talking to you. . . .

Catalina. Oh, don't stop on my account. I suppose you mean something superior? Well, I am afraid I'm dreadfully romantic, and I haven't got much fire in my blood—not a bit of it, in fact, although sometimes I do get hot when I think . . .

Augusto. Of a man? Is it some man you already

know, or one you would like to know? Tell me, what sort of man would you like for your husband?

CATALINA. Now, don't be offended. I would like a real man, not as elegant as you are, but one who seems like a man, and who knows something—about art, for instance, and is willing to travel—to Rome, if necessary, and become famous. He might be a painter. I don't care whether he is noble or not; he might belong to the people —no, not to the people, either, but his mother might be a school teacher—

AUGUSTO. [*Seizing both her hands.*] Really? You are an angel!

CATALINA. What?

AUGUSTO. [*Transported.*] An archangel, an extraordinary woman!

CATALINA. [*More and more alarmed.*] Oh! It is true, then. You do want to marry me?

AUGUSTO. No, positively I do not.

CATALINA. Then why do you say all these things?

AUGUSTO. That's it exactly—because I don't want to marry you, because you don't love me, because you love somebody else.

CATALINA. I do not.

AUGUSTO. Yes, you do, though you may not know it. I have no idea who he is—apparently a painter or something of that sort, thank God! Now don't be offended; I don't love you either, although I think better of you than I did, and I am grateful beyond measure. Thank you again, oh, thank you! Thank you! [*Kissing her hands.*]

CATALINA. [*Allowing him to kiss her hands, so completely indifferent that she attaches no importance to it.*] It certainly is a great relief to us both. But wait till mamma hears!

AUGUSTO. [*Distressed.*] And papa!

CATALINA. [*Tapping the ground with one foot.*] She says I ought to take you because you are a vizconde.

Augusto. Yes, and then, you know you are rich. But I'd rather throw in my title for nothing.

Catalina. And you could have all my money. However, that is impossible.

Augusto. I fear so. What shall we do?

Catalina. Think of something; you're a man.

Augusto. I? I can't think.

Catalina. [*Having an inspiration.*] No, we had better ask father. He's not awfully enthusiastic about it, either. Come and find him—or, perhaps, I had better go alone; you can slip out by the orchard gate. Mother and Don Luis will believe, then, that we are still together. How do you like that?

Augusto. Perfect! Hurry and separate and fool them both.

Catalina. Hurry, while I get my hat. [Augusto *runs out behind the house. As* Catalina *reaches the steps, she notices her mother's parasol, which leans against a chair, where it has been forgotten.*] This parasol will do. What's the difference? [*An automobile horn is heard.*] An automobile! [*Distressed.*] Who can it be? [*Hesitating.*] Oh, well! Never mind. [*As she is disappearing,* Galatea *enters.*] Oh, Madame Galatea! [*Going up to her pleasantly.*] How do you do?

Galatea. [*Frigidly.*] How do you do?

Catalina. [*After looking at her.*] Something is the matter—Mother is inside. Won't you step in?

Galatea. Thanks. I've business with you, first.

Catalina. With me? Won't you sit down?

Galatea. [*Walking nervously to and fro, looking about in all directions.*] I'm easier as I am.

Catalina. [*Curiously.*] Perhaps you have lost something?

Galatea. [*Brusquely.*] Yes, and you have picked it up.

Catalina. I?

GALATEA. My dear, think it over, or all these sweet dreams of yours may turn out to be nightmares.

CATALINA. [*Amazed.*] Nightmares?

GALATEA. Depend upon it, as long as I'm alive, that man is never going to marry anybody but me.

CATALINA. [*Astonished and shocked.*] What man?

GALATEA. So you want me to stage this little scene, do you?

CATALINA. I? What scene? Unless you make it a good deal plainer, I shan't understand one word you say.

GALATEA. You want me to make it plainer, eh?

CATALINA. Yes, make it plainer.

GALATEA. Well, is this plain enough? You think you're going to be a damn countess.

CATALINA. Why, I never heard of such a thing!

GALATEA. What are you doing with Augusto, anyway?

CATALINA. Oh! So it's Augusto, is it? Is that what you're so mad about? Do you want to marry him?

GALATEA. That's my business.

CATALINA. I think so, too. Well, if you love him, and he loves you, go ahead and marry him. Count me out of it.

GALATEA. Don't you love him?

CATALINA. No, and I never did. I can't stand a man who parts his hair with a ruler.

GALATEA. [*Offended.*] Parts it with a ruler?

CATALINA. Yes, that's what he does. And he wears corsets and rouges—although you do yourself, so you've nothing on him there, as far as that goes.

GALATEA. [*Uncertain whether to be pleased or not.*] But there must be some mistake. I thought—I heard that you . . .

CATALINA. Perhaps. I heard it myself, but you can't always believe what you hear.

GALATEA. No, but when you're fond of a man . . .

CATALINA. Are you fond of him, honestly?

GALATEA. I'm fond of him all right.

CATALINA. It is hard for me to believe it.

GALATEA. However, I understand your position. A woman cannot get along without love. She may suffer, she may wish she was dead, and worry until she has not one hair left on the top of her head, but, after all, when you come down to it, love is love. There's nothing else like it.

CATALINA. [*Absorbed.*] I feel as if you might be a great help to me. Have you been engaged very long?

GALATEA. [*Depressed.*] I've never been engaged.

CATALINA. Never engaged?

GALATEA. And it's too late now. I was starving, and needed the money.

CATALINA. Do you really mean you were hungry?

GALATEA. [*Smiling at her innocence.*] Oh, that was a long time ago. But I could starve all my life for that man. You're a lucky girl! Some day you will have a sweetheart yourself, and be engaged. You'll understand, then, what love means.

CATALINA. [*Earnestly.*] I hope I will.

GALATEA. [*Preparing to leave.*] We all go through it. However, there is no need for you to worry.

CATALINA. Are you in a hurry? Won't you wait for Augusto?

GALATEA. No, I guess he's safe with you. But remember! . . . [*Goes out.*]

CATALINA. Don't forget, yourself. [*Puzzled, watching* GALATEA *as she disappears.*] She's in love. Just imagine it! Ah, before you can be in love, you have to find somebody who is willing!

> [ALBERTO *enters. He is dressed as an artist, by which it is to be understood that he wears a flowing tie and broad-brimmed hat.*]

ALBERTO. Good morning. [*Advancing.*]

CATALINA. [*Startled and happy.*] Oh!

ALBERTO. Don't be afraid. [*Disconcerted himself.*]

CATALINA. But . . . I didn't know you were there.

ALBERTO. [*Dreadfully embarrassed, but making an effort to maintain his dignity.*] Yes . . . that is . . . I was in the street, looking for you.

CATALINA. For me?

ALBERTO. [*Apologetically.*] No, not for you—for Don Guillermo. I wish to thank him. Don't you know?

CATALINA. Ah, yes! Of course!

ALBERTO. The gate was open, so . . . But I frightened you?

CATALINA. [*Hesitating.*] Then you did win the prize?

ALBERTO. Yes, thanks to Señor de Armendáriz.

CATALINA. That wasn't the only reason. The picture had to be good, too.

ALBERTO. It wasn't bad, although they said the subject was a little worn out.

CATALINA. Jacob wrestling with the angel.

ALBERTO. Yes, I should never have won the prize on that. The other pictures were good, too—there were two or three good ones; but Don Guillermo preferred mine, because . . .

CATALINA. Because why?

ALBERTO. Because . . . because he thought the angel looked like you.

CATALINA. [*Overcome.*] The angel?

ALBERTO. [*Apologizing.*] Yes, but you mustn't think that I did it on purpose.

CATALINA. [*Disappointed.*] Oh, didn't you?

ALBERTO. No, I just had you in mind. I seemed to see you, that was all. Your head is so characteristic—and your curls, and your wonderful eyes! After I had seen you, and we had talked a little—it came to me as a revelation, just like that.

CATALINA. [*After a pause.*] I suppose you are awfully anxious to go to Rome, aren't you?

ALBERTO. Awfully.

CATALINA. [*After another pause.*] You must be very happy.

ALBERTO. Yes; that is, I should be, very—because I have done what I set out to do. It is my career. Italy is my dream!

CATALINA. [*Sadly.*] I know.

ALBERTO. But, then, I am sorry to go. Honestly, I should rather not. [*Manifestly embarrassed.*]

CATALINA. Why not?

ALBERTO. [*Repenting his indiscretion, before it is too late.*] Because . . . because I am awfully fond of Madrid.

CATALINA. Oh! Are you?

ALBERTO. However . . .

CATALINA. [*Hopefully.*] However?

ALBERTO. However, I am fond of it, and so are you, although you don't live in Madrid any more.

CATALINA. No, I live in the country.

ALBERTO. Yes, in the country!

CATALINA. Are you fond of the country?

ALBERTO. I am fonder of it than I am of Madrid.

CATALINA. Are you? Why?

ALBERTO. Because . . . [*Catching himself.*] There are so many trees in the country.

CATALINA. Are you fond of trees?

ALBERTO. Very—if you are.

CATALINA. [*Touched.*] Oh, yes indeed! [*Restraining herself.*] If you are.

ALBERTO. I am fond of everything that you are, because . . . because you have such excellent taste.

CATALINA. I? What makes you think so?

ALBERTO. Because . . . [*Throwing restraint to the winds.*] Because you have such beautiful eyes!

CATALINA. [*Overwhelmed.*] Have I?

ALBERTO. [*Embarrassed.*] No, excuse me. Yes, you have. They are blue.

CATALINA. Do you like blue eyes?

ALBERTO. Immensely.

CATALINA. [*Coquettishly.*] But my eyes are not blue. That is, they are not entirely blue.

ALBERTO. No, not entirely.

CATALINA. Can you see any green in them?

ALBERTO. Yes, green—decidedly; but it makes no difference to me.

CATALINA. Of course it makes no difference to you.

ALBERTO. [*Fervently.*] Absolutely not.

CATALINA. What do you care what color my eyes are, anyway?

ALBERTO. That is quite different.

CATALINA. Is it?

ALBERTO. Yes. [*Hopelessly embarrassed.*] If you were nothing to me, of course I shouldn't care. Pardon my saying so, but you can never be nothing to me. You could not be indifferent.

CATALINA. Oh! Couldn't I?

ALBERTO. [*Impetuously.*] Never! I must tell you—I know it's not right, but I am very unhappy. You are rich and I am poor—only a poor artist. All I have is my future—a hope of glory, merely a hope, that is all. It is little enough to offer a woman in exchange for happiness.

CATALINA. [*Wishing to appear oracular.*] It may seem little enough to you, but it's an awful lot right now to me.

ALBERTO. No!

CATALINA. Because I have money, you think I must be hard to please, and want the earth, besides. Men always think they know so much, they imagine that they are the only ones who have ideals, or can dream about the future, and things that can never be. Well, let me tell you, women do it, too. Though they may be ignorant, they are just as anxious to go to Rome as men are. [*She begins to cry.*]

ALBERTO. [*Deeply moved.*] Catalina!

CATALINA. [*Without raising her eyes.*]   Here am I.

ALBERTO. [*Drawing nearer.*]   Catalina!

CATALINA. [*Discovering* DON GUILLERMO, *who enters.*] Papa!

DON GUILLERMO. [*Without noticing* ALBERTO.] Hello! Are you here? I was waiting for you.

CATALINA. [*With a tremendous effort.*]   Alberto is here, papa.

DON GUILLERMO. Alberto?

ALBERTO. [*Advancing.*]   Alberto Jiménez y Vergara, sir, at your service.

DON GUILLERMO. [*Slightly surprised.*]   Ah, yes! I am delighted . . .

ALBERTO. I have come to thank you for . . . for . . .

CATALINA. [*Interrupting.*]   For his prize. [DON GUILLERMO *makes a deprecatory gesture, indicating that it is not to be mentioned.*]   And while we are about it, I thought I would tell you that he has asked me to go to Rome with him.

DON GUILLERMO. To Rome? With him? Impossible!

CATALINA. [*Blushing.*]   We can get married before we go.

DON GUILLERMO. Outrageous! [*To* ALBERTO, *angrily.*]   I demand an explanation, sir.

CATALINA. It was all my fault.

DON GUILLERMO. Your fault?

CATALINA. Yes, he was poor, so he was afraid to ask me, because I am rich, so I had to ask him. It's the same thing, anyway. I love him, and he loves me.

DON GUILLERMO. This is too preposterous.

CATALINA. And if you won't let us marry, I am going to die, or shut myself up in a convent.

[*While* DON GUILLERMO *and* CATALINA *are speaking,* DON LUIS *and* MADAME PEPITA *enter from the house.* MADAME PEPITA *listens in amazement, and turns, unable to restrain her indignation.*]

Madame Pepita. [*To* Catalina, *seizing her by the arm.*] What is all this nonsense?

Don Guillermo. [*Calmly.*] They are in love and want to get married.

Catalina and Alberto. [*In unison.*] Yes, we want to get married.

Madame Pepita. But Augusto?

Don Luis. Yes, what about Augusto?

Catalina. [*Heroically.*] He doesn't love me and he is out of it. He is in love with another woman.

Madame Pepita. You don't know what you are talking about.

Catalina. He is in love with Galatea. She's just been here, and she swears Augusto will never marry any one else as long as she is alive.

Madame Pepita. Galatea? That shameless hussy?

Don Luis. Leave her to me. I shall attend to her case.

Don Guillermo. [*Interrupting.*] No, it has been attended to already.

Don Luis. We shall see.

Don Guillermo. As long as your activities in this house were confined to checking up lime and bricks, I remained silent; I hesitated to arouse my wife. Now, however . . .

Don Luis. Do you dare to insinuate . . . ?

Don Guillermo. [*Paying no attention to the interruption.*] As I am infinitely more interested in Catalina's happiness than in her mother's bricks, I shall not tolerate any further interference from you.

Don Luis. Then you imply, sir . . . ?

Don Guillermo. That the time has arrived for you to go. Remove yourself! We are not in the habit of discussing family affairs in the presence of strangers. [*Turning his back.* Madame Pepita *is struck dumb.*]

Don Luis. Very well! I shall retire. What shocking bad taste! Pepita, you will regret this. You will think of me when I am gone and you are pining away, alone

with this man. Remember! You have my sympathy.
[*Goes out.*]

MADAME PEPITA. [*To* CATALINA.] Because Augusto
may have made a few slips, is that any reason why I
should permit you to—

CATALINA. [*Interrupting.*] Certainly, mamma.

MADAME PEPITA. [*Looking scornfully in* ALBERTO'S
direction.] With that man?

CATALINA. Certainly, mamma.

MADAME PEPITA. My daughter, the daughter of a
Russian duke, marry a clerk, who is a retailer?

CATALINA. He's an artist.

DON GUILLERMO. In a few years, he will be famous—
I guarantee it. He will paint pictures, win medals, and
in the course of time be elected to the Academy—[*Sadly.*]
perhaps in my place. Some families seem predestined to
glory. You will have a great man for your husband, as
your mother has had before you.

MADAME PEPITA. [*Sighing.*] All the same, a title
would have done no harm, if we could have had it thrown
in. I don't want anybody to say I am an unnatural
mother.

CATALINA. [*Embracing her.*] Nobody ever accused you
of that, mamma.

ALBERTO. We are much obliged to you for what you
have done.

MADAME PEPITA. [*Deeply affected.*] Children are a
constant source of anxiety.

ALBERTO. But I must not miss my train. I am nervous. If there is nothing I can do . . . Madame Pepita,
Don Guillermo . . . I can never thank you sufficiently.

DON GUILLERMO. My wife deserves no thanks.

MADAME PEPITA. God help us both!

ALBERTO. *Adiós,* Catalina.

CATALINA. *Adiós.*

[*They look at each other, too embarrassed to move.*]

ALBERTO. I must be going . . .

CATALINA. Yes, you really must.

ALBERTO. If I am to return—the very first thing in the morning.

CATALINA. Be sure you don't forget!

[DON GUILLERMO *smiles.*]

ALBERTO. [*Confused.*] I am going. I am going now . . . *Adiós!*

[*Disappears.* CATALINA *gazes after him, without daring to follow.*]

DON GUILLERMO. Run along and see him off, if you want to. Everybody is willing.

[CATALINA *runs out.*]

MADAME PEPITA. Well, she seems happy, I must say. This has been a great day. She is going to leave us.

DON GUILLERMO. [*Pacing up and down, as he repeats his wife's words.*] Yes, she is going to leave us. [*Suddenly realizing their significance.*] Going to leave us? True! She is going to leave us!

MADAME PEPITA. The poor dear!

DON GUILLERMO. [*Startled, staring at his wife as if discovering her for the first time.*] And I am left alone with this woman!

MADAME PEPITA. [*Coyly.*] Guillermo . . .

DON GUILLERMO. What luck! [*Fiercely.*] Catalina is going to marry—naturally, she will live with her husband. Then what will become of me? I have nothing to detain me here. There is no time to lose! I have an invitation to visit Egypt to conduct excavations.

MADAME PEPITA. Not in Egypt?

DON GUILLERMO. Yes, of long standing.

MADAME PEPITA. But you can not go alone? [DON GUILLERMO *nods.*] What is to become of me?

DON GUILLERMO. [*Uneasily.*] You? [*She assents.*] You can stay behind—the trip would be too fatiguing. Besides, you could never make up your mind to leave all these objects of art.

MADAME PEPITA. [*On the verge of tears.*] True, I

forgot. Aren't they lovely? I know you only want to get rid of me.

DON GUILLERMO. Nonsense! How could I?

MADAME PEPITA. It mortifies me to think that my husband—

DON GUILLERMO. Although, strictly speaking—

MADAME PEPITA. But you grow fond of a dog when you live with him. After my experience with that man, it never occurred to me that I could love another. But my heart is tender, and I couldn't help seeing what you were. You happened along, and after all, you are my husband, though I am not the one to say it, and I am your wife, and . . . and I love you!

DON GUILLERMO. Pepita, do not prevaricate.

MADAME PEPITA. No, I love you! I wish to God that I didn't, but it's too late now, and I love you. [*Bursting into tears, she sinks into a chair.*] And there you are!

DON GUILLERMO. [*Dumbfounded.*] Pepita! But, Pepita! Come, come, I had no idea . . . [*Going up to her.*] Don't cry now. You unman me.

MADAME PEPITA. [*Sobbing.*] I am nobody, and you are a philosopher, and you belong to a different class, but I love you! I don't care whether you love me, only it isn't my fault. Don't go away, because I can't bear it. I have lived alone all my life, without anybody to take care of me—my first husband ran away, but I had my daughter, and I shared her with you because you said you needed her. But now she is leaving me, and if you leave me, too, you take the heart out of my life!

DON GUILLERMO. Pepita!

MADAME PEPITA. There is nothing left.

DON GUILLERMO. Please forgive me. A man may be an egotist, but not to that extent. I was not thinking of you. You are alone in the world, you have been deserted; but so have I. I do not ask you to love me; it is more than I could wish . . .

MADAME PEPITA. But you deserve it.

DON GUILLERMO. I know. You have no idea what it means to a man to have a wife at his side. Old age is coming on, when it is sad to be alone. No, I cannot refuse the offer of a generous woman's hand.

MADAME PEPITA. [*Sitting up.*] Guillermo, this is so sudden!

DON GUILLERMO. [*Stifling a sob.*] We might spend our honeymoon in Egypt and conduct explorations by the way.

MADAME PEPITA. Guillermo! [*And they fall into each others arms.*]

> [CATALINA *enters, flushed and confused with the remorse of the first kiss. Her eyes open wide as she discovers her mother with* DON GUILLERMO. *After hesitating a moment, she smiles discreetly, smoothing her disordered hair.*]

CATALINA. Papa and mamma! [*Tiptoeing out.*] Something new.

CURTAIN

THE KINGDOM OF GOD

THE KINGDOM OF GOD

And Other Plays

BY

G. MARTINEZ SIERRA

IN ENGLISH VERSIONS WITH AN
INTRODUCTION BY

HELEN AND HARLEY GRANVILLE-BARKER

NEW YORK
E. P. DUTTON & CO., INC.

First published ....April, 1923
Reissued with introduction.......February, 1929

CONTENTS

	PAGE
INTRODUCTION	vii
THE KINGDOM OF GOD	3
THE TWO SHEPHERDS	109
WIFE TO A FAMOUS MAN	171
THE ROMANTIC YOUNG LADY	223

CONTENTS

INTRODUCTION

While there may be much to say, there is really very little
to explain about the plays of Martínez Sierra, for they have
in the first place the supreme dramatic virtue of explaining
themselves. They are not (those at least now under
review) strikingly novel in technique. They certainly carry
no abstruse philosophical message. But they are notable,
the present writer holds, for simple excellence as plays, for
the directness with which they set out to—and the fine
economy with which they do—achieve their purpose. And
what better in this sort, can be said? Take for instance
"The Cradle Song." Sierra has the idea—the charming,
unrecondite idea—of a foundling baby thrust upon the mer-
cies of a convent of nuns, who bring her up, spend upon her
all they can recover of their suppressed motherly instincts,
give her to a young man in marriage, and so back to the
world. Mark his means to this effect. The foundling, a
varied chorus of nuns—among them one who is emotionally
the play's protagonist, an old doctor (the child must acquire
a legal parent) and the young bridegroom. No intrigue,
no thesis, no rhetorical enlargements; two acts because his
theme needs two, and no convention-satisfying third, which
it does not need. The whole result is a story perfectly told
for the sake of its innate humour and feeling, a picture filled
and rounded. And—not that this affects the matter—it is
interesting to note that with the Spanish public this play
conceding little or nothing to what is usually understood
to be the popular demand in such things, was yet a great
success—interesting from the point of view of public and
theatre-manager. The playwright at this juncture stands
aside; his work is done, he bows with one emphasis or

another to success or failure, advising himself merely of the future. But the *elements* of success—this is the important conclusion if it may be drawn—are probably pretty constant, though its incidentals may vary from country to country and year to year; and it might pay theatre managers to keep a tame crowd-psychologist or so to analyse them. Then all the English-speaking public—that part of it at least which has developed some taste and judgment—would not always be left asking, as they read translated, instead of hearing in their native tongue, plays like "The Cradle Song," why— in the name of "What the public wants"—they should be fobbed off, time after time, with entertainments which, with every well-tried appearance of being entertaining, do not *entertain*. To return however to Sierra, less occupied as a playwright with theatrical economics even than with an obtruding philosophy, though as a theatre manager—a second and successful occupation that has unluckily been thrusting aside his playwriting lately—his opinion on this point would be worth having.

"The Two Shepherds" may be coupled with "The Cradle Song." It has the same simplicity of scheme, the same directness of approach. It is perhaps the more remark-able in that its action swings upon a stark fidelity of vision. And here is the chief of Sierra's dramatic (distinct for the moment from "theatrical,") virtues; he paints faithfully the thing he *sees*. Once he has his outline clear and true he may sentimentalise a little in filling in the detail; it is a ve-nial fault. We could forgive, if need were, even more affec-tionate weakness on his creator's part for snuffy, frowsy, garlic-smelling old Don Antonio with his frayed cassock and his battered image of the Virgin, pummelling (as he says) his ill-conditioned village flock into righteousness, dragging them up to God by the scruffs of their dirty necks. Again Sierra needs his two acts and no more, seventy minutes, perhaps, of playing time, but in that space he shows us a dozen characters, individual and alive, and a picture of a

Spanish village so consistent that, experience apart, we know it to be true. Mr. Sam Weller remarked that if instead of eyes he had been gifted with a pair of double hextra million magnifying glasses he might have been able to see through two brick walls and a door, but having only eyes his vision was limited. Sam, though not given to literature was a bit of a genius, apt, as his creator was, at seeing the realities of cockneydom through things even more opaque to most sights than walls and doors. It is the one gift worth having. Sierra translates for us his Spanish village in terms, no doubt, of his own happy, humorous, ironic temperament. But he has seen it first without illusion, seen it naked, seen it true and, thanks to him, so can we—and have our fun into the bargain.

Lirio entre espinas ("Lily among Thorns") and *El enamorado* ("The Lover"), one-act plays, sound dominantly the note of irony, the one in its elaborately developed situation, the other in its treatment of the character of the Lover himself. The chancing of the timid little nun into the house of ill-fame, the circumstance by which her healing touch at a sudden sick-bed brings the inmates like good little children fetching and carrying at her call, disposes of the rowdy patrons in a sulky silence—all that is ironic and amusing enough; and (a carping critic might continue) we have had that sort of thing before (Maupassant!) and many another playwright could make as much effect with it! But mark again, the clarity of vision. Sierra has seen each single figure and has informed it with a life of its own before he started the mere making use of it for his group. Even the rather fantastically unpleasant little figure of the half-witted child (it reminds one, dependent for knowledge of Spain chiefly on books and pictures, of a Velázquez dwarf) has a pitiful little individual place—and a purpose. For—and this is what every clever dramatist fired with a good idea would not give us—one is struck with the fine humanity of Sierra's treatment of his theme. No condescension either! He writes about the nun and the fallen women and the gay young blackguards, their visitors, alike without vulgar astonishment, unselfconsciously, with a perfect courtesy of mind. He writes as a gentleman should.

The saliency of "The Lover," as a study of the entirely absurd gentleman who spends his life regardless of his personal affairs, in rapt and unregarded worship of the Queen is technically the sureness of the touch—it is drawn in spare outline so that one false stroke might be fatal—and above and beyond that the fearlessly comic treatment of the subject. No spice of ridicule is spared. The fellow has even a foolish sounding name; he ran a margarine factory before he ruined himself trapesing over the world after his Dulcinea (*aliter visum*); cruelest stroke of all, he has to confess that as he watches in the palace grounds through winter nights for the Queen to come out at dawn to feed her pigeons, he has, lest he perish with cold, to seek the comfortable cage, the friendly society of the orang-outang. He has a ridiculous collection of souvenirs, for which he has refused some Englishman's offer of a good round sum, (Englishman = eccentric, *c. f.* of course, the Danish gravedigger's "They are all mad there." How odd—an Englishman writes—that *this* should be still the typical European joke about us!); he refuses the costly ring the Queen offers him—for after all, while her courtiers stood by helpless with etiquette, this preposterous being did really save her life. He asks to be allowed to kiss her hand. Is he, then, to turn heroic after all? No! for his final request is a free pass over the State railways that he may continue his foolish, useless trapesing as before.

Surely that is good art. And, with the courageous consistency, note the final effect. The fellow wins us, we take off our hats to him; the Queen is stirred to a passing emotion she never felt before. "She feels" (it is also a warning to the actress of the part not to tumble into sentiment)

"that for the first time in her life she has really been loved."
Sierra is not Cervantes' countryman for nothing; and,
quoting that great name, we need enlarge the general argument no further.   But, glancing at the purely dramatic value
of irony it is perhaps worth while to consider for a moment
the peculiar difficulty of its use in the theatre.   This
resides, of course, mainly in the natural constitution of the
actor himself.   It is not, as some contemptuous critics of the
art would say, an objection to being made ridiculous
(though let us admit that one may now and then meet that
in the self-conscious or over-popular actor), so much as a
far more reasonable desire that his audience should, from
the beginning, have no doubt of his intentions, should be
sure that, however big a fool he is making of himself, he is
doing it deliberately with his eyes open.   There is nothing
the actor hates more than to be at cross purposes with his
audience.   Hence the practical difficulty for a dramatist of
the gradual disclosure of an ironic purpose, but the necessity of a ruthless consistency, by which the end shall justify
both the beginning and the means.   And we rule out of
course any concluding claptrap of a sudden direct sentimental appeal for sympathy.   "The Lover" is a simple
admirable example of what an ironic play should be.   For
it is by the sustaining of the irony that our proper sympathy is won.   The actor can round off his performance, the
play's last scheme come full circle.   Still something more
than technique is involved.   If Sierra did not love his man
well enough to want to tell the truth about him and love
him the better for truth being told, the silly fool could not
touch the Queen's imagination and ours as he does.   It is
respect for poor humanity that counts.   Sierra has that.

El Reino de Dios ("The Kingdom of God") is in some
ways the most considerable of Sierra's work.   He devises
for himself a larger canvas than usual and, if for nothing
else, the play would be remarkable for the number, variety,
fidelity, vitality of the sketched characters with which it

is so economically filled. He demands great assistance from his actors, no doubt, but he sets them no problems of psychology, no modelling, so to speak, is asked of them, they have but to colour in "on the flat" the firm outlines of his drawing. And, for more immediate effect he places them against a background which is in itself dramatic, which in itself and in its changes, develops the action and purpose of the play. The action itself is unconventional more or less—though there is little in the shape of transgression against the unities which has not been tried in the post-Ibsen period of European drama by one dramatic experimentor or another. We mark Sierra yet once more as the accomplished man of the theatre by the ease and certainty with which he transgresses. He sacrifices everything to his purpose and contrives to sacrifice nothing. The play has, as its main thread, the story of a girl—in her girlhood, her middle and old age—who gives up her share in the things of this world to ensure, rather than seek, such a portion as she may snatch in this life of the kingdom of God. She joins a sisterhood. We find her in her girlhood ministering in an asylum for old men, foolish, tiresome and—if a stray peseta opens the door of an inn to them—drunken old men. Womanhood brings her to a home where the children of fallen women come into the world, a sadder beginning of life than was the preceding picture—so pitifully comic—of life's end. She refuses release from it in marriage (the vows of her order are not final) to a worthy doctor who worships her, with the flashing phrase "And you dare to talk to me of love . . . *here!*" Old age finds her the Mother of an orphanage, with one of God's adopted returning in laurelled triumph as a bull fighter to lay his trophy —his first bull's ear—at her feet (How one envies a Spanish dramatist that scene, but with an admiring envy for Sierra's quite perfect treatment of it!) and as a crown and ending to the play we have her passionate plea with a young revolutionary in embryo (Spain has no immediate copyright in these at least) to abjure violence, to seek his kingdom of God in pity and in love. A very stirring play; and it is instructive to the student of drama to note the use made of the material, the means by which Sierra appeals—and most legitimately—to our emotions. He is not concerned (as an English dramatist choosing such a theme to-day would almost certainly be) with the growth or wane of the woman's religious belief, nor yet—but for that one flash already recorded—with her mental reaction to the social conditions she faces, not even with developing her "character"; in fact, it is part of his theme that she does not bother, as certain of our self-conscious philanthropists do, with any such self-righteous thing—so why should he? He relies upon making as clear in his picture to us, as in the reality it was clear to her, the human needs and their claim upon us of disreputable age, sordid sins of the flesh, and of childhood, that will bate no claim, and should not, since upon it all the claims of the world must fall. And that he does so in terms which not the simplest soul in his audience can mistake, nor the most sophisticated deny, is, it may be claimed, an achievement—complete of its kind—in the reality of art.

La mujer del héroe ("Wife to a Famous Man") makes far fewer pretentions. It is a sound playable play, little more, interesting to us mainly for the peep that it takes into working class Madrid. The dramatist, in fact, frankly tells us in a spoken epilogue that it is a passing tribute to the virtues of the Spanish woman of the people as you may walk down any street in any city to find her—as you might find her, *bien entendu*, had you Sierra's power to see and show beauty, pathos, humour in this laundry, and in the kindly, rough-tongued, honest-minded woman earning her family's living there; as good fun and as great a beauty, so felt and seen, as some of us go seeking in remoter places. He selects the rest of his material a trifle carelessly, perhaps; he has used some of it before. But it is an admirable notion, this, of a national hero made in a moment out of the winner of an air-race (this was in the days before the war) ; a common fellow, reckless and stout of nerve, but with a head which, though he can keep it in the air, is only made to be turned on earth; not too much of a hero to have lived on the laundry, rapidly too spoilt to live contentedly in it.

Sierra might have added in his epilogue almost as legitimately that the play is tribute in the shape of opportunity to the actress upon whom the chief burden is to fall. But this again might be remarked of all his work (though surely it should not call for particular remark in any dramatist!) how grateful his plays are to the actor. It comes of course partly from the extreme simplicity of his method and from his never trying to force into a play more matter than it will easily hold. He seems incapable of writing anything ineffective, though now and then he may yield to the too obvious effect. That is a venial fault—in the actor's eyes at least. And Sierra, one may judge from this, does genuinely like, admire and understand the art of acting.

It is a taste that every dramatist should have. It may sound superfluous to say so, but of late years there seems to have developed in certain dramatists a distrust, even a positive dislike of acting, an unreasoning, if sometimes excusable anger with the actor himself and all his works. Now this reflects quite inevitably upon their own work and its result is to be seen in a stiff unyieldingness, a drabness and dryness, a self-sufficiency, as if to say "You actors are my megaphone merely. Please don't presume." Upon such a perverse misunderstanding of what the free and full collaboration between actor and dramatist should be, the drama can never flourish. The trouble springs partly, one fears, from the quite uncalled-for acclaim of the modern dramatist as "a literary man." He bows, a bit snobbishly, to the intended compliment and then from literature's present pontifical height is apt to begin to look down on the motley theatre. In a short time, if he's not careful, he'll soon be writing plays fitter for the study than the stage. There is no good play of which that can be said. There are good plays enough that need better acting than our present theatre with its stupid system and its artistically uneducated public, by whose favour it must live, can be expected to supply. But no progress is possible in the art as a whole unless all concerned—dramatists, actors, yes, and public too—such a selection from the mob as can form a conscious third—move forward together. In England we are still far from that happy state of things. The theatre is commercially prosperous, artistically at cross purposes. Dramatists may complain of their actors, but actors are bitterer about managements, and managements alternately curse at and despise the public—save, of course, during the runs of luck that most of them, gambling long and good-temperedly enough, may look for. Spain no doubt has her theatrical troubles too; we are not here concerned with them. But it is at least a sign of artistic good health to find such plays as Sierra's among its living drama, apt above all things for acting, and for such acting as, one is sure, is bread and meat to the appetite of the audience, wholesome and familiar fare that they know the good and the bad of.

If one comments no further it is not for lack of material. The author's works, his plays alone (there are novels and poems besides. He is forty. What is the secret of this amazing fecundity of the Spaniard?) would take a page or more only to list.

Plays like *Madame Pepita, Mamá, Sueño de una noche de agosta,* (played in English as "The Romantic Young Lady," and the little fantasy *Hechizo de amor* ("Love Magic") are of a content to which we are more accustomed in the French and English spoken drama of to-day. There are yet others, less usual in form and content too, but these will find their way to translation some day and may then more appropriately be dealt with. This must suffice now, an inadequate introduction, perhaps, to a playwright whose adequacy is, in any case, beyond question.

H. GRANVILLE BARKER

THE KINGDOM OF GOD

PLAY IN THREE ACTS

TEATRO DE NOVEDADES, BARCELONA
1915

STRAND THEATRE, LONDON
1927

ETHEL BARRYMORE THEATRE, NEW YORK
1928

CHARACTERS

First Act.	*Second Act.*	*Third Act.*
SISTER GRACIA.	SISTER GRACIA.	SISTER GRACIA.
SISTER JULIANA.	MARGARITA.	SISTER DIONISIA.
SISTER MANUELA.	CANDELAS.	ENGRACIA.
MARÍA ISABEL.	QUICA.	THE INNOCENT.
LULU.	CECILIA.	PAQUITA.
DON LORENZO.	THE DUMB GIRL.	LORENZA.
TRAJANO.	SISTER CRISTINA.	MORENITO.
GABRIEL.	SISTER FELICIANA.	FELIPE.
LIBORIO.	ENRIQUE.	JUAN DE DIOS.
TWO OLD MEN.		VICENTE.
		POLICARPO.
		SEVERAL CHILDREN.

The first act takes place in an asylum for poor old men; the second in a maternity home; the third in an orphanage.

In the first act SISTER GRACIA *is 19, in the second 29, and in the third act she is 70.*

It should be noted that SISTER GRACIA *is not a nun. She belongs to the order of St. Vincent de Paul, which is dedicated to the care of the sick and the teaching of children. The Sisters take their vows year by year, and they may renew them or not as they wish.*

1

ACT I

*The garden of a ducal palace that has been converted
to a home for poverty-stricken old men. The garden itself
is still both stately and charming. We are in a part of it
that is walled with clipped hedges of box and myrtle; upon
the left is a bower of cypress; in the half distance a
screen of plane trees and chestnuts. In the middle is a
fountain surrounded by beds of flowers. And in the arbour and behind the fountain are marble benches of classic
design. Upon the right stands the ci-devant palace which
is reached by marble steps across a terrace that is of marble
too. Upon this terrace open the long windows of the rooms
which were once the salons, but are now the dormitories
and living-rooms of the present inmates. Below the terrace
a little service door shows the way into the lower regions
of the house.*

*It is autumn. The leaves of the plane trees and chest-
nuts have already turned red and gold. Over the terrace
balustrade is twined a flaming creeper. In the flower beds
are dahlias and chrysanthemums, and upon the rose trees
a few last roses cling. Dead leaves drift upon the walks
and steps where the autumn wind has blown them.*

*It is the afternoon of a clear bright October day in
Castile. The sun soon begins to set; the sky is lit by flaming colours which fade after a little to a pallor that is
brightened, then, by the evening star.*

*GABRIEL, one of the old pensioners, is sitting on a bench
cracking pine-nuts with a stone. He is a very thin old
man, shrunk within his blue uniform. But he is as sharp*

3

*as a needle and as lively as a lizard; and his eyes are al-
ways expressionlessly ablink. He eats the pine-kernels with
all the pleasure of second childhood.*

TRAJANO, *a still older inmate, is walking backwards and
forwards evidently somewhat out of temper. He has a
fine, rather apostolic, head; he limps a little from rheumatism.*

Another old man, passing at the back, salutes them both.

THE OLD MAN. Good afternoon, gentlemen.
GABRIEL. Same to you.
    [*The old man passes on.*]
GABRIEL. And a beautiful afternoon it is. Good to
sit and warm one's bones in such an October sun.
    [*He gives a little shrill laugh.* TRAJANO, *for all
    that he was spoken to, makes no pause in his walking
    and gives no answer but a grunt.* GABRIEL *goes on
    cracking his nuts and, as* TRAJANO *passes him, holds
    one out, ready peeled.*]
GABRIEL. Have one?
    [TRAJANO *looks him up and down with quite an
    Olympic disdain.*]
TRAJANO. What is that, pray?
GABRIEL. A pine nut.
TRAJANO. [*Contemptuously.*] A pine nut!
    [*For all his contempt, however, he takes—not the
    one offered him, but a whole handful that are lying
    there cracked, and munches them as he talks.*]
TRAJANO. And how did you come by these, may I
ask?
GABRIEL. Sister Josefita gave them to me.
TRAJANO. The cook! Oh indeed . . . filched them
out of our tomorrow's dessert, did she?
GABRIEL. No, she did not. These are not Asylum pine-
nuts. They are some that were specially given to the
Sisters by the Warden . . . God bless him. [*He politely
lifts his hat.*]

TRAJANO. [*With ill-concealed envy.*] I say, I say
. . . is that a new hat you've got?

GABRIEL. [*With mischievous satisfaction.*] Yes indeed . . . it's a new hat. I had it dealt out to me this
morning.

TRAJANO. Sister Martina gave it to you, did she?

GABRIEL. [*Delighted that* TRAJANO *is losing his
temper.*] Yes, Señor . . . Sister Martina.

TRAJANO. That's flat favouritism! There are hats
about much worse than your hat was.

[GABRIEL *smiles even more maliciously, and* TRA-
JANO *begins to walk up and down again, grumbling
to himself.*]

TRAJANO. But as long as you can get round the Sisters . . . ! Pull . . . that's all it is . . . pull! [*Suddenly stopping in front of* GABRIEL.] Look here now . . .
how do you work it . . . every Sister in the place ready to
black your boots for you?

GABRIEL. [*Still highly delighted.*] The Sisters do
treat me better than I deserve, no doubt . . . because, I
should say, they are ladies who know how to value good
breeding. And . . . though I say it that shouldn't . . .
I have breeding!

TRAJANO. You're a snob . . . that's what you are.

GABRIEL. Well, I'd sooner be a snob than an anarchist!

TRAJANO. Are you referring to me?

GABRIEL. If the cap fits you can wear it.

[TRAJANO *again looks him up and down with supreme disdain, and then resumes his pacing, while* GA-
BRIEL *goes back to cracking his nuts.*]

GABRIEL. Not walking out this afternoon?

TRAJANO. Are you addressing me?

GABRIEL. [*Urbanely.*] Yes . . . if I may so far presume.

TRAJANO. [*Relaxing a little.*] No, Señor . . . I am
not going out.

GABRIEL. For a very good reason, I'm sure.

TRAJANO.   I have no wish to go out.

[GABRIEL *laughs slyly.*]

TRAJANO.   And what the devil are you grinning at?

GABRIEL.   Oh . . . I'm staying in just for the same reason.

[TRAJANO *interrogates him with a haughty stare.*]

GABRIEL.   For where can a man go to without a penny in his pocket?

TRAJANO.   Thank you . . . I have all the money I need.   And enough to take you with me . . . if I wanted to.   Look here!

[*He takes out his pocket-book, and out of the pocket-book a folded piece of paper, and with great care he produces a silver coin.*   GABRIEL *darts up and gazes at the money as if a miracle had just been performed.*]

GABRIEL.   A peseta!

TRAJANO.   [*Folding it away again as if he feared it might evaporate.*]   Yes, Señor . . . and earned by honest toil . . . not by licking people's boots, mark you . . . like some I know.

GABRIEL.   Licking people's . . . !   Do you mean that for me?

TRAJANO.   Aha, my friend . . . if the cap fits you can wear it.

[*This time* GABRIEL *sits down in a sulk,* TRAJANO, *cheered by his little revenge, starts his pacing again and flourishes out his words like a very Cyrano.*]

TRAJANO.   A peseta . . . Yes, Señor Gabriel, [*He pronounces the name with utter contempt.*] yes, indeed . . . a peseta.   The Warden gave it me . . . God bless him [*and he takes off his hat in ironic imitation*] for mending a lock for him.   I've no need to lower myself to praying to the Saints when I don't believe in them . . . so that the Sisters shall run after me and spoil me.   Trajano Fernandez' conscience is not to be bought with a handful of pine-nuts.   [*Then follows a solemn pause till he says.*] And if I do not walk out this afternoon . . . and it re-

mains to be seen whether I do walk out or not . . . I have
not the remotest intention of first asking leave from any
lady-bishop alive.

GABRIEL.   Lady-Bishop!   My good man . . . when you
want to speak of Sister Manuela can't you call her by her
proper name as every other well-mannered person does?

[GABRIEL *rises, very fussed. But* TRAJANO *only
laughs.*]

GABRIEL.   Don't laugh . . . don't laugh, please. It
makes me very angry.

TRAJANO.   I didn't confer the title on her!   The chaplain calls her that . . . and the Warden . . . God bless
him.   And so do the parish priest and the doctor and all
the other sisters.   And quite right too . . . for a more
dictatorial woman was never born.

GABRIEL.   And so she should be.   What else is she the
Superior for?

TRAJANO.   But as for yours truly he takes no orders
from any Sister of Mercy.   Don't the rules lay it down
that we have a right to walk out on a Sunday afternoon?
Do they or don't they?   Well if they do . . . it'll take
a ton of pine-nuts to make me go asking leave from a lot
of petticoats . . . as if I was a schoolboy.   Thank you
. . . I left school some time ago.

GABRIEL.   [*Between his teeth.*]   Where they didn't
teach you manners anyhow!

[*He begins to pick up the nutshells that* TRAJANO
*has scattered and puts them with his own into a blue
and white checked pocket-handkerchief.*]

TRAJANO.   What's that you're doing?

GABRIEL.   Picking up the nutshells you threw about.
You know well enough that Sister Manuela doesn't like
to see rubbish lying around.

TRAJANO.   [*Grumbling.*]   There again!   Tidy up!
I'm fed up with being told to tidy up.   Don't throw nutshells about!   Don't spit!   Wipe your boots before entering a room . . . so that the lady-bishop can show off her

nice waxed floors to the visitors. Wash your face once a day . . . and your hands twice a day at least . . . and your feet every Saturday, rain or fine! And as if that weren't enough . . . take a bath every two months! Am I a man or a frog? Water . . . water . . . water! Give me wine. Yes, indeed . . . a glass of wine for dinner . . . that's what we need . . . as I keep on saying. What an idea to put a place like this in the charge of Sisters of Charity! Women do not understand men. Am I right or not?

GABRIEL. [*Sighing in spite of himself.*] Well . . . about the water . . . and about the wine . . . why, yes, I think you are.

> [*At this moment a little burst of women's laughter is heard; and* SISTER GRACIA *and* SISTER JULIANA *come along the path at the back carrying between them —and hardly able to carry—an immense basket of potatoes. They are laughing because, as the basket is so full, some of the potatoes keep rolling out on to the ground.* SISTER GRACIA *is a girl of nineteen, pretty, fragile, and very gay.* SISTER JULIANA *is about the same age, but commonplace to look at, her face high-coloured. She talks rather affectedly and self-consciously, trying to appear refined.*]

SISTER GRACIA. There go some more good potatoes. Oo . . . this basket's heavier than a mortal sin.

> [*She lets go the handle, but as* SISTER JULIANA *keeps hold of hers quantities of potatoes roll out as the basket tips.*]

SISTER GRACIA. [*Still laughing.*] Now we've done it!

SISTER JULIANA. Aie . . . ! Sister . . . Sister . . . don't laugh like that. Some one might hear you.

> [GABRIEL *rushes forward to help pick up the potatoes.*]

SISTER GRACIA. Thank you, Gabriel.

GABRIEL.   Don't mention it, Señorita.

SISTER GRACIA.   Señorita!   Why ever must you call me that?

GABRIEL.   Oh, Señorita, I beg your pardon . . . Sister Gracia I meant to say.   But I'm so used to think of you as . . . you see.   And though you do wear the habit now, I can never forget that you're the Marquis's granddaughter . . . rest his soul.

SISTER GRACIA.   I'm nobody's granddaughter here, Gabriel.   I'm a Sister of Charity . . . and that's all you need to remember.   [*Then to* TRAJANO *who stands by majestically indifferent.*]   And you might help too . . . mightn't you?

SISTER JULIANA.   He help us!   He's an atheist.   He'd like to see us all killed and eaten.

TRAJANO.   I am not an atheist . . . I want no one killed and eaten.   I am a Radical and a Freethinker.

GABRIEL.   [*Maliciously.*]   And a Freemason.

TRAJANO.   [*Rounding on him.*]   Yes . . . and a Freemason . . . and proud to be one.

SISTER JULIANA.   [*Crossing herself in terror.*]   Ave Maria . . . hold your tongue . . . hold your tongue.

[TRAJANO *turns very oratorical and solemn.   He is glad to have shocked her, as he dislikes her extremely.*]

TRAJANO.   And of the Scottish Rite . . . as is the German Emperor . . . and the King of England . . . and King Victor Emmanuel . . . who in 1870 made Rome the capital of Italy.

SISTER GRACIA.   [*Rallying him affectionately.*]   Quite so . . . most suitable company for you, I'm sure.

TRAJANO.   [*Gallantly.*]   And I was in your father's company too.

SISTER JULIANA.   Holy Virgin!

TRAJANO.   [*Rounding on her.*]   Yes, Señora . . . in the company of Lorenzo Benevidez . . . an honoured

tribune of the people . . . and a spiritual heir of that
great republic that said to the negro slave, "Arise, be free
. . . you also are a man."

SISTER GRACIA. [*A little sadly.*] Quite so, quite so
. . . that'll do.

TRAJANO. But what is there to sigh about in that?
Your father and those like him . . . though indeed there
aren't many like him . . . are the only hope of Spain.
And thanks to them there shall one day be no more social
injustice. But rich and poor will feast together . . .

SISTER JULIANA. And there'll be lots of wine on the
table.

TRAJANO. [*Turning on her viperously.*] A little more
than we get here . . . yes, let's hope so. [*Then to* SISTER
GRACIA *again.*] No more privileged classes . . . no
aristocrats . . . no convents.

[*He begins to get excited, and* SISTER GRACIA, *to
quiet him, says pleasantly and gaily.*]

SISTER GRACIA. Well, I daresay not . . . but you
needn't choke over it. And if you'll pick up some of these
potatoes God will reward you for that.

TRAJANO. [*As he stoops with some difficulty.*] I pick
up these potatoes for your father's daughter. But . . .
[*The blood is rushing to his head.*] for all that, a day will
come . . . a day will come . . .

SISTER GRACIA. When you and your King of England
will cut off our heads . . . we're quite aware of that.
Yes, you'll cut off our heads and then we shall go straight
to heaven . . . and be very glad to get there. And once
we're there we shall pray to God for you and get you to
glory in spite of yourselves. And with that beard and
bald head of yours they may even mistake you for St.
Peter . . . who knows! [*Then as she takes the potatoes.*]
Many thanks.

TRAJANO. [*Wheezing and coughing.*] The . . . Social . . . Revolution . . . will come . . .

[*He sinks on a bench, half choking with asthma.* SISTER GRACIA *goes to him and wipes the sweat from his forehead.*]

SISTER GRACIA. Come now . . . here's a Marquis's granddaughter wiping your forehead for you. How much further can your Social Revolution take you?

[SISTER JULIANA *and* GABRIEL *are putting the last potatoes in the basket. She looks up suddenly and then says.*]

SISTER JULIANA. Sister Manuela!

TRAJANO. [*Trying to struggle to his feet and like a scared schoolboy.*] The lady-bishop!

[SISTER GRACIA *rests her hand on his shoulder to quiet him as* SISTER MANUELA *comes majestically down the marble steps. She is a woman of fifty, energetic, a little harsh of speech but good at heart. She wears spectacles.*]

SISTER MANUELA. [*To the two girls.*] What are you doing here?

SISTER JULIANA. Picking up the potatoes . . . the basket upset.

SISTER MANUELA. Couldn't the gardener have carried it for you?

SISTER GRACIA. Well . . . it's Sunday you see . . . and he was in such a hurry to get down to the village. There's a dance on and his sweetheart was waiting for him. So we told him . . . begging your pardon . . . that we could manage it ourselves quite well.

SISTER MANUELA. Well . . . don't let it happen again. You know that I don't like the Sisters to carry such heavy loads. We all have our appointed tasks . . . and God keeps us from failing in those.

SISTER GRACIA. Yes, Reverend Mother.

SISTER MANUELA. [*To the two old men.*] You two can carry it to the kitchen. A little exercise won't do you any harm.

[TRAJANO *and* GABRIEL *lay hold of the basket, and* SISTER MANUELA *is passing on when* SISTER GRACIA *detains her by saying*:]

SISTER GRACIA. Reverend Mother.

SISTER MANUELA. What is it?

SISTER GRACIA. May I ask a favour? Will you give Trajano leave to go into town? This is the day for it.

SISTER MANUELA. Why doesn't he ask me himself?

SISTER GRACIA. [*Glancing at* TRAJANO *out of the corner of her eye.*] He doesn't like to.

SISTER MANUELA. [*Assuming a tone of great severity.*] Because . . . I suppose . . . the last time he went he came home drunk.

TRAJANO. [*Feebly protesting.*] Not drunk, Señora . . . no, not really drunk.

SISTER MANUELA. As drunk as an owl. Have you forgotten, pray, that you tried to proclaim a Spanish Republic in the middle of supper?

SISTER GRACIA. But he won't get drunk today. I'll answer for him. [*To* TRAJANO.] That's so, isn't it? If you may go out you won't touch one drop . . . now will you?

[TRAJANO *gestures his promise by kissing his crossed fingers, and with mock solemnity she copies him.*]

SISTER GRACIA. There . . . the daughter of the tribune of the people has gone bail for you.

SISTER MANUELA. Well . . . I haven't much confidence in him. However, he can go out if he likes. What I do not like, though, is his going alone.

GABRIEL. [*Quickly.*] If the Reverend Mother would graciously permit me I should be most happy to accompany him.

TRAJANO. [*Only half to himself.*] Parasite!

SISTER MANUELA. [*Looking at* GABRIEL.] And I haven't much faith in him either. However . . . be off, both of you. You must be back before dark . . . remember that. [*She looks* TRAJANO *up and down and he trembles*

under her eye.]   And perhaps you'd oblige me by making
yourself look a little respectable before you go.   You're a disgrace to the institution.   [TRAJANO *surveys himself, puzzled and confused.*]   How long since you washed your
beard? There are wild beasts in that jungle I expect.
My fault! I should have made you shave like the rest.

TRAJANO.   [*Much offended.*]   Let me assure you,
Señora, that this venerable beard has never harboured . . .

SISTER MANUELA.   You put it in the basin next time
and soap it well.   And now . . . take that away [*The
potato basket.*] at once.

> [TRAJANO *and* GABRIEL *go out carrying the basket
> between them,* TRAJANO *saying between his teeth* . . .]

TRAJANO.   Before they made her a lady-bishop she must
have been Grand Inquisitor of Spain . . . !

SISTER GRACIA.   Thank you, oh, thank you, Reverend
Mother . . . and God reward you.

SISTER MANUELA.   He'll come back as he always does
. . . and you'll be to blame.   Well, that'll teach you not
to be so soft-hearted.   [SISTER GRACIA *looks abashed at
this.*]   Cheer up . . . there are visitors coming for you.

SISTER GRACIA.   For me?

SISTER MANUELA.   Your family telephoned they'd be
here this afternoon . . . and quite soon.   You can receive
them in the garden here, if you like.

SISTER GRACIA.   Yes . . . thank you, Reverend Mother.

> [SISTER MANUELA *now passes on and away.*
> SISTER GRACIA *sits on one of the benches, and after a
> moment sighs pensively.*]

SISTER GRACIA.   . . . coming to see me!

SISTER JULIANA.   [*Rather officiously.*]   Well, aren't
you glad?

SISTER GRACIA.   Oh yes . . . of course . . . I shall be
glad to see them . . . very glad.   Though Mother will
give me a bad ten minutes as usual.   She can't make up
her mind to my being here.   [*Then with an almost childish vexation.*]   Well, no more can anyone else for that

matter. No one will believe that I have a vocation.
Good heavens . . . why ever shouldn't I have! I know
I'm not a saint. But . . . [*Very simply.*] God makes
his choice from among us as he thinks best, after all. Besides we needn't wait for God to call us, need we? If
we call to him, he'll answer . . . even though in ourselves
we're of no account. That is so, don't you think? [*She
gets up from the bench and passes her hands across her face
as if to brush away the shadow of melancholy.*] Well,
well . . . we can all feel certain of ourselves if we want
to . . . and if we don't, so much the worse for us.

SISTER JULIANA. [*Looking at her as if hypnotised.*]
Of course. . . .

SISTER GRACIA. Why are you looking at me like that?
[*She looks down as if something might be wrong with her
dress.*]

SISTER JULIANA. What a wonderful complexion you
have! [*She goes up to* SISTER GRACIA *and takes her hand.*]
What do Society ladies use to get themselves a skin like
that?

SISTER GRACIA. [*Drawing her hand away.*] Soap and
water . . . just what we have here.

SISTER JULIANA. Nothing else?

SISTER GRACIA. [*A little amused at the other's passionate curiosity.*] Well . . . it was all I was ever given.

SISTER JULIANA. [*Still more eagerly.*] I say . . . was
your grandfather a Marquis?

SISTER GRACIA. Yes, he was.

SISTER JULIANA. And your father's a most important
person in Parliament?

SISTER GRACIA. Well, yes . . . he's one of the people
who make most noise there.

SISTER JULIANA. I say . . . [*Whenever she uses this
phrase she half chokes with eagerness.*] Did you ever see
the King?

SISTER GRACIA. Yes . . . often.

SISTER JULIANA. Close to?

SISTER GRACIA. Quite close. About a fortnight before I came here on probation I was dancing with him.

SISTER JULIANA. [*Her eyes starting from her head.*] Dancing with him!!

SISTER GRACIA. [*Quite simply.*] Yes . . . at a fête some San Sabastian ladies gave for the shipwrecked seamen.

> [SISTER JULIANA *is torn between her fear of discussing something she thinks sinful and her desire to know it at all hazards.*]

SISTER JULIANA. Was it . . . fun?

SISTER GRACIA. For the King?

SISTER JULIANA. For you.

SISTER GRACIA. For me! Oh . . . when I hear the hand organ that stops outside the gate every morning . . . if you only knew how hard it is to stop myself taking a turn round the room with the nearest chair!

SISTER JULIANA. [*Professionally scandalised.*] Mother of God . . . don't say that. [*But after a moment, more curious than ever.*] And at the . . . at that ball . . . did you wear a dress with a train to it?

SISTER GRACIA. No . . . they're not in fashion.

SISTER JULIANA. [*With such an effort; as if she were hauling a bucket out of a well.*] But . . . your dress was cut low, wasn't it?

SISTER GRACIA. Just a little . . . down to here . . . that's all.

SISTER JULIANA. [*Crossing herself.*] Blessed Jesus . . . weren't you ashamed? I say . . . did you put rouge on?

SISTER GRACIA. Why on earth should I?

SISTER JULIANA. [*Lowering her eyes hypocritically.*] They say all Society ladies do.

SISTER GRACIA. Well, if they think they look too pale I daresay they do.

SISTER JULIANA. I say . . . and have you ever been to a theatre?

SISTER GRACIA. Well, of course.

SISTER JULIANA. Yes, of course . . . when you were in the world you did as they all do. [*Then she asks, very fearfully, so monstrous does it seem.*] And you've read novels?

SISTER GRACIA. [*A little impatient at last.*] Well . . . haven't you?

SISTER JULIANA. [*Scandalised.*] I? Why, you know I was an orphan and brought up in a convent . . . so I never had a chance. [*Then, her conscience pricking her for the lie.*] That's to say . . . once, a long time ago, I did read one. Another girl brought it in, hidden in her dress and lent it us. [*Prudishly, but still with a little pleasure remaining.*] Blessed Jesus . . . I wish I could forget about it. "Claudine's Adventures in Paris" it was called.

[SISTER GRACIA *goes off into peals of laughter, much to the other's annoyance.*]

SISTER JULIANA. What are you laughing at? Have you never read that?

SISTER GRACIA. The girls I was brought up amongst didn't read books of that sort.

[*She laughs still, and* SISTER JULIANA *gets up most offended.*]

SISTER JULIANA. Sister . . . you upset me exceedingly by laughing like that.

[*And she goes towards the house with much dignity.*]

SISTER GRACIA. Oh, don't be angry . . . please. I didn't mean to offend you . . . Sister Juliana . . . listen!

[*But* SISTER JULIANA *has vanished.* SISTER GRACIA *is on the point of following her, when she meets* TRAJANO *and* GABRIEL *coming out arm in arm.*]

GABRIEL. [*Very gallant.*] Any commissions to execute in town for the most beautiful of Sisters?

SISTER GRACIA. Nothing, thank you. Have a good time and don't waste your money.

GABRIEL. [*With an insinuating laugh.*] No affair of mine! Señor Trajano is the capitalist today.

[*Trajano is in a very bad humour because of the company that has been forced on him.*]

TRAJANO. I shall spend my money if I want to . . . but I shall spend it on myself!

GABRIEL. [*Magnanimously.*] Man alive . . . who wants your money?

[*The bell at the front gate is heard ringing.*]

GABRIEL. Some one at the gate. Visitors.

[DON LORENZO'S *voice is heard saying, "Don't trouble yourself, Sister, please. We know the way."*]

SISTER GRACIA. [*With suppressed joy.*] Father!

[DON LORENZO, MARÍA ISABEL, *and* LULU *come along the path.* SISTER GRACIA *unrestrainedly throws her arms round her father's neck, and then kisses her mother and sister.*]

SISTER GRACIA. Father . . . Father, how good to see you! Dear Mother! Lulu!

TRAJANO. Lorenzo Benevidez . . . friend of the People. [*He goes up and takes off his hat in fine style.*] I salute the Tribune.

[TRAJANO, *having accomplished this, goes his way with great dignity.* LORENZO *is a little surprised, but most amiably returns the salute.*]

LORENZO. Good-afternoon.

SISTER GRACIA. [*To her mother.*] How warm you look. [*Then to* LULU.] So do you. Sit down . . . it's shady here.

MARÍA ISABEL. [*As she sits, fanning herself.*] Oh, my dear child . . . the heat . . . and the dust! And the road . . . seven times at least I thought the car had broken in two. It shows how much we must want to see you . . . when we take such a terrible journey.

SISTER GRACIA. But if you've a saint in the family you must expect to make these hard pilgrimages. But it's so good to see you.

María Isabel. Oh . . . much you care whether we come or not.

Sister Gracia. Don't say that, Mother, please.

María Isabel. Mother! Don't call me Mother. Call me Mamma as you did at home.

Sister Gracia. Yes, Mamma, I will.

[*She is sitting by her mother, gentle, affectionate.*]

María Isabel. Oh . . . your hands! What makes your fingers like that?

Sister Gracia. Peeling potatoes.

María Isabel. You have been peeling potatoes!

Sister Gracia. Why, of course. You see, when it's my week in the kitchen . . .

María Isabel. No, please . . . I don't want to hear about it.

[Trajano *has departed, but* Gabriel *lingers, surveying the group; and now he approaches* María Isabel, *with great elegance of deportment.*]

Gabriel. Will you allow me to wish you a good afternoon, Señorita María Isabel?

María Isabel. [*Blankly.*] Good afternoon.

Sister Gracia. Don't you recognise him? It's Gabriel.

Gabriel. Gabriel, Señorita . . . valet to the late Marquis . . . now in glory, and God rest his soul! Doesn't the Señorita remember me? I'm not so young as I was, of course, and . . . [*He looks himself up and down with a little laugh.*] the livery here isn't quite so fine as the Marquis's . . . now in glory. Not that I want to grumble . . . no indeed, one might be much worse off.

[*While* Gabriel *stands talking to* María Isabel. Sister Gracia *goes to her father who is pacing up and down, silently slips her hand in his, and walks with him, as if she were a little girl. He is moved by this, holds her hand very tight, looks down at her tenderly. But he is silent too.*]

María Isabel. Yes, indeed you might. You have a palace to live in, and a garden that a millionaire might envy you. What things are coming to, I don't know. An alms-house! Think of all the money that was spent on this place . . . the famous parties they gave here, when I was a girl . . . everybody used to talk about them.

GABRIEL. Yes . . . even from the pulpit. The Duke of Torre Blanca's palace . . . these high places of our Modern Babylon . . . that's what his Grace the Arch-bishop said.

MARÍA ISABEL. If these trees could speak!

GABRIEL. [*Chuckling.*] They'd have some pretty stories to tell! Look here, Señorita . . . this arbour used to be called the Bower of Venus. And it had a statue in it which his Grace the Duke had brought from Italy . . . a very female statue . . . the Señorita will understand me. And now, you see, the Sisters have put the blessed Saint Cayetano there instead . . . our mediator in heaven. [*He chuckles again.*] But the ghosts that come walking back here must give him some very queer nights of it. Oh, but all the best gentlemen of Madrid used to come here. . . .

MARÍA ISABEL. And the worst women!

GABRIEL. Well . . . God created the one lot to bal-ance the other, I suppose. And a fine lot they were, I tell you . . . worth staring at. They made the house what it was . . . and what it is. [*He grows confidential and important.*] For when his Grace the Duke went and died . . . his Grace, now in glory . . . probably . . . oh, they say they're not very hard on you up there when it has only been petticoats . . . when his Grace the Duke died here . . . for it was here he came back to die after trapesing all over the world . . . he'd hardly drawn his last breath when his two latest lady friends . . . one was fair and one was dark, and a pretty picture they made, I can tell you . . . they started to fill all the baskets and trunks in the place with whatever they could lay their hands on . . . clothes, pictures, mirrors, books, china . . . why, they took the very quilt off the poor gentleman's bed, a satin quilt it was, as thick as that, and embroidered

in colours with history-pictures two hundred years old!
They didn't let the grass grow under their feet . . . the
baggages. Why, it was like the day of judgment. And I
saw it. For I'd been sent to enquire after the sick man
by the Marquis . . . now in glory . . . and he was just
at his last gasp when I got here . . . and there was the
undertaker driving up at one door and the wagon full of
things . . . piled high with them . . . driving off from
the other. If they left the walls standing it was only that
they shouldn't dirty their pretty hands with the bricks
and mortar.

SISTER GRACIA. [*From her father's side.*] Gabriel . . .
you'll lose Trajano.

GABRIEL. Quite right, Señorita . . . and I won't
trouble the Señorita María Isabel any longer . . . and I
hope she'll forgive me having taken the liberty. . . .

MARÍA ISABEL. Not at all . . . I'm glad to see that
you're so happy here.

SISTER GRACIA. [*Quietly to her father—more a gesture
than a sentence.*] Give him something.

GABRIEL. A very good afternoon to you, Don Lorenzo.
LORENZO. God be with you.

[*He gives him a coin.* GABRIEL *protests as he
takes it.*]

GABRIEL. No, no . . . I couldn't think of it . . . I
really couldn't. There's nothing that we want here . . .
thank you, thank you! [*He glances furtively at the coin,
and is overwhelmed.*] Two pesetas . . . oh, a thousand
thanks!

SISTER GRACIA. Run along now . . . run along.

[GABRIEL *disappears, contemplating the coin and
murmuring ecstatically "Two pesetas!"* MARÍA
ISABEL *remains seated on the bench, musing over what
she has just heard.* LULU *gets up and goes to peep
through the foliage into the arbour.* SISTER GRACIA
still holds her father's hand.]

SISTER GRACIA. How silent you are, Father. Talk to me a little.

LORENZO. What about?

SISTER GRACIA. About yourself. What are you busy at now?

LORENZO. The usual things. I'm rather pressed with . . . lots of things to think about . . . and getting to feel rather old.

SISTER GRACIA. Old . . . you! Since when, pray?

LORENZO. Ever since a certain little witch gave up coming into my study and untidying my papers for me. [*His voice turns a little husky, but he keeps it firm.*] There's a vacant place there, young lady.

SISTER GRACIA. Ah . . . don't say that to me . . . don't say that.

LORENZO. [*Smiling again.*] There, there, never mind! When I'm quite decrepit I'll petition the authorities to admit me here . . . and then you will look after me, won't you?

> [*She doesn't answer; just kisses his hand. There are tears in his eyes.*]

LORENZO. As long as you're content . . . that's all that matters.

SISTER GRACIA. I am, Father . . . indeed I am.

LORENZO. Truly?

> [*She lifts her face like a child, so that he may see she is not lying, and he looks her in the eyes.*]

SISTER GRACIA. Yes, look at me . . . truly, truly. And more than content today . . . because you've come to see me.

> [*Without answering he rests his hand affectionately on her shoulder.* MARÍA ISABEL *surveys her husband and her daughter with a mixture of envy and commiseration.* LULU, *who has gone into the arbour, now gives a sudden cry, and rushes out again. They all turn to her.*]

María Isabel. What is it . . . what has happened?

Lulu. There . . . in the arbour . . . a man . . . or an animal . . . I don't know. But with eyes all burning . . . and it growled.

Sister Gracia. Don't be frightened. [*She goes and looks into the arbour.*] Oh, poor thing . . . it's Liborio. [*She calls gently.*] Come here. What are you doing in the arbour? Come out now . . . come out.

[*She pulls out a decrepit, pitiful, huddled up, trembling old negro, and draws him to a bench, talking the while.*]

Sister Gracia. This is the unluckiest of them all, poor fellow. He's . . . not quite right [*She taps her forehead.*] . . . but he's harmless.

[*María Isabel surveys the old thing with horror, and Lulu with disgust, Lorenzo with some interest.*]

Sister Gracia. [*Speaking as to a child.*] Look . . . you've frightened this lady. There now . . . take off your hat to her.

Liborio. Liborio . . . not take off his hat . . . nobody loves him here . . . this not his country.

Sister Gracia. Yes it is . . . oh yes, it is.

Liborio. [*Getting a little excited.*] No . . . oh no . . . not his country. His country lost . . . Cuba was lost. [*To Lorenzo*] That true, Señor? . . . yes . . . Cuba lost. [*Very mournfully.*] Liborio born in Cuba . . . no Cuba . . . so can't go back . . . no doubt of that . . . is there, Señor? [*Then a strange tone comes into his voice.*] No . . . not lost . . . the sea swallowed Cuba. But where's the sea . . . there's no sea either . . . no sea here. Only roads . . . roads . . . and Liborio walks . . . walks . . . walks. Oh, where is the sea? No sea . . . no sea. But policemen . . . and they beat you . . . and it's so cold . . . it's always cold here [*He is almost crying.*] . . . Liborio's cold.

Sister Gracia. [*Putting her arm round his shoulders as if really to warm him.*] No, no, you're not cold . . .

that's all imagination. There . . . sit down now . . .
and don't shake so [*Then, over her shoulder, to her
father.*] Give me a cigar.

[LORENZO *takes out a cigar.*]

SISTER GRACIA. Look, Liborio . . . just look what this
gentleman is giving us.

LIBORIO. [*His eye kindling a little.*] A cigar . . . a
cigar!

SISTER GRACIA. [*As pleased as he.*] Yes, a cigar . . .
and look at the band on it . . . that says it's from your
country . . . from Cuba.

LIBORIO. What—what then . . . Cuba not lost?

SISTER GRACIA. Why no . . . how can it be lost?
Now off with you and light it . . . and see how warm the
smoke will make you.

LIBORIO. [*Like a child.*] Yes . . . yes.

SISTER GRACIA. And then go to the kitchen . . . and
tell Sister Juliana that I said she was to give you a cup
of hot coffee.

LIBORIO. Coffee!

SISTER GRACIA. Yes . . . black coffee . . . as black as
you are. Come along . . . I'll take you as far as the door,
so that you shan't lose yourself. [*To her family.*] I'll
be back in a minute. Come along.

[*She takes the old negro out through the little doorway that leads to the kitchens.*]

MARÍA ISABEL. What a horrible man . . . he must
have the palsy . . . it gives one the creeps to look at
him.

LULU. And he smelt! How can she go near him!!

MARÍA ISABEL. The girl's stark mad. Lorenzo, we
must get her away from here at all costs.

[SISTER GRACIA *comes back and goes straight to her
father. She is still full of her care for the poor
creature.*]

SISTER GRACIA. Look here, Father . . . you're going to
send me some cheap cigars . . . some of those confiscated

smuggled ones they sell off . . . and you're to keep all the bands from your Havanas, so that I can put them on the others . . . and then the poor thing can imagine. . . .

María Isabel. [*Suddenly breaking out.*] What your father will do if he has one ounce of common sense . . . for you haven't . . . is to take you home with him this very minute.

Sister Gracia. [*Startled and grieved.*] Mother!

María Isabel. My dear child . . . this has been a very pretty whim . . . but it has lasted long enough. Three months in a hospital dressing people's sores and laying them out when they were dead. Six months a probationer . . . making yourself look such a fright with that thing on your head. And now here . . . among these disgusting old men . . . why, they may be lepers! No . . . no more of it . . . Home you come with us this very minute.

Sister Gracia. [*Her eyes cast down . . . but her voice firm.*] No . . . I can't do that, Mother.

María Isabel. Why can't you, pray?

Sister Gracia. I have taken a vow.

María Isabel. Oh yes . . . for a year.

Sister Gracia. In my heart . . . I took it for all my life.

María Isabel. Don't talk nonsense.

Sister Gracia. It's not nonsense, Mother.

María Isabel. It is ridiculous affectation. You're a spoiled child . . . you've always been given your own way. And now you want to play at being a nun . . . just as you used to play sweethearts.

Sister Gracia. Mother!

María Isabel. But please remember, my dear, that you're not of age yet. Your father can have something to say to this.

Sister Gracia. Father gave his consent.

María Isabel. He did not . . . and you know that perfectly well. He let you go and said nothing about it

. . . which is not the same thing at all. You took very good care to leave the house when he wasn't there. And why? Because you were afraid he'd stop you.

SISTER GRACIA. That wasn't the reason.

MARÍA ISABEL. Wasn't it? Then perhaps it was because you hadn't the courage to say goodbye to him. Well . . . answer me.

SISTER GRACIA. Yes, that was why.

MARÍA ISABEL. Oh, you never found it very hard to get round people. [*Then to her husband.*] Well, here's your spoilt baby . . . Papa's darling . . . always in his pocket . . . crying if her dear father left home without saying goodbye to her . . . couldn't go to sleep at night unless he came in to kiss her . . . was to grow up to be the comfort of his old age. Well, here you have it . . . the comfort and happiness she promised you. And because she calls her conduct by a fine sounding name . . .

SISTER GRACIA. But, Mother, I've done nothing wrong.

MARÍA ISABEL. [*With a final fling of sorrowful wrath.*] And this is what children are given us for!

LORENZO. [*Quietly intervening.*] María Isabel . . . children are not an idle gift.

MARÍA ISABEL. What do you mean?

LORENZO. I mean that they are not our own just to do as we like with.

MARÍA ISABEL. So like a man! Easy to see that you don't suffer to bring them into the world.

LORENZO. [*Gravely.*] We sweat blood though, sometimes, to keep them alive in it. But we owe them more than that. Did we so deliberately plan to bring them into the world? They are ours through our frailty.

MARÍA ISABEL. Frailty!

LORENZO. What else? And if they are the fruit of our happiness what right have we to deny them their own . . . unless they seek it in evil ways?

MARÍA ISABEL. And you believe she'll find happiness here?

LORENZO. She has made herself believe so. What then can I say?

SISTER GRACIA. But I haven't *made* myself believe it, Father . . . I haven't indeed.

MARÍA ISABEL. Petted and brought up in luxury as she has been!

LORENZO. You were brought up in just such luxury. You were rich and came of a great family and you were nineteen as she is now. Every sort of pleasure was yours for the asking, and life promised you very many of them. Then you met me . . . a good for nothing, a firebrand . . . so your family told you. And certainly I was a nobody. But you gave up everything to endure privations and persecutions and suffering by my side. Isabel, have you forgotten the courage with which you faced it all . . . just for the sake of the love that we so believed in? Our first child was born in an attic . . . that's twenty-five years ago. Have you forgotten? I've not forgotten my debt to you. [*He kisses her hand.*] Ah, my dear . . . don't give your own nature the lie when you see it again in your daugher.

MARÍA ISABEL. What I did, I did because I loved you. That was very different.

SISTER GRACIA. Mother . . . I do this for love.

MARÍA ISABEL. [*Recovering her ill-temper.*] Love . . . who for? God! D'you imagine you're Saint Teresa?

SISTER GRACIA. No, Mother . . . I don't imagine any such thing. I know that I'm nobody. But then you don't need to be anybody here . . . for we're all nobodies together. Here, you see, we gather in people that the world has no more use for . . . no one loves them or wants them . . . they've nowhere to go . . . the poor, the sick, the homeless. Well then, one needs to be a nobody to be of any use to them . . . it's so much better to be a nobody . . . for the less you count in the world yourself . . . the closer you come to them.

MARÍA ISABEL. You need not live among poor people in order to help them.

SISTER GRACIA. Oh yes, Mother . . . oh yes, you must.

MARÍA ISABEL. Not at all. You can be charitable . . . you can give alms.

SISTER GRACIA. [*Quite carried away now.*] Give alms! No . . . no . . . oh, no! Where's the good in giving away a little of what you have too much of . . . and keeping the rest . . . and not caring . . . spending money amusing oneself . . . while they have so much to endure . . . and you do nothing for them, nothing at all. Because giving alms is nothing . . . oh, I don't mean one shouldn't give alms. But no . . . [*To her father.*] oh, isn't this true . . . for you've said so a thousand times . . . that one must give one's life, one's whole life . . . to the last breath and the last drop of blood, if one wants to atone for the wickedness of the world. For misery is wickedness and want is a crime . . . because God gave his world to us all alike . . . and our daily bread. And if his children starve and are homeless . . . that's a crime, yes, a crime. And the man who keeps more than he needs robs the man who's in need. Turn away your eyes when your brother is dying . . . and you're an accomplice in his death. Oh, Father, Father . . . when I've heard you speak . . . if only I could have been a man, a man like you . . . to speak like that so that people must hear me . . . and plead the cause of the oppressed, stand up for them, make laws that will help them! But of course I'm only an ignorant girl. What can I do? I might stand and shout for ever, and no one would listen. I'm no use. I'm nobody. I've nothing to give but my happiness . . . so I want to give that, you see, to those that have none.

LORENZO. My dear . . . my dear . . .

SISTER GRACIA. Because no one seems to think of giving that. Food, oh yes . . . but happiness! Why, if it's only

to amuse them a little . . . to joke with them . . . and
then to make believe, so that just for a little they *may* believe that there's still something left for them to hope
for . . . that they still count for something in the world
. . . that they're human beings still. That's what matters,
isn't it, Father?

LORENZO. Yes, you're right. That's to say. . . . Ah
yes, my dear . . . believing as you do you are right to be
doing what you do.

MARÍA ISABEL. And you say that, do you . . . when
you believe in nothing at all.

LORENZO. I may not . . . but then she does.

MARÍA ISABEL. [*To* SISTER GRACIA.] You show great
consideration . . . for everybody but us.

SISTER GRACIA. But you don't need me.

MARÍA ISABEL. And to think that when you were so
high . . . how I cried and cried when they said you might
die of diphtheria . . . and I took a vow to wear a peni-
tent's dress for a year . . . and I cut off all my hair that
your father was so fond of . . . and now . . . this is
what happens. [*She begins to cry.*] One never does
know what one is really asking God to grant.

SISTER GRACIA. [*Putting her arms round her mother,
but smiling in spite of herself.*] Oh, mamma, don't say
that . . . just because I'm still alive.

[LULU, *when this discussion began, had moved away
to a further bench and begun to read a letter she took
from her bag. She puts it away now, and rejoins
the group.*]

LULU. Well . . . is the storm over? [*To* SISTER
GRACIA.] Oh, my dear . . . mothers are very hard
things to understand, aren't they? She's angry with you
because you want to be a nun . . . and just as angry with
me because I want to get married. [*Then with juvenile
superiority.*] The fact is, I suppose, that if older people
couldn't amuse themselves by upsetting themselves about
nothing, they'd be bored to death . . . poor things!

María Isabel.   What's that you say?

Lulu.   [*With her soubrettish air.*]   Oh . . . each time of life has its own sort of trouble.   Young people are desperate because old people won't let them have their own way, and the old people are furious because the young ones won't do what they think right.   So nobody's content.

María Isabel.   What has come over these girls . . . [*To her husband.*]   And you listen to this so calmly. . . .

Lulu.   Papa always listens calmly when one's in the right.

Lorenzo.   But even if you're in the right you could put it more prettily.

[*Sister Manuela comes back along the path.*]

Sister Gracia.   The Superior, Mother.

Sister Manuela.   Good afternoon.

[*She looks at everybody and can tell well enough what has been going on.   One should note that Sisters of Charity in Spain do not shake hands with men, though they may embrace their fathers and mothers.*]

Lorenzo.   Good afternoon, Señora.

María Isabel.   Good afternoon.

[*She rises, still a little disturbed.   Lulu salutes Sister Manuela who acknowledges it.   The sun has now set and it begins to grow dark.*]

Sister Gracia.   My mother . . . my father . . . my sister.

Sister Manuela.   So pleased.   Well . . . at last you have made up your minds to come.   Sister Gracia must be delighted . . . she has been longing to see you.   So have we.   She has been with us five weeks now . . . and though you're so near you've not been to visit her . . .

María Isabel.   [*A little aggressively.*]   You can understand, I think, that it isn't very pleasant for a father and mother to come only to make up their minds to their daughter burying herself alive in such a depressing place as this.

SISTER GRACIA. Mamma!

SISTER MANUELA. [*With a touch of irony.*] Oh, it
isn't so bad. We have our small share of the pleasures of
life too. Blue sky . . . fresh air . . . sunshine . . . and
if you listen you can hear the birds singing quite contentedly before going to bed.

LULU. It is a beautiful garden.

SISTER MANUELA. Do you think so? Would you like,
perhaps, to follow your sister's example . . . and come to
us too?

MARÍA ISABEL. No, no . . . for heaven's sake! One
crack-brain in the family is enough. Our only hope is
that this one will recover her senses and come home again.

SISTER MANUELA. Well . . . she always can, of
course. Our order takes no perpetual vows. Our sainted
founder thought well to account for the weakness of human
will. If any one of us finds her chain too heavy she can
break it whenever she likes.

LORENZO. [*Smiling.*] Yes . . . it's an ideal union, no
doubt. A heavenly marriage . . . with divorce at the discretion of one of the parties.

SISTER MANUELA. [*Taking this quite well.*] Oh
really, really! But if you knew how very seldom anyone
wants to leave us. . . .

LORENZO. Why, of course . . . easy divorce makes marriage lasting.

SISTER MANUELA. Ah . . . don't talk like that, please.
But do sit down.

MARÍA ISABEL. No, thank you . . . we must be going.
And I'm sure you've lots to do . . . both of you.

SISTER MANUELA. As it's Sunday the dinner bell won't
ring till half past five. And Sister Gracia's on duty . . .
so she has to wait in the garden till all the old men that
have been out for their walk are safely back again. You
can quite well keep her company here if you like.

MARÍA ISABEL. No . . . no, thank you . . . we really
must go.

SISTER MANUELA. Well, come this way. We'll go through the greenhouse and I'll ask them to pick you a bunch of flowers. Sister Gracia always tells us how fond her mother is of flowers. So am I. That's a worldly failing I brought here with me twenty years ago . . . unconquered still.

[THE MOTHER SUPERIOR *goes on with* LORENZO *and* MARÍA ISABEL. SISTER GRACIA *and* LULU *follow them. Just as they disappear* SISTER JULIANA *can be seen at the little kitchen door looking after them curiously. She has a kitchen apron over her habit, a knife and a loaf in her hands, for she is slicing the bread for supper.*]

SISTER JULIANA. Oh . . . how pretty they look. And what hats!

[*She sighs and goes back to the kitchen. The dusk is deepening now. After a moment three old men pass along on their way in. The first, leaning heavily on his stick, does not stop. The second pauses at each bench he comes to, and sits down, wiping it first very carefully with his handkerchief. The third stops at every other step, gesticulating, talking to himself as if he were addressing some one else. First he argues, hotly, wrathfully. Then he looks at his supposed adversary with pitying condescension and assents ironically to what the fellow has been saying, as if he were humouring a madman. Finally he takes off his hat and bows, as if to let him pass. And then when the phantom has turned his back, he laughs, shrugs, watches him disappear, and then goes on his own way with the greatest complacency. Then a Sister of Charity passes with some flowers in her hand. And then* LIBORIO *comes from the kitchens, with his cigar still in his hand, and singing in great content. . . .*]

LIBORIO. Far off I see the Cuban mountains. . . .

[*The bell calling the Sisters to their refectory begins to ring.*]

LIBORIO. Bell! Sisters now going to supper. Sunday! chicken! Chicken and ham! Let them have chicken and let them have ham. Good women . . . give me coffee . . . and tobacco. [*He kisses the cigar.*] Aha . . . brown darling . . . brown darling . . . I kiss you because you were born . . . so happy . . . over there.

> [*He goes on his way. The horn of a motor car is heard; and then* SISTER GRACIA *comes back looking anxiously about.*]

SISTER GRACIA. Oh . . . it's nearly dark . . . and those two are not back. [*Calling.*] Trajano! Gabriel!

> [TRAJANO'S *voice is now heard, for he is singing at the top of it. After a moment he appears. He is a little drunk and in high good fellowship with* GABRIEL, *who is very cheery and a little drunk too, and has his arm protectingly round* TRAJANO'S *shoulder.*]

TRAJANO. [*Trolling it out.*]

> Democracy's bright sword shall shine,
> Its dauntless trumpet blow;
> The blood of noble and of priest . . .

SISTER GRACIA. What's that you're singing?

> The throne shall be the first to fall,
> The church the last to end . . .

GABRIEL. That's right! Hurrah for the Republic! Glory be to the Goddess of Liberty!

SISTER GRACIA. Oh, Trajano! Oh, Gabriel . . .

> That wildest beast of all no more
> The Nation's heart shall rend!

SISTER GRACIA. Well, this time you've surpassed yourself, Trajano! This is how you keep your word to a lady! Drunk again!

TRAJANO. [*With the utmost dignity.*] I . . . drunk!
Well . . . let me see now, let me see. Are you drunk,
Trajano? Speak the truth, now. Yes, Señor Trajano
Fernandez is undoubtedly drunk. But he is a free citizen
. . . so what has any one to say to that? And what has
the lady-bishop to say to that? Bring her here . . . fetch
her right out here . . . the lady-bishop, so that I can drink
her health in the name of the most worshipful Republic.

GABRIEL. In the name of her royal highness the Republic . . .

[GABRIEL *laughs foolishly and then pretends to open
a carriage door and to bow the lady out.*]

GABRIEL. Will your royal highness the Republic be
pleased to step in? If your royal highness will be good
enough to give me your card, I will immediately acquaint
the Warden . . . whom God preserve.

TRAJANO. I drink to the lady-bishop! Can't you see
that I'm drinking to the lady-bishop?

SISTER GRACIA. Oh . . . for God's sake, Trajano . . .

TRAJANO. [*Solemnly.*] For whose sake? Will you
please to remember that my god is not the god of Sinai?
No, indeed! [*Then to* GABRIEL.] Is there a brotherhood
of man, or is there not?

GABRIEL. Brotherhood-a-man? Please to step in, Señor
Brotherhood-a-man. If your excellency would be kind
enough . . .

TRAJANO. Is there a brotherhood of man or is there
not?

SISTER GRACIA. Yes, by all means . . . only do be quiet
or I shall get so scolded.

TRAJANO. Oh no . . . I'll not have that. If they attempt to scold you I shall raise an insurrection . . . I say
that I will raise an insurrection.

SISTER GRACIA. Yes, yes . . . but quietly.

TRAJANO. I will raise that insurrection because I wish
to raise that insurrection . . .

SISTER GRACIA. What you'd better do now at once is

to go and put your head under the pump and see if cold
water won't sober you. Then no one need find out the
state you came back in.

[*She takes him firmly by the arm and tries to get
him away.*]

TRAJANO. Water . . . cold   water! Never! Death
rather than submission to tyranny.

SISTER GRACIA. [*Trying not to laugh.*]   Oh dear, oh
dear!

[LIBORIO *comes back. He is crying.* GABRIEL
greets him ceremoniously.]

GABRIEL. Will your grace the duke kindly step in? If
your grace will be kind enough to hand me your card . . .

SISTER GRACIA. Now what's happened to you?

[TRAJANO *looks at* LIBORIO *curiously and slowly
goes up to him.*]

LIBORIO. Liborio cold . . . Liborio's cold.

SISTER GRACIA. Cold . . . on a beautiful evening like
this? Why . . . didn't you smoke the cigar I gave you?

LIBORIO. Liborio not smoke . . . they beat him . . .
they steal cigar.

SISTER GRACIA. Stole the cigar . . . who did?

TRAJANO. The government stole it, Señora . . . this
damned tax-gathering government stole it. [*To* LIBORIO.]
Now, don't you put up with it . . . you rise in rebel-
lion.

SISTER GRACIA. [*To* TRAJANO.] Now you be quiet.
[*To* LIBORIO.] Who stole it?

LIBORIO. White man . . . Spanish man . . . down in
orchard.

SISTER GRACIA. In the orchard! Was it the gardener?
The brute! There, don't cry . . . I'll make it all right.

LIBORIO. So Liborio no smoke it . . . Liborio no smoke
it.

SISTER GRACIA. But you shall. Tomorrow I'll give
you a cigar as big as . . . that.

[*The three old men are round* SISTER GRACIA *looking at her attentively.* LIBORIO *is sitting on a bench and she holds his hand.*]

LIBORIO.   No tobacco here . . . no tobacco here.

SISTER GRACIA.   Never mind then . . . we'll go to your country to find some.

LIBORIO.   No, no . . . not my country.   Cuba lost . . . Cuba lost.

SISTER GRACIA.   Yes, I know it was.   But now it has been found again.

LIBORIO.   Where?

[SISTER GRACIA *looks round at a loss.   Then, with an inspiration, she points to the evening star that is just visible in the sky.*]

SISTER GRACIA.   There . . . look . . . look at it.

LIBORIO.   Where?

SISTER GRACIA.   There . . . up there . . . the star. Don't you see how beautiful it is . . . all alone . . . as it used to be on your flag.   Look how it shines.   There . . . there's your country.

LIBORIO.   The star . . . the star!   That Cuba?

SISTER GRACIA.   Yes . . . didn't I tell you it had been found again?   So now shall we go there . . . you and I together?

TRAJANO.   And I?

GABRIEL.   And I?

SISTER GRACIA.   Yes, all four of us.   We'll sail away in a boat . . .

LIBORIO.   No sea left now. . . .

SISTER GRACIA.   But what do we want with the sea? We'll sail our boat through the air . . . tonight when the moon rises.   So come along now.

TRAJANO.   Yes indeed . . . 'tenshun . . . quick march!

> Democracy's bright sword shall shine
> Its dauntless trumpet . . .

[GABRIEL *sees* SISTER MANUELA *at one of the windows and whispers in terror.*]

GABRIEL. The lady-bishop!

TRAJANO. What?

[*He is as dumbfounded, and looks round wondering what to do or say. Then a happy thought strikes him and he breaks gently into a different song.*]

TRAJANO. Oh . . . bleeding heart of Mary,
            Our succour and . . .

SISTER MANUELA. [*From the window.*] Who's that singing?

[*The old men now hold their breath in anguish.*]

SISTER GRACIA. It's Trajano. He's here with me, Reverend Mother.

SISTER MANUELA. Is any one missing?

SISTER GRACIA. No, Reverend Mother . . . they're all back now.

SISTER MANUELA. Bring them in then, or they'll take cold in this night air.

SISTER GRACIA. Yes, Reverend Mother.

[SISTER MANUELA *disappears, and the old men breathe again.*]

SISTER GRACIA. Come along now . . . come along.

[*She goes first with* LIBORIO. *The two others follow her.* TRAJANO *singing in a whisper and hushing* GABRIEL, *apparently under the impression that it is he.*]

TRAJANO. Democracy's bright sword shall shine . . .
            Sh! . . .
            Its dauntless trumpet . . .
            Sh! Sh! . . .

GABRIEL. The most serene lady-bishop is served.

SISTER GRACIA. Come along now . . . quietly.

LIBORIO. The   star . . . the   star . . . Cuba   not lost . . .

TRAJANO. The blood of nobles and of priests . . .
            Sh! . . .

Unceasingly shall flow . . .
The throne shall be . . .
Sh! . . . Sh! . . .
[*They go out by the little kitchen door. It is now
quite dark.*]

CURTAIN

ACT II

A large patio which serves as a place of recreation for the inmates of a maternity home (for women who have "come to grief"), which has been established in some old noble mansion in the north of Castile.

The patio has thus something of the cloister about it, with its covered corridor, high gallery and great doors that open to the rooms which are now the eating and sleeping rooms of the institution.

The centre of the patio was once a garden, no doubt; now it is nothing but a jungle of uncared-for shrubs, lilies, celandine, hawthorn, and a tree or two, a walnut, a chestnut tree. On one side there is a well with its bucket and wheel and a stone trough that serves for a washing place. It is springtime, and some of the shrubs are in flower. On their branches though, hang sets of babies' clothing, aprons and handkerchiefs.

CANDELAS, CECILIA *and the* DUMB GIRL *are in the patio.* CANDELAS *is a swarthy young woman, with a bit of the devil about her. She has fine black-green eyes, and looks serpentlike when she moves about. She is poorly dressed, in a calico skirt which has been much turned, a blouse, and a knitted handkerchief crossed over her breast and tied at the back. Her voice is harsh. She has put a flower in her hair. Her sleeves are turned up over her brown arms while she washes some handkerchiefs in the trough. And she sings . . .*

CANDELAS. Aie!

> I asked a sick man the complaint
> Of which he was to die;
> "Of loving you . . . of loving you,"
> The sick man made reply.

[CECILIA *wearily lets fall the stocking she is knitting.*]

CECILIA. Aie!

CANDELAS. And what's the matter with you?

CECILIA. Nothing. I know that song.

CANDELAS. Well . . . singing scares away your troubles.

CECILIA. That depends on what they are.

CANDELAS. [*Mockingly.*] Oh, Holy Mother . . . depends on what they are, does it? What *are* your troubles, I should like to know? You fell in love and you had a baby. Well . . . what else are women for? Then he deserted you and they took you in here out of charity . . . and your character's gone . . . but that had gone a bit earlier, hadn't it? What you've got to do, my girl, is to make the best of a bad job . . . there's no help for it now, anyway. Besides . . . things happen because they're meant to . . . and you make them no better by crying about them. The day that your mother bore you your steps in this world were all counted . . . from your first to your last one.

[*She goes on with her washing . . . vigorously.*]

CECILIA. [*Half to herself.*] Oh . . . if I'd known how it was all going to end. . . .

CANDELAS. Yes, my girl . . . it's all been settled beforehand, every bit of it . . . and you've only to wait for it to come to pass. And nothing happens to any one that hasn't happened sometime to some one else. I tell you this world's like a road with a lot of inns along it . . . and if you're not cheated in one of them, why, you will be in another . . . and whichever one of them it is someone's always been cheated there before you. But I know . . . once you're all dressed up and ready to start you think you know everything . . . and nobody can advise you!

[*She keeps at her washing more furiously than ever and begins her song again.* SISTER CRISTINA, *a Sister of Charity, aged about 45, comes into the patio. She is the head of the Home, and is a sympathetic, well-bred woman, with an unaffected motherly dignity about her. But she thinks of the women under her charge as lost souls, for all that she pities them, as a woman may who knows what life is.*

The great door by which she enters the patio has written over it in black letters the word "Lactantia." She unlocks and locks it again with the large key which is hung with the rosary at her belt. She crosses the patio slowly, taking in everything at a glance, picking up a little child's cap that has fallen from one of the branches and replacing it. She comes up to the group of women. CANDELAS, when she sees her, leaves her washing and dries her hands on her apron. CECILIA picks up her stocking again. The DUMB GIRL does not move.]

CECILIA. [*As she rises.*] Here's the Superior.

[*SISTER CRISTINA goes to the dumb girl and putting a hand on her head, says kindly.*]

SISTER CRISTINA. Good mornïng, my child . . . getting some fresh air . . . you're feeling stronger today.

[*The DUMB GIRL presses the baby she has in her arms to her breast and makes a queer unintelligible but rather frightened sound.*]

SISTER CRISTINA. Why, I'm not going to take him away from you! Don't hold him so tight . . . you'll smother him. Yes, he's your very own . . . don't be afraid. But let me look at him. What a beautiful boy. [*Then she turns to CECILIA.*] And what about yours?

CECILIA. [*Hanging her head.*] He's asleep.

[CECILIA's *baby is in a basket turned cradle close beside her. As she goes to take it out SISTER CRISTINA bends over and says.*]

SISTER CRISTINA. Why, he must be nearly suffocated with all those clothes on him. Here, give him to me. Why, you don't even know how to dress a child. Little angel! So . . . let the air get to his head . . . then he

may grow up with a few more brains than his mother has.
Here . . . take him now.

> [*She takes the heavy shawl from the child's head
> and after tidying him gives him back to* CECILIA, *who
> immediately puts him back in the basket again.*]

SISTER CRISTINA. What . . . back in his basket again!
Don't you feel like walking him up and down a little . . .
or making some clothes for him . . . or even washing his
face? What have you been doing all the morning . . .
lying here like a log!

CECILIA. I've been crying . . .

SISTER CRISTINA. Crying! It's too late for that now.

CANDELAS. That's just what I tell her.

SISTER CRISTINA. Ah . . . and I've something to say to
you too.

CANDELAS. Yes, please Señora . . .

SISTER CRISTINA. Yes, please, Señora! . . . but it goes
in at one ear and out at the other.

CANDELAS. Oh no, Señora. Have I done something
wrong? Honour bright . . . I never meant to.

SISTER CRISTINA. Never meant to glue your face to the
dormitory window-grating and begin shouting at the top
of your voice to those men, whoever they were, passing
along the road?

CANDELAS. Muleteers they were . . . and they came
from my village.

SISTER CRISTINA. Indeed! You're very anxious to let
your village know that you're in a place like this.

CANDELAS. Well, it's no disgrace.

SISTER CRISTINA. Oh, not the least in the world, of
course.

CANDELAS. [*Passionately.*] Why, this isn't a prison,
is it? The police didn't bring me here for stealing or murder or doing any harm to anyone. I came because I chose
to . . . and because I was unlucky enough to go loving a
man far better than he deserved. And as I wasn't born

a Duchess or an Infanta of Spain myself I couldn't get my baby born into gold swaddling clothes, could I?

SISTER CRISTINA. Very well . . . don't get excited about it.

[*She is going on her way. But* CANDELAS *stops her.*]

CANDELAS. Sister Cristina!

SISTER CRISTINA. What is it?

CANDELAS. When are you going to let me go?

SISTER CRISTINA. You know well enough . . . in another four months' time.

CANDELAS. [*Sullenly.*] I've been here two already.

SISTER CRISTINA. Quite so . . . you have been here two, and there are four to come. That makes the six you have to stay.

CANDELAS. [*Protesting.*] Have to!

SISTER CRISTINA. [*Quietly and gravely.*] Yes . . . have to, young lady. The institution receives you, cares for you, doctors you, gives you all that you need. And in return you have to stay here and nurse a child. You were told that when you came.

CANDELAS. But mine's dead.

SISTER CRISTINA. And therefore you nurse someone else's . . . a poor little foundling. You have no child, and he has no mother, and our Charity brings you together. But aren't you glad to be doing a good deed?

CANDELAS. [*Passionately.*] Devils . . . heartless she-devils . . . to leave a baby on your doorstep like a dog. Mother of God . . . if mine had lived wouldn't I have walked out of here with my head high . . . and him in my arms.

CECILIA. That'd have been a fine sight, I'm sure!

CANDELAS. [*In a fury.*] A fine sight, would it? Well, I'd come here over again, so I would, if I could have him alive. Oh, let me go, Sister Cristina, do! Let me get away from here . . . for the love of God, let me.

Look, I'll take the one I'm nursing now away with me, and treat it like my own . . . I will.

SISTER CRISTINA.   And next week you'd leave it on the doorstep here and be off and up to your tricks again as gay and as careless as you please.   No, my girl, no . . . I'm an old hand now and know you, all of you . . . much better than I could wish.   Here you stay your four short months . . . for they'll be the only ones you'll live as God meant you to. . . . [*She turns.*]   What's this?

> [SISTER FELICIANA, *a much older woman, comes through one of the doors, unlocking and locking it again with her key.   She brings with her* QUICA, *a woman from some Castilian village, ugly, dirty and unkempt.   She is holding a black shawl up to her mouth, and has a cotton handkerchief roughly tied round her head.*]

SISTER FELICIANA.   Here we have quite an unexpected guest to entertain!   [*Then to* QUICA, *who is hanging back in pretended shame.*]   Come here, woman, and don't go on like that.   You ought to be used to it by this time.

QUICA.   Good afternoon, Sister Cristina.

SISTER CRISTINA.   [*Recognising her.*]   You . . . Quica . . . you!

SISTER FELICIANA.   [*Sarcastically.*]   Yes, Señora . . . and in all her glory!   And it's so long since we last had the pleasure of her company, isn't it?

SISTER CRISTINA.   [*Very angry.*]   But . . . here again . . . for the fourth time!   And not a year since you left us!

QUICA.   [*Her head down but smiling ingratiatingly.*] Well . . . I can't see that we're to blame . . . for the poor little brats being so anxious to come into the world. We don't want 'em . . . you may take it from me.

SISTER CRISTINA.   Hold your tongue!   Have you no shame?

QUICA.   Well . . . anyone can make a mistake, I suppose.

SISTER CRISTINA. One mistake . . . yes. But three! And at your age too! You ought to know better.

SISTER FELICIANA. [*With brutal sarcasm.*] And with that face . . . and got up as you are . . . a sight for sore eyes, I must say!

QUICA. Well, you'd have to be precious ugly not to find someone that'd look at you.

[SISTER FELICIANA *departs.*]

SISTER CRISTINA. Has the doctor seen you yet?

QUICA. Yes, Sister. Sister Feliciana has got the form filled out.

SISTER CRISTINA. Well, then . . . go and wash your face and tidy your hair. You don't earn enough by your wicked life, I see, to buy a brush and comb.

[QUICA *approaches* SISTER CRISTINA, *wheedlingly, stoops and tries to kiss the crucifix that hangs from her rosary.*]

QUICA. Sister Cristina . . .

SISTER CRISTINA. You know the way. No . . . I don't want to have anything to do with you.

QUICA. Oh, don't be angry with me, Sister Cristina. It's me that's got to suffer after all.

SISTER CRISTINA. Yes, my girl, that's true . . . and it seems as if you were all so anxious to get to hell that you didn't mind what you went through to make your way there. [*Then to* CANDELAS *as she walks away.*] And don't you stay here washing till the day of judgment. No one has asked you to. And if you catch cold we shall only have to take care of you.

CANDELAS. I want to earn the bread that I eat here . . . that's why I do it.

SISTER CRISTINA. [*Smiling.*] You're very scrupulous all of a sudden.

CANDELAS. Well, we've all got our pride!

SISTER CRISTINA. There . . . don't be touchy. Our duty here is to befriend you whether you deserve it or not. [*Then to* CECILIA.] Look after that child now, addle-

pate. Goodness, woman . . . no one would think it was
your own!

> [*She crosses the patio and goes out, locking the door
> behind her.*]

CANDELAS. Look there now . . . bolts and bars so that
you shan't run away. Mother of God . . . if I could fly
. . . I'd be a carrion crow!

CECILIA. She never sees you without scolding at you.

QUICA. [*Who has dropped her false shame and now
seems rather pleased with herself.*] Yes, and she can scold
. . . because she knows what she's scolding about. Before
she put that dress on she was a woman the same as any
of us . . . and she knows the world . . . not like the
others . . . shocked at every mortal thing. [*Confidentially
to* CANDELAS.] She was a widow, she was . . . and they
say that she loved her man more than the apple of her eye
. . . so did he her . . . and when he died she turned herself
into a nun just so that she shouldn't love anyone else ever
again . . . and she wasn't more than twenty-five!

CANDELAS. [*Passionately.*] Well, she was right . . .
for when you've lost your own man, the world's a deal too
full of the rest of them.

QUICA. Oh, it all depends. Is this your first time
here?

CANDELAS. First and last . . . I take my oath.

QUICA. [*Cheerfully.*] But it's not so bad. To start
with it doesn't cost you a cent . . . and you've a good doctor . . . and then there are the Sisters . . . and though
they do think you the lowest of the low they look after you
for dear charity's sake as if you were a queen. Why as
soon as you're put·to bed they kill a chicken for you . . .
they do indeed. You get soup and your glass of sherry and
chocolate and sponge cakes . . . and you've nothing to do
for months but nurse a baby. And if you care to stay another six and nurse another they'll pay you four dollars a
month for it. What more could you ask for? I've nursed
seven already . . . counting my own and other people's.

I've lived four years and six months for nothing . . . and I've had about a thousand pesetas out of them.

CANDELAS. Well . . . I wouldn't come back for a million pesetas. I'd sooner die in the gutter like a dog . . . starve and freeze there . . . and be free. Why . . . here am I chained up for six months . . . and he with all the world to himself to do as he likes in . . . and forget me . . . if he gets a chance.

QUICA. Needn't ask who he is, I suppose?

CANDELAS. No, Señora . . . he was the father of my son.

QUICA. Well, I shouldn't worry. If you do find he's forgotten you . . . you can find someone else to remember you quick enough. There are men in the world and to spare.

CANDELAS. There's only one for me.

QUICA. Perhaps you're right . . . and they're all alike anyway! [*Then to* CECILIA.] That's so, isn't it?

CECILIA. I've never known but one . . . and he was a cur. That's his baby. [*She points to the basket.*] . . . because it *is* his . . . though his devil of a mother does say it isn't. There it is in a basket and wrapped up in a few old rags like a kitten . . . and he riding in his carriage. Five dollars he gave me when the old lady threw me out of the house. Five dollars! And him with stacks of money. [*She started speaking quietly enough, but now her voice has risen with excitement.*] Just think what I was when I went into service there . . . and then where I was when I left it! And then on the top of it all she had the face to say to me . . . the old swine . . . that I'd gone and seduced her son . . . because he wasn't of age! I know now what the old devil was up to. Wasn't of age! What about me? I wasn't eighteen. And I know what I ought to have done instead of coming here like a fool . . . made a scandal and put the two of them in gaol . . . yes, him and his mother both. For she knew well enough what was going on . . . and as long as there wasn't a baby coming she was quite pleased for the boy to be getting his fun at home . . . for then he didn't want to get married . . . for when he gets married he gets half all their money, and that doesn't suit her at all. Curse him . . . and his mother . . . and his child . . . and me too for a fool to trust what he said to me . . . when he wanted to get his way. Said he was the master so he was . . . and all that he had he'd give me. It didn't cost him much, when his mother threw me out of the house to get out of that little promise. Think of it . . . think. Five dollars! Five dollars for life . . . and me with a baby on my back. And if I leave it behind me here I'm a bad mother. And if I take it I'm marked down a bad lot wherever I turn.

QUICA. Why don't you send it to its grandmamma by parcel post?

CANDELAS. [*Muttering gloomily to herself.*] Oh . . . if mine had lived . . .

CECILIA. [*Bitterly.*] Five dollars!

QUICA. Yes . . . if it was money you were after you did make a good bargain, didn't you!

CECILIA. And some women get motor-cars. . . .

QUICA. [*With confident philosophy.*] Ah . . . you're too young for that yet. Nobody gets anything out of it the first time . . . except [*She points to the baby in the basket.*] just what you've got out of it. Well, I'd better be off to my ward or Sister Cristina will be after me.

[*As she turns to go she literally tumbles over the* DUMB GIRL, *who, with her queer cry of alarm, clasps her baby tight to protect it.* QUICA *herself is startled for the moment.*]

QUICA. Saints in Heaven! Sorry . . . I didn't see you. But whatever do you mean by sitting listening there . . . as if you hadn't a mouth to open?

[*The* DUMB GIRL *glowers at her suspiciously.*]

CANDELAS. She *is* dumb.

QUICA. [*With cheerful cynicism.*] Dumb is she! And they say that it's getting into talk with men is the

ruin of you. Didn't make much odds to her! But there
. . . when it's God's will you've only got to nod your head.
[*She turns again to the dumb girl reinforcing what she says
with much gesture.*] What . . . was he a handsome fellow, eh? . . . baby's father?

CANDELAS. Don't waste your time . . . she doesn't
know a thing you're saying. You can make signs and write
things to her in Spanish and French and everything else
. . . there's nothing they haven't tried. One of the Sisters
that's been in a deaf and dumb school asked her and asked
her who she was and where she came from and such like
. . . and she didn't even wink. The Warden says she's
an idiot. But the doctor says she isn't . . . and that it's a
mystery . . . and she must come from some country . . .
I forget where . . . but it's a long way away and the sun
shines there in the middle of the night.

QUICA. [*A little uneasily.*] But however did she get
here?

CANDELAS. Nobody knows. One fine morning about
two months back they opened the street door and found
her lying flat on the ground in a faint . . . half starved
she was and nearly dead with the cold. So they brought her
in and the baby was born before she ever came to . . . and
there she was at death's door for three weeks and longer.
And now here she is . . . always staring at the baby as if
she couldn't make out wherever it came from. And if you
go near her she starts to howl like a perfect wolf for fear
you're going to steal it from her.

[QUICA, *looking curiously at the child, almost by
instinct takes a couple of steps towards* THE DUMB
GIRL *who gives her queer cry of alarm.*]

CANDELAS. There . . . I told you so!

QUICA. All right . . . don't get scared, my girl. Nobody wants to steal another mouth to feed.

[*But* THE DUMB GIRL *still looks at them all with intense suspicion.*]

CANDELAS. [*Enviously.*] And the little brat's so pretty,

what's more . . . got a skin like milk and hair on its head
that's the colour of corn . . . just like its mother's. Mine
had fair hair too . . . though where he got it from I don't
know . . . for I'm pretty dark . . . well, you should see
his father!

> [*Suddenly she draws her arm roughly across her eyes
> and then goes back to the trough, plunging her hands
> in the water. And, sharply and defiantly, as if she
> meant to stop herself crying, she begins to sing again.*]

CANDELAS. Aie . . .

> Girl of the Mountains,
> You made too free
> When to ruin yourself
> You ruined me.

> [SISTER GRACIA *comes into the patio followed by two
> women carrying a large basket of rough-dried clothes.
> She points to the linen on the bushes.*]

SISTER GRACIA. Gather up all that too, and take it to
be ironed. It must be ready by this afternoon.

> [*The women collect the linen in silence and go out
> again carrying their basket with them.* SISTER GRACIA
> *is now 29. She is pale and evidently tired and over-
> strained, though she does her best to hide this by her
> smiles. When the women have gone she turns towards*
> THE DUMB GIRL *and her companions, but on the way
> to them she stops, gives a little sigh, and murmurs "Oh,
> Blessed Jesus." Then she leans against one of the pil-
> lars and closes her eyes. She is half fainting.* CAN-
> DELAS *sees and goes up to her anxiously.*]

CANDELAS. D'you feel ill? Oh . . . what's the matter?

SISTER GRACIA. [*Pulling herself together.*] Nothing,
thank you . . . nothing at all. Don't be frightened.

CANDELAS. [*To* CECILIA.] Here . . . you! Go and
fetch her a chair, can't you. D'you want some water?

[CECILIA *goes out and doesn't return.* QUICA *takes* THE DUMB GIRL'S *chair—she has risen too—and brings it to* SISTER GRACIA.]

CANDELAS. Sit down now.

SISTER GRACIA. [*Only anxious to get away from them.*] No, there's nothing the matter indeed. Please take no notice.

CANDELAS. Now, do sit down . . . won't you?

SISTER GRACIA. Oh . . . very well then.

[*She sits down and as soon as* CANDELAS *sees her safely in the chair, she dashes out to the right.*]

QUICA. But whatever is the matter, Sister Gracia?

SISTER GRACIA. [*Recognising her amazedly.*] You here again?

QUICA. [*Complacently.*] Yes, Señora.

SISTER GRACIA. And didn't you promise when you went away that you'd never so much as look at a man again?

QUICA. Well, there it is . . . you can't be sensible all the time!

SISTER GRACIA. [*With a sigh.*] God's will be done!

[THE DUMB GIRL *now comes slowly to* SISTER GRACIA *and kneeling puts her baby in her lap, leaves it there and remains looking at her and smiling.*]

QUICA. There . . . see what a present the dumb woman's brought you.

SISTER GRACIA. [*Smiling.*] Thank you . . . thank you . . .

QUICA. [*To* THE DUMB GIRL.] So you're not afraid of her!

[*The dumb girl looks from one to the other and smiles again at* SISTER GRACIA. CANDELAS *comes back, followed by* ENRIQUE. *She is carrying a glass of water.*]

CANDELAS. Look at her now . . . with the child on her lap! Isn't she beautiful? She's like the Blessed Virgin of Carmen. [*Then she goes down to* SISTER GRACIA, *very pleased with herself.*] Here's the doctor.

[*The doctor,* ENRIQUE, *is a man of about 35, pleasant, quite good looking. He is dressed in a plain dark suit.* SISTER GRACIA *jumps up on seeing him.*]

SISTER GRACIA. Oh, good heavens! [*Then to* CANDELAS.] But . . . what nonsense! Whoever told you to . . . ?

CANDELAS. Take what the saints provide, I say. What's the good of the doctor being here if we're not to call him when you're ill?

SISTER GRACIA. [*Giving* THE DUMB GIRL *back her child.*] Here.

ENRIQUE. [*Anxiously.*] But . . . were you really taken ill?

SISTER GRACIA. No, Señor, of course not . . . it was nothing but this girl's foolishness.

CANDELAS. [*A little slyly.*] And I tell you she was, Don Enrique. She leaned against that pillar . . . so. And she shut her eyes . . . so. And she went as white as a sheet, and if I hadn't got to her she'd have fallen flat on the ground.

ENRIQUE. Well . . . now let's see. What was the matter?

SISTER GRACIA. Nothing, nothing . . . take no notice. I spent the whole morning in the laundry where it's half dark . . . so when I came out into the patio the light dazzled me and made me dizzy . . . that was all. But this silly girl [CANDELAS.] is always making a fuss.

CANDELAS. I'm sure I meant well.

ENRIQUE. You really don't need me at all?

SISTER GRACIA. No really. Of course, if I do . . . ! I'm so sorry you've been disturbed.

ENRIQUE. That's nothing. If you do want me, I'm in the convalescent ward. Goodbye.

[*He goes out without looking back. But he caresses* THE DUMB GIRL'S *baby in passing and she looks at him smilingly too.*]

QUICA. He's a handsome man.

CANDELAS. And what a way with him . . . hasn't he, Sister Gracia?

SISTER GRACIA. You know all about such things, I'm sure.

CANDELAS. You're not cross with me, are you?

SISTER GRACIA. Yes, I am. Fancy going and worrying the doctor over a thing like that.

CANDELAS. Well, what else is he for? Besides, as it was you, he was only too glad to come [*To* QUICA.] wasn't he?

QUICA. Trust him. He's got eyes in his head.

CANDELAS. That he has . . . for I've seen him once a day going on for two months now . . . and I know he's got eyes in his head. He'll pass near a particular person and be knocked all of a heap, poor thing! Oh, every-one's noticed that. [*Then she looks at* SISTER GRACIA *and says coaxingly.*] You've an angel's face . . . that's a fact.

SISTER GRACIA. What *are* you both talking about?
[QUICA *bursts into laughter.*]

SISTER GRACIA. And what are you laughing at, pray?

QUICA. Oh . . . nothing at all, Señora. Don't be angry . . . I meant no harm.

CANDELAS. But what I say is that coifs can't hide faces . . . and in woman's face is man's perdition.

QUICA. Yes . . . and a woman's in a man's. . . .

CANDELAS. And if she looks all pale and sad and seems just to be crying out for someone to take care of her. . . .
[*The two are talking to each other, but with glances at* SISTER GRACIA, *who says very severely.*]

SISTER GRACIA. Will you please be quiet?

CANDELAS. We didn't mean you . . . for you're a saint . . . everyone knows that . . . but it's the very rea-son why I hate to see you here.

SISTER GRACIA. Do you indeed!

CANDELAS. I tell you, Sister . . . you don't know what you're missing.

QUICA. You don't . . . she's right . . . you don't.

SISTER GRACIA.   [*Turning away.*]   You're talking nonsense.

CANDELAS.   Would I be a woman . . . and young and
pretty . . . and be shut up here washing other women's
babies' faces . . . when I might be having my own?   Yes,
Señora . . . it's her own babies . . . and their father's,
the man she could love and who'd be mad about her . . .
that's what a woman wants . . . so I tell you.

SISTER GRACIA.   You've nothing more to do here, have
you, either of you?   So be off now, to the refectory, it's
nearly dinner time.

CANDELAS.   [*To herself, to* QUICA, *to the things she
collects to carry off with her.*]   Holy Mother . . . you
don't know whether she's more beautiful to look at when
she's angry or when she's pleased.   Eyes like that . . . in a
place like this . . . where no one has a chance look at
them. . . . [*Then she sings again.*]

> Oh, quickly drop your lids
> To keep me in your eyes,
> For there I've seen myself
> At last . . . in Paradise.

SISTER GRACIA.   [*Irritably.*]   Be quiet . . . be quiet.
You have a voice like a watchman's rattle.

CANDELAS.   Have I?   It was my voice though that first
brought him running after me . . . for all that he has
gone and left me now!   Oh, Holy Mother! . . .

> I have a grief, a grief
> Which if I longer bear . . .

SISTER GRACIA.   Really, you seem to have taken leave
of your senses today.   And haven't I told you to be off
to the refectory?   It's time our private patient took her
walk.

QUICA.   Oho . . . have we got a private patient here?

CANDELAS. Very private . . . for though she's done just what we all have, she can't possibly come and breathe the same air that we do . . . oh dear no!

QUICA. Well . . . people of position must do something to keep it up. We've no shame at any time, have we! Nor have they before things go wrong . . . but they have after . . . and that's always something. [*She laughs impudently at her own wit.*]

SISTER GRACIA. Are you both going . . . or are you not?

QUICA. Yes, Señora . . . this very minute. . . .

[*As she is turning to go she comes against the basket cradle.*]

QUICA. Well . . . just look what that girl's done . . . left her baby here!

SISTER GRACIA. Take it with you then.

CANDELAS. Yes, Señora . . . Aie . . . don't look at me as if I'd committed a crime!

SISTER GRACIA. Oh, be off . . . be off!

CANDELAS. Holy Mother. . . .

> I have a grief, a grief
> Which if I longer bear . . .
> A coffin and a grave
> For me they can prepare.

[*The song dies away. Left alone, SISTER GRACIA leans a moment against the stone trough to rest. Her face is drawn and sad, but after a little she smiles to herself and then goes to a door that has not been opened yet, opens it and disappears and then comes back with MARGARITA, saying.*]

SISTER GRACIA. You can come out now.

MARGARITA. There's no one here?

SISTER GRACIA. No one at all. They've all gone to dinner.

[MARGARITA *is a delicately pretty girl of 20. Her*

*plain dark dress and the large silk scarf of blue and
black that she wears stamp her as belonging to the
middle classes. The settled look on her face speaks of
a medley of shame and anger, and her voice is sometimes sad and sometimes sharp with a sort of despair.
She comes in not lifting her eyes, sinks into the first
chair she finds and murmurs half articulately.*]

MARGARITA.   Mother of God. . . .

[SISTER GRACIA *goes to her and speaks very gently,
very kindly.*]

SISTER GRACIA.   Now, my child . . . you mustn't torment yourself any more.   Look what a wonderful day it
is.   Aren't you glad of this sunshine after all the cold and
rain?

[MARGARITA, *her eyes on the ground, makes no reply.
SISTER GRACIA goes to one of the blossoming trees and
breaks off a little branch which she throws lightly into
the girl's lap. Still no movement, no reply. Then
SISTER GRACIA puts a hand to her forehead and lifts
the sunk head.*]

SISTER GRACIA.   Lift that head now.   What do you
want with your eyes always fixed on the ground?   Look
up at the sky.   God is there, and he'll comfort you.

MARGARITA.   [*Stubbornly.*]   God won't look at me.

SISTER GRACIA.   [*Still kind, but a little more sternly.*]
Won't he?   Is your sin too great . . . or do you think his
mercy is too small?

MARGARITA.   God is merciful to you, isn't he, when
your heart is softened.   Mine has only been broken.

SISTER GRACIA.   No, don't say that . . . you mustn't
say that.

[MARGARITA *hides her face in her hands and begins
to cry.*]

SISTER GRACIA.   Now don't cry . . . you know how it
upsets you . . . it's very dangerous. . . .

MARGARITA.   Oh . . . I'm not going to die . . . no
fear of that.   You never do die when you want to.

SISTER GRACIA. [*Smiling.*] Hush now . . . or Death
may hear . . . and come for you.

MARGARITA. I wish it would . . . Oh, I wish it would.
If I could just die and forget . . . yes, die here . . . in
this infamous place . . . and then no one would ever hear
of me again! If I could be buried here and forgotten . . .
with my shame and my wrongs. . . .

SISTER GRACIA. [*A firm hand on her shoulder.*] And
with your child too?

MARGARITA. [*Fixedly.*] Yes . . . my child too.

SISTER GRACIA. [*Horror-struck.*] Blessed Jesus!
[*But she rallies her kind smile again.*] How sorry you'll
be that you said that, once he's born and you hold him in
your arms.

MARGARITA. My punishment.

SISTER GRACIA. No, no, no . . . a son can never be his
mother's punishment.

MARGARITA. Not when he is her dishonour?

SISTER GRACIA. The child's no dishonour . . . only the
sin is that.

MARGARITA. It's the same thing.

SISTER GRACIA. It is not. When God sends you a child
he offers you pardon for your sin.

MARGARITA. Pardon. . . .

SISTER GRACIA. Why yes. Would you have left sinning if the child had not come to convince you that you
were sinning? God puts redemption in your arms.
Don't miss the chance of it. Oh, think what it can mean
to you to live and suffer for your child . . . and to teach
him to be good. God in his mercy is calling to you . . .
and you must answer . . . you must not turn away. Oh
yes . . . cry if you want to because you repent . . . but
not because you're in despair. And in a little while now
an angel will come to dry your tears.

> [*But* MARGARITA *makes no answer, her eyes still
> stubbornly upon the ground. Defeated,* SISTER

GRACIA *gives a sad little shrug to her shoulders and looks up.*]

SISTER GRACIA. Oh Dear God . . . !

[*Then she moves away, and taking her knitting from her pocket works as she stands there. After a moment,* MARGARITA *says in a hard voice.*]

MARGARITA. He'll have no father. He'll have no mother.

SISTER GRACIA. No mother, did you say? Did you say that? D'you mean you're thinking that you'll turn your back on him and leave him here . . . as these poor wretched women leave their children?

[*She has dropped her work and is so vehement, so shaken with indignation, that* MARGARITA *gets up, a little frightened.*]

SISTER GRACIA. Oh no, no! You can't mean that . . . you couldn't do such an infamous thing. To give up your child   altogether . . . oh,   think . . . think!   No,   you couldn't do it . . . you couldn't. Promise me that you'll take him with you . . . and give him your name . . . and the love that he has a right to. Promise me.

MARGARITA. I can't.

SISTER GRACIA. Why not?

MARGARITA. My father knows nothing about it. We've told him that I've a vocation for the Sisterhood and he thinks that I'm here on probation. If he knew, he'd die of the shame of it.

SISTER GRACIA. And your mother . . . ?

MARGARITA. I've no mother. I've a step-mother.

SISTER GRACIA. She knows?

MARGARITA. Yes, she knows. She has helped me deceive my father and hide here. Not that she cares much for me! But at least she's a woman . . . and understands.

SISTER GRACIA. A woman, is she . . . and understands? Understands what? Has she never had children . . . ?

[*At this moment* SISTER FELICIANA *comes across the*

*back of the patio carrying some letters. On seeing
her* MARGARITA *begins to tremble with excitement and
runs to her crying.*]

MARGARITA. Sister Feliciana . . . is that the post . . .
is there anything for me?

SISTER FELICIANA. I'm sure I don't know. The Superior will give it you soon enough if there is.

[*She is going her way, but* MARGARITA *desperately
catches at her habit.*]

MARGARITA. Oh, for the love of God, let me see them.
I won't ask you for the letter . . . I won't indeed. I
only want to know. Oh . . . please . . . won't you?
Oh . . . I'll go on my knees . . .

SISTER FELICIANA. But . . . !

[*While* MARGARITA *kneels and clings to her, she
questions* SISTER GRACIA *with a look, which says, "Is
this girl mad?"*]

SISTER GRACIA. Let her look.

[MARGARITA, *when she gets the letters, runs through
them with feverish anxiety and passes from hope to
despondency and to despair.*]

MARGARITA. No . . . yes? No . . . no . . . no!
Nothing . . . oh, my God . . . nothing!

SISTER FELICIANA. Well . . . God's will be done, you
know.

[*She philosophically packs the letters together again
and departs. But* MARGARITA *is left like a mad creature.*]

MARGARITA. Nothing . . . nothing . . . nothing!

SISTER GRACIA. My child, my child . . . keep calm.

MARGARITA. Not one word! I'm not worth even a
word from him . . . and I've brought myself to this for
him. He knows where I am . . . he knows . . . oh, he
knows!

SISTER GRACIA. [*To say something.*] He'll write tomorrow.

MARGARITA. He won't. I shall die here . . . alone.

For he doesn't love me . . . he never did. I was the one
. . . I . . . oh, God help me!

> [*She breaks down again, sobbing helplessly.* SISTER
> GRACIA *goes to her and says gently.*]

SISTER GRACIA. There, there now . . . don't think of
that any more.

> [*Suddenly* MARGARITA *stops crying and looks fixedly
> in front of her.*]

MARGARITA. He's wicked and heartless . . . everybody
says that. Yes . . . wicked! No . . . no, he's not. It's
only that he doesn't love me. And I didn't know how to
make him love me. But there were those that did. Well
. . . what more could I do? I gave myself to him, body
and soul . . . and even that wasn't enough. For he was
false to me. Oh, those women that took him away from
me! And when I cried, all he said was . . . "But if you
really loved me." [*She echoes distractedly.*] "If you really
loved me! If you really loved me!"

> [*She has ranged through tears and anger to the cli-
> max of an almost hysterical scream. And now she gets
> up and goes up to* SISTER GRACIA.]

MARGARITA. You don't know what it is to be jealous.

SISTER GRACIA. I never want to know.

MARGARITA. It's hell. It's like being burnt alive. It's
like having one's heart torn out. "If you really loved me."
Ay de mi . . . ay de mi! As if I didn't . . . better than
anyone else would.

SISTER GRACIA. [*Very moved.*] Yes . . . yes. Keep
quiet now.

MARGARITA. For haven't I risked salvation . . . look
what I've brought on myself just to please him. And I
cried . . . I prayed God I might die . . . and it meant
nothing to him. But there was one day . . . yes, just
one . . . when he did love me. And I tell you, I'd lose
my soul and see him lose his, to have that day over again!

SISTER GRACIA. Don't blaspheme!

MARGARITA. Oh, I tell lies about it all . . . I do nothing but lie. For I'm not sorry for the sin and the shame of it . . . I'm not. If he wants me, what do I care about honour or dishonour . . . he's my life . . . I've no other.

SISTER GRACIA. Be quiet . . . be quiet, I tell you. Are you mad . . . or do you want to lose your last hope of salvation?

[MARGARITA *loses all self control whatever. She clings hysterically to* SISTER GRACIA *and kneels to her without in the least knowing who she is.*]

MARGARITA. Where is he? For the love of God where is he? Tell me where he is so that I can go to him . . . barefoot . . . on my knees. . . .

SISTER GRACIA. Let me go.

MARGARITA. Carlos . . Carlos! We're here . . . both of us . . . your child . . . and I'm here. Carlos . . . love . . . life . . . Carlos . . .

[*She falls to the ground in a violent fit of hysterics.* SISTER GRACIA *is really alarmed, and calls out.*]

SISTER GRACIA. Help . . . help!

[ENRIQUE *comes in by one door, and by the other* SISTER FELICIANA.]

ENRIQUE. What is it . . . what has happened?

SISTER FELICIANA. Who was that calling . . . ah!

[*She goes to succour* MARGARITA, *while* SISTER GRACIA, *very distressed, hardly knowing what she is saying, crying indeed like a child, just manages to get out.*]

SISTER GRACIA. This woman . . . this woman . . . !

ENRIQUE. There now . . . don't be frightened . . . it's nothing.

[*He lifts up* MARGARITA, *who grows quieter, little by little, sighing out "Ay . . . ay," and gradually getting some control over herself. He takes the glass of water that has been left by the trough and gives it to* SISTER FELICIANA *saying.*]

ENRIQUE. Sprinkle a few drops in her face. Keep quiet,

girl, keep quiet.   Hysterics are over, I think.   Now get on
your feet.

> [SISTER FELICIANA *helps her up.*]

ENRIQUE.   That's right.   Now take care you don't begin again . . . d'you understand?

> [*Though he talks to* MARGARITA *he is looking rather
> anxiously at* SISTER GRACIA, *who is leaning against one
> of the pillars still crying though she tries to control
> herself.*]

MARGARITA.   Yes . . . I will . . .

ENRIQUE.   [*Taking a little bottle from his pocket.*]
Take a sniff of this.   And now you're all right . . . wasn't
anything serious, was it?   [*To* SISTER FELICIANA.]   Now
. . . take her to her room . . . give her a little orange
flower water . . . shut out the sun, and keep her quiet.

SISTER FELICIANA.   Come along then . . . don't cry
any more.

> [*She takes* MARGARITA *away and* SISTER GRACIA,
> *hardly herself even yet, is instinctively following them,
> when* ENRIQUE, *gently authoritative, stops her.*]

ENRIQUE.   Where are you going?

SISTER GRACIA.   I . . . I was going with them.

ENRIQUE.   No.

SISTER GRACIA.   Why not?

ENRIQUE.   Because it's quite possible that in a moment
she'll have another attack . . . and you may have one too
if you're there.

SISTER GRACIA.   I?

ENRIQUE.   Yes . . . these nervous crises are very con-
tagious things . . . Besides you're thoroughly upset . . .
you're shaking all over.   Sit down.

SISTER GRACIA.   But. . . .

ENRIQUE.   Sit down, please.   Doctor's orders.

> [SISTER GRACIA *sits down and after a moment tries
> to speak.   But she is still so upset that she hardly
> knows what she is saying.*]

SISTER GRACIA. Blessed Jesus . . . that poor girl . . . she seemed possessed . . .

ENRIQUE. Don't talk . . . rest. Close your eyes a moment.

[*She obeys him. He then begins to walk up and down, but going no nearer to her. After a moment she says.*]

SISTER GRACIA. Can I open them now?

ENRIQUE. Are you quite yourself again?

SISTER GRACIA. Yes, I am.

ENRIQUE. Quite?

SISTER GRACIA. Quite. Don't be afraid . . . I've never had hysterics yet.

[*She gets up as if to go. Then he moves a step nearer.*]

ENRIQUE. Sister Gracia. [*Struck by his tone she looks at him curiously.*] How old are you?

SISTER GRACIA. Oh . . . really, I hardly remember. Twenty-nine, I ought to be, I think, on my next birthday. Yes . . . that's it. Ten years I've been professed . . . and I was eighteen.

ENRIQUE. You've been here since you were eighteen?

SISTER GRACIA. Oh no . . . I've only been here four years and a half. I started in an Asylum for old men. Oh, poor old things . . . if you knew how miserable it made me to leave them . . . really it was almost worse than leaving my own home. They were so fond of me . . . and I was of them. Hard luck they'd all had! And they were so old . . . and I was such a child. They used to pretend . . . some of them . . . that I was their granddaughter . . . and sometimes I'd find myself thinking of them as if they were my dolls. Such fun we used to have together!

ENRIQUE. There's not much fun to be had here.

SISTER GRACIA. I think that all the sorrow in the world is to be found here. These women . . . I don't know whether it makes me more wretched to have them suffer so . . . or for them to think nothing of it at all. And the babies . . . the ones that are born here . . . and those that they bring here . . . outcasts every one . . . with people only thinking how best they can be rid of them . . . as if they were something unclean and shameful altogether. And . . . oh, my God . . . a month ago, while you were away . . . one night when I was on duty, someone put a dead child into the basket at the gate. That is . . . it hadn't died—its throat was cut. I shall never forget it. With big blue wide open eyes that seemed to be asking . . . But why . . . but why?

ENRIQUE. This can't go on, you know, Sister Gracia.

SISTER GRACIA. What do you mean?

ENRIQUE. You can't stay on here.

SISTER GRACIA. Where?

ENRIQUE. Surrounded by this misery and pain . . . misery of the body and of the spirit too. For you're right . . . the whole world's unhappiness is centred here . . . we're at the very heart of its corruption. Vice or cowardice it may be . . . degeneracy, self-will . . . but over it all, despair. For what have they to look forward to . . . any of them?

SISTER GRACIA. I know, I know . . . there's nothing . . . and that's what is so horrible. My poor old men now . . . who cared what became of them? But it was so easy to take them out of themselves . . . why, if I'd promised them the moon to play with, they'd have felt quite sure of getting it . . . because I'd promised. But these wretched souls . . . what visions can one give to them? Some of them are callous, and some only wish they were dead, and some just want to be revenged. But there's not one . . . not one that even *wants* to rise above it all. And, if they did . . . what could we promise them? They leave here . . . and what is waiting for them? More misery . . . more hunger . . . more vice . . . more shame. Do you know, I think sometimes . . . oh, not very often, but sometimes I can't help thinking . . . that if one of these women would only lift up her head, take her child in her arms,

and outface what the world calls her dishonour . . . why,
God at least would forgive her. For he always does forgive us if we call on him. But then . . . they don't know
how to call on him. How should they? No one has
taught them. They hardly know that he exists. Then
how can one sin against a God one doesn't know? And if
they've not knowingly sinned . . . how should they feel
the shame, and why . . . oh why . . . should such punishment fall upon them? God . . . God . . . but who is
to blame then for so much misery?

ENRIQUE. Sister Gracia . . . Sister Gracia!

SISTER GRACIA. What am I saying . . . what have I
said? Oh, forget it please. And God forgive me . . .
blessed Jesus! . . . thy will be done . . . and as you have
willed it . . . then so it should be. As it is . . . it is
right . . . although we cannot understand. Have pity on
us and forgive us all . . . Lord . . . Lord!

ENRIQUE. But . . . why are you crying then?

SISTER GRACIA. Oh, indeed I'm not . . . well . . .
no, I'm not quite myself yet. That girl . . . like a mad
creature . . . like some fury from another world. You
mustn't think I'm generally so impressionable as this. But
today . . . well, you'll forgive such foolishness . . . and
. . . another time. . . .

[*She starts to go.*]

ENRIQUE. Wait . . . wait a little.

SISTER GRACIA. No, really . . . there is so much to be
done. . . .

ENRIQUE. Wait . . . please . . . just for a minute.
I want to speak to you . . . of something that may touch
you very nearly.

SISTER GRACIA. That may touch me . . . !

ENRIQUE. Well then . . . that does touch *me* very,
very nearly . . . that means more to me than anything
in the world. [*At a gesture from her.*] No . . . for
God's sake don't be offended.

SISTER GRACIA. Let me go, please.

ENRIQUE. You guess what it is?

SISTER GRACIA. No.

ENRIQUE. Ah . . . but you do. [*He is deeply moved for all that he speaks quietly and stands very still; she, trembling rather, stands as still, to listen.*] Sister Gracia . . . you can't go on leading this life. How can you endure to be sunk here in this pit of bitterness and despair? Well then . . . I can't endure that you should be. For three years now I've been coming here and seeing you every day . . . and from the first day I've cared for you . . .

SISTER GRACIA. Oh, God in heaven, don't say that . . hush, hush!

ENRIQUE. Why? I have cared for you . . . felt for you more and more . . . and more deeply. For you are all that I believe a woman should be . . . you are good, you are true, you have sense . . . and you are full of joy . . . you were when I knew you first. And if you're unhappy now . . . why then, indeed, you are not yourself. You are a sick woman now.

SISTER GRACIA. I . . . !

ENRIQUE. Yes . . . the foul breath of this place has poisoned you. All the tears that you have seen shed are heavy on your heart. And all the suffering you've seen and all the blasphemies you've heard have beaten back into your body and your mind. But you need the bright sky above you and the fresh air to breathe . . . and on your horizon some gleams of hope.

SISTER GRACIA. No, no . . . oh, no!

ENRIQUE. Yes, yes . . . and that's what I bring you when I bring you . . . my love.

SISTER GRACIA. Oh, for God's sake. . . .

ENRIQUE. My love. We must call things by their names.

SISTER GRACIA. And you dare to speak to me of love . . . here . . . where we see how it all ends.

ENRIQUE. It isn't love that comes to such an end . . .

that has eaten like a cancer into these lives. True love between men and women is health and strength to both.

SISTER GRACIA. That is enough!

[*And she turns away determinedly.*]

ENRIQUE. No, don't go away . . . listen . . . there's nothing I'm saying that need offend you. Love that is worthy of the name brings peace of mind and harmony . . . clear thoughts and steadfastness. And work to be done . . . and shared . . . oh, anxious hours enough . . . but with their burden lightened by just half. Day after day of toil and weariness . . . but at the end of each the comfort of a heart that beats near yours. Come out of this prison and learn to laugh again. Take off that habit which is black like death and that coif . . . it's like the cloth that you lay on a dead woman's face . . . and honour me by trusting me to make you happy.

SISTER GRACIA. I am happy. God knows it.

ENRIQUE. But won't you be as happy with me? And I should be so happy with you. Ah . . . forgive that from a man who really isn't used to being selfish. I'm not offering you what's called a life of pleasure . . . mine's austere. I'm not well off, and I'm a doctor and you'd be brought close enough, if you were my wife, to all the ills of mankind. Don't be afraid that you'd have no chance of doing good. I live for my work . . . and though I don't worship science for its own sake . . . I do believe it can help me to help my neighbour. Won't you help me too? You have grown wise in charity. Working together we could give such life to our work . . . won't you try? I'm a free man . . . and you are free . . .

SISTER GRACIA. I . . . free! How can you say that?

ENRIQUE. Why, you wouldn't be the first to leave the hard road you chose when you were young and full of illusions for a simpler way . . . the human way, you know, that love makes easier.

SISTER GRACIA. I have given my love once and for all.

I abide by that vow. I live for that love and I will die in it.

ENRIQUE. Sister Gracia. . . .

SISTER GRACIA. Oh yes, you're right . . . I am unhappy . . . unhappier than you can think. And I'm tired, and perhaps I'm ill . . . poisoned . . . oh no doubt, as you say. But God, who has my love, is with me. I may not see him, but he is with me. And while I love him he will not leave me. Oh yes, it's true that just now he has put bitterness in the cup . . . but he has given me so much other happiness . . . that I have so little deserved. And he will again . . . I know that he will. And even if he does not I have given myself for ever.

ENRIQUE. Sister Gracia . . .

SISTER GRACIA. For ever . . . for ever. And no one has the right to try and turn me from my way. My love and my sorrow are my God's. No, don't speak and don't come near me. Don't ever speak or ever think of this again.

ENRIQUE. Is that your last word?

SISTER GRACIA. My last . . . and my only one. Good-bye.

[*She is more than a little shaken by all this, by the violence she is doing to herself. Once again she turns to go.*]

ENRIQUE. Well, at least let me as a doctor give you some advice. I really think you are ill . . . you are worn out.

SISTER GRACIA. Don't let that trouble you. The Superior is responsible for my good health. What I need she will order. Good-bye.

ENRIQUE. Good-bye.

[*He bows and goes without turning his head. SISTER GRACIA turns now to go out on the left and so she has to cross the whole patio. She is quite broken with emotion and physical fatigue; she moves very*] *slowly and rests wherever she can, by a tree, a chair, a pillar. Half way across she can hear the impudent, sensual voice of* CANDELAS *singing.*]

> I asked a sick man the complaint
> Of which he was to die,
> "Of loving you . . . of loving you,"
> The sick man made reply.

[SISTER GRACIA *stops to listen and there comes over her, like an agony, all the temptation of love and its happiness. She wrings her hands, then crosses them on her breast, and stands there trembling. Then she lets her arms fall and stands for a moment with closed eyes. Then she pulls herself together, takes the crucifix from her sleeve, looks at it for a little, presses it to her breast and says*:]

SISTER   GRACIA. Jesus . . . beloved   saviour . . . do not leave me without help!

[*She starts on her way again, and, as she reaches the door, meets the* SUPERIOR *coming out.*]

SISTER GRACIA.   Sister Cristina.

SISTER CRISTINA.   What is it?   Why, what's the matter?   You're shaking all over.   Are you ill?

SISTER GRACIA.   No, indeed.   But I want to ask a favour.   Will you be so kind as to write today . . . today, please . . . to the authorities and ask them if they will transfer me. . . .

SISTER CRISTINA.   But. . . .

SISTER GRACIA.   Please . . . please!   I want to leave here at once . . . and without anyone knowing . . . or knowing where I go!   I beg you . . . for the love of God! It is a case of conscience . . .

CURTAIN

ACT III

The kitchen of an Orphanage. It is a large white-washed room, divided in two by a wooden barrier. In the back part, which is a little higher than the front, separated from it not only by the barrier but by one or two steps, is a great stove with large saucepans fitted into it; and they have taps in them. On the ground, close to t'e stove, are four large two-handled pots.

The front of the room is arranged as a dining-room, with tables and benches of plain deal. There are two of these tables, one on each side of the room.

In the wall on the right is a large doorway; the door stands open all the time and through it one can catch a glimpse of the great patio. In the left wall are two smaller doors which lead to other dining-rooms, one for the girls, the other for the little boys; it is the big boys that eat in the kitchen.

At the back are high windows through which trees and sky can be seen. Beneath the windows is a shrine, and in it an image of the Virgin and Child. Two flower-pots with artificial flowers also adorn the shrine. SISTER DIO-NISIA *is in the kitchen; a Sister of Charity, aged about 35, a country woman, uneducated and taciturn, but full of common sense and sturdy practical virtue, possessing too, great physical powers of work. She is by the stove and has just finished putting the four large pots in a row.*

ENGRACIA *and* LORENZA *come in carrying a deal box with cord handles which is full of hunks of bread. They are inmates of the orphanage, very poorly dressed, cotton skirts, hemp sandals, sleeved aprons of striped cloth, and on their heads cotton handkerchiefs which they take off once they are in the kitchen, and tie loosely round their necks.* ENGRACIA *is very pretty and delicate in her movements,* LORENZA *is a rather ugly country girl.*

ENGRACIA.   Here's the bread for supper.

[*They carry the box, which they had dropped for the moment while they untied the handkerchiefs from their heads, towards the door.*]

SISTER DIONISIA.   You've cut very little.

LORENZA.   [*Sullenly.*]   That's all the bread there was.

[*To this* SISTER DIONISIA *makes no reply.* LORENZA *and* ENGRACIA *start taking out the bread with two great metal scoops, and putting it into the four great pots.*]

SISTER DIONISIA.   Put a few extra in that . . . it's the little ones'.

LORENZA.   Yes, Sister.

ENGRACIA.   [*Looking at the stove.*]   Is the water hot?

LORENZA.   Not boiling yet.

SISTER DIONISIA.   Lots of time . . . it's only four o'clock.

ENGRACIA.   I'll go and fetch the plates.

[*She goes out by one of the doors on the left.*]

SISTER DIONISIA.   Get the ladle . . . and we'll put in the dripping.

[LORENZA *takes out of a cupboard in the corner the vessel containing the dripping, and a large iron ladle.*]

SISTER DIONISIA.   Take care you don't burn yourself.

[LORENZA *starts to ladle in the dripping.   Then she stops, surprised.*]

LORENZA.   Sister Dionisia!

[SISTER DIONISIA *knows what the matter is, and in self defence looks severe.*]

SISTER DIONISIA.   What's the matter?

LORENZA.   You've forgotten the peppers.

SISTER DIONISIA.   No, I've not forgotten them.

LORENZA.   Oh yes, Sister.   Look, the dripping's not coloured at all.

SISTER DIONISIA.   I tell you I've not forgotten them . . . there aren't any.

[LORENZA, *horror struck, puts down the dripping and stands with the ladle in the air.*]

LORENZA. No peppers!

SISTER DIONISIA. [*Ill-humouredly, to hide her own vexation.*] No, child, there aren't any. We used up the last this morning.

LORENZA. Well . . . we needn't waste time making the broth then . . . for they won't eat it.

SISTER DIONISIA. What else can they do . . . if it's all there is?

LORENZA. I know the big boys won't eat it. They'll go to bed starving. If there aren't peppers in the broth . . . they won't eat it.

SISTER DIONISIA. Come along now . . . the dripping will be cold . . . and if it's put with the bread like that the whole thing turns to glue.

[*She goes on apportioning the dripping to the pots. LORENZA puts it in while SISTER DIONISIA stirs it. ENGRACIA now comes back with a pile of tin plates which she puts on the table.*]

ENGRACIA. The plates!

[*And she goes out again.*]

SISTER DIONISIA. Now, put the lids on.

[*She carries the dripping back to its corner.*]

LORENZA. If you've things to do we'll look after the water boiling.

[ENGRACIA *comes back again with a basket full of tin mugs and wooden spoons.*]

SISTER DIONISIA. Well . . . even if it does boil don't pour it out or you'll burn yourselves . . . you'd better call me. I'm going to the bakehouse to see if they've done kneading.

[*She goes out through the wide open door.* EN-GRACIA *has been setting out the plates, with a mug and a spoon by each.*]

ENGRACIA. [*Mocking.*] The table's laid . . . the silver plate is on.

LORENZA. [*Coming from the back.*] And as for the
banquet . . . why, the King himself never had the like.
Bread soaked in hot dripping just for a change . . . and no
peppers with it either.

ENGRACIA. I don't know which way makes me sicker
. . . with them or without them.

LORENZA. [*Philosophically good-humoured.*] My
child, when you can dip your bread in good pepper broth
that turns it red, at least you can pretend that it tastes of
sausage.

ENGRACIA. Sausage! You're a nice one.

LORENZA. Oh my . . . what wish would I have
if. . . ! Now look . . . suppose the blessed Saint Cayetano
were to work a miracle, so that when we put in the ladle
instead of bringing out hunks of bread and water we got
. . . sausages . . . and boiled codfish . . . or beans and
bacon . . . or lentils. Holy Mother, I want to forget
there's such a thing as lentils in this world.

[ENGRACIA *is sitting on a bench, her elbows on the
table, looking fixedly at some sort of little card she has
taken from her pocket.*]

ENGRACIA. Oh . . . there are such a lot of things in
this world that you want to forget about.

LORENZA. What's that you're looking at?

ENGRACIA. Nothing . . . a picture out of a match-
box.

LORENZA. Let's see. [*She takes it and reads.*]
"Juanita la Serana." Oh, my dear . . . isn't she handsome? Is she an actress?

ENGRACIA. Yes . . . one of those that sing and dance
and have motor-cars and silk dresses!

LORENZA. And how her hair's done! Now who is it
she looks like?

ENGRACIA. Like me.

LORENZA. [*Scandalised.*] Like you! Well . . . yes
she is . . . if you wore your hair right high up like she does
. . . and your skirts short. Oh . . . !

ENGRACIA. What are you laughing at?

LORENZA. Oh . . . think of all the lentils you could have to eat, if you were an actress with your picture put on match-boxes.

ENGRACIA. Hold your tongue . . . someone's coming.

LORENZA. Only the Innocent.

ENGRACIA. Here . . . give it me!

[ENGRACIA *seizes the picture and puts it back in her pocket.* THE INNOCENT *comes in. She is what is sometimes called a "natural," a grown woman with the undeveloped brain of a child. She has however an old woman's face and her hair is grey and bristly. She is dressed like the other orphans. As she comes in she produces a screw of greasy paper, and takes from it after a moment the drumstick of a chicken.*]

THE INNOCENT. Girls . . . want some chicken?

LORENZA. [*In fascinated amazement.*] Chicken!

THE INNOCENT. [*With all the pride of great possession.*] Chicken! Don't it smell good. [*She holds it close to* LORENZA'S *nose, and as suddenly snatches it away again.*] Ah . . . don't you wish you may get it! [*Then turning generous.*] All right . . . take it, greedy. But don't eat it all . . . give her a bit . . . she looks pretty hungry.

LORENZA. [*To* ENGRACIA.] Have some?

ENGRACIA. [*In great disgust.*] No, thank you!

THE INNOCENT. Not like chicken! Have a cutlet.

[*She now produces from the screw of paper a cutlet bone with a little meat left on it.* ENGRACIA *looking upon this no more favourably she goes on cheerfully.*]

THE INNOCENT. Try some fish!

[*And out comes a bit of fried fish.*]

ENGRACIA. No, no . . . take it away.

THE INNOCENT. [*Amazed.*] No? Well, have a sweet?

ENGRACIA. [*A little moved.*] Oh . . . well . . . perhaps.

THE INNOCENT. Here you are . . . cokernut!

[ENGRACIA *takes the sweet delightedly, puts it to her mouth, then takes it away again.*]

ENGRACIA. Oh, no . . . it makes me sick!

THE INNOCENT. What . . . the sweet too!

ENGRACIA. [*With growing excitement.*] The sweet too . . . and everything else besides. Yes, I'm hungry . . . like everybody else here . . . well, I was . . . oh no, I'm not. I haven't been able to get through a meal for these two days . . . and it does turn me sick to see you with all that. Goodness knows I'd like something to eat . . . but not food! I'd like something very sour and very sweet . . . and cold . . . no, hot . . . oh, I don't know. Coffee with lots of sugar! Salad with lots of vinegar! No, nothing to eat . . . I'd like to sleep. Mother Mary, if I could go to bed this very minute and not ever have to get up again. For oh, I am sleepy!

LORENZA. [*With rough kindness.*] Now you just listen to me. People that don't eat, die . . . and that's what's going to happen to you . . . going on like this. And I tell you . . . that if you throw your supper under the bench again I'll tell Sister Dionisia, so I will . . . and she'll get it down you . . . see if she doesn't!

[ENGRACIA *bursts into tears.*]

LORENZA. Oh . . . don't cry!

ENGRACIA. Let me be!

LORENZA. Where are you off to?

ENGRACIA. Let me alone, can't you?

[*She goes to the end of the table, sits down, hides her face in her hands, and quietly proceeds to have her cry out.* LORENZA, *much distressed, turns to the* INNOCENT.]

LORENZA. There . . . she's all upset again. Some days she fires up at you because she's sure she must be a Marquis's daughter . . . or why are her hands so white, and her feet so something or other? Other times she's wild because she can't go on the stage! And last night in the dormitory she jumped out of bed in her sleep and was walking about

with her eyes tight shut . . . a bit more and she'd have
been out of the window. She's going off her head . . .
that's what I think.

THE INNOCENT. Where's the sweet? Don't let it get
lost.

> [*She takes the sweet from the table where it has
> dropped—it is a sugar-coated one—and gazes at it al-
> most with adoration.*]

THE INNOCENT. Yes, you'd like it yourself, wouldn't
you? Don't you wish you may get it? But it's for
Morenito. [*She fishes out another.*] Though this is even
nicer . . . it's got rum inside.

LORENZA. Where did you get all this?

> [THE INNOCENT *carefully puts the sweet away
> again and screws up her parcel.*]

THE INNOCENT. Don't you tell the Superior! I went
out to take a letter to the Warden's daughter's sweetheart
who's from Madrid, and stopping at the New Inn. And the
cook there said she'd make me a present . . . because they'd
had a big dinner on for the Town Council. Oh, my girl
. . . but don't they just stuff themselves! Rice . . .
chicken . . . cutlets . . . fish . . . ham in syrup . . .
cheese! And all because a gentleman they call a Minister
has come down . . . and they'd made him a free something or other of the city . . . and then this morning to
celebrate it they've given him a funeral.

LORENZA. [*Amazed.*] A funeral!

THE INNOCENT. Well, it must have been. They put
him in a coach and took him all through the streets in a procession . . . and there's been a stone put up with his name
on it in gold letters . . . just like the ones in the cemetery.
And they hung wreaths . . . and everybody was in black
clothes and high hats . . . all the Council and the Mayor
. . . and the College professors and the Governor of the
province and the Bishop. And I suppose it was just to
make it all not seem so dreadful that they gave him a
dinner. And there's a bull-fight too . . . just for him.

They've gone there now. And, what's more . . . Juan de Dios, that used to be here, is fighting.

ENGRACIA. Juan de Dios!

THE INNOCENT. Look here . . . it says so.

[*She produces a crumpled handbill and they all three scan it excitedly.*]

ENGRACIA. The Bull-ring. . . .

LORENZA. In honor of His Excellency. . . .

ENGRACIA. Six magnificent bulls. . . .

LORENZA. Bull fighters. . . .

THE INNOCENT. Here . . . here!

ENGRACIA. . . . whose place will be taken by Juan de Dios Garcia, the Foundling . . . from the Orphanage of San Vincente de Paolo.

LORENZA. From our orphanage . . . does it put that?

THE INNOCENT. Yes . . . and he made them put it . . . so as to show that he wasn't ashamed of being brought up here.

ENGRACIA. [*Enviously.*] Fancy flourishing it back at them like that when they meant it as a disgrace. Foundling! And perhaps his father will be watching him fight . . . and he may see him killed! He'll be one of those in a black coat and a high hat who's been at the dinner. Foundling! That's what I'll call myself, Engracia the Foundling . . . and if I'm a success I'll make some of the gentlemen in high hats pay pretty dear for the use of the name. Foundling! Foundling!

[*Most of this is muttered between her teeth. Meanwhile from the patio the sound of a quarrel can be heard; a man's voice, unsteady, half sober; a boy's, high in indignation; and the frightened cries of a child. This is* MORENITO. *It is* VICENTE *that calls out, "What are you up to . . . hitting a child like that?" and* POLICARPO *that replies, "I'll hit him if I choose. Take that! I'll learn you to laugh at me . . . on the other side of your mouth!" Then* MORENITO *screams again.*]

ENGRACIA. What's the matter . . . what's happening?

[*The three girls all rush to the door.*]

LORENZA. It's that tailor! He's thrashing one of the little ones . . .

THE INNOCENT. It's Morenito! [*She calls out in great distress.*] Morenito . . . Morenito . . . come here.

[MORENITO, *a little boy of 10 who seems even younger he is so pallid and fragile, runs helplessly in.* POLICARPO, *the tailor, is close at his heels. He is a hunchback, a drunkard, debased, almost ape-like in his movements.* VICENTE *comes too, one of the orphans, a well set up boy of 16.*]

VICENTE. . . . And I'll break your head open because I choose. So now!

POLICARPO. [*In great disdain.*] Oh, you will, will you?

VICENTE. Yes, I will. Let that child alone. Let him alone, I tell you.

[MORENITO *yells with terror.*]

VICENTE. Will you let him alone . . . ?

[VICENTE *sends* POLICARPO *flying. He staggers and falls against the screen.* MORENITO *escapes and takes refuge with the* INNOCENT, *who comforts and pets him, and stops his crying by giving him a sweet.* POLICARPO *struggles to his feet and scowls at the five of them.*]

POLICARPO. Scum! Charity brats!

VICENTE. D'you want another? Oh yes . . . . you're plucky enough to hit a poor child like that . . . you won't stand up to a man.

POLICARPO. Him and you and all the lot of you . . . sons and daughters of trollops and thieves . . . that's what you are!

VICENTE. Say that again!

POLICARPO. I'll say it whenever I choose.

VICENTE. Say it again, and I'll throttle you.

POLICARPO. Aha . . . that gets you on the raw, does
it? Yes, my lad . . . because it's true. You're the sons
and daughters of . . .

[VICENTE, *with a yell, flings himself upon* POLI-
CARPO. LORENZA *and the* INNOCENT *rush to separate
them.* ENGRACIA *shouts with joy.*]

ENGRACIA. Throttle him, Vicente . . . throttle him!

LORENZA. Vicente . . . Vicente!

THE INNOCENT. Help . . . help!

ENGRACIA. Throttle him!

LORENZA. Now you be quiet!

[*While* MORENITO, *still quietly sobbing a little, looks
on and sucks his sweet as if it were all no affair of his.
At this moment* SISTER GRACIA *comes in.*

*She is now an old lady of 70. She supports herself
with a stick, suffers from rheumatism and wears spectacles, but she is lively and merry all the same. As a
rule she speaks gently enough, but she can get excited
and be very angry too. And happening on this quarrel
she raps out with great authority.*]

SISTER GRACIA. What's going on here? Policarpo!
Vicente! Get away from each other at once. What is all
this about?

[*The fighters separate.* LORENZA *and* ENGRACIA
hang their heads. Only MORENITO, *feeling quite safe
now that* SISTER GRACIA *is there, breaks out into renewed lamentations.*]

MORENITO. Aie . . . aie . . . aie! He hit me . . .
so he did!

[*In response to* SISTER GRACIA'S *severely questioning look, both* POLICARPO *and* VICENTE *break out angrily.*]

VICENTE. The coward . . . he was thrashing the
child. . . .

POLICARPO. The young blackguard . . . trying to
throttle me!

MORENITO. Aie . . . aie . . . aie!

Sister Gracia. [*To* Morenito.] Keep quiet now. [*Then she thumps the floor with her stick.*] Silence!
> [*There is dead silence. Then she turns to* Poli-carpo.]

Sister Gracia. Whatever could such a child do to you to make you ill-treat him like that? Answer me.

Policarpo. [*Sullenly.*] What they all do . . . all the time. Sit idling and laughing in a man's face.

Morenito. [*Perking up.*] He tries to make me learn to sew with a needle that's got no point.

Policarpo. You broke the point, you mean . . . so that you needn't learn to sew.

Morenito. [*To* Sister Gracia.] Oh . . . you tell him that's a lie. He gave me a needle that hadn't any point just so that I couldn't sew and then he hit me, he did . . . because he hates me because he says I called him a name. And I didn't call it him . . . and it's not a name, what's more . . . for it's true and everybody calls it him . . . the Sisters call it him. Policarpo the hunchback. Hunchie . . . hunchie . . . hunchie! [*He jumps up and down as he cries it out.*]

Policarpo. See if I don't twist your neck for you!

Sister Gracia. Quiet now [*She raps with her stick again. The child's indignation amuses her, though she does her best to look severe.*] Morenito, I'm surprised at you. Go and stand this very minute with your face to the wall till you have learnt to be respectful to your elders. Is that the way a child should talk? Take care I don't shut you up in the cellar and let the rats eat you.

Morenito. Aie . . . aie . . . aie!

Sister Gracia. And as for you, my good Mr. Tailor . . . I have told you a thousand times that the children are not to be beaten.

Policarpo. Oh, I'll give him goodies!

Sister Gracia. When they misbehave you are to come and complain to me . . . and I will punish them as they deserve.

POLICARPO. Why . . . you and the Sisters are all the
same . . . always backing them up . . . and so they do
just as they please. A pretty state my workshop would get
into if I didn't take them in hand a bit myself!

SISTER GRACIA. There are four workshops besides yours
. . . and none of the other masters find they have to ill-
treat the children before they can make them behave.

POLICARPO. Then they're cleverer than I am.

SISTER GRACIA. Or less fond of brandy perhaps.

POLICARPO. There you go . . . always bringing up the
brandy against me.

SISTER GRACIA. Well, my friend . . . don't you put it
down and then I shan't have to bring it up. Heavens . . .
what a man!

POLICARPO. [*Muttering.*] Heavens . . . what an old
woman!

SISTER GRACIA. What's that you say, you insolent fellow?

POLICARPO. [*Insolently indeed.*] What I do in my
workshop is my own affair. I'm not the Sisters' servant.
I'm an employee of the Board. Let's understand that.

SISTER GRACIA. Really. And have you never heard of
an employee of the Board being out of employment sometimes?

POLICARPO. I've got some influence there though . . .
and you may as well know it.

SISTER GRACIA. And so have I . . . and you may as
well know it. You lay another finger upon one of these
children and we'll see who counts for most . . . your
friends the publicans, or mine in the Church. And now
you take yourself out of my sight.

POLICARPO. So one's to treat these charity brats as if
they were the sons of dukes. . . .

SISTER GRACIA. They are the sons of God . . . and
that's a higher title still.

POLICARPO. [*To* MORENITO.] Oh, well . . . come
along now, you little imp.

Morenito. Aie . . . aie . . . aie!

Sister Gracia. No, Señor . . . he'll not go along . . . he'll stay here with me.

Policarpo. Going to teach him his trade, are you?

Sister Gracia. That's no concern of yours.

Policarpo. [*As he goes angrily to the door.*] Women's place is in the kitchen . . .

Sister Gracia. Quite so . . . and men's in the tavern . . . and there we have the world nicely divided up, haven't we? [*Then she turns to* Vicente, *who has been standing quietly in a corner.*] And you now . . . what are you doing here?

Vicente. [*A little uneasily.*] Nothing . . . oh, nothing. I was just walking across the patio. . . .

Sister Gracia. I know that. But how did you come to be walking across the patio at this time of day . . . past the tailor's shop where you have no business to be? Who gave you permission? Who opened the door for you?

[Policarpo, *who had about disappeared, suddenly thrusts his head back with a jeering laugh.*]

Policarpo. He didn't need it opened . . . he's got a key . . . a skeleton key . . . like a burglar.

[*After spitting this out he vanishes.*]

Vicente. Curse him. . . .

[*He starts to pursue* Policarpo, *but* Sister Gracia's *voice brings him to a stand.*]

Sister Gracia. Stop! A skeleton key. Is that true?

Vicente. [*Meekly.*] Yes, Señora.

Sister Gracia. [*Drily.*] Give it to me.

[Vicente *takes a key from his pocket and hands it over.*]

Vicente. Here it is.

Sister Gracia. And what are you doing with a skeleton key? Answer me.

[Vicente *stands silent.*]

Sister Gracia. Let's see now. Oh . . . I understand. You come across the patio past the tailor's shop to

geτ to where the girls are working. So we have a sweetheart, have we? Answer. Who were you going to see?
Don't make me angry now, Vicente, or it will be the worse
for you. Who did you come here to see?

> [VICENTE *looks on the ground and does not reply.*
> SISTER GRACIA *turns to the girls, who are a little dis-*
> *concerted.*]

SISTER GRACIA. It'll be a miracle if you're not concerned in this, Engracia.

ENGRACIA. [*Hastily.*] No, Señora . . . it wasn't to
see me . . . no, Señora, indeed.

SISTER GRACIA. But you know who it was. I can tell
by your looks . . . all three of you know. Come along
now . . . let's have it . . . quickly.

> [*The three of them hang their heads and stay silent.*
> SISTER GRACIA, *with a gesture of impatience, raps*
> *on the ground with her stick.*]

MORENITO. [*Piping up from his corner.*] The Innocent won't say because Vicente has promised to stand her a
glass of anisette presently.

> [VICENTE *glances at the child as if he could mur-*
> *der him, but* MORENITO *goes on quite imperturbably.*]

MORENITO. But she knows . . . because she's the one
that takes the letters to Paca. . . .

SISTER GRACIA. [*To* VICENTE.] To . . . to which
Paca?

MORENITO. To little Paca . . . that works in the
bakery . . . she's his sweetheart.

SISTER GRACIA. Send Paca here to me at once . . .
and you [*To the girls.*] run along . . . run away.

> [ENGRACIA *and* LORENZO *vanish precipitately, and*
> *the* INNOCENT *is following when* SISTER GRACIA *stops*
> *her.*]

SISTER GRACIA. No, no . . . you stay. I've to settle
accounts with you too. Letters . . . glasses of anisette,
indeed! A pretty business. This is what comes of trusting

you and letting you go out. You carry letters to Paca, do you?

MORENITO. [*Very pleased with himself.*] I took her one one day . . . and she baked me a little loaf of bread for it . . . all to myself.

SISTER GRACIA. Hold your tongue! Do you know what happens to children who speak when they're not spoken to? They have their tongues cut right out. Into the corner and down on your knees this very minute.

> [MORENITO, *much taken aback, kneels down in the corner and weeps.* PAQUITA *appears in the doorway, a pretty girl of 17, dressed like the others. She is evidently a little troubled, but as evidently has her mind made up. She does not venture in, but stands, glancing sideways, first at* SISTER GRACIA *and then at* VICENTE.]

SISTER GRACIA. Come in . . . you.

> [PAQUITA *comes in. The* INNOCENT, *who had retired to a corner, little by little, edges her way to* MORENITO, *and sits down on the floor to comfort him. After a while they are to be seen playing knucklebones together.*]

SISTER GRACIA. Well . . . [*Nodding to* VICENTE.] here he is. And can you tell me why he was making his way through the second patio by the help of a skeleton key?

PAQUITA. [*Seeing that denial is useless.*] Yes, Señora . . . to see me.

SISTER GRACIA. Well, I'm glad you confess it. You're pluckier about it than he is.

PAQUITA. [*With childish petulance.*] I suppose I love him better than he does me.

VICENTE. [*Just as childishly distressed.*] Oh . . . you've no right to say that!

PAQUITA. Well . . . if you're ashamed to say that you love me. . . .

VICENTE. I'm not . . . why should I be? And if I didn't tell, it was so as not to get you into trouble. And you know perfectly well that I love you every bit as much as you do me . . . and more, if it comes to that!

PAQUITA. [*With a shy smile.*] Well . . . if you say so . . .

[*It would seem that they had completely forgotten* SISTER GRACIA, *who with a burst of half humorous anger interrupts them.*]

SISTER GRACIA. That's right . . . that's all right, children! Go on sweethearting . . . don't attend to me! Well, this is the last straw!

VICENTE. Oh . . . we don't mean to be rude. But we . . . she . . . you see . . .

SISTER GRACIA. Yes, I see her . . . and I see you . . . and a pretty pair of noodles you are! And what do you think is going to happen now, I should like to know?

[*She starts to get up, and with her rheumatism that's not easy, so* PAQUITA *goes to help her. But with all the impatience of an old lady who hates to be reminded of her infirmities.*]

SISTER GRACIA. Let me be . . . let me be! Well . . . I like your impudence. One little angel of light mentions quite casually that he has made himself a skeleton key . . . and this girl confesses as calmly as you please that it's for clandestine meetings with her! And instead of being ashamed of yourselves and asking forgiveness . . .

PAQUITA. But it isn't a sin to love people.

SISTER GRACIA. But it's hardly a virtue, is it . . . to go making skeleton keys?

VICENTE. Oh . . . she knows I never wanted to.

PAQUITA. No . . . because you haven't the courage of a mouse.

SISTER GRACIA. [*Banging on the ground with her stick.*] Goodness gracious me . . . what a pair of children! May I ask if I'm to be allowed to get a word in edgeways?

VICENTE. Yes, Señora.

SISTER GRACIA. Much obliged, I'm sure! Well now
. . . how long have you two been romancing like this?

VICENTE. It's since St. James day . . . that's the Warden's birthday . . . and Paquita went there with the Innocent to wait at table . . . and I was there seeing to the
lock of the cupboard. And we started talking and I said
to her . . .

SISTER GRACIA. Thank you. I can guess what you said
to her . . . and what she answered.

PAQUITA. [*With great dignity.*] No, Señora . . . I
didn't answer him at all till the Eve of Our Lady's Day,
when I was in the bakehouse with the Innocent . . . and
he came in with the chopped wood . . . and then I
said. . . .

VICENTE. She said I could make the key.

SISTER GRACIA. Excellent! And now what happens?

PAQUITA. We're going to get married.

SISTER GRACIA. At once?

PAQUITA. Yes . . . just as soon as he can get fifty dollars to buy the furniture.

SISTER GRACIA. Oh . . . and then what?

PAQUITA. Then . . . ! We're used to going hungry.
It won't be so bad to go hungry together.

VICENTE. And I'm sure I don't know why you need say
you'll have to go hungry . . . when you know perfectly
well you won't have to with me there to look after you.
I can work . . . and though I say it that shouldn't, I know
my trade with the best . . . I'm worth five pesetas a day
anywhere. And I'd be earning it now and have the fifty
dollars saved if it wasn't. . . .

SISTER GRACIA. That's the thing. Tomorrow we'll find
you some work and we'll get you a lodging.

PAQUITA. What . . . send him away!

SISTER GRACIA. Yes, if you please. It doesn't suit me
at all to have such a good locksmith living here.

VICENTE. [*To* PAQUITA.] There . . . what have I always told you!

PAQUITA. Send him away! Yes . . . you'll save your fifty dollars right enough . . . but who'll you spend them on then?

VICENTE. Why, whatever should I want fifty dollars for . . . but to spend it on you?

PAQUITA. Oh, you say that now . . .

VICENTE. I say it now . . . and I always shall . . . and God may strike me dead else.

SISTER GRACIA. [*Very angrily.*] And we've learnt to swear, have we? I've had enough of this. You be off to the bakehouse again . . . and you [*To* VICENTE.] get back to your work. Hurry up. Tomorrow I shall have a talk to the Warden about you . . . and that's the end of that.

VICENTE. [*Meekly.*] You won't tell him about the skeleton key, will you?

SISTER GRACIA. [*Pretending to be very angry.*] I shall tell him just exactly what I choose. Of all the impudence! Get along with you.

[VICENTE *and* PAQUITA *linger, gazing at each other.*]

SISTER GRACIA. Will you both be off . . . when I tell you?

VICENTE. [*Very meekly.*] Yes, Señora. [*He turns to go and then back to* PAQUITA *with* . . .] Goodbye, Paquita.

PAQUITA. [*As she turns away unresponsive.*] And a nice mess we've got into! This is what comes of trying to be happy!

[*As she goes out she meets* SISTER DIONISIA *in the doorway.*]

SISTER DIONISIA. Well . . . and where have you been hiding . . . and what about your oven? Oh, I beg pardon, Sister Gracia.

SISTER GRACIA. That's all right.

SISTER DIONISIA. May we serve supper? Come along
. . . come along.

> [*This last to* ENGRACIA *and* LORENZA *who are be-
> hind her with a basket filled with hunks of bread.
> They put it on the table, and join* SISTER DIONISIA *at
> the stove where they all three serve out the dripping-
> bread and broth.* SISTER GRACIA *sits down on a bench,
> crosses herself, and says a Paternoster in a low voice.
> On ending it, she takes a little stone from her pocket
> and throws it out into the patio.*]

SISTER GRACIA. Eah! The first Paternoster I've been
able to say all day. [*Picking up the crucifix from her side
and smiling at it lovingly.*] Ah . . . sweet Saviour, it's
little time we get to talk to each other, you and I. But
we're an old couple now.

> [*She kisses the crucifix in simple affection, then, as
> in sudden reminder, turns to* SISTER DIONISIA.]

SISTER GRACIA. Sister Dionisia . . . did the peppers
come?

> [SISTER DIONISIA *leaves the girls at the stove.*]

SISTER DIONISIA. No, Señora.

SISTER GRACIA. Didn't you send for them?

SISTER DIONISIA. I went to the shop myself . . . with
the Innocent.

SISTER GRACIA. And they wouldn't give them you?

SISTER DIONISIA. No . . . the man said that if it was
for anyone of position or for the Sisters even he'd give
credit . . . but that he wouldn't trust the Orphanage
Board because they owed him for fourteen bags already
and he's sure they won't pay.

SISTER GRACIA. God's will be done. But the flour
. . . that came?

SISTER DIONISIA. Yes, Señora . . . yesterday afternoon.

SISTER GRACIA. Well . . . that's something.

SISTER DIONISIA. But you can't knead the dough it makes. Half of it's the commonest rye and half of it's nothing but bran. Just look what the bread's like.

[*She takes a bit of the black bread from the basket.*]

SISTER GRACIA. Mother of God!

SISTER DIONISIA. [*Lowering her voice.*] And there were cockroaches in some of the bags.

SISTER GRACIA. [*Her temper rising.*] Then it must all be sent back at once.

SISTER DIONISIA. But we sent it back last time . . . and it did no good. The contractor's on the Board, you know . . . and, as if that wasn't enough, his brother-in-law's the Party chairman.

SISTER GRACIA. I'm going to the Town Hall this very minute . . . and they shall hear what I have to say . . . yes indeed. Here . . . Innocent . . . give me my cloak . . . and you're to come too.

SISTER DIONISIA. You won't find anyone . . . they're all at the bull-fight.

SISTER GRACIA. That's true . . . oh, very well then.

[*She sighs. The* INNOCENT *who has jumped up, goes back to her corner.* LORENZA *comes from the stove to the bell-rope by the door.*]

LORENZA. Supper's ready. Shall I ring?

SISTER DIONISIA. [*To* SISTER GRACIA.] Do you think perhaps we'd better wait till everyone's back? Some of them, you know, had leave to go and stand near the bull-ring, to hear about the fight.

SISTER GRACIA. [*A little fussed.*] What? . . . oh yes . . . certainly, we'd better wait. To stand near the bull-ring! I don't like it a bit. They'll come back excited as usual . . . and so difficult . . .

[SISTER DIONISIA *is back at the stove.* ENGRACIA *and* LORENZA *stand looking out of the patio door, while* MORENITO *has come to sit at* SISTER GRACIA'S *feet.*]

SISTER DIONISIA. [*Half to herself.*] He's fighting to-day.

ENGRACIA. [*To* LORENZA.] And won't he be proud
. . . all dressed up like that!

SISTER DIONISIA. Come along now . . . take the basket
. . . put out the bread for the children. Innocent . . .
you can come with me.

[ENGRACIA *and* LORENZA *carry off their basket and*
SISTER DIONISIA *goes off by the other small door with
the* INNOCENT. *Seated on her bench,* SISTER GRACIA,
*though still a little fussed, begins to pray in a low
voice, while* MORENITO, *at her feet, fingers her rosary
and looks at her in silence for a little.*]

MORENITO. Are you saying your prayers?

[SISTER GRACIA *smiles and nods.*]

MORENITO. Are you praying for Juan de Dios to do
well?

[SISTER GRACIA *still smiles.* MORENITO *hesitates
a little and then asks a most important question.*]

MORENITO. Tell me . . . is there any Saint that was
a bull-fighter?

[*At this moment a great noise of cheering begins
to be heard. As it grows,* SISTER DIONISIA, EN-
GRACIA, LORENZA, *the* INNOCENT *and a lot of the girls
come out of the other dining-rooms. The sound of
the cheering comes nearer; the crowd is evidently in
the patio itself by now, and one can hear the shouts of
"Hurrah for Juan de Dios! Hurrah for the Foundling!" and* JUAN DE DIOS' *voice "Where's Reverend
Mother?" and cries of "This way . . . she's here!"*]

SISTER GRACIA. What's all this . . . who's making all
this noise? Go and see, Sister Dionisia.

[SISTER DIONISIA, *obeying, meets* JUAN DE DIOS
at the patio door.]

JUAN DE DIOS. Where is she? Reverend Mother . . .
Reverend Mother. . . .

SISTER DIONISIA. Oh . . . it's Juan de Dios!

[*And the girls cry out his name too. He is an attractive lad of 20, dressed in a bull-fighter's gala cos-*

tume, which has lost its freshness, for indeed it is one that he has hired for his first fight.]

JUAN DE DIOS. Sister Gracia . . . oh, Reverend Mother . . . where are you?

[*He runs and kneels at her feet and puts his arms round her waist. SISTER GRACIA, surprised and a little embarrassed, but very pleased, pushes him away, exclaiming.*]

SISTER GRACIA. Here . . . here! What is all this? Get away!

JUAN DE DIOS. I've come . . . oh, congratulate me!

SISTER GRACIA. Juan de Dios! There . . . get up.

[*He sits on the bench by her side. She leans on him a little.*]

JUAN DE DIOS. Why . . . what is it? You're not ill?

SISTER GRACIA. [*Smiling.*] No . . . no. . . .

MORENITO. [*Jealously, pulling at her skirts.*] Reverend Mother . . . Reverend Mother!

[*The girls at the back are all exclaiming among themselves, "Oh, what clothes!" "Oh, doesn't he look handsome!"*]

JUAN DE DIOS. The porter didn't want to let us in. A fine thing to have had the door shut in my face . . . today of all others!

[*Some of the bigger boys of the Orphanage that were with JUAN DE DIOS come in from the patio, some little ones come from the other dining-room. And the crowd that followed him helps fill up the patio door. And they all cheer him "Hurrah for the Foundling!" JUAN DE DIOS is beside himself with joy.*]

JUAN DE DIOS. D'you hear that . . . d'you hear that? "Hurrah for the Foundling!" And in the Bull-ring . . . you should just have heard them shouting it there. They threw me cigars and they threw their hats in . . . and all the beautiful young ladies in the boxes stood up and applauded me . . . they did. And before you can say 'knife' I'll have all Spain applauding me . . . and adoring me

. . . and shouting . . . every one of them . . . "Hurrah
for the Foundling" . . . and that's me . . . that's me . . .
who hadn't any father or a name of his own . . . but went
hungry and cold . . . ! Oh, Reverend Mother, I have
dreamed of this day . . . and I've kept myself for it . . .
yes, I have . . . like one of God's blessed angels.

SISTER GRACIA. Hush, hush . . . don't talk like that.

JUAN DE DIOS. [*Very seriously.*] But I have . . . I
swear it. And look here. . . .

[*He now proceeds to show* SISTER GRACIA *by a
lively pantomime how he disposed of his bull, the
present spectators cheering him at every point with cries
of "Olé! Olé!" He pulls out his handkerchief for
a muleta (the red cloth by which the bull is distracted).*]

JUAN DE DIOS. The muleta . . . so! One pass . . .
over his head to blind him. Then a high one to get my
position. That leaves me exposed . . . so four more over
his head, quickly, one after another. Then one to turn
him . . . one from down on my knees right at his horns.
And then . . . the thrust! And you should have heard
them shout. I tell you . . . they went mad! And if you
had only been there too . . . with a white mantilla on
. . . and I could have dedicated my bull to you.

SISTER GRACIA. Quiet . . . quiet . . . you heretic!

JUAN DE DIOS. But for all that, I've brought you . . .
a present. Give it here . . . give it here.

[*One of the boys gives him something that is carefully wrapped up in a silk handkerchief.* SISTER
GRACIA *hesitates a moment before she takes it.*]

JUAN DE DIOS. Take it . . . you deserve it . . . better than anyone else does. Open it . . . open it.

[SISTER GRACIA *undoes the handkerchief, and discloses a bull's ear . . . all bloody still.*]

SISTER GRACIA. Mother of God . . . what's this?

SISTER DIONISIA. [*Innocently.*] Why . . . it's an ear
off a cow!

JUAN DE DIOS. [*Very offendedly.*] What d'you mean by a cow? It's the bull's ear, Señora . . . my bull that I killed . . . and this is his ear to prove it!

[*Once more the whole assemblage bursts into cheers.*]

JUAN DE DIOS. And there were fifty people at least came and asked me for it as a souvenir. But it's for you . . . just for you . . . to hang in your room . . . and everyone that sees it there will envy you.

SISTER GRACIA. Thank you . . . my son.

[*She cannot think what to do with her present, but* ENGRACIA *takes it and does it up again with the greatest care.*]

JUAN DE DIOS. And look . . . look at the tie-pin his Excellency threw me. Isn't it wonderful . . . isn't it, Sister Dionisia . . . and all of you . . . aren't you proud . . . and happy . . . isn't this a wonderful day for our Orphanage?

[*The boys and girls agree enthusiastically.*]

JUAN DE DIOS. But do look happy, Reverend Mother. [*He puts his arm round her and calls to the people in the doorway and out in the patio.*] For she is my mother . . . she is . . . she is! The other one left me in a basket on the doorstep . . . but she took me in and brought me up and cared for me. And Hurrah for our Reverend Mother . . . she's all the mother I ever want.

[*Tremendous cheering.*]

SISTER GRACIA. Be quiet now. Tell them all to be quiet.

JUAN DE DIOS. But why don't you look happy? Oh, . . . haven't you made up your mind yet to my being a bull-fighter? I know . . . I know! Oh wasn't she just set on my staying a carpenter all my life!

SISTER GRACIA. But suppose a bull kills you, my son?

JUAN DE DIOS. Well . . . if a bull kills me after I've done my duty by him, they'll give me a finer funeral than they would the Prime Minister.

Sister Gracia. Mother of God!

Juan de Dios. And whether or no . . . I have a good time and everybody talks about me and all the women go mad about me and I get lots of money . . . yes, I'm going to be rich . . . do you know that? I got nothing for fighting today . . . because it was the first time. But I did so well that for next Sunday they're giving me a thousand pesetas . . . one thousand pesetas!

[*This creates an enormous sensation. The orphans stare and comment upon the marvel in low, impassioned tones. And* Juan de Dios *adds impulsively.*]

Juan de Dios. And fifty of them for you . . . and then Sister Dionisia can cook you such a dinner. Hurrah, girls, hurrah! Meat for dinner next Sunday!

[*They all cheer ecstatically.*]

Juan de Dios. But I must be off . . . they're waiting for me. [*To* Sister Gracia.] Oh . . . come as far as the gate with me, so that everybody can see us together.

Sister Gracia. My son . . . I never heard of such a thing!

Juan de Dios. Please . . . please . . . for it's the happiest day of my life. Good-bye, everybody . . . good-bye!

[Engracia *suddenly darts up to him.*]

Engracia. Well . . . good luck to you, Juan de Dios!

[Sister Gracia *lets him lead her to the door, where everyone makes way for them, and out into the patio, where the cheers are tremendous. "Hurrah for the Foundling! Hurrah for our Reverend Mother!" Gradually the crowd disperses and the cheers die away.* Sister Dionisia, *the girls, the little ones, and* Morenito *are left in possession of the room.*]

Sister Dionisia. Come now . . . come everybody . . . back to work. Back to your refectory. [*Then to* Lorenza *and* Engracia.] You can serve supper.

[Engracia *does not stir.*]

SISTER DIONISIA. And what's the matter with you, stupid? D'you want to be a bull-fighter too? Ring the bell now.

[ENGRACIA *without a word goes to the bell-rope and pulls it.* MORENITO *likewise stands very aloof.*]

SISTER DIONISIA. And what's come to you, pray? Sit down in your place.

MORENITO. And aren't I a Foundling too?

[*He seats himself at the head of one of the tables. The bigger boys now begin to filter in again through the patio door. And in the further rooms can be heard the chatter of children who will have come in to their meal by some other way. The big boys talk and gesticulate excitedly as they make their way to their places at the table, jostling and stepping over each other or crawling even under the tables.*]

FIRST BOY. Get out . . .

SECOND BOY. Get out yourself!

THIRD BOY. Stop it, will you . . .

FIRST BOY. That's my place.

SISTER DIONISIA. [*Rapping upon the screen with a wooden spoon.*] Order there . . . order . . . keep order and silence. Take your proper places at once.

SECOND BOY. Precious stuck up, wasn't he?

FELIPE. And well he may be! He's going to get more rosettes off bulls yet . . . and make millions at it.

FIRST BOY. Well, we shall see . . . or perhaps we shan't!

FELIPE. We've seen enough to know, Señor!

SECOND BOY. Oh, don't tell me! He's only a phenomenon.

FIRST BOY. Anyone can be that!

FELIPE. Can they? Well, let's see anyone else that can give the last thrust like he did . . .

[*He proceeds to illustrate the way it was done and all the others applaud him with cries of "Olé! Olé!"*]

SISTER DIONISIA. Silence there!

FIRST BOY. Well . . . if he keeps on doing it that way see how long it'll be before he finds himself stuck on the horns of the bull.

FELIPE. Don't you believe it!

FIRST BOY. A bit of a suicide . . . that's what he'll be!

SECOND BOY. Still, he's a plucky fellow.

FIRST BOY. Being plucky isn't bull-fighting.

FELIPE. It's being a hero.

THIRD BOY. It's being a man anyhow.

SECOND BOY. Hurrah!

FIRST BOY. Oh, stop it!

SISTER DIONISIA. [*In despair.*] Now . . . now . . . now! Do sit down and be quiet . . . your supper's getting cold.

THIRD BOY. You know just as much about bull-fighting as a potato!

SECOND BOY. I know more than you do, anyway.

SISTER DIONISIA. Silence . . . silence! Now. In the name of the Father and of the Son and of the Holy Ghost . . . Amen.

> [*And she crosses herself, as do the girls. Some of the boys do so, carelessly enough, and some go on talking.*]

FIRST BOY. I bet anything you like that he started in to kill the bull too soon . . .

SISTER DIONISIA. Silence!

> [*And now she prays while the boys mumble after her.*]

SISTER DIONISIA. Bless, Lord, the food that we are about to receive. Preserve us from the sin of gluttony. And be thou unto us, by thy grace, the eternal food of our souls . . . Amen.

THE BOYS. [*In a hurry to begin talking again.*] Amen.

> [LORENZA, ENGRACIA, *and the* INNOCENT *have been serving out the supper.*]

SISTER DIONISIA. Be careful with that saucepan now!

ENGRACIA. [*To a boy who has joggled it.*] Look here
. . . you keep your hands to yourself.

THIRD BOY. Me!

ENGRACIA. Yes . . . you!

THIRD BOY. You're off your head, my dear!

FIRST BOY. Well . . . she's not all there anyway . . .
poor girl!

ENGRACIA. Clumsy lout!

THIRD BOY. Why, how much more do you want of her?

SISTER DIONISIA. What's all that now? Don't you hear
me tell you to be quiet?

FIRST BOY. Where's my bread?

THIRD BOY. Who's got my spoon?

MORENITO. Aie . . . they've taken my mug!

SISTER DIONISIA. Will you start your suppers . . . yes
or no?

FELIPE. [*Having dipped his spoon in.*] Look here . . .
what sort of stuff is this?

FIRST BOY. It's got no peppers in it!

   [*And several of the boys repeat protestingly, "No
   peppers! It's got no peppers!"*]

SISTER DIONISIA. [*Gently apologetic.*] Now my children . . . what difference does it make?

FELIPE. Well . . . I'm not going to eat it.

   [*He gets up in protest and all the others do the same,
   crying, "Nor am I!" "Nor I!" . . . all but
   MORENITO, who says nothing, but stays in his corner
   calmly eating away.*]

SISTER DIONISIA. [*Very distressed.*] But, my children,
if there's nothing else . . . why, for the love of God . . .
eat this!

   [FELIPE *stands upon a bench and shouts.*]

FELIPE. We don't want it and we won't eat it! We've
had enough of eating bread and water for the love of God!

   [*A chorus of shouting approbation.*]

SISTER DIONISIA. But boys . . . boys . . . boys!

FELIPE. Always shaking a crucifix at you . . .

[*More approbation.*]

FELIPE. . . . whenever they want to cheat you out of something!

[*There is enthusiastic agreement with this.*]

SISTER DIONISIA. Oh boys, do be quiet . . . just because I ask you to. You're quite right . . . but do eat your supper. What good will it do you to go to bed hungry? You shall have something better tomorrow. Now be good . . . be patient . . . sit down . . . oh, please do as I tell you!

[*Some of them, thus appealed to, are sitting down when* FELIPE *says:*]

FELIPE. The boy that puts his spoon in his plate is a coward.

SISTER DIONISIA. Now you be quiet!

FELIPE. I won't be quiet. I say that he's a coward and a sneak.

[*Those that are down get up again and thus reinforced they all protest, loudly, that "They won't! No, they won't!"*]

SISTER DIONISIA. Sit down . . . sit down!

FELIPE. And the boy that sits down to table again is a disgrace to us all!

[*A great clamour; cries, stamping and hammering on the tables.*]

SISTER DIONISIA. [*To* FELIPE.] Will you be good enough to leave the room this very minute?

FELIPE. Oh, I'm going! But I'm not going alone. Come along, all of you! Anyone that's not afraid and wants something to eat . . . follow me!

[*They cheer him and cry that they will, and they are moving off.* SISTER DIONISIA *darts to the door and tries to block the way.*]

SISTER DIONISIA. But where are you going . . . what are you going to do?

FELIPE.   What men do . . . take by force what we can't get by asking nicely.

[*Loud cheers and great readiness to be gone.*]

SISTER DIONISIA.   No . . . no . . . no!

FELIPE.   Now you stop interfering or it will be the worse for you.   Come on, boys!   They keep us penned up here as if we were brute beasts.   We may shout as loud as we like and we shan't be heard . . . they've forgotten us.   And we're just starved.   Well . . . there's bread outside . . . and there's meat outside . . . and there's wine outside . . . so come outside and get it.   If it has to be stolen we'll steal it . . . and if killing's what's needed . . . well, we'll do some killing!

[*Tremendous enthusiasm.*]

SISTER DIONISIA.   Blessed Jesus . . . Ave Maria . . . help!

FELIPE.   [*Beside himself.*]   Into the street with you! We'll let them see . . . we'll let them hear.   It's an ever-lasting disgrace the way that we're treated.   Well then . . . let's make them treat us better.   Throw their bread and water back in their swine's faces!   We weren't born different to anyone else, were we?   Well then . . . we've a right to be as well fed as everyone else is.

[*They cheer wildly and are marching off.* SISTER DIONISIA *struggles with them in vain, crying, "Get back!   Get back!" and then rushes to the bell-rope and pulls it violently.   The girls scream.* FELIPE *turns back to them.*]

FELIPE.   Well, aren't you coming too?   All of us . . . all together . . . where are the rest?   Let's have the whole orphanage out in the streets to demand its rights.   If we're nobody's children . . . why, we're everybody's children. Come along then . . . March!

[*At this moment* SISTER GRACIA *appears in the door-way.*]

SISTER GRACIA.   What's all this?

[*At the sound of her voice and the sight of her, there is something of a lull in the storm, and voices can be heard exclaiming "Reverend Mother! . . . Sister Gracia!"*]

SISTER GRACIA. Oh yes . . . it's Sister Gracia! And what is all this terrible fuss about?

[*The girls have drawn back already and so have some of the boys. The rest stand their ground and the noise has by no means ceased.*]

SISTER DIONISIA. Aie . . . Sister! People must have been giving them wine in the Plaza . . . and there's no holding them.

SISTER GRACIA. So I see. Well . . . we live in a revolutionary age! [*To the girls.*] What . . . you too! [*Then she faces the malcontents.*] Have you had your supper yet?

SISTER DIONISIA. They . . . they didn't like. . . .

SISTER GRACIA. Let me talk to them. Have you had your supper yet?

FELIPE. That's where we're going . . . to get our supper. Well . . . what are you all waiting for? Come on!

SISTER GRACIA. Tsch . . . tsch! [*Looking* FELIPE *squarely in the eyes.*] To get your supper indeed? Where, pray?

FELIPE. Wherever it's to be found.

SISTER GRACIA. And when you've found it . . . do you fancy its owners'll give it you?

FELIPE. If they don't, we'll take it.

[*The few enthusiasts that are left reinforce this with what boldness they can muster.*]

SISTER GRACIA. People keep things that they value locked up, my son.

FELIPE. Then we'll break open the locks.

[*The enthusiasts applaud this also.*]

SISTER GRACIA. [*Quietly now and kindly.*] And do you think if there were any locked door that would open I shouldn't have been there by this to knock at it for you?

FELIPE. Yes . . . but you go asking so prettily. We're going to try if a few stones won't make them attend.

SISTER GRACIA. My son . . . the answer to a stone is often a bullet.

FELIPE. [*Defiantly.*] So much the better! Far better to be left dead in the street once and for all than to stay here and starve to death bit by bit.

SISTER GRACIA. [*Sternly.*] You don't know what you're talking about. And none of you know what you're doing. Now, there has been enough of this . . . and everybody will be quiet and sit down . . . because I tell them to.

> [*They are quiet . . . but they can't make up their minds to obey altogether.*]

SISTER GRACIA. Did you hear what I said? Sit down.

> [*The boys go slowly towards the benches.*]

SISTER GRACIA. Come now . . . be quick about it.

> [*They slowly sit down.*]

SISTER GRACIA. [*To* FELIPE.] And you.

> [*Last of all and much against his will* FELIPE *sits down too.*]

SISTER GRACIA. Now, Sister Dionisia . . . is there any more broth in the kettle?

SISTER DIONISIA. [*Who is still rather frightened.*] Yes, Señora.

SISTER GRACIA. Well then, serve that out . . . then they'll have their supper hot. And let everyone keep quiet. I don't want to have to punish anybody tonight.

> [SISTER DIONISIA *and the girls put more broth in the plates. Then after a moment* SISTER GRACIA *goes on talking . . . quietly and kindly now, but masterfully still.*]

SISTER GRACIA. And d'you think you're the only folk in this world who don't get all that they want to eat? No, my children, no. There are people worse off than you . . . some of them so poor that they'd think your plate of supper a luxury. You'll have a roof over your head tonight and a mattress to sleep on and a blanket to cover you. Think of the people who'll sleep in a ditch by the roadside with no roof but the sky, and only the hoarfrost to come down and cover them. Think of the sick people . . . of people without a friend . . . stumbling through the world with not a hand held out to them . . . nobody caring. While you have a home and all the love we can give you. You are sheltered . . . you are taught . . . you are kept in right paths. And then think if you don't owe a few thanks to God after all.

FELIPE. To God . . . to God! There is no God!

[*A stir of horror among the children.* SISTER DIONISIA *crosses herself and exclaims, "Blessed Jesus!"*]

SISTER GRACIA. And whatever do you think you mean by that, you little fool?

FELIPE. Because if there were . . . would he think this was all right?

SISTER GRACIA. God does not think this is right. Men break his laws. He made them brothers. Is it his fault if they turn wolves and devour each other? God does not think it right that his children should go hungry . . . and the innocent are not ever disgraced in his eyes. It is by no will of his that some are poor and neglected while some are set up in pride. For God is Love and he loves us all and to each one he gives a share in heaven and in this earth.

FELIPE. Don't listen to her . . . she's just preaching lies to you. Nuns have all sold themselves to the rich. Do they ever go hungry? And as long as they can get us to keep up the sham they're let stuff themselves with food in peace.

SISTER GRACIA. I am not lying to you. I am telling you the truth and the whole truth. God does not smile upon the injustice of this world. He endures it . . . for how long? . . . ah, that we do not know. But he does not think it right.

FELIPE. Well then . . . let's go and break the heads

of those that do . . . and God will thank us for that.

[*A few of the boys cheer up at this and approve.*]

SISTER GRACIA. Ah, no, no . . . all that can be done for this wicked world is to help to make it good.

FELIPE. And who's going to?

SISTER GRACIA. You . . . you . . . not by hating but through love. Yes, all of you will help do that. For, when you are men . . . and go away from here, it will be because you have suffered from injustice that you'll know how to make . . . and want to make . . . laws that are just. Oh yes, my sons, yes . . . the world is yours . . . for you have won it by hunger and by suffering and pain. So when you hold it in your hands, make it what it ought to be. God is watching you . . . his hopes are all in you. You suffer now that you may succour his world then. God sees you . . . God hears you. Now say with me. Lord, Lord, we thank thee for this food which is given us in thy name. There is not much of it, it is not very good, and we will not forget the taste of this bitter bread. And by thy precious love we swear that thy children on this earth shall eat of it no more . . . say it with me . . . say it . . .

[*The boys repeat after her solemnly and quietly.*]

SISTER GRACIA. Jesus, Son of God . . . Christ, son of man, by the divine blood that thou didst shed for us we swear to spend our own to the last drop when we are men . . . that children may not be forsaken any more . . . that no more mothers may be wronged and go hungry and be ashamed to carry their children in their arms. My sons . . . my sons, promise me that when you are men you'll try to bring these things to pass . . . that you'll help to build on earth the Kingdom of God.

[*Very quietly, very solemnly, they murmur "Yes."*]

SISTER GRACIA. Thank you, my children . . . thank you. And now . . . supper's over . . . go to bed and sleep in peace.

[*The boys go slowly out. Only FELIPE does not*

move. *He is sitting on his bench, head buried in his arms, and crying.* SISTER GRACIA *goes to him and puts a hand upon his shoulder.*]

SISTER GRACIA. Don't cry . . . for men don't cry, you know. And they don't complain. They suffer . . . but they work and hope.

CURTAIN

THE TWO SHEPHERDS

COMEDY IN TWO ACTS

TEATRO LARA, MADRID
1913

CHARACTERS

Doña Paquita.	Don Antonio.
Lucia.	Don Francisco.
Doña Gertrudis.	Don José María.
The Schoolmistress.	Don Juan de Dios.
The Mayoress.	Juanillo.
Rosita.	Mateo.
Niña.	Demetrio.
A Young Lady.	Niceto.
Another Young Lady.	The Mayor.

The Colonel of the Civil Guard.

The Play Takes Place in a Castilian Village of Today.

ACT I

The Scene is the garden of the priest's house. The house itself is simple, almost humble; and the scene is dominated by the side wall of the church in which there is a small door, used by the priest himself for going to and from his duties. In another wall which divides the garden from the street, there is a gate. There are a few flowers and a fruit tree or two . . . but all as simple as the house itself. At this moment too, the laundry, personal and ecclesiastic, has been hung out to dry, some amices, an alb, a surplice, besides table cloths, dinner napkins and things. And when the play begins, Juanillo, *a young rapscallion of fifteen, is taking them down under the direction of* Doña Paquita, *the priest's sister, a woman of sixty-five, and helping her to put them into two open baskets. His attention wanders and he dodges the work.*

Doña Paquita. Juan, you little nuisance! What are you up to? Come here at once!

Juanillo. Coming, Señora! I say, aren't we in a temper all of a sudden!

Doña Paquita. And aren't you a more impertinent little idler than ever? Take down that rochet, it ought to be dry by this.

Juanillo. [*Picking up the rochet throws it above his head, singing a stave of an evidently ribald song.*]

Doña Paquita. Silence, you young heathen. And put the rochet in the basket. Sacred things are not for playing about with.

Juanillo. [*Throwing the rochet into the dark basket.*] There she goes!

109

Doña Paquita. Not in that one. That's for the house linen, can't you see?

Juanillo. Oh my gracious goodness me! What would a rochet say if it found itself alongside a table napkin.

Doña Paquita. Will you listen to what *I* say, please? Everything in its place and reverence where reverence is due! But what does that mean to you, young limb that you are. If you feared either God or the Devil—God keep us from him [*Crossing herself.*] . . . ! Shoo off that sparrow now, or he'll dirty the altar cloth. [Juanillo *scampers round after the sparrow with great gusto.*] But don't run, you little fiend. The linen will be a nice sight, won't it? with all the dust that you're raising. Take down the amice now.

Juanillo. I'll get the chair. [*From the chair he can see* Lucia *who is going along the street.*] So long, Lucia!

[Lucia, *a pretty, demure minx of eighteen, pauses at the gate, and looks in. She is carrying a laundress's basket.*]

Lucia. Good afternoon, Godmother. I'll be with you in a minute. I'm going to the sacristy to get the linen.

Doña Paquita. God go with you, my dear. Don't be too long about it.

Juanillo. [*To* Lucia.] Father Antonio's been asking for you.

Lucia. [*With alarm.*] For me?

Juanillo. Yes . . . and you're not to go without seeing him. He wants to talk to you!

Lucia. To me?

Juanillo. Get along with you to the church then. It's just where you ought to be, asking God on your knees to forgive you for taking those walks, as you do, all alone in the woods with Mateo. [Lucia, *without a word, disappears.* Juanillo *goes on in great delight.*] Aha, look at her, look at her! Did you see how she blushed? So it's true!

DoÑa Paquita. Will you be quiet?

Juanillo. Oh yes, I'll be quiet. But it's true. Besides . . . I've seen them.

DoÑa Paquita. All right then . . . all right! Unfasten the altar cloth. Take care it doesn't drag! [Juanillo, *after unfastening the altar cloth, jumps to the ground.*] Help me stretch it. Take hold of that end. Pull! Carefully!!

Juanillo. And to look at her you'd say that she didn't know a goose from a gander! But that's women all over. Follow their fancies and when things go wrong, then it's the Saints must get them out of the mess. Not that I wouldn't rather like to be a Saint and have the dear repentant creatures come and tell me all about it.

DoÑa Paquita. You imp of Satan . . . can't anything or anyone be free from that wicked tongue of yours.

Juanillo. Wicked tongue, indeed! I should think it was wickeder to commit the sin than to talk about it.

DoÑa Paquita. Should you! Well, the Church tells us to keep silent about the faults of our neighbours. How do we know that the stories are true?

Juanillo. [*With a very wise and ancient air.*] Now, how have you managed to grow so old and to remain so very stupid!

DoÑa Paquita. You are a very rude boy!

Juanillo. Oh, please don't be angry. Not stupid then . . . but so easily taken in. Why, of course all the stories you hear are true. So are a great many more that you don't!

DoÑa Paquita. Juanillo, you horrify me! I can't think how such a piece of wickedness as you got loose in the world.

Juanillo. Well . . . father and mother managed it somehow.

[*A tumbling of bells is heard; the sound of people, presumably coming out of the church, and the voices of children who are crying: A baptism! A baptism!*]

JUANILLO. [*Throwing away an amice which he has in his hand.*] The christening's over. They're coming out of church. They'll be throwing the pennies.

[*He disappears into the street.*]

DOÑA PAQUITA. Juanillo! Off like a greyhound! My amice on the ground! [*Picks up the amice, and goes to look over the wall.*] Oh, but the godmother's smart, I must say.

[*The noise outside increases. Copper coins are heard falling, footsteps, the shouts and disputes of a crowd of children.*]

A VOICE. Long live the godfather!

VOICES. A christening! Show us the baby!

A VOICE. Throw us the pennies!!

VOICES. A christening . . . a christening!!

1ST VOICE. That's mine!

2ND VOICE. I saw it first!

1ST VOICE. I picked it up!

VOICES. A christening!

3RD VOICE. Chuck us another one!

VOICES. [*Singing.*]

> He'll never grow up a Christian boy,
> This little baby won't,
> Nor his father's pride, nor his mother's joy.
> For why? For why?
> They christened him *under* the font!

1ST VOICE. That's mine!

JUANILLO. Oh, you want them all, don't you?

1ST VOICE. It *is* mine!

JUANILLO. Not if I know it!

[*A noise of blows and boys' voices.*]

3RD VOICE. Let him have it!

2ND VOICE. Coward!

4TH VOICE. One for his nob!

[*During all these happenings* Doña Paquita *is look-ing over the wall, crossing herself and making at the right moment the following comments.*]

Doña Paquita. Ay Jesus! Now somebody's going to get their head broken. I do wish people wouldn't throw them money. That always raises the devil. Juanillo, *will* you come here when you're told? Yes, when he wants to, he will . . . not before. . . . Holy Virgin! They'll kill each other! Let go, you murderous little ruffian!

3rd Voice. Look out . . . here's the sexton!

Doña Paquita. Oh, Benito, do pull them apart!

Voice of the Sexton. Now then, you young scoundrels . . . off with you!

Voices. [*Singing.*] Where does the sexton get the wax
For the tapers he sells in bundles?
When he has bolted the door you
can see through the cracks.
What? What?
He's nicking it off the candles.

[*A sound of cries and of children scampering.*]

Doña Paquita. Be off! Run away home all of you!

[Juanillo, *much ruffled from his fight, comes back.*]

Doña Paquita. Good God, he's bleeding!

Juanillo. [*Cleaning himself off with his sleeve.*] Don't be frightened. It's nothing to hurt.

Doña Paquita. You'll have no face left soon . . . nothing but scratches and bruises. And a nice way to spend your time, isn't it? Fighting . . . in the street!

Juanillo. Call this a bruise? If you want to see bruises go and look at him. And he won't forget the kick he got from me either. No, by . . . !

Doña Paquita. Don't swear! It's a mortal sin to swear.

Juanillo. And all for a halfpenny! That's a nice sort of godfather for you. And Papa was just as stingy. A shillingsworth of coppers. It's worth more than that

I should think to walk along with your nose in the air behind the baby . . . even if the brat *isn't* your own after all!

DOÑA PAQUITA. What's that you say?

JUANILLO. Take it from me.

DOÑA PAQUITA. If you don't shut your wicked mouth you'll be struck dead by lightning, so you will. And suppose anyone going by had heard you say that . . . in the priest's own house too?

[DON ANTONIO, *the priest, comes out from the church. He is sixty years old, and has a benevolent, but at the same time, energetic air. He has rough white hair. He wears a cassock and carlotte. He is carrying a small, very ancient figure of the Virgin and child.*]

DON ANTONIO. Well, another little lamb in the fold. [*He says this quite simply as if it were a current phrase.*] And what's the matter with you, Paquita? You look very upset!

DOÑA PAQUITA. What's usually the matter? This Judas Iscariot of a boy will be the death of me!

DON ANTONIO. God bless my soul! What has he done now?

DOÑA PAQUITA. Ask him!

JUANILLO. [*Humbly.*] Nothing . . . nothing at all, Father. I was only picking up one of the coins thrown for the christening . . . and some stone or other must have hit me. But women always exaggerate, don't they . . . especially old women!

DOÑA PAQUITA. Old women! Do you hear that?

DON ANTONIO. [*Smiling.*] Ladies . . . and, when absolutely necessary . . . elderly ladies . . . would sound better. And how many thousand times have I told you to speak of my sister respectfully?

DOÑA PAQUITA. Respectfully!

DON ANTONIO. Now go in and wash that place clean and put some court plaster on it.

JUANILLO. No need. It's too hard to crack. [*He hits his head to give evidence of this.*]

DON ANTONIO. I know that. But do as you're told.
[JUANILLO *goes into the house.*]

DOÑA PAQUITA. Delightful! Yet let him off without a word. Of course he's a little angel . . . still it might do him some good to have his wings clipped.

DON ANTONIO. But what's the use of punishing him because he has had his head broken?

DOÑA PAQUITA. Oh, it isn't his broken head. It's his viper's tongue. But you're used to that by now, I suppose.

DON ANTONIO. I've got used to hearing you say so . . . for these five years.

DOÑA PAQUITA. And I'm to keep on saying it for another five, am I?

DON ANTONIO. But what do you want done with the lad? He has neither father nor mother nor anyone else. Wasn't it our duty to take him in, and how could we turn him out now? He's a good boy at bottom.

DOÑA PAQUITA. He's a perfect little earthquake.

DON ANTONIO. Sister, sister, we must learn to be patient. Rome wasn't built in a day . . . and it's more than a mile to heaven.

DOÑA PAQUITA. Well, well . . . I'm not a saint like you!

DON ANTONIO. Has Don Juan de Dios come yet?

DOÑA PAQUITA. No.

DON ANTONIO. That's very odd. His train must have been in this half hour.

DOÑA PAQUITA. He'll come by the last.

DON ANTONIO. I think not. When he started this morning he said he only meant just to call in at the Bishop's palace to find out what was going on, and then that he'd come straight back . . .

DOÑA PAQUITA. As if you didn't know what he is. He'll be stopping at every church he comes to to say the Stations of the Cross.

Don Antonio. I daresay he will. He gets to be more and more devout.

Doña Paquita. And whose was the christening? For the baker's baby? Well, they might at least have asked you to the Breakfast! After all, but for you, the father would be rotting in jail at this very moment.

Don Antonio. Woman, woman, they *did* ask me! They did all that they ought to do. But I didn't happen to want to go.

Doña Paquita. And quite right not to, considering the sort of orgy it's likely to be. I should doubt if even the baby will finish up sober!

Don Antonio. Charity, charity, Paquita!

Doña Paquita. Do you want your chocolate?

Don Antonio. Thank you, I don't think I feel like it.

Doña Paquita. Aren't you well? Have you got a pain?

Don Antonio. No.

Doña Paquita. Worried?

Don Antonio. Now, why should I be!

Doña Paquita. Shall I send to the Convent and ask if Don Juan de Dios has got back?

Don Antonio. No, we shall hear soon enough.

Doña Paquita. Well, I do think the Archbishop might find some other way of amusing himself and leave his parish priests in peace.

Don Antonio. And what do you know of such things, pray? Be quiet, Paquita.

Doña Paquita. One needn't know much to know that there's no sense in making men of your age pass examinations as if they were charity schoolboys.

Don Antonio. His Grace knows what he's about. He wants to take stock of his shepherds and find out in what sort of hands his flocks are.

Doña Paquita. Then let him come here and see for himself! Here, among the flock is where the worth of the shepherd is known. Examinations in Latin and Theology, indeed! Let him come here, I say, and hear what this village was thirty years ago . . . and then see what it is today. Thanks to you and your toil and the heart's blood you've poured out for the sake of these sticks and stones . . . may God forgive me! And what do you gain by it?

DON ANTONIO. Heaven. Is that so small a thing to gain?

DOÑA PAQUITA. Oh yes, it'll pay you hereafter, no doubt. But what about *now?* Till this very moment has it ever occurred to the Archbishop to give you a thought? And here you've been slaving for thirty years . . . as *locum tenens* too. A *locum tenens* for thirty years! So that they could keep you on half pay!

DON ANTONIO. Quite so! And His Grace when he came to the diocese found so many of us in like case, men who passed years and years working as parish priests and never being regularly made so, and therefore, as you say, on half pay . . . and he wanted to put that all right. After we've been examined we shall all be regular priests . . . on full pay. So cheer up!

DOÑA PAQUITA. A lot it will matter to me! For however much money comes into this house. . . .

DON ANTONIO. I know . . . there's always somebody wanting it, isn't there? So in any case, it won't come amiss.

[DOÑA PAQUITA, *while they are talking, has finished picking up the linen and folding it.*]

DOÑA PAQUITA. And you don't want your chocolate? Then I'll hurry up supper. Are you coming in?

DON ANTONIO. I think I'd sooner sit out in the air.

DOÑA PAQUITA. Shall I take away the Virgin?

DON ANTONIO. No. Tell Juanillo to get out the tool box. I want to repair her crown. There are a few stones out of it.

[DOÑA PAQUITA *goes into the house, carrying one of the two baskets.* DON ANTONIO *sits down by the table upon which he has placed the Virgin; takes off*

*her crown, extracts from his pocket a paper in which,
carefully wrapped up, there are two or three imitation
stones, and spreads it open.* NICETO *and* DEMETRIO
appear at the gate. NICETO *is plainly a very ignorant
sort of fellow.* DEMETRIO *is smooth, more effeminate
and he makes many gestures. Both are men of the
people.*]

DEMETRIO. Glory be to God!

DON ANTONIO. Amen!

NICETO. May we . . . ?

DON ANTONIO. Yes; come in.

NICETO. Good afternoon.

DON ANTONIO. Good afternoon to you.

DEMETRIO. My respects to you, Father.

DON ANTONIO. Well, what's the news?

DEMETRIO. Precious little, Father.

NICETO. And that's bad.

DON ANTONIO. God's will be done, you know. Sit down.

DEMETRIO. Thank you kindly. [*He sits.*]

NICETO. I'm well enough as I am.

DON ANTONIO. Just as you like, my son. Well now,
what is it?

DEMETRIO. I suppose, Father, we'd better begin at the
beginning . . . because, as the saying is, there must be a
beginning to everything. Therefore . . .

NICETO. Don't waste your time listening to him, Father.
When he has got all his fine words off his chest it'll only
have to be told all over again.

DEMETRIO. Well, tell it your own way then.

NICETO. If I hadn't had patience enough not to use
my fists on you, you wouldn't be here to tell it at all . . .
and if you weren't such a lath and plaster image of a man
that anyone breaking your head for you would only be
called a coward . . .

DEMETRIO. Which means that you are too much of a
coward to try. . . .

NICETO. Am I! [*Looking at the priest.*] You think you're safe now behind *his* petticoats. . . .

DON ANTONIO. Yes, yes . . . but come to the point. Use fine words or any other sort you can find. [*To DEMETRIO.*] You!

DEMETRIO. Well, it's like this. I was the proprietor . . . with all due respect to you, Father . . . of an ass.

NICETO. Well, I suppose we must call it one.

DEMETRIO. And what do mean by *that?*

NICETO. You can judge what a precious jewel of a beast it was when he sold it to me for three dollars and a half.

DEMETRIO. If you bought it for three dollars and a half, it couldn't have been so bad.

NICETO. I wanted something to work the pump, and I wasn't going to buy a young racehorse, was I? And even at that the poor beast was dear.

DEMETRIO. Dear or not, you took him away. And not a penny of the money have I seen.

NICETO. But didn't we agree that the money shouldn't be paid till I'd sold my pigs?

DEMETRIO. I don't remember that.

NICETO. Well, I do. For if I'd paid you the money down there and then, the half dollar was to have come off . . . making it three dollars cash.

DEMETRIO. Then as you didn't pay, the ass remained mine.

NICETO. Mine . . . because I'd settled to pay you, and I'm ready to stand to my word.

DON ANTONIO. But what in the name of ten thousand devils does all this matter? You've got him . . . and you're to be paid for him.

NICETO. No . . . no one has got him now, Father.

DON ANTONIO. How's that?

NICETO. He's dead.

DEMETRIO. Since yesterday, six o'clock.

DON ANTONIO. Ah . . . and in your possession when he died?

NICETO. Yes, I'd had him three days, Father.

DON ANTONIO. Well . . . pay for him then. And get along with you.

NICETO. That's what I say. Ready money. Here they are. Three dollars and a half.

[*He starts to pay it down on the table.*]

DEMETRIO. Keep your money.

NICETO. You won't have the offer of it again.

DEMETRIO. Three dollars and a half! Yes, a nice little bargain for you, isn't it?

DON ANTONIO. But . . .

NICETO. And I wouldn't pay you that, if he hadn't died as he did.

DEMETRIO. There, that's the sort of man he is, Father!!

DON ANTONIO. Now, do let me understand. What did the ass die of . . . and what has that to do with it?

NICETO. Well, Father, here's just how it was. Yesterday afternoon Paca . . . my wife . . . was bringing him home from where he's been having a bit of a feed. And such a state he was in even then . . . even *then* . . . that he hardly could stagger along. Well, as luck would have it, along comes a motor and frightened the brute, and he got in its way. And it hit him just about here [*Indicating the priest's head.*] saving your presence. And as he wasn't what you might call strong . . . well, he lay where he fell. Then Paca . . . *you* know what women are, Father . . . started to weep and to wail, calling out she was ruined and that the ass was all that she and the children had to live on . . . and "What about the police" and "What had the law to say to it" . . . so the people in the car . . . they must have been weak in the head . . . just to put a stop to her noise, gave her a twenty dollar note and made off as quick as they could.

DON ANTONIO. Well, what more?

NICETO. Nothing more! Only now this fellow says that the twenty dollars are his.

DEMETRIO. Weren't they paid for the ass? And wasn't the ass mine?

NICETO. But hadn't I bought him from you?

DEMETRIO. But you hadn't paid *me*.

NICETO. Haven't I been trying to pay you these last two hours?

DEMETRIO. Thank you, but I've changed my mind. I don't care about selling him now.

NICETO. No, a bargain's a bargain.

DEMETRIO. Have you got it in writing?

NICETO. Writing! I'll write it out on your skin with my stick and seal it on your skull with my fist, so I will!

[*And a fight begins.*]

DON ANTONIO. Stop that now! Keep your hands off each other and be quiet.

[*They separate.*]

DON ANTONIO. Now what did you both come to me for?

NICETO. Well, we always do come to you, don't we, Father . . . to have you say which is in the right? And that's me! For this fellow didn't want to come . . . and he can't deny that.

DEMETRIO. I didn't want to trouble his reverence about such a thing.

NICETO. And why on earth shouldn't he be troubled? What else did he learn to be a priest for!

DON ANTONIO. Very well then. The ass was yours by legal right.

DEMETRIO. But Father, Father, consider a moment . . .

DON ANTONIO. I am considering . . . so be silent. Therefore the twenty dollars . . . though they were fraudulently obtained . . . are yours too.

NICETO. [*Turning away.*] Thank you . . . good afternoon.

DON ANTONIO. Wait. There's no doubt they are yours. But we will consider also that this man who was your friend trusted to your honour and handed you over the ass without getting his money for it. And ran the risk . . . you've told us so yourself . . . of never getting it at all if the beast had died on your hands. Therefore as the twenty dollars fell to you by chance, and you did not a thing for them, share them with him. Instead of the three and a half you owe him, pay him seven dollars . . . and let me hear no more about it.

NICETO. Seven dollars indeed . . . as if I was made of them!

DEMETRIO. What . . . and he gets thirteen!

DON ANTONIO. Yes, and you're three and a half to the good. And if you don't like my decision, go to law about it.

NICETO. No doubt . . . and be done out of the whole twenty dollars for costs. You're law enough for this village, Father.

DON ANTONIO. Very well then . . . fork out.

NICETO. But. . . .

DON ANTONIO. What *now?*

NICETO. What's my wife going to say when I tell her I've parted with seven dollars?

DON ANTONIO. A lot you care what she says!

NICETO. Oh Father, you don't know what women are. . . . How should you?

DON ANTONIO. Are you master in your house or is she?

NICETO. I am! But it takes a lot of argument to convince my wife.

DON ANTONIO. Yes . . . and I've noticed that the stick's what you like to argue with . . . if she so much as opens her mouth to you.

NICETO. Well, Father, it's odd . . . but the more you beat 'em the more they seem to get their own way.

[DON FRANCISCO, *the village doctor, a man about* DON ANTONIO'S *age, is seen in the gateway.*]

DON ANTONIO. Who goes there?

DON FRANCISCO. Friend!

DON ANTONIO. Ah, doctor . . . come in. How are you?

DON FRANCISCO. What are you up to?

DON ANTONIO. Settling a quarrel, as usual.

DON FRANCISCO. Gratis?

DON ANTONIO. Of course. That's their only reason for preferring my judgment to the magistrate's. [NICETO *and* DEMETRIO *laugh.*] Isn't that so, you scoundrels?

NICETO. Yes, Father. . . .

DON ANTONIO. Then . . . be off with you!

DEMETRIO. Good afternoon.

NICETO. Afternoon!

DON ANTONIO. Can't you even take the trouble to say thank you?

DEMETRIO. Oh . . . beg pardon, Father, I'm sure.

NICETO. But you know that we mean it, don't you!

[DEMETRIO *and* NICETO *go out.* JUANILLO *comes in and sets a box on the table in which various tools, a hammer, pliers, etc. are neatly set out.*]

JUANILLO. Here is the tool chest. Anything else you want?

DON ANTONIO. Show the doctor your hurt.

JUANILLO. But it's nothing . . . I've cured it.

DON FRANCISCO. [*Going up to* JUANILLO *and taking off the handkerchief which he is wearing on his head like a turban.*] Let's have a look. What did you put on it?

JUANILLO. A slice of onion, salt and vinegar. What else should I put on it?

DON FRANCISCO. Kill or cure!

JUANILLO. Was that wrong?

DON FRANCISCO. Put your head in that water-butt. Wash the place well. [JUANILLO *obeys.*] Now come here. Dry yourself. [*He puts on a piece of court-plaster.*] There . . . that'll last till your next fight. Weeds are mighty hard to kill.

DOÑA PAQUITA. [*In the house.*] Juanillo, bring in the black basket.

JUANILLO. Coming, Señora.

[JUANILLO *takes up the black basket, and goes into the house, taking his time.*]

DON FRANCISCO. Where's your water jar?

[*He goes to fetch the round earthen jar with its spout and handle, which is under one of the stone seats beneath the arbour, and takes a long drink.*]

DON ANTONIO. It's warm today, isn't it?

DON FRANCISCO. The country's so hot it might be on fire. And I've had to walk all the way from the Venta Vieja. [*Again drinks copiously.*] Ah, nothing like a good drink of cold water when you're thirsty. [*He puts the water jar on the stone seat and goes up to the table.*] Nature has been very wise in giving us the greatest pleasures in life for nothing. We poor people should give thanks for that.

DON ANTONIO. [*Smiling.*] To Nature . . . or to God, Señor don Francisco?

DON FRANCISCO. To whichever you please, Señor Don Antonio. You and I are not going to quarrel over a word. Any news yet about that affair of yours?

DON ANTONIO. Nothing more so far. But I'm expecting Don Juan de Dios any minute. He went off to the Archbishop's this morning to find out what he could. Who's ill at the Venta Vieja?

DON FRANCISCO. The old grandfather. You'd better look in.

DON ANTONIO. Is he very poorly?

DON FRANCISCO. Blood poisoning. Anyone else would die of it. But he mayn't.

DON ANTONIO. What have you given him?

DON FRANCISCO. Oh, the usual thing. A bath. And plenty of water to drink with lemon juice squeezed in it.

DON ANTONIO. Well, that won't do any harm.

DON FRANCISCO. Or any good either, d'you think?

Don't be too sure. Water's not touched him inside or
out since the day he was christened. He has worked in
the fields all his life. He's burnt up with wine and sun.
Water . . . just for a change . . . may work a miracle.

DON ANTONIO. Perhaps you're right.

DON FRANCISCO. I've seen it happen. People talk of
these "cures" . . . Anything may be a cure . . . for something. Yesterday they installed a regular medicine man
in the dispensary. He has just got through his examinations in Madrid with flying colours . . . and he seems a
clever boy. A little pedantic . . . but that's only natural
. . . for he knows such a lot . . . such a devil of a lot.
To hear him talk about serums and injections and immunity
and all the while giving me a look from the corner of his
eye as much as to say, "Now's your chance to pick up a
tip or two." And I sat and laughed to myself. "Talk
away, my lad," I thought. "These clodhoppers here are
made of another clay than the sort your Madrid professors
like to meddle with. Once upon a time I had book learning at my fingers' ends too. Wait a little, and you'll be
glad enough to put your faith in lemon juice and water."
Why, *you* might as well ask them when they come to confession, whether they'd been committing the unforgivable
sin against the Holy Ghost. No, no . . . What good
would the silk purse be to the sow anyway . . . she's better
off with her ear. Leave learning to the learned!

DON ANTONIO. And theology to the Bishops. To get
these folk to heaven I've to drag them by the scruffs of
their necks . . . I know that!

DON FRANCISCO. Well, I have to vaccinate 'em by main
force to keep them on earth a little longer. I went into
the school yesterday afternoon, shut the door, and left
El Tuerto in front of it with a thick stick. "Now,"
I said, "not a child leaves this room till he's been vacci-
nated." Lord, you should have heard them yell. Well
. . . I'd had three of them die on my hands in two days
and there's no mortal way of knocking sense into their

mothers. The savages! When they're ill they still think they're possessed by the devil. I am . . . when I have to write small-pox on a death certificate. And now if one of these children that I stick a little calf lymph into goes and dies after all, the village will want to lynch me. So I ask myself . . . and you . . . for we're both in the same boat . . . since we get neither pay nor thanks . . . why on earth do we make such fools of ourselves?

DON ANTONIO. For the love of God, my dear doctor.

DON FRANCISCO. Or is it that we just can't leave ill alone.

DON ANTONIO. Well, do you wonder? When most human beings . . . God forgive me for saying so . . . are hardly better than brute beasts, what should we do, if by God's grace we're a little less so, but lend them our strength and our brains. For it's not their fault, poor things.

DON FRANCISCO. Don Antonio, Don Antonio . . . be careful. That sounds very like an attack upon Providence.

DON ANTONIO. Not at all! God made us all, and as he made us it is good to be. He has his reasons for all that he does.

DON FRANCISCO. He may have . . . but I wish he'd confide 'em to us sometimes.

[LUCIA *comes in from the street, and crosses the garden rapidly, making signs to someone outside, who can not be seen, to wait for her. She is carrying a flat wicker basket, covered with a white cloth.*]

DON FRANCISCO. Hullo, Lucia!

LUCIA. Good afternoon, Don Antonio . . . good afternoon, Don Francisco. [*She wishes to go on her way without being stopped.*] Is my godmother in?

DON FRANCISCO. You're in a great hurry.

LUCIA. I've brought the surplices.

DON ANTONIO. Come here . . . I want to talk to you.

LUCIA. [*Nervously.*] Yes, Father.

Don Antonio. Put that down. [*The basket.*] Who
are you making signs to?

Lucia. No one . . . no, indeed, Father. [Don Antonio *looks fixedly at her.*] . . . that's to say, only to
Mateo, who's waiting outside for me. But don't
think. . . .

Don Francisco. Mateo? Oho . . . so you mean to
be my lady Mayoress, do you?

Lucia. I?

Don Francisco. Well, he'll be Mayor, I daresay, when
his father dies. . . . So . . . it stands to reason . . . sauce
for the gander is sauce for the goose, isn't it?

Lucia. What an idea!

Don Francisco. Oh . . . then you don't mean to
marry him. It's a pity in that case you go so many walks
with him in the woods of an evening.

Lucia. I?

Don Francisco. Yes, Miss . . . you. And he! Now
don't deny it, because you've been seen.

Lucia. Who by?

Don Francisco. By me. So now!

Don Antonio. Listen to me, Lucia. I have heard of
these walks too.

Lucia. Oh yes . . . from that little tell-tale Juanillo.

Don Antonio. Never mind how . . . for sooner or
later, one way or another, it was bound to be known.

Lucia. Yes, I suppose so . . .

Don Antonio. Even then it's not people knowing it
that matters . . . but that there should be anything to
know. Do you understand me?

Lucia. Yes, Father.

Don Francisco. Well, that's something.

Don Antonio. And what do you think will be the end
of this love-making in secret . . . ?

Don Francisco. . . . More or less . . . rather less by
this time.

Lucia. Well . . . you see . . .

DON ANTONIO. You are as poor as a church mouse.
He is well off. You're an orphan. His father's the Mayor
of the village. Is he going to marry you for the sake
of your pretty face?

[LUCIA *doesn't answer.*]

DON ANTONIO. Well?

LUCIA. I love him.

DON ANTONIO. And does he love you, pray?

LUCIA. He says so . . .

DON ANTONIO. You don't seem very sure of it.

LUCIA. Well, you know what men are, Father!

DON ANTONIO. I suppose what you mean is that you
think you do. Then what on earth are you about, throwing
your reputation away in this insane fashion?

LUCIA. I suppose I've a right to live my own life in
my own way, haven't I?

DON ANTONIO. And what in Heaven's name do you
mean by *that?*

LUCIA. Oh, of course I'm nobody. I'm a country girl.
I'm poor and I haven't been educated. But he's no better
born than I am, and it isn't much good that his going to
school has done him. Of course he has got money, or
rather his father has. But is that any reason his mother
should treat me like the dirt under her feet?

DON ANTONIO. Now what has his mother to do with
it?

LUCIA. Didn't she come on the feast of the Virgin a
year ago last August when I was dancing with Mateo in
the Square . . . and that was no crime, was it? . . . and
say before everybody that her son was too good for me
. . . too good to be dancing with me, if you please? Well,
I know that I'm poor, but why should that stop me from
doing what I want to do? So I swore that I'd get the
better of her for that . . . and I have.

DON ANTONIO. Can't you see that it's you will get
the worst of it all?

LUCIA. Yes, I suppose so. But I have made her angry.

DON FRANCISCO.   Which is always a comfort.

DON ANTONIO.   Come here, you poor little fool.   Here's a good lady that has done you no harm, and just to annoy her you think it worth while to disgrace yourself.   Don't you know that your only dowry is your virtue and your good name, the fact that no one can say a syllable against you? And can't you understand, you feather-brain, that if when you're a good girl the Mayoress doesn't think you good enough for her son, you'll be good enough for nobody if you're a bad one?   Where will you be I should like to know when everybody refuses to have anything to do with you?   And if you could keep your shame a secret from them, can you keep it secret from God?   You are a Christian, you have been dedicated to the Virgin Mother. You are committing deadly sin.   Our Lady is watching you from Heaven with very sorrowful eyes.   [LUCIA *hangs her head.*]   Well, what is it now?

LUCIA.   I did tell Mateo that you'd think it very wrong if you knew.

DON ANTONIO.   And what did he say to that?

LUCIA.   [*With much candour.*]   He said it was none of your business.

[*The Doctor laughs.*]

DON ANTONIO.   [*With almost comical indignation.*] None of my business!   Whose business is it then I should like to know?   You've no father, your mother's a helpless cripple.   You're my sister's godchild.   And even though you were not, I have known you since you were born . . . I baptised you . . . I've taught you the little catechism you know . . . your silly head wouldn't hold more . . . I gave you your first absolution . . . ah, and that's true, since Easter . . . four months ago, you haven't been to confession.

LUCIA.   No . . . Mateo says he doesn't like me to go to confession.

DON ANTONIO.   And why not, pray?

LUCIA.   Well, he says that after all priests are only men

just like he is . . . and they might easily take advantage of an innocent girl like me.

Don Antonio. Wrath of God!

Don Francisco. Ho . . . ho! . . . he prefers to confess you himself, does he, under the pine trees.

Don Antonio. [*To the shabby old figure of the Virgin.*] Mother of God . . . do you hear this? Give me patience. Don't let me be driven to violence. [*To Lucia.*] Take yourself out of my sight! No, come here. Now understand me once and for all. This scandalous nonsense is over, over and done with. For the future . . . from tonight . . . you will live here with your godmother, and she will see that you are kept properly employed. Your mother will go to the Hospital, where the Sisters will look after her far better than ever her gadabout daughter has done. As for Mateo, he can amuse himself by taking care of the kitten, for not so much as the tip of your skirt shall he ever touch again, I'll see to that.

Lucia. [*Almost crying.*] Oh no, Father . . .

Don Antonio. Now, what is it . . . what's the matter?

Lucia. I can't.

Don Antonio. What do you mean?

Lucia. I simply can't.

Don Antonio. Why can't you?

Lucia. [*Sobbing.*] Because I don't want to . . . and because I simply can't . . . now that there . . . isn't any help for it.

Don Antonio. What?

Don Francisco. What's that?

Lucia. [*Without stopping her crying.*] Well, you see . . . now . . . now . . .

Don Francisco. Young woman . . . look me straight in the face. [*Then he smiles.*] Oh, so that's it, is it? We've been sitting down to dinner before the bell rang!

[*She cries like a child without answering.*]

DON ANTONIO. You? You! Answer me . . . is this true? You, Lucia!

LUCIA. [*Choking.*] Yes . . . yes, Father. But you see I . . . that is, he said . . .

DON ANTONIO. Child of sin. Oh, but you're all alike. And wanting to keep your good name into the bargain. He said . . . ! Wait and see what'll be said to you now! Lord God . . . what is to be done with this village full of swine!

LUCIA. [*Weeping, but rather for the sake of the conventions, because, at bottom, she is glad to have got out of her difficulty.*] Ay . . . Ay . . . Ay!

DON ANTONIO. Don't cry! And with that angel face! Too innocent if you please, to come to confession . . . and now we hear this! Well, and what are you going to do? Aren't you overwhelmed with shame? Where are you going? Who's to take care of you now . . . ?

LUCIA. [*Knowing that she is sure of being looked after, but believing it an obligation upon her to show intense distress.*] Ay . . . Ay! Whatever will become of me!

DON ANTONIO. Until . . . until . . .

LUCIA. Ay . . . ay . . . ay!

DON FRANCISCO. Come now, come . . . you mustn't go on like this. I'll let you know when it's time to start crying.

LUCIA. Yes, Señor!

DON ANTONIO. [*Gruffly.*] Go into the house . . . and stop making an exhibition of yourself . . . here in the street almost. Paquita!

LUCIA. Ay . . . don't tell my godmother.

DON ANTONIO. She'll know soon enough, won't she, whether we tell her or not? Paquita!

DOÑA PAQUITA. [*Appearing.*] What is it?

DON ANTONIO. The Doctor has a case for you.

DON FRANCISCO. [*Supporting* LUCIA.] Come along now, child . . . come along.

Doña Paquita.   What's the matter . . . what has happened?

Don Francisco.   Nothing more than usual, Señora. The flesh is weak, you know.

[*The three go in.*]

Don Antonio.   Holy Mother . . . Holy Mother! [*He addresses the Virgin, then turns and calls.*]   Mateo! *As there is no answer, he goes out into the street and calls again.*]   Mateo!   Come in.   I want to speak to you.

Mateo.   After you, Father.

Don Antonio.   Go in.

Mateo.   If you say so.   May I ask what it is you want?

Don Antonio.   Yes.   I want you to go tomorrow morning and take out a license and bring it to me, so that I may send it to the Vicar of the Province.   Because on Sunday the first banns must be published.   You will be dispensed from the rest . . . and the week after you will be married.

Mateo.   I?

Don Antonio.   Yes, you.

Mateo.   Who to?

Don Antonio.   Who to!   God bless my soul . . . to the mother of your child.

Mateo.   So that cat's out of the bag, is it?   I might have expected it.   I believe if Lucia held her tongue for ten minutes she'd burst.

Don Antonio.   But as if it could be kept a secret . . .

Mateo.   Well, that remained to be seen, didn't it?

Don Antonio.   [*Indignantly.*]   What's that you say?

Mateo.   [*Shamefacedly.*]   Nothing, Father.

Don Antonio.   So much the better for you.   But you know what you've to do now anyhow.

Mateo.   Look here, Father.   I quite hate to disappoint you . . . but I'm really afraid that I can't.

Don Antonio.   Can't you indeed!   And why "can't" you, I should like to know?

MATEO. Well . . . a man can't . . . so to speak . . . go against his own nature, can he?

DON ANTONIO. I see. And it's yours to behave like a scoundrel, is it?

MATEO. You needn't insult me.

DON ANTONIO. Well, please tell me what *you'd* call a man who just seduces an innocent girl, and then refuses to do his plain duty by her?

MATEO. Oh . . . innocent, Father. Come now . . .

DON ANTONIO. Yes . . . innocent beside you . . . and all such young blackguards. Shame on you, and doubly shame to speak like that of a woman that you yourself have disgraced. Yes, innocent till you came along . . . and an honest girl, till you dishonoured her. And if this is what men are like, why ever do women drag their skirts in the mud for them? That's what I ask! Your mother must be proud of you . . . very proud of the gentleman she has for a son!

MATEO. Look here . . . you know you can tell me I'm not a gentleman, and I've got to put up with it, because you're . . . what you are. But I wouldn't from any-one else. I mayn't be anything very out of the way, but my honour's all right.

DON ANTONIO. Indeed! And will it be when your child has been born fatherless, and his mother is drudging to keep him, or begging bread for them both in the streets . . . or worse?

MATEO. She shan't. They shall both be looked after as long as I live.

DON ANTONIO. As long, I daresay, as you're your own master. But wait six months . . . wait till you marry some woman of your own class, who can bring you the one thing on earth that you want no more of . . . the one thing this other poor girl hasn't got . . . money . . . money! Then you'll have other children, and a very good father you'll be, I don't doubt. Nothing that you and their mother can think of will you deny them. But this one, your first and more yours than the others can ever be, for he is to be the child of your youth and your illusions, he will go barefoot and hungry, with a bricklayer's hod on his shoulder . . . he'll go to prison, maybe, someday, for stealing his bread from his brothers . . . his own brothers.

MATEO. Father . . .

DON ANTONIO. Oh . . . no doubt you can answer . . . It's none of my business . . . she should have thought of all this sooner . . . and how am I worse than other men? . . . can I go against my nature . . . ?

MATEO. Father, it's not fair, to speak of me as if I were a . . . as if I weren't a . . .

DON ANTONIO. As if you were a scoundrel? You are! As if you weren't a gentleman? You are not!

MATEO. I am. . . . I tell you I am. And I love her. . . . I tell you I love her. I swear it before those two [*The Virgin and Child.*] And I can never love any woman else . . . that's true too. And the day that she told me . . . you know . . . about the baby . . . before ever it struck me what a mess I was in . . . I felt pleased . . . I did indeed . . . and almost proud . . . as if till that moment I'd never really known what . . . well, how would you put it now . . . what life was.

DON ANTONIO. [*Gently.*] And after that you still mean to leave her to her fate?

MATEO. But I don't! It can all go on just as before. I love her . . . I've said so.

DON ANTONIO. Not a bit of it, my son. You'll do what's right by her now, or you won't set eyes on her again. She may have made one mistake, but she's not a bad woman, I know . . . and you shan't see her again.

MATEO. Of course I'd marry her like a shot . . . but my father . . .

DON ANTONIO. Well?

MATEO. He's dead against it. And as for Mother . . . she says if I marry Lucia she'll die of it. And it's just the sort of thing she would do.

Don Antonio. All right! If she does, I'll give her Christian burial. But there's not much fear of that.

Mateo. You don't know her!

Don Antonio. I think I know you all . . . to my sorrow . . . and an evil worthless lot you are. Now, no more shuffling, my lad. You're going to get married. That's your duty, and it'll be the best thing for you too. The mother of your child is your wife by rights . . . there's no getting away from that. As to your mother . . . you leave her to me. And you can tell your father this to go on with . . . tell him I told you to . . . I know all about that business of the municipal slaughter houses . . . and there's more than one road by which a man may find himself in prison. He'll understand. So be off and break it to your parents . . . and I'll be by presently and assure them the news is true. Tomorrow before noon remember, I shall expect the license.

Mateo. All right.

[*He goes.*]

Don Antonio. [*To the Virgin.*] Holy Mother, that's what these people are like. But you know it, you know it well. Stupid, cunning, greedy of money, their hearts as hard as their heads are empty. What can we do to save them? Holy Mother, whatever can we do? But remember, won't you, that sometimes in the end they do the right thing . . . why, now and then, even, you might almost think that one of them was a man. It costs us sweat and blood, Mother, doesn't it, to lead them to the right path? But we must just be patient and keep on. Can your blessed Son ask more of us? Ah no; he knows, none better, the sort of flock that he has given to our care.

[Juanillo *has entered.*]

Juanillo. It always sounds as if you were singing little songs to the Virgin.

Don Antonio. Now what do *you* want?

Juanillo. I was listening to you . . . [*Looking at the*

Virgin.]   Do you like talking to her . . . when she never answers back?

DON ANTONIO.   And how do you know she never answers back?

JUANILLO.   [*With terror.*]   Does she?

DON ANTONIO.   She'll answer you someday . . . somewhere. . . .

JUANILLO.   [*Incredulously.*]   How does she do it? Does she give you a sign?

DON ANTONIO.   What should Our Lady want, my child, with signs or words?   She speaks to the soul, and in our souls we hear her voice.

JUANILLO.   The soul . . . ?

DON ANTONIO.   You'll know what that means someday. There's nothing kept from her and nothing that she doesn't understand.   She never listens to idle gossip, and she never judges by appearances, and so her judgment is always right. And there's always good counsel on her lips for him who asks it from his heart . . . and healing in her heart if we bring our troubles to her. . . .   She gives us her hand and asks her son to pity us . . . for we want so to serve him and yet we stumble . . . then she prevents our fall. Our Lady is our queen, you see.   Well, we all want to be worthy to work for her in her kingdom.

JUANILLO.   But what a silly face the child has, hasn't he?

[DON JUAN DE DIOS *appears at the gate.*]

DON JUAN.   Ave Maria Purissima. . . .

JUANILLO.   Oh . . . it's Don Juan de Dios.

DON ANTONIO.   . . . *Concepta sine.*   Come in.

DON JUAN.   May God make the rest of the day a blessing to us.

DON ANTONIO.   What about your journey?

[DON JUAN DE DIOS *has a very troubled air.   He is very nervous and keeps on turning his hat in his hands while repeating almost all his words.*]

DON JUAN.   Good . . . oh good!   That is, the journey

itself was good. A little warm, . . . one can't deny that.
But good . . . oh good . . . thanks be to God . . . so to
speak.

Don Antonio. And did you find out anything?

Don Juan. Yes . . . oh yes, my friend. I did. Well
. . . God's will is . . . is not always, quite naturally . . .
does not always accord with the expectations of men . . .
desires which seem, so to speak, quite natural, that is, and
legitimate. So that . . . well now I'm afraid . . . so to
speak . . . that there's nothing more to do . . . but to
bow . . . bow, you know . . . to the decrees of Providence.

Don Antonio. You mean that . . .

Don Juan. Frankly . . . yes . . . frankly I do. And
of course . . . submission . . . that's what it must come to
in the end, mustn't it . . . so what's the use now . . . of
saying . . . so to speak . . . anything? And I myself . . .
well, I too . . . naturally . . .

Don Antonio. But you . . .

Don Juan. Oh yes . . . both of us, I assure you . . .
that's some comfort, isn't it . . . both of us, dear friend
. . . both of us are suspended from office.

Don Antonio. You say they have suspended me from
office!

Don Juan. And me . . . and me! Oh yes, both of
us . . . that's the truth.

Don Antonio. Are you quite sure?

Don Juan. Oh, the secretary himself so to speak . . .
his grace the Archbishop's secretary told me . . . that is,
naturally in confidence, of course . . . but he told me.
And the official communication . . . so to speak . . . will
be sent next week.

Don Antonio. But what *for?*

Don Juan. In my case . . . Latin, I'm afraid. . . .
Yes, it was, so to speak, Latin. My translation . . . of
St. Augustine. You, I fear, failed . . . that is . . . well,
yes . . . failed in Theology.

Don Antonio. In Theology!

Don Juan. Dogmatic . . . yes, dogmatic Theology. The secretary . . . well the secretary said that your answer to the question, "De vitiis religionis appositus per defectum . . ." was really . . . yes, "per defectum," was really almost a heresy.

Don Antonio. A heresy!

Don Juan. Well, frankly . . . yes . . . he said . . . that from lack of true doctrine . . . of true doctrine . . . these villages were forgetting . . . so he said . . . the very alphabet of religion. Yes, that's how he put it.

Don Antonio. The very alphabet . . .

Don Juan. For myself . . . I don't resent it . . . so to speak . . . no, I don't resent it. God's punishment on me, no doubt . . . for pride . . . yes, for pride. A mere humble chaplain such as I, who thought . . . yes . . . that he could save souls. *Peccavi . . . peccavi!* My nuns though, my nuns of St. Clara . . . they'll resent it. Because they thought that they had as their chaplain a Chrysostom . . . so to speak . . . oh yes indeed a perfect Chrysostom . . . as it were.

Don Antonio. [*First rebellious, then depressed.*] Suspended! Suspended! [*Then with serene resignation.*] God's will be done.

Don Juan. Why, of course, yes . . . God's will be done.

[Don Francisco *and* Doña Paquita *come out of the house.*]

Don Francisco. Mostly nerves now! In ten minutes give her another glass of linden-flower water, and let her go home.

Doña Paquita. Good heavens . . . what a nuisance these girls are!

[Juanillo *has been in a corner listening to the conversation of the two priests, goes up to* Doña Paquita *before she has finished coming down the door steps,*

and, taking hold of her skirts, says in almost tragic
affliction.]

JUANILLO.   Doña Paquita . . . they've suspended him!

DOÑA PAQUITA.   What!   What's that you say?

JUANILLO.   They have!   They've suspended him from
office for failing in the examination.   Yes, Señora . . .
Don Antonio . . . and Don Juan de Dios . . . they've suspended them both.

DOÑA PAQUITA.   It's not true!   Oh, don't talk such
nonsense.   [*To her brother.*]   It's not true, is it?

DON ANTONIO.   Yes, it's true, Paquita.   And there's
nothing to be done.   We must just be patient.

DOÑA PAQUITA.   D'you mean to tell me that you're no
longer priest of this village?

DON ANTONIO.   No . . . I've no right here at all.

DOÑA PAQUITA.   And who will have . . . may I ask?

DON ANTONIO.   Probably some young priest will be sent
. . . who can pass the examination.

DOÑA PAQUITA.   And you'll be put out in the street?

DON JUAN.   Oh no . . . no, indeed . . . I'm sure
that the Archbishop . . . that His Grace the Archbishop must take into account the years . . . so to speak
. . . years of service.   And he'll give him a chaplaincy
. . . in an asylum, no doubt . . . or to a Convent . . .

DOÑA PAQUITA.   Chaplain to a lot of nuns!

DON JUAN.   Well now, I assure you it's not
so bad.   I have always found my sisters . . . very good,
oh yes, indeed.   A little tedious at times, perhaps . . .
well, yes, I must confess . . . tedious . . . but very good.

DOÑA PAQUITA.   Oh, please be quiet

DON FRANCISCO.   [*To* DON ANTONIO.]   How has it
happened?

DON ANTONIO.   Well, I'm afraid there's no doubt, that
when it comes to dogmatic Theology . . . one has dropped
a little behind.   As we were saying just now, you know

. . . with one's struggle, year in and year out, with these savages for their salvation, one forgets all about the sort of things that they put in examinations . . .

JUANILLO. [*With indignation.*] Well, of course you do. . . . And here's the Virgin that knows everything . . . why, they'd stump her with their damned questions . . .

CURTAIN

ACT II

The same scene as in the first act. Doña Paquita, *the* Doctor *and* Juanillo *are in the garden.* Doña Paquita *is seated, with an air of profound sadness, on one of the stone seats by the door:* Juanillo *is doubled up on the step of the little door leading into the church, which is half open. The* Doctor *is walking up and down the garden with his hands behind his back.*

A ringing of bells is heard as the curtain rises.

Don Francisco. [*Looking into the air, as if he were speaking to the sound of the bells.*] This is a great day.

Doña Paquita. [*Almost in tears.*] Oh . . . a great day indeed!

> [*There is a pause, the sound of an organ inside the church can be faintly heard.*]

Doña Paquita. [*Sighing.*] There . . . they've reached the Te Deum now.

Juanillo. Yes . . . and hark at the organist flourishing away! . . . just to show off before the new priest!

Don Francisco. Here . . . why aren't you in your surplice?

Juanillo. Why should I be?

Don Francisco. Aren't you an acolyte?

Juanillo. Are we any of us anything now?

Don Francisco. No indeed . . . no indeed, we're not!

Juanillo. They've turned you out too . . . haven't they?

Don Francisco. Yes, my lad, yes . . . they've turned me out too.

Doña Paquita. [*Rebellious and bitter.*] God will judge them for it.

Don Francisco. Well, he may! . . . but what can

141

we all expect in this progressive world? Is this enlightened
village of ours the only one to be left behind in the great
race of the millennium? We must follow the fashions, we
must be brought up to date whether we like it or not!
And what are our Town Councillors for but to push us
along the path? So when it came to those seven illustrious gentlemen who read the papers once a week and are
deep in the secrets of the Government, having to choose between an old doctor who had brought most of them into
the world, by the grace of God and the exercise of his common sense and a brand new medical gentleman who was
ready to help them die in the very latest and most scientific
style, hall marked by Paris and Berlin—well, once again,
what could you expect? Señora Doña Paquita. . . . We
must be cosmopolitan, up to date. Hurrah for Progress!
And if you don't like it get out of the way . . . or be run
over, if you like that better!

Doña Paquita. Well, then . . . God's will be done.

Don Francisco. And the vote was unanimous . . .
why the question, so they tell me, wasn't even argued. As
with one voice they called aloud for the very latest thing!
The first time, I believe, that they have ever agreed upon
anything. Blessed progress . . . all-conquering youth!

[*There is another pause.*]

Juanillo. Andreson's wife, at the inn . . .

Don Francisco. Well?

Juanillo. She's having her baby today.

Don Francisco. How do you know, pray!

Juanillo. I saw that new doctor go by. They've
called him in because he's a specialist . . . that's what he
is . . . an acc—acc—something or other. Anyhow he
went by on his motor bicycle like greased lightning.

Don Francisco. Yes, he'd better not waste time. She
doesn't.

Doña Paquita. Well, she's used to it . . . it's her
seventh.

Don Francisco. Eighth . . . the fourth time it was

twins. Think of it! That's the first baby for twenty-five years to come into this world and this village without asking my leave!

[*He tries to speak jestingly, but doesn't make a success of it.*]

JUANILLO. And they say that that boy of Juana la Fea's was just dying . . . but the new doctor put water into him with a syringe and he got well at once.

DOÑA PAQUITA. [*Thinking* DON FRANCISCO'S *feelings will be hurt.*] Hold your tongue now!

DON FRANCISCO. Are you going away this very day?

DOÑA PAQUITA. This very evening . . . as soon as they've finished in there [*Indicating the church with a glance, but without moving.*] The van with the furniture has gone on already.

DON FRANCISCO. [*To* JUANILLO.] How much longer will they be?

JUANILLO. There's the sermon to come still . . . he's just going up for it now.

DOÑA PAQUITA. Aren't you going in to hear it ?

DON FRANCISCO. No, thank you!

JUANILLO. They say he's no end of a preacher. Well, since he's preached himself in here and preached us all out into the street I suppose it's true. He gets ten dollars a sermon. And the other day in the Cathedral at the Novenary of Souls he preached and he preached until the Canons almost died of it [*He is at the Church door.*] And what a voice he has! You can hear it through the door. [*Repeating with gestures of admiration what it may be supposed he hears said by the preacher.*] "Honoured servants of the Sanctuary . . . worthy authorities of this godly village . . . best beloved brothers, all, of the Sacred Heart of Jesus and the Sweetness of Mary." What rot!

[*He hides himself behind the door so that he can go on listening.*]

DOÑA PAQUITA. Shut that door . . . they don't want to hear every noise from the street in there.

Don Francisco. It's a large congregation.

Doña Paquita. Every soul in the village. That's
what novelty will do. Some of those people haven't set
foot in the church for a matter of fifty years or so. The
Mayor's there and the Schoolmaster and the Colonel of the
Militia . . . even   the   district   Judge . . . though   he
stands, if you please, for Sunday work at the Universities.
. . . [Crossing herself.]   God save us from that at least!

Don Francisco. But it seems that he is a bit of a
prodigy.

Doña Paquita. Who . . . the judge?

Don Francisco. No . . . our new priest.

Doña Paquita. He certainly is. [Disdainfully.] He
arrived today in a motor car.

Don Francisco. Yes, the place will smell strong of
petrol now . . . that's one sure sign of progress.

Juanillo. [Popping round the door.] He says that
the village is going to be a garden planted with carnations
and roses and [Scratching his head and trying to remember.] . . . that he . . . he means to be the gardener . . .
and he'll make a nosegay of the gently opening flowers and
suck from it honey for the honey comb . . . which is the
Church. He's a one-er ain't he? [He disappears again.]

Doña Paquita. A garden of roses! With a few
thorns among them he'll soon find.

Don Francisco. These ceremonies take a long time.

Doña Paquita. Don't talk about it. First the Installation . . . then the Supplicatory Procession. Then a
Te Deum . . . a sermon . . . and Heaven knows what
else! Still this is the finish of it all, thank God. I tell
you, what with one thing and another, we've had a pleasant four months.

Don Francisco. Yes . . . the powers that be at the
Archbishop's were a long time making up their minds.

Doña Paquita. Yes . . . and nobody pleased at the
end. For don't imagine the young man likes coming here
any more than the old man likes leaving. Do you notice

that he uses a cigarette holder, so as not to stain his fingers? He will like it, won't he, when all the dirty nosed little children come kissing his hand?

DON FRANCISCO. Not quite the village, is it, for fastidious fingers to meddle with?

DOÑA PAQUITA. No, nor for his shiny shoes with their silver buckles. He's here because he's been put here and he has to do as he's told. Why, he has buttonholed everyone from Rome to Santiago to get himself into some church in Madrid. Preaching's what he likes. Showing off, getting talked about . . . he thought he'd be made a Bishop in no time. That's where he was wrong. He tried to be too clever . . . put things in the offices, they say, which were more than even they could stand. So like this world, isn't it? They take the old man from the corner he belongs in because they say he knows too little and they send the young one to eat his heart out in a far off village because they think he knows too much.

DON FRANCISCO. What else does one expect!

DOÑA PAQUITA. Oh well, time will put things right for the young man . . . but only death can do that for the old one.

DON FRANCISCO. Nonsense . . . what are you talking of . . . I never heard such nonsense! What your brother needs at his age . . . is a little rest . . . and peace and quiet.

DOÑA PAQUITA. Rest! You know him. He'll rest in his grave . . . not before. What has his life been? From morning till night, never stopping . . . was ever a single thing done in the village if his hand wasn't in it? Well, can you see him as chaplain to an old woman's almshouse . . . saying mass for them . . . sitting by while they gabble their prayers . . . hearing their confessions; the dreadful things they said to the cat when it stole the milk. He'll fret himself to death. Why you've only to look at him . . . ever since he knew it was settled. He says nothing . . . but what he's thinking and feeling! I know him

so well. But so do you, oh, so do you. But he's all I have
in the world, you see . . . he's brother and father and son
to me, all in one. And I can't sit by and watch him suffer
like this. I can't . . . I can't. What's to become of us!

[JUANILLO *comes from behind the door and turns
towards the gate.*]

DOÑA PAQUITA. Where are you going? Is the sermon
over?

JUANILLO. No, Señora . . . there's a woman been taken
ill . . .

DON FRANCISCO. [*Instinctively standing up; business-
like.*] Where?

DOÑA PAQUITA. Who?

JUANILLO. I don't know . . . just someone in there.
She was kneeling . . . and then she fell right over on the
floor.

DOÑA PAQUITA. Fainted . . . they'd better bring her
here.

DON FRANCISCO. Let me see . . . let me see.

[*At this moment* LUCIA *comes in supported by* MATEO
and the MAYOR, *and followed by the* LADY MAYORESS.
*She is half fainting, or, rather pretending to be. She
wears a black brocade silk dress, her wedding dress,
very elaborate, a lace mantilla, a filigree rosary, diamond ear-rings and brooch, a mother-of-pearl fan and
a lace handkerchief. She has all through the scene
the manner of a very affected fine lady.*]

DON FRANCISCO. What's the matter?

DOÑA PAQUITA. What has happened?

JUANILLO. Well . . . if it isn't Lucia!

MATEO. [*Very worried.*] Get a chair please, somebody!

THE MAYOR. Please get a glass of water!

[JUANILLO *goes to the back to fetch the water and*
DOÑA PAQUITA *pulls out a chair.*]

DOÑA PAQUITA. Loosen her dress.

MATEO. [*Who hasn't noticed* DON FRANCISCO.] Will
somebody please go for a doctor . . . at once.

DON FRANCISCO. Now don't be frightened. Let's see what's the matter. Give her a chance to breathe.

THE MAYOR. [*With a mixture of confusion and annoyance.*] Oh . . . oh . . . it's you, is it? Still here!

DON FRANCISCO. Yes, Señor Alcalde . . . though not officially.

MATEO. [*At* LUCIA'S *side and afraid that this is going to be the death of his wife.*] Don Francisco . . . for God's sake . . .

DON FRANCISCO. Don't worry . . . don't worry . . . I *am* here.

[*He goes up to* LUCIA *who continues her pretence of a fainting fit.*]

MATEO. [*Anxiously.*] What's the matter with her?

THE MAYORESS. Nothing whatever.

DON FRANCISCO. She fainted with the heat. She's coming to. It's all right.

MATEO. I warned her . . . I did warn her that in her most delicate condition she must not go into that crowded church!

LUCIA. [*Coming to very prettily.*] Where am I?

MATEO. Here . . . safe with your husband.

LUCIA. [*Affectedly.*] Oh!

JUANILLO. Here's the water.

MATEO. Try to drink some, my darling.

THE MAYOR. But slowly . . . slowly.

LUCIA. Oh . . . my fan!

MATEO. [*Rushing to pick it up.*] Here it is.

THE MAYOR. Shall I fan you? [*He takes his wife's fan for the purpose.*]

LUCIA. No, please . . . I can't bear it. My handkerchief.

THE MAYOR. Here it is!

MATEO. Take mine.

LUCIA. Oh! Wipe my forehead please! Oh!

MATEO. Are you in pain?

THE MAYOR.   Aren't you better?

MATEO.   Would you like to go home?

THE MAYOR.   Shall we have the carriage brought round for you?

LUCIA.   No, no . . . I'm better now, thank you. [*She gets up.*] Oh . . . how my head swims!

MATEO.   Sit down . . . *please*.

THE MAYOR.   Keep still, child . . . just a little longer.

THE MAYORESS.   Oh . . . for all our sakes! Suppose anything should happen to our precious jewel!!

LUCIA.   Mateo . . . Mateo!

MATEO.   What is it?

LUCIA.   Your mother . . . your mother is insulting me . . . again.

THE MAYOR.   My dear . . . *will* you be quiet?

THE MAYORESS.   Yes, I will be when I choose!

MATEO.   A nice thing, isn't it, to upset her now! Suppose anything happens . . .

THE MAYOR.   . . . in her delicate condition!

THE MAYORESS.   Delicate fiddlesticks! I've brought seven children into the world and never fainted over one of them.

LUCIA.   No doubt, Señora . . . but some of us are more sensitive, I suppose.

THE MAYORESS.   I didn't hear of your fainting three months ago before you were married when you were still washing clothes in the river. And I understand that you'd every right to feel just as delicate then.

LUCIA.   [*Collapsing.*] Oh, Mateo! Oh Father, dear Father! Oh!!! [*She affects the classic attack of nerves.*]

MATEO.   [*Furious, while he supports her on one side.*] If it weren't that you are my mother . . .

THE MAYOR.   [*Threatening, while he supports her on the other.*] If it wasn't that we are . . . where we are . . .

THE MAYORESS.   And if you men weren't so easily taken in . . .

DOÑA PAQUITA.   Please . . . please don't make so much
noise.   Every word you say can be heard in the church.

THE MAYORESS.   By a dolly draggle-tail who was scrub-
bing floors three months ago and now if you please she can't
lift a feather duster!

LUCIA.   Oh—oh—oh!   Mateo . . . my heart!

DON FRANCISCO.   [*Who is losing patience.*]   Look here
—young lady—will you stop this nonsense or shall I throw
a bucket of water over you?

JUANILLO.   Shall I go and fetch one?

LUCIA.   [*Taking hold of the doctor's hand.*]   Oh, dear,
dear Don Francisco!

JUANILLO.   Turned into a fine lady in double-quick time,
haven't you . . . fainting fits and all!   You're no fool . . .
I'll say that for you.

LUCIA.   Is that Juanillo?

JUANILLO.   Oh yes . . . the same old Juanillo as ever
. . . and will be for ever and ever, amen!   We can't all
get up in the world by coming a cropper like you.

LUCIA.   You are an impertinent boy.

JUANILLO.   That's right—keep it going!—You do it very
well.

MATEO.   Get out of here . . . or I'll kick you out.

JUANILLO.   All right . . . consider me kicked!

DOÑA PAQUITA.   Well, Lucia . . . so you're better?

LUCIA.   [*A little shamefaced.*]   Yes, Señora.

DOÑA PAQUITA.   Let's have no more of these scenes then
. . . unless you want to send your mother-in-law into a
fit.

LUCIA.   Suppose you ask her to stop driving me mad!

JUANILLO.   [*Who has returned to his post by the small
door leading to the Church.*]   The service is over!   They're
coming out . . . they're all coming . . .

[*A movement of curiosity on the part of everyone.*
LUCIA *entirely forgetting her faint, goes forward with
the others toward the church door.   At the same time
there come in from the street with huzzas,* DOÑA GER-

TRUDIS, *a lady of fifty summers, pretentiously dressed in black silk, with a mantilla;* THE SCHOOL MISTRESS, *a blue-stocking of twenty-five or thirty;* ROSITA, *a young girl of the village, about eighteen; a little girl; the Colonel of the "Guardia Civil"; and various other ladies, married and unmarried.   Also some men.*]

JUANILLO.   [*As the ladies appear, in a stage whisper.*] Ha—hum . . . enter the wise Virgins!

DOÑA PAQUITA.   Be quiet . . . you blasphemous boy!

DOÑA GERTRUDIS.   May we . . . ?

THE SCHOOL MISTRESS.   Will you allow us to . . . ?

DOÑA PAQUITA.   Yes . . . come in, come in.

DOÑA GERTRUDIS.   Forgive us, dear Doña Paquita, won't you, for bursting in on you like this.   But these girls . . . they felt they just must kiss our new Priest's hand and . . .

THE COLONEL.   Only the girls . . .

DOÑA GERTRUDIS.   Now . . . don't   be   mischievous, Colonel.

ROSITA.   [*To* DOÑA PAQUITA.]   And you weren't there for the sermon.   Oh, I never heard one like it.

DOÑA GERTRUDIS.   Such feeling!

THE SCHOOL MISTRESS.   And such erudition.

      [*They all talk.*]

ROSITA.   But what happened to you, Lucia?

LUCIA.   It was nothing, dear . . . I felt a little faint. The heat I daresay . . .

THE MAYOR.   She's so very delicate . . .

THE MAYORESS.   And of course we were frightened . . .

DOÑA GERTRUDIS.   And I'm sure that the sermon stirred you very deeply.   Such depths of wisdom.   You lost all the best of it.

ROSITA.   What I liked best was the part about "godly womanhood."

DOÑA GERTRUDIS.   Ah no, no!   Remember "the mellifluent sweetness of our Redeemer's heart . . ."

THE SCHOOL MISTRESS.   The best of all though was that

passage about the soul as a butterfly taking flight, drawn
by its intense desire to be consumed in the flame of the Love
Divine.   [*She looks softly at* THE COLONEL.]

A LADY.   And his voice . . . !

A YOUNG LADY.   Such gestures . . . !

DOÑA GERTRUDIS.   And what a beautifully embroidered
rochet!

ROSITA.   Made . . . was it not . . . from the fabric of
the nipa-palm?

A LADY.   It had lace half a yard wide.

THE COLONEL.   Well . . . and did our respected school-
mistress enjoy herself?

THE SCHOOL MISTRESS.   We all did!

THE COLONEL.   Ah, but you discriminate.   A thing must
be really good before it pleases you.

DOÑA GERTRUDIS.   Well, he brought tears to my eyes
more than once . . . more than once!

LUCIA.   Oh . . . he's coming!

[DON ANTONIO *and* DON JOSÉ MARÍA, *the new
priest, come out of the small church door. The latter is a young man of about twenty-eight, he wears
his mantle beautifully, elegantly gathered up in one
hand, and in the other he is carrying his plush hat,
small and tasselled. His hands are very white and
perfectly cared for. He wears patent leather shoes
with silver buckles. He comes forward slowly and
bows with suave inclinations of the head. His eyes
are cast down and he is smiling with honeyed sweetness.
The actor must be careful to have the necessary affecta-
tions, without the slightest approach to caricature.*
DON ANTONIO, *as in the first act, is wearing a sotana
and threadbare cassock, with elastic boots and has a
breviary in his hand and an ordinary tile hat.*]

DOÑA GERTRUDIS.   So modest too!

ROSITA.   Oh . . . but doesn't he remind one of St.
Luiz Gonzaga.

THE COLONEL. Say something, Señora Dominie.

THE SCHOOL MISTRESS. [*Coquettishly.*] Colonel, Colonel, you know my name, don't you?

DON ANTONIO. This is the garden, you see . . . and that is the house. Shall we go in?

DON JOSÉ MARÍA. No . . . no thanks. Time enough . . . time enough!

DON ANTONIO. It's very convenient . . . one can come this way . . . without having to go through the street.

DON JOSÉ MARÍA. What a pretty garden . . . and how well kept!

DON ANTONIO. It has amused my sister to grow a pot-ful of vegetables . . . and a bunch of flowers: Paquita . . . Don José María . . . My sister. [*He introduces them.*]

DON JOSÉ MARÍA. So pleased, Señora . . .

DOÑA PAQUITA. Señor . . .

DON JOSÉ MARÍA. You're a great gardener, I see.

DOÑA PAQUITA. Oh . . . I love flowers. And the earth will always give something in return for one's care of it, will it not? It is easier to strive with than the hearts of men.

[*She moves away.*]

DON JOSÉ MARÍA. And these ladies and gentlemen?

DON ANTONIO. They all want to pay their respects to you, I think . . . if you don't mind.

DON JOSÉ MARÍA. No, no, of course . . . on the contrary . . .

DON ANTONIO. Don Francisco . . . [DON FRANCISCO *has been alone at the back.*] I have the honour to present to you Doctor Don Francisco Lasada . . . my best friend . . . my most valued comrade.

DON FRANCISCO. Your servant.

DON JOSÉ MARÍA. So delighted to know you.

DON ANTONIO. And I have never met his equal.

DON FRANCISCO. [*Smiling.*] Well . . . one's as good as one knows how to be!

DON ANTONIO. You'll come to value him too.

DON JOSÉ MARÍA. You're the Officer of Health for the village, of course.

DON FRANCISCO. I was . . . till a short while ago.

THE MAYOR. [*Putting in his oar where it isn't needed.*] Yes, there's been a new appointment. A younger man . . . your own age . . . and very clever . . .

DON ANTONIO. Our Mayor.

[DON FRANCISCO *and* DOÑA PAQUITA *retire together to one side.*]

DON JOSÉ MARÍA. And so to remain, I hope, for many years.

THE MAYOR. Ah well . . . I'm on the way down hill now, you see. But here's my son [*Indicating* MATEO, *who comes forward with a certain perturbation.*] ready to seize the staff of office . . . when I let it go.

MATEO. [*Not knowing what to say.*] What nonsense, Father!

THE MAYOR. Why, of course, you are . . . ready and anxious too. Don't be ashamed of it. Ready to put the whole world to rights, these young folk, aren't they? And quite right too . . . quite right [*To his wife.*] Come here, my dear. Oh come along, come along . . . nobody's going to eat you. My wife!

DON JOSÉ MARÍA. Delighted to meet you, Señora.

THE MAYORESS. [*Bashfully kissing his hand.*] Oh no . . . I mean yes . . . the pleasure is yours . . . I mean mine . . .

[*A little whispered laughter in the group of women.*]

THE SCHOOL MISTRESS. [*Quietly to the others.*] Now the Lady Mayoress has made her customary happy remark!

THE MAYOR. [*Taking* LUCIA *by the hand.*] And this is our daughter-in-law. Now you can boast that you know all the family. Now make him a pretty speech since you've got yourself up for the occasion.

LUCIA. I . . . oh yes, of course . . .

[*She kisses the priest's hand.*]

THE MAYOR. And we shall want your services soon. There's a christening coming! Ha, ha!

THE MAYORESS. [*Furious.*] Oh, of course . . . we don't escape *that* remark!

THE MAYOR. And remember . . . my house is yours . . . and everything in it. No compliments . . . I mean it.

DON JOSÉ MARÍA. [*Wanting to make an end.*] You are most kind . . . I'm much obliged . . .

DON ANTONIO. [*Presenting* DOÑA GERTRUDIS.] And here is the President of the Sisterhood of Our Lady of Sorrows.

DON JOSÉ MARÍA. Señora . . .

DOÑA GERTRUDIS. [*Kissing his hand.*] Your very devoted servant, Father. And we have such a beautiful image . . . oh but you must have noticed it . . . in the church.

DON JOSÉ MARÍA. I have indeed.

DOÑA GERTRUDIS. Ah, but she's not at her best now . . . as dowdy, I'm afraid as . . . well, as I am. We fully meant her to have a new mantle for the Novena. But it couldn't be managed. No, as usual, these girls [*Indicating* ROSITA.] got everything.

ROSITA. [*Offended.*] Oh, you shouldn't say that!

DON JOSÉ MARÍA. I beg your pardon . . .

DON ANTONIO. This young lady, you see, is President of the Association of the Daughters of Mary.

ROSITA. Your reverence . . . [*She too kisses his hand.*]

DON JOSÉ MARÍA. God bless you.

DOÑA GERTRUDIS. [*Persisting.*] But it is so . . . the Daughters of Mary get everything that's going. And I suppose it's natural, because they're young, and when it comes to begging, of course, people give more readily to a young girl than to an old woman.

ROSITA. Oh, but don't you think it's a little because our Virgin is so much prettier?

DOÑA GERTRUDIS. Certainly not, child . . . our Virgin is far more distinguished . . . and far more appealing too . . . with those tears on her cheeks.

ROSITA.   [*To* DON JOSÉ MARÍA.]   Well . . . you must
be the judge, Father . . .

DON JOSÉ MARÍA.   [*Smiling.*]   Ladies, ladies, there is
but one Holy Virgin and her joy is the same in the worship
offered to her through every one of her images.

THE SCHOOL MISTRESS.   Oh, it's no use, Father, you'll
never get them to believe that.   It's to these villages one
must come, I'm afraid, to find true materialism.

[DON JOSÉ MARÍA *looks at her with some alarm.*]

DON ANTONIO.   [*Smiling at the poor girl's inoffen-
sive pedantry.*]   This lady is the head of our elementary
school.

THE SCHOOL MISTRESS.   Yes . . . only a school teacher,
and your humble parishioner, Señor.   [*She kisses his hand.*]

THE MAYOR.   But she knows Latin!

DON JOSÉ MARÍA.   [*Without enthusiasm.*]   Does she
indeed!

THE SCHOOL MISTRESS.   A few words, oh, hardly more.
Just enough to let me read the works of the Fathers in my
moments of leisure.

DON ANTONIO.   [*Going on with the introduction.*]   Our
commandant here, Colonel Manuel Ramirez of the Civil
Guard.

THE COLONEL.   At your command!

DON JOSÉ MARÍA.   Señor . . .

[*They all surround him now, while he bows and smiles
and the women kiss his hand in fierce rivalry.*]

A LADY.   Welcome . . . welcome from us all, Señor
Cura . . .

A YOUNG LADY.   And we hope that you'll stay here many,
many years . . .

ANOTHER.   And that you'll be so happy among us . . .

DEMETRIO.   And preach us lots more sermons like today's . . .

NICETO.   May we all be spared to hear 'em!

THE MAYOR.   Come, come now . . . we mustn't tire him
out.

Don José María.   Oh indeed, you do nothing of the sort!

Doña Paquita.   [*A little bitterly to* Don Francisco.] They'll come to blows over him in a minute.

Don Francisco.   Children with a new toy!

Don José María.   Dear ladies . . . gentlemen . . .

Several People.   He's going to speak . . . he's going to speak!

Doña Gertrudis.   Sh! Sh!

The Mayor.   Hear, hear! Hear, hear!

Don José María.   No, really . . . I had no intention . . .

The School Mistress.   Oh yes, yes, Father . . . say a word to us.

Don José María.   Why, I have nothing to say . . . [*But already he has dropped into his honeyed rhetorical tone.*] . . . except that I am deeply, deeply grateful for the kindness . . . so little merited by me . . . and the warmth of my welcome to this enlightened village and for the trust with which it so readily begins to honour me . . .

The Mayor.   The honour is ours . . . the honour is ours!

The Mayoress.   [*Pulling his cloak.*]   Don't interrupt him!

The Mayor.   Don't interrupt *me!*

Don José María.   To-day . . : this past hour . . . and above all this passing moment stamp an ineffaceable memory in my heart. I bring to your service little power of mind, no store of knowledge, much unworthiness . . . but leaning, in my feebleness upon the strength of Him to whom all things are possible I do believe that I shall not quite utterly betray the hopes on which you build when with a simple and a touching faith, springing from the pure depths of love and fellowship, you hold out such a welcome to this unworthy servant of the Most High.

Juanillo.   [*Admiringly.*]   Good Lord . . . you'd think he must have learnt it all by heart before.

Don José María. But I . . . I ask your aid. Together we must labour in the mystic garden of our souls'
Beloved. Alone I can do little. It will be your task . . .
as when of old Aaron and Caleb so stood by Moses on the
mountain . . . to strengthen and sustain the drooping hands
I lift to God!

Several Low Voices. Yes, yes, indeed.

Niceto. That's the sort of priest for me!

Demetrio. Look out . . . there's the old one's sister
listening . . .

Don José María. But let me . . . taking up the staff
that makes me shepherd of your fold . . . add now a word,
inadequate I know, of gratitude and praise to him whom
I succeed. For many years he has watched over you with
patience and with skill that has indeed not had to be its
own reward. The Will that orders all things calls him
to well-earned repose. From his hands I take my sacred
charge. In your name and my own I ask him, in the peace
of his retreat, the evening of his days not to forget to pray
for his old flock and for their new shepherd.

[*He gives his hand to* Don Antonio *with signs of
great emotion. There are murmurs of admiration.*]

Don Antonio. God help you through your task.
You'll find other things than roses in the garden . . . sometimes.

The Mayor. Well, come now . . . what have you had
to complain of?

Don Antonio. [*Serene and grave.*] God did not ask
me for complaints. We have been together—I among you
all—for thirty years. I came so young . . . now that I
leave you I'm so old that somehow all my life is left behind
. . . I wish I could have laid my body here as well. But
God has willed that otherwise . . . blessed be His name.
Forgive me for the things in which I have offended you.
I always wished you well. We all make mistakes. And
I forgive, with all my heart indeed, any unkindness that
has been done to me. And I'll never forget you . . . any

of you . . . nor the village . . . as long as I live . . .
because . . . I can't go on . . . I . . . God keep and help
us all.

JUANILLO. [*To steel himself against tears.*]
Damn . . . !

[*There is a deep silence; no one moves, nor gives
the least sign of approbation. After the flowers of
rhetoric of the new priest, the other's simple speech
leaves the assemblage cold.* MATEO, *alone, after a
moment, goes up to the old man and presses his hand.*]

MATEO. [*With a little embarrassment.*] You know
just how we feel . . .

DON ANTONIO. [*More touched than he wants to show.*]
Thank you . . . thank you, my dear boy.

THE MAYOR. [*After another brief moment of silence.*]
Well, well . . . we mustn't waste time here. There's a
small—ah—collation ready in the Town Hall. [*To* DON
JOSÉ MARÍA.] You must honour us by coming.

DON JOSÉ MARÍA. Oh . . . but to go to all that
trouble! With pleasure . . . with the greatest pleasure.

THE MAYOR. Let's be off then . . . or the chocolate
will be getting cold. Come along, come along, everyone's
welcome . . . plenty there for us all.

DON JOSÉ MARÍA. [*To* DON ANTONIO.] Señor . . .

DON ANTONIO. No . . . forgive me if I don't come.
I've a few little things still to pack . . . and my train goes
at six.

DON JOSÉ MARÍA. But . . . are you going today?

DON ANTONIO. Yes indeed . . . my sister will give the
house keys to the sacristan.

THE MAYOR. [*Wishing to appear polite.*] But there's
no hurry, you know . . . at least as far as the house is
concerned. Don José María can consider himself my guest
for as long as he pleases. [*As* DON JOSÉ MARÍA *bows dep-
reciatingly.*] No, I mean it, I mean it.

DON ANTONIO. No, I've finished everything now.
Besides . . . [*With a little smile.*] my old ladies will be

expecting me. There's my installation to think of, you
know.

THE MAYOR. That's right . . . each in his turn!
Well . . . till we meet again.

DON JOSÉ MARÍA. Good-bye, good-bye. And remember . . . anything I can do for you . . . at any time . . .

DON ANTONIO. Yes, yes. Good luck to your work
here.

DON JOSÉ MARÍA. [*To* PAQUITA *who bows but does
not speak.*] Señora. . . . [*To* DON FRANCISCO.] Good
afternoon, doctor.

DON FRANCISCO. Good afternoon.

> [*They are all going out,* LUCIA *with the others,
> without paying any more attention to those who are left
> behind.* MATEO *detains her.*]

MATEO. [*To* LUCIA, *with a little reproach in his
tone.*] Say a word to your godmother.

LUCIA. [*As a duty and wanting to get it over.*] Anything I could do for you . . . if I stayed . . . ?

DOÑA PAQUITA. No, child, thank you . . . everything's
done.

THE MAYOR. [*From the gate.*] Lucia . . . Mateo
. . . come along.

LUCIA. I'm just coming.

DOÑA PAQUITA. Yes . . . off with you!

MATEO. I shan't say good-bye . . . we'll be down at
the station.

DON ANTONIO. All right . . . run away . . . run
away!

> [*Everyone goes out, except* DON ANTONIO, DON
> FRANCISCO, DOÑA PAQUITA *and* JUANILLO. *They
> don't speak. A gay peal of bells is heard; they are
> setting off rockets in the street, and a band of music,
> supposed to be stationed there, begins to play a quick-
> step, in front of the church, awaiting the exit of the
> new priest.*]

JUANILLO. [*Who, on hearing the music and the rockets,*

forgets everything else, and dashes toward the street.]
Rockets!

DOÑA PAQUITA. [*With deep reproach.*] Juanillo!

DON ANTONIO. Why . . . let him go, Paquita.

JUANILLO. [*Very conscience-stricken.*] No, Father, I
wasn't going . . . I wasn't really.

DOÑA PAQUITA. [*Making an effort to appear calm.*]
I'll make sure that nothing has been forgotten. [*To
JUANILLO.*] You come with me.

DON ANTONIO. Very well . . . fetch me when you're
ready.

> [DOÑA PAQUITA *and* JUANILLO *go out. The
> sound of music and bells goes on for an instant. The
> last rockets are fired off.* DON ANTONIO, *overcome
> by emotion, falls on a chair, and leaning his head on
> the stone table sheds a few tears; afterwards he makes
> a great effort to be calm, and succeeds.*]

DON ANTONIO. [*In a broken voice.*] God's will be
done . . . His will be done. [*He dries his eyes with his
bare hands.*] Ay . . . ay! [*To* DON FRANCISCO *bitterly.*]   all that my courage really comes to, you see.   Don't
despise me.

DON FRANCISCO. Well—if you mean to begin trying to
hide things from me at this time of day . . .

DON ANTONIO. Our work's done, my friend.

DON FRANCISCO. Yes, indeed . . . over and done
with.

DON ANTONIO. Oh, this village . . . this village!

> [*They both speak excitedly and with emotion, and
> at first, each one as if he were talking only to himself
> and with himself.*]

DON FRANCISCO. [*Walking from one side to another.*]
I remember the day I came. What a hideous and impossible place I thought it. I said to my wife—I won't stay
here a week. Well . . . that's thirty years ago.

DON ANTONIO. More.

DON FRANCISCO. [*A little grudgingly.*]   And the odd

thing is that one ends by having some sort of feeling . . .
an affection . . . for all the savagery and indecency of it.

DON ANTONIO. And for this hard dry land beyond . . .
and . . . oh the harder hearts of its people.

DON FRANCISCO. Yes . . . I suppose if we labour at
the plough long enough the ass-thistles in the furrows get
to look like roses . . . we see no others.

DON ANTONIO. Well . . . at least we *have* laboured!

DON FRANCISCO. We have! When I think how I've
travelled these roads . . . in the glaring sun . . .
not a tree on all the length of them . . . summer after
summer . . .

DON ANTONIO. And these hearts of stone . . . knocking at them day by day. . . .

DON FRANCISCO. I sold my horse yesterday. Well,
I've no use for him now. My wife cried when they took
him away.

DON ANTONIO. And you're staying on, are you . . . to
watch your successor? That takes some courage.

DON FRANCISCO. Does it! But where am I to go at
my age? The boys will be breaking loose—they've their
own way to make. I have a bit of land, you know. My
wife and I can live very simply . . . and she thinks stopping on in the house where they were born . . . where they
were children . . . will be almost like having them with
her still. Women will indulge themselves in these fancies.
But there's nothing else left for me . . . except to be lazy
while the other man does his work . . . my work . . . !
and to console myself by thinking—though it mayn't be
at all true—that I should be doing it better. Time heals
all wounds!

DON ANTONIO. God heals them, Señor Don Francisco.

DON FRANCISCO. The same thing!

DON ANTONIO. [*Passionately.*] It is not . . . it is
not the same thing. Do you think if I didn't *know* it was
the will of God that I could be patient while my life . . .
my whole life . . . was torn up by its roots?

Don Francisco. Well, you know . . . what can't be cured must be endured.

Don Antonio. Yes . . . if God gives us strength to endure. Beneath the wings of his pity we are still. His will be done, we say.

Don Francisco. Oh yes, we keep still because a wise instinct teaches us that keeping still is the proper prescription for dangerously wounded men.

Don Antonio. And you are content to believe, are you, . . . even in such an hour as this . . . that there's no God watching over you . . . that you must stand in this friendless world alone?

Don Francisco. I'm not alone! What about my wife? We've been happy together these forty years. What about you? And if I lost everything else I'd have my conscience still.

Don Antonio. But doesn't that whisper to you . . . doesn't it? . . . of something beyond and above, something more enduring that can give us the answer to this desperate riddle of our life?

Don Francisco. I shall be quite content to have lived it honourably.

Don Antonio. I don't understand . . . no, I do not understand how you can so have lost your faith.

Don Francisco. Bless you, I haven't . . . I never had any . . . and never felt the need of it.

Don Antonio. You've never prayed . . . your heart has never turned to God . . . you mean to die and not to ask him to go with you upon that unknown journey?

Don Francisco. When I was a child I used to pray with my mother . . . to please her. I still have the rosary that she said so many paternosters over . . . and that I fell asleep over so many times. When I was first married I went to Mass with my wife . . . to please *her*. If I die first, I'll have them call a priest . . . to set her mind at rest. If she has gone before me, I shall die quietly enough,

without ceremony. What is there to fear? One will
fall asleep like a child in his mother's arms.

DON ANTONIO. Oh, Señor Don Francisco.

DON FRANCISCO. No, believe me, dear old friend . . .
there's only one thing that matters . . . to be an honest
man. And I'm sometimes afraid that is settled for each
of us . . . whether or no . . . when we're born. And
everything else is illusion . . . hysteria in some people
. . . gross superstition in others. Your dreams are very
beautiful, my friend, because . . . well, it is your own nature makes them so. You have faith in God, you hope
for Heaven. But tell me now, truthfully . . . suppose
you were to lose all faith, all hope, could you, for any price
the world might offer . . . could you do a wicked thing?

DON ANTONIO. [*Humbly and sweetly.*] I don't know
. . . really I don't know. We are all weak creatures.

DON FRANCISCO. Weak . . . and brave!

DOÑA PAQUITA *and* JUANILLO *enter.* DOÑA PA-
QUITA *is carrying the image of the virgin, a small bag
and a case containing a chalice and paten.* JUANILLO
*has a basket with food for the journey and other pack-
ages.* DOÑA PAQUITA *shuts and locks the door of the
house.*]

DOÑA PAQUITA. [*Turning the key.*] There . . .
that's done.

DON ANTONIO. Everything?

DOÑA PAQUITA. Every single thing. I'm going to hand
over the keys. [*She calls into the Church.*] Benito! Benito! [*There is no answer.*] Juanillo, take them to the
Sacristy.—Here.

JUANILLO. He's off to the Town Hall . . . if there's
chocolate going.

[*He starts to go out with the keys and the basket.*]

DOÑA PAQUITA. Leave that basket now. If you lose
that we'll have no lunch. [JUANILLO *goes off.*] Have
you anything to put in the bag?

DON ANTONIO. My breviary.

[*He gives her the breviary which is bound in coarse
black cloth and* Doña Paquita *packs it in the bag.*]

Don Francisco. [*Taking up the case with the chalice
in it.*] What's this?

Doña Paquita. His chalice. That's our only valuable.

Don Antonio. My godmother gave it me when I said
my first Mass. Yes . . . it had better go in the bag.

[Doña Paquita *packs the case with the chalice in
the bag.*]

Doña Paquita. I'll wrap the Virgin in a handkerchief
. . then she can go in too.

Don Antonio. No, no . . . I'll carry her.

Doña Paquita. Here's the carriage already.

Don Antonio. Well now . . . you go on with Juanillo . . . and I'll walk. That won't be so conspicuous.

Doña Paquita. We shan't be noticed anyway if we take
the short cut. [*To* Don Francisco.] Are you coming?

Don Francisco. Yes, Señora.

[Juanillo *comes back.*]

Juanillo. [*Licking his lips.*] Oh yes . . . he was
there! And I tell you they're having no end of a time.
They gave me a meringue through the window.

[Paquita *suddenly breaks down, and bursts into
tears.*]

Doña Paquita. Oh God . . . Oh God!

Don Antonio. [*Trying to quiet her.*] Come now, Paquita . . . Come . . .

Doña Paquita. We're so old . . . we're all so old
. . . such a little time left us. Surely . . . surely . . .
you'd think they could have waited . . . just for a little.

Don Francisco. Young people have no patience, Señora.

Doña Paquita. [*With passionate grief.*] No, nor
pity.

Don Antonio. Remember that God knows what is best
for us, my dear. There now, go along . . . and don't let
them see you crying.

Don Francisco. Yes . . . yes. Come . . . come.

[*He gives his arm to* DOÑA PAQUITA, *and picks up the bag*—DOÑA PAQUITA *takes some of the packages, and they go.*]

JUANILLO. [*Breaking out uncontrollably.*] I can't stand it . . . I won't stand it! And that brute in there stuffing himself with sweets and wine and everything! Shall I go wait at the Plaza and throw a stone at him when he comes out? Shall I? Shall I?

DON ANTONIO. [*Horrified.*] God preserve us . . . certainly not! Do you know what you are saying! [*He gently draws the lad to him.*] Now listen, my child. This that has happened is God's will . . . and no one . . . do you understand? . . . no one is to blame. Never speak like that again. And never think of committing such a mortal sin.

JUANILLO. [*Vaguely comprehending, from the priest's agitation, that he has said something atrocious.*] No, Father . . . I won't . . . If you say so . . . but I . . . [*He bursts into tears.*]

DON ANTONIO. There then . . . run along . . . take the basket . . . we'll say no more about it.

[JUANILLO *takes the basket and goes out.* DON ANTONIO *remains alone for a moment, takes a long look about the garden, as if to say good-bye to it, sighs, and going slowly to the table, takes the image of the Virgin in his arms, and says to it, with love and resignation, but simplicity.*]

DON ANTONIO. And now . . . we must go too, Holy Mother.

[*He lifts the little statue and goes.*]

CURTAIN.

WIFE TO A FAMOUS MAN

COMEDY IN TWO ACTS

TEATRO DE APOLO MADRID
1914

CHARACTERS

MARIANA.
SEÑORA ANDREA.
THE APPRENTICE.
CARMEN.
LOLA.
JULIETA.
NATI.

JOSÉ MARÍA.
SEÑOR RAMÓN.
A REPORTER.
SEÑOR JULIÁN.
A POSTMAN.
SEVERAL NEIGHBOURS.

ACT I

The ironing-room in a public laundry. At the back the door and the show-window look out on a street in Madrid. At the right is a door which leads into the other rooms. There are a table and stove for heating irons, and another table with baskets in which linen garments may be placed, some ironed, some ready to be ironed. There is also a wardrobe, with a looking-glass, of white enamelled wood.

In the foreground, at the left, is a clothes-horse, and near it an armchair in which SEÑORA ANDREA *is sitting. Two laundresses and a girl apprentice are working at the ironing table. At* SEÑORA ANDREA'S *right and near the clothes-horse is a wooden cradle in which a baby is lying. There is a display of ironed linen in the show window.*

At the rising of the curtain there can be heard in the street the noise of voices and of people running. The three work-women leave their ironing and dash to the door.

THE VOICES. [*In the street.*] Yes! . . . Oh yes! . . . There! . . . Up there! . . . yes . . . no. . . .

THE WORKWOMEN. [*Running to the door.*] Let's see! . . . Oh, let's see!

ANDREA. Here . . . you . . . Carmen . . . Lola!

> [*The girls pay no attention to her. She tries to get up and go after them, but is prevented by her rheumatism, and sits down again.*]

Oh, these legs of mine! [*To the child in the cradle, who is supposed to be crying.*] Will you be quiet . . . you little

171

demon! [*Anxiously, to the laundresses.*] Is it coming? Is it coming?

CARMEN. Yes, Señora . . . yes! . . . yes! . . .

LOLA. No, Señora . . . no! . . . no! . . .

ANDREA. Well, which do you mean?

THE APPRENTICE. It must have been a comet or something.

ANDREA. Get back to your work then . . . wasting time like this! You'll see what your mistress will have to say to you presently. [*Then to the child again.*] Oh, be quiet, you limb of Satan!

A NEWSBOY IN THE STREET. Extra! Herald! Extra!

ANDREA. Here . . . you . . . Carmen, Lola, get a paper!

> [CARMEN *goes out and comes back with the paper.*]

CARMEN. Here it is!

> [*They all crowd round* ANDREA.]

ANDREA. Read it . . . read it!

CARMEN. [*Reading.*] "Aviation   Race . . . Nice, Marseilles, Barcelona, Madrid. . . ."

ANDREA. Go on . . . go on!

CARMEN. [*Reading.*] "Cuenca, 4 p. m. The Bleriot monoplane piloted by the Spanish aviator, José María Lopez, is now passing over the town . . . flying rapidly."

ANDREA. [*In rapture.*] Oh, . . . my darling boy!

CARMEN. [*Reading.*] "He should reach Madrid in about twenty minutes."

ANDREA. Oh . . . my precious one! The first! Will he come in first?

LOLA. It looks like it now . . . yes, Señora.

ANDREA. Oh . . . my José María!

THE APPRENTICE. If he does get in first . . . he'll have a good handful of dollars.

LOLA. The first prize . . . a hundred thousand *pesetas.*

CARMEN. And five hundred from the Mayor!

LOLA. And a cup from the King!

CARMEN. And another from the Aero Club!

THE APPRENTICE. And then won't you give yourself airs, Señora Andrea?

ANDREA. [*To the child.*] Will you lie quiet . . . or won't you? [*To* THE APPRENTICE.] Here, you . . . take the little wretch and walk him up and down. See if that'll quiet him.

THE APPRENTICE. [*Taking the baby and walking to and fro.*] There, darling . . . hush, my pretty one . . . my little poppet. Father's going to be ever such a famous man . . . ever . . . such . . . a . . . famous . . . man. [*But apparently the child is not comforted.*]

LOLA. He's hungry.

ANDREA. Well, then, where's his mother?

CARMEN. A lot of use she'd be to him, with the suspense she's been in!

THE APPRENTICE. [*Who wants an excuse to get out.*] Shan't I take him out in the street? That might quiet him.

ANDREA. Oh, take him to the devil if you like! And the rest of you, get on with your work. The irons will be in a fine state, won't they?

CARMEN. Oh, but today's not like any other day, is it, Señora Andrea?

THE APPRENTICE. [*Who was on the point of going out, but stopped seeing the approach of* RAMÓN.] Here's Señor Ramón.

[RAMÓN *comes in from the street.*]

ANDREA. What's happened? What are you back for? There's nothing wrong?

CARMEN. Has he got in yet?

RAMÓN. [*Very solemnly.*] Not yet. He is about to. No, Señora Andrea, nothing has happened. I have come to fetch a fan and a bottle of smelling salts for my poor daughter . . . who is in a state of nerves. . . .

CARMEN. Well . . . I don't wonder!

LOLA. I'll get it!

[*She goes out of the door at the right.*]

ANDREA. [*In a sarcastic tone.*] Oh, of course . . .
hurry . . . hurry! Suppose the poor delicate creature goes
off in a faint!

RAMÓN. Well, if she can't go off in one today, I should
like to know when she can!

THE APPRENTICE. [*With conviction.*] So should I!

CARMEN. What with the suspense . . . !

RAMÓN. Why shouldn't she be faint seeing it's the first
time in his life her husband ever did anything for anybody.
It's enough to make her . . . faint with surprise.

ANDREA. [*Very irritated.*] Is that an insult?

RAMÓN. I don't know, Señora . . . but it's the truth.

[CARMEN *returns to the ironing-table, and* THE
APPRENTICE, *with the baby in her arms, goes out by
the street door.*]

ANDREA. May I ask what you expect of my son?

RAMÓN. I don't expect anything; but three *pesetas* a
day to keep house on might not be too much perhaps for my
daughter to look for?

ANDREA. Your daughter . . . poor unlucky woman!
Picked out by the handsomest man in Madrid!

RAMÓN. And the greatest scamp ever born in Spain!

ANDREA. Oh . . . then you come from foreign parts?

RAMÓN. Señora Andrea. . . .

ANDREA. I didn't know!

RAMÓN. Is a woman like my daughter to marry and
then work her fingers to the bone to support her husband?

ANDREA. Well, since before she was married she had
the pleasure of supporting her father, it mayn't seem so very
odd to her after all.

RAMÓN. She supported *me?*

ANDREA. And hasn't had a chance to break herself of
the habit!

RAMÓN. Señora Andrea. . . .

ANDREA. [*Looking him up and down.*] Why bless me
. . . I thought so . . . if you haven't bought yourself a
new cap!

RAMÓN. [*Surveying her from top to toe also.*] And I notice that you've got a pair of new shoes . . . though what use they are to you . . . sitting here all day long . . . !

ANDREA. One takes a fancy to a thing sometimes. . . .

RAMÓN. [*Regarding the shoes.*] They must have cost seventeen *pesetas*.

ANDREA. Twenty.

RAMÓN. Fancy . . . yes, fancy's the word! [*Maliciously.*] A present from your son?

ANDREA. No, Señora; nor from your daughter.

RAMÓN. Then I suppose you're in debt to the shoemaker.

ANDREA. I'm in debt to nobody. I paid for them out of my own pocket.

RAMÓN. [*Incredulously.*] Four dollars, all at once?

ANDREA. Six; I won a prize in the lottery last week.

RAMÓN. Then I think you might have given your friends a treat. . . .

ANDREA. And who did you treat with the nine *pesetas* you won at cards the other day, I should like to know?

LOLA. [*Coming in.*] The smelling salts!

RAMÓN. [*Taking the bottle.*] All right.

[*He is just about to leave as* MARIANA, *accompanied by three or four women neighbours, comes in by the street door.*]

1ST NEIGHBOUR. He's got here! He's arrived!

[*They all rush to meet* MARIANA.]

ANDREA. Mariana!

RAMÓN. My child!

THE LAUNDRESSES. Señora!

[THE APPRENTICE *enters behind* MARIANA, *with the baby in her arms.*

ANDREA. But you're alone!

MARIANA. Yes . . . yes. . . .

RAMÓN. Why . . . how is that?

[MATI *and* PEPITO, *two of* MARIANA'S *children,
aged seven and nine, have come in with her. They
both seize hold of their mother.*]

MATI.   Mama!

PEPITO.   Mama!

[MARIANA *caresses the two children.*]

THE APPRENTICE.   [*Giving her the baby.*]   Here's
another one! He's been howling for you.

MARIANA.   Darling! Precious! Angel!

[*She is in such a state of emotion and excitement that
she can hardly speak.*]

CARMEN.   [*Bringing a chair.*]   Sit down, Señora.

[*They all surround her.*]

RAMÓN.   Here are the smelling salts.

MARIANA.   A little late, aren't they?

1ST NEIGHBOUR.   Take a sniff anyway, it never does you
any harm.

LOLA.   Yes . . . and you all upset!

THE APPRENTICE.   [*Taking away the baby from her.*]
And you're in no state to bother with him, I'm sure!

ANDREA.   Oh, tell us all about it . . . tell us what happened.

MARIANA.   Nothing . . . it . . . it just came [*To her
father.*] after you went away.

RAMÓN.   My luck . . . when I'd waited for him seven
hours!

ANDREA.   Well, go on . . . go on. What else?

MARIANA.   Nothing else. It came. It flew up like a
great bird, fast and high, and you could scarcely see it, and
then it dropped down, down . . . all the way down, and
then it stopped . . . and there he was . . . so jolly as ever!

RAMÓN.   Oh, he's always jolly!

ANDREA.   [*In ecstasy.*]   There's nobody to touch my
son!

RAMÓN.   Indeed!

ANDREA.   Well, but where is he now?

MARIANA.   He's in the grand stand with the King and

the Queen and the government and the people from the
Aero Club, and a whole crowd of ladies and gentlemen.
They're all drinking champagne and eating cakes.

THE APPRENTICE. Did he speak to you?

MARIANA. Of course!

LOLA. What did he say?

MARIANA. Oh, nothing!

RAMÓN. And you came away and left him?

MARIANA. Looks like it!

ANDREA. But isn't he coming?

MARIANA. Of course . . . as soon as they'll let him.

1ST NEIGHBOUR. Well, my dear . . . you must be a
happy woman!

MARIANA. Yes . . . I am.

2ND NEIGHBOUR. With all the money he'll make . . .
you'll have nothing to worry about now!

1ST NEIGHBOUR. Why, you'll be giving up the laundry.

MARIANA. Yes . . . I suppose I shall.

1ST NEIGHBOUR. They'll give him a decoration.

RAMÓN. Of course they will.

CARMEN. And a banquet!

LOLA. And his picture will be in all the papers!

THE APPRENTICE. Do you know . . . our district
councillor said that, as he's the first Madrid man to win
an aeroplane race, they're sure to name a street after him,
as soon as he's been dead ten years.

CARMEN. I wouldn't trust 'em to keep it in mind that
long.

THE APPRENTICE. Oh, but they can't do it till he's dead
. . . because they say they've been taken in so often.

RAMÓN. Well, that's true. Just as sure as you name
a street after a man, he goes and disgraces himself afterwards . . . and of course that may happen to anyone . . .
then they get the blame.

1ST NEIGHBOUR. That's true!

RAMÓN. Wait till a man turns up his toes, I say, before
you call him a hero.

ANDREA. Will you please stop talking about turning up toes?

1ST NEIGHBOUR. [*Taking her leave.*] Well, congratulations, Señora Andrea.

ANDREA. Thank you very much, I'm sure.

2ND NEIGHBOUR. Mine too, Mariana.

NEIGHBOURS. [*Taking their leave.*] Good-bye . . . good-bye . . . good-bye. . . . Good luck to you . . . best wishes . . .

MARIANA. [*Going with them to the door.*] Thanks . . . thanks.

[*The neighbours go out.* MARIANA, *who is still very nervous, begins to talk to the laundresses and to her children—who follow her about like dogs—all in the same breath.*]

MARIANA. Get on with your work now . . . all of you! The irons must be in a fine state. And you [*To the children.*] go and put on your pinafores; you mustn't mess up the only decent clothes you've got.

[*The children go out by the door on the right, and return shortly with their pinafores on.* MARIANA, *in the meantime has taken off her crape handkerchief and put it away in the wardrobe with the mirror, afterwards putting the key in her pocket. Then she turns to the* APPRENTICE.]

MARIANA. Give me the baby [*She takes the child from her.*] and get the linen ready for 57 Carmen Street. It's got to go back this afternoon without fail.

[THE APPRENTICE *places some freshly ironed shirts, collars, and cuffs in a basket and covers them with a cloth.*]

MARIANA. Hurry up now . . . it's getting late . . . and of course you've not done a thing because I've been away!

RAMÓN. My child, you are a regular demon for work!

ANDREA. Yes indeed . . . whoever else would go on slaving like this?

MARIANA. Well, someone has to. How else d'you think the world goes on?

RAMÓN. But why worry now? You're going to be rich!

MARIANA. Oh, going to be no doubt. But till I am someone's got to pay for the dinner . . . haven't they? [*Seeing that the* APPRENTICE *is about to go out with the basket.*] Here, let's have a look. [*Examining the ironing.*] Who ironed those collars? It'll be a miracle if they're not sent back. Get along now . . . and hurry back.

ANDREA. [*To the* APPRENTICE.] Child!

THE APPRENTICE. What is it?

ANDREA. As you are going out, bring me back a lamb pasty. What with all this commotion . . . I'm famishing!

THE APPRENTICE. The cheap sort, or the best?

ANDREA. Oh no, bring the best, the others are nothing but pastry. Give her the money, Mariana, please, then I shan't have to change a dollar, and that's all I have.

[*She says this after searching her pockets, but with the evident intention of not producing anything.*]

MARIANA. [*Resignedly giving the money to the* APPRENTICE.] Here you are.

RAMÓN. Here, child.

THE APPRENTICE. [*Returning from the door.*] What is it?

RAMÓN. As you're going that way, bring me a packet of cigarettes . . . and see they're the best . . . and that they're not damp now. Ah, and a box of wax matches. Well . . . what are you waiting for?

THE APPRENTICE. The money. They don't give credit.

RAMÓN. Here you are! . . . [*He searches in his waistcoat, but doesn't take out anything.*] I must have left it in my other waistcoat! Ask your mistress . . . she's going to be rich now.

THE APPRENTICE. Señora?

MARIANA. [*Giving her the money.*] Oh, take it, and

be off with you. [*She walks from one side to the other with the baby in her arms.*] Now, where did I put the order book?

ANDREA. Oh, do sit down and rest a minute, woman, if you can. It makes me dizzy to see you.

RAMÓN. [*Taking away the order book which she is turning over.*] Let it alone now. Aren't you ashamed of yourself? Haven't you ever been taught that a hundred thousand *pesetas* are twenty thousand dollars and don't you know that from today on all this laundry and ironing won't matter any more than a drop of water in a pond?

[*A man is seen standing at the street door. He is a newspaper reporter.*]

REPORTER. May I . . . ?

MARIANA. Come in. What can I do for you?

REPORTER. Does José María López, the aviator, live here?

MARIANA. Yes, Señor, he lives here; but he's not at home.

REPORTER. [*Pompously.*] Thank you, . . . I know that. I have only just left him. Could I speak to his wife for a moment?

[*Through all this the laundresses are coming in and going out, busy with their work.*]

MARIANA. [*First amazed and then horrified.*] With me? What's the matter? Great Heavens! Has anything happened to him? . . . Has he been hurt? . . . Oh, José María! [*Begins to cry.*] What? . . . What? . . .

ANDREA. [*Also weeping.*] Oh, my boy . . . my precious boy! . . .

MARIANA. And I saw him not five minutes ago . . . safe and sound!

ANDREA. Oh! Holy Mother of Sorrows!

[*At this point the laundresses, from the ironing table, also begin to shriek.*]

REPORTER. [*Alarmed and trying to quiet them.*] Ladies . . . for God's sake . . . do be calm. Nothing has happened . . . I swear to you that nothing has happened.

MARIANA. Honestly . . . nothing?

ANDREA. Nothing?

REPORTER. Absolutely nothing.

MARIANA. Well . . . you might have said so sooner!

ANDREA. You gave us a very bad turn, young man!

REPORTER. [*Confused.*] But, my dear ladies . . . how was I to suppose that you'd take it into your heads that . . . I'm very sorry.

RAMÓN. Women always expect the worst! Take a seat, please.

MARIANA. Sit down, Señor, do! And please excuse us, because with all that's going on today we're in such a state that we don't seem to know what will happen next.

REPORTER. Thank you. I haven't time.

MARIANA. Well . . . tell us what we can do for you.

REPORTER. You must forgive my coming like this when I haven't the pleasure of knowing you. . . .

MARIANA. Oh . . . the pleasure is mine.

RAMÓN. The pleasure is ours.

REPORTER. But I am from the *Evening Herald*. . . .

RAMÓN. [*With admiration.*] A reporter!

REPORTER. A reporter.

RAMÓN. Sit down. Sit down, Sir.

REPORTER. [*Sitting down to escape more invitations.*] Thanks! Well, you know . . . we want . . . in tonight's edition, before anyone else gets ahead of us . . . to have a full account of the great event . . . and it seemed to me no one could give me better help in making a good story of it than the wife of our famous man himself.

MARIANA. Do you mean me?

REPORTER. I do, Señora. So, if you don't mind . . . [*He has his note-book out.*]

RAMÓN. Oh, why should we mind?

REPORTER. Tell me now . . . what emotions have been aroused in you by your husband's brilliant triumph?

MARIANA. Oh . . . what am I to say?

ANDREA. Say what comes into your head.

MARIANA. Well, that's just it . . . nothing does.

RAMÓN. Suppose I ask her. She looks as if she could
eat you . . . but she's really only shy. What the gentleman wants to know is if you're pleased that he won the first
prize?

MARIANA. Well . . . of course!

REPORTER. You didn't expect it, did you?

MARIANA. No, Señor.

REPORTER. But why didn't you?

MARIANA. Well . . . because I didn't.

RAMÓN. I will tell you; she didn't expect it because, up
to today, she's only been used to having him make a mess of
everything. There . . . that's why. And when he left
home two months ago, without telling her, she was very
angry, and though Señor Julián (who keeps the wineshop at
the corner) told her that he had gone off to France to learn
flying . . . no, she wouldn't believe it! And when he wrote
to her from France, asking her to forgive him, and telling
her (just as it has happened) that he'd fly back, still she
wouldn't believe it. No . . . she'd got it in her head (for
she's as stubborn as a mule) that *that* José María López
wasn't her José María López. And now she's actually seen
him flying back through the air, and seen that it really is he
. . . well . . . she has almost died from the fright! And
that's how men get a bad name.

MARIANA. [*Offended.*] I'd never give anyone a bad
name . . . least of all him.

ANDREA. Well, I'm sure you've no reason to now!

MARIANA. And even if I had, it would be nobody's business but mine.

REPORTER. One can see that you're a wonderful wife to
him.

MARIANA. And that's his business . . . I should hope.

RAMÓN. Don't pay any attention . . . she's upset.

REPORTER. I believe that our famous man is a son of
Madrid . . .

ANDREA. Yes, Señor, of Madrid; and of his father and me.

REPORTER. Ah! You are his mother?

ANDREA. And very proud to be.

REPORTER. Now how old is he?

ANDREA. Thirty-three . . . that's to say, he won't be until Our Lady's day in August. That's why he's called José María . . . because we didn't expect him until the first of September. Ah, one might almost say that the Blessed Virgin took a fancy to his being born on her own special day!

REPORTER. [*To* MARIANA.] Have you been married long?

MARIANA. Ten years.

[*The children come in and go up to* MARIANA.]

ANDREA. [*Interrupting.*] They were married on Our Lady's day in March . . .

REPORTER. And was that a fancy of the Blessed Virgin's too?

RAMÓN. No, Señor, it was mine. Because this girl's mother (now in glory) was called Candelas, and . . . not to flatter her . . . she was a perfect woman.

REPORTER. And I see that you have progeny?

MARIANA. Have . . . what?

RAMÓN. He means your family, child!

MARIANA. Oh! Yes, Señor, yes . . . two boys and a girl.

RAMÓN. And more to come.

MARIANA. Now . . . what do *you* know about it?

RAMÓN. Well . . . don't fly out at me.

MARIANA. Well, I should have thought this mattered about as much to your newspaper as the price of my stockings.

REPORTER. Señora, everything in the life of a famous man is of interest.

MARIANA. Oh well, of course . . . if that's so. . . .

REPORTER. Señora, did your son take an interest in mechanics from his childhood?

ANDREA. Well . . . while his father was alive he went to school but he learnt nothing, because he had far too much imagination, the teacher said.

REPORTER. And after . . . ?

ANDREA. You can guess . . . with his father gone, there wasn't much money for schooling . . . though I'd my profession . . . and if I say it as shouldn't, I was a hairdresser . . . so we got along somehow. And indeed he wanted for nothing and never should have while I could do a day's work.

RAMÓN. No, nor afterwards either, because, when this lady here was done in by her legs giving out (begging her pardon) he married my daughter who keeps this laundry, and, not to flatter her, there's no better ironing done in Madrid than there is here. Did you notice the shirt that the Minister of Education was wearing this afternoon? On that very table it got its polish!

[*A noise is heard in the street. A motor horn sounding, and cries of "Viva! Viva!"*]

MARIANA. [*Rushing to the door.*] Oh, he's here, I do believe!

ANDREA. [*Trying to get up.*] My boy! My precious boy!

[*JOSÉ MARÍA comes in, accompanied by various men neighbours. Those on the stage mingle with them; the REPORTER remains on the left taking notes. After a little he goes away.*]

JOSÉ MARÍA. [*Embracing his mother.*] I'm all right, Mother! [*To his wife.*] Mariana! What did you run away for? Why didn't you wait for me?

MARIANA. [*Timidly.*] Whatever should I be doing among all those celebrities . . . and ladies . . . and gentlemen?

JOSÉ MARÍA. [*With condescending affection.*] Get along with you! You're the queen of the world for me . . . don't you know that?

MARIANA. [*With emotion.*] Oh, José María! . . .

JOSÉ MARÍA. Give us a kiss, woman! Don't be shy about it. We were married in Church, they all know that. [*Kissing her.*] Look at her . . . blushes like a girl . . . after ten years of it . . . and three babies . . . !

MARIANA. [*All blushes and tenderness.*] Silly!

JOSÉ MARÍA. [*Laughing.*] Well, here's a husband dropped from the moon for you. I tell you it's cold up there!

RAMÓN. [*Explaining.*] As one rises the temperature falls.

JOSÉ MARÍA. Well . . . youngsters! Are you scared at me . . . because I look so fine? [*Picking up the baby and kissing it.*] Look at the little chap! Why, he's got the aviator's face on him already. [*His mother, his wife, and the neighbours laugh at his jokes. To the workwomen.*] Hello, girls, you're all just as ugly as ever, I see! [*To* MARIANA.] But what's happened, woman? Isn't there going to be a glass of something . . . to drink the healths of our friends here? Have you gone bankrupt since I went away? Gentlemen! You see what happens! . . . a man shouldn't take to flying . . . that's evident!

MARIANA. [*To* CARMEN.] Run and buy some bottles of beer . . .

JOSÉ MARÍA. Beer! Women are stingy creatures! You get some rum from La Negrita and some anisette . . . and two packets of the best cigars they've got.

RAMÓN. Ah, I rather think I'll go for the cigars; women know nothing about them.

JOSÉ MARÍA. [*To Mariana.*] Here . . . don't look so scared, my girl . . . it's all right. I've got the money to pay for it. You're not walking in your sleep, are you?

RAMÓN. Why, Mariana . . . you're regularly dazed.

JOSÉ MARÍA. Oh well, oh well . . . it's not to be wondered at. This sort of thing doesn't happen every day . . . [*Going up to her.*] Come now . . . would you like me to give you a present? What's it to be? The

best Chinese shawl in Madrid? Or a necklace of those
imitation diamonds? Or will you go in a 40–60 Hispano-
Suiza, and have supper at the Puerta de Hierro?

MARIANA.   No, I just want you to love me.

JOSÉ MARÍA.   Oh I say, I say . . . that's something
new! Now however d'you suppose I'm to manage to do
that!

> [CARMEN *enters with the bottles and puts them
> down on the table.*]

CARMEN.   Here's the rum.

JOSÉ MARÍA.   Pour it out.

> [RAMÓN *arrives with the cigars.*]

RAMÓN.   And the cigars. [*Then quietly to* JOSÉ
MARÍA.] They're the best. But this isn't a time for
doing things by halves. [*He begins to pass round the
cigars.*]

JOSÉ MARÍA.   Quite right . . . quite right! Now,
Gentlemen. [*He takes one of the filled glasses in his hand.*]
Your health!

SEVERAL VOICES.   [*The others drinking.*] And yours!

SEÑOR JULIÁN.   Madrid's greatest aviator!

ALL.   Viva!

JOSÉ MARÍA.   Thank you . . . thank you . . . thank
you all!

SEVERAL VOICES.   A speech! A speech!

JOSÉ MARÍA.   Oh, I can't make speeches . . .

RAMÓN.   [*Very solemnly.*] My boy, you must say a
few words.

JOSÉ MARÍA.   Well . . . if you like . . . Ahem!

SEVERAL VOICES.   Hear, hear . . . silence . . . quiet
them!

JOSÉ MARÍA.   Ladies and gentlemen . . .

A VOICE.   [*As if he had been inspired.*] Hear, hear!
Very good!

JOSÉ MARÍA.   I am very grateful to you . . . for this
display . . . of enthusiasm.

SEVERAL VOICES.   Hear, hear! Hear, hear!

José María. Appropriate indeed to the occasion . . . though it sounds wrong for me to be the one to say it . . .

Voices. No! No!

José María. Well, then . . . thank you again! But, Ladies and Gentlemen . . . and because this business of conquering the air is the last word of modern science . . .

Ramón. That's true . . . that's very true.

José María. And I don't care who says it isn't!

Ramón. Right! Hear, hear!

José María. For whoever says it isn't . . . well, never mind him. But I am *very glad* to have given one proud day to my native place . . . and that's Madrid. And, what's more, to the Calle de le Madera, which had the honour of having me born in it. . . .

Voices. Bravo!

José María. Me . . . my children . . . and the mother of my children! [*Explosion of "bravo" and applause.*] Therefore . . . ladies and gentlemen, long live the Calle de la Madera, and long live Madrid and may it never be beaten at flying. And whoever don't like that can lump it!

Voices. Very good! Very good!

Señor Julián. Very good indeed!

Andrea. That boy's an orator!

Ramón. That's what science and democracy can do for a man!

José María. Have another glass?

Señor Julián. Thank you, I will. [*To the others.*] We'd better be getting off . . . they'd like to be left by themselves a bit. [*Going up to shake hands with* José María.] Well . . . once more. . . .

José María. Thank you . . . thank you!

Someone. Congratulations.

Another. Good-bye.

Another. Till next time. . . .

José María. [*Importantly.*] Tomorrow, you know, I go up from the Aerodrome.

Señor Julián.   Oh, I shan't fail to be there.

[*All the company go out.*]

Andrea.   Come and let's have a look at you, my dear!
How handsome you are in that uniform!

José María.   [*Peacocking up and down.*]   Well . . .
it's not one of the most becoming.

Mariana.   But you must be just tired out.   Don't you
want a change . . . or a brush?

Ramón.   Oho, there wasn't much mud on the road he
came by, my child!   [*And he laughs at his own joke.*]

José María.   No . . . good . . . no indeed, there
wasn't much mud on that road!   But I must change all
the same, because they'll be here for me in a minute.

Mariana.   Here for you . . . Who?

José María.   Some gentlemen that are giving me a dinner.

Mariana.   [*Disconsolately.*]   Tonight?

José María.   Yes, tonight.

Mariana.   You're not going to have supper at home?

José María.   But it's a dinner in my honour . . . it's
been got up by the Aero Club.

Ramón.   That's what popularity means, my child.

Mariana.   [*Sighing.*]   Oh, very well then . . . you'd
better hurry and get dressed.

[*So* José María *goes off to do so.   The scene which
follows must be very lively.*   Mariana *keeps on taking garments from the wardrobe, and giving them to
her father and the children, who go rapidly in and
out.   A laundress cleans the shoes.*   Andrea *puts the
studs and link in the shirt, aided by the other laundresses.*]

Mariana.   Here you   [*To the little boy.*]   get some
warm water!   . . . Now, where did I put the key of
the cupboard?   [*She finds it in one of her pockets, opens it
and takes out a cake of soap.*]   Here's the scented soap.
[*To the little girl.*]   There, you can take it to him.   [*Turning round.*]   And where's his shirt . . . with the em-

broidery? [*Discarding one for another.*] No, not this
one . . . this with the pleats . . . it's more the fashion
now to have pleats. [*Taking out a towel.*] Here . . .
take him this towel. [*She gives it to the little boy who is
back from fetching the water.*] And he'll find the Eau de
Cologne is on the dressing-table.

ANDREA. Give me the shirt. I can be putting in the
studs.

MARIANA. Here. [*Then she goes back to the cupboard.*] His black suit. . . . [*She takes it out. Then she
sneezes.*] Achiss!

ANDREA. Have you taken cold?

MARIANA. It's the pepper . . . for the . . . m . . .
m . . . moths . . . [*Giving the suit to her father.*] You
take it to him. [*He sneezes too.*]

RAMÓN. Achiss! [*He goes out with the suit and immediately returns.*]

MARIANA. And his patent leather shoes. [*To one of
the laundresses.*] Take a cloth and clean off the dust.

PEPITO. [*Coming in.*] He wants his shirt!

ANDREA. All ready! Take it, child.

MARIANA. [*At the wardrobe with the cravats in her
hands.*] Now which tie will be best . . . the blue or the
red?

RAMÓN. White is what's fashionable in the evening.

MARIANA. With evening-clothes.

RAMÓN. Yes . . . that's so. Well, give him the red
one . . . it's more democratic.

[PEPITO *comes back having delivered the shirt, and*
NATI *goes off with the red tie.*]

MARIANA. But suppose they're all Dukes and Marquises
that are giving him the dinner.

RAMÓN. So much the better! A chance to show his
colours.

MARIANA. Now, let's see! . . . A handkerchief.

[*She takes one out.* JOSÉ MARÍA *comes in. He
has changed but is still in his shirt-sleeves.*]

José María. I say . . . button this for me. You starch things as stiff as a board here.

Ramón. You must look a credit to the laundry now!

Mariana. I can manage it with a hairpin. That's it! Now . . . how'll you have your tie . . . a bow, or a knot?

[José María *sits down to put on his patent leather shoes, and while he does so his wife inspects the way his hair is brushed.*]

José María. Whichever you like.

Mariana. Your parting's crooked. [*To one of the children.*] Bring me his coat. [*She helps him on with it.*]

José María. Yes . . . I never can see a thing in there.

Mariana. Now, a brush.

Ramón. Where's his hat?

Mariana. [*To* The Apprentice.] Brush that carefully now! [*To* José María.] And your handkerchief . . . a bit stuck out. So! And keep this in your pocket in case you want one to use.

Ramón. Fold it tight, and then it won't show.

Mariana. No, no . . . it's fashionable to have it rumpled. [*Sniffing at it.*] It hasn't got much scent on it!

Andrea. [*To* Lola.] Here . . . you . . . go fetch the Eau de Cologne.

Mariana. No, wait now! I've got a bottle of scent that's never been opened. I won it in a raffle. We'll have that. [*She gets it from the wardrobe.*]

The Apprentice. Here's the hat.

[José María *puts on his hat.*]

Carmen. Put a little scent on your moustache as well . . . so that you can smell it while you're in the motor car.

Andrea. Some on your hair, too.

Mariana. There now! Look at yourself in the glass. Turn round.

José María [*Walks proudly about.*] Well . . . what do you say to it . . . eh?

MARIANA. [*With emotion.*] Isn't he handsome!

ANDREA. The very image of his father. Oh, but you're a lucky girl, my dear!

JOSÉ MARÍA. [*To the laundresses, who are looking at him.*] Yes . . . look as hard as you like . . . there aren't many to touch me!

LOLA. Oh indeed . . . you should see my young man!

RAMÓN. You should have seen me when I was your age!

JOSÉ MARÍA. I don't believe you! Well, good-bye, all!

ANDREA. Good-bye, my boy. Have a fine time!

CARMEN. Mind you enjoy yourself!

MARIANA. Don't forget me, José María!

JOSÉ MARÍA. Look here, you know . . . just because I'm going out, you mustn't miss your treat. Give yourselves a supper, with something tasty to it. Have a steak in from the café . . . and some prawns . . . and one of those custard puddings . . . have anything they've got. And ask the girls to stop, if you like. They deserve it.

ANDREA. What a good heart he has!

[*The sound of a band is heard outside.*]

MARIANA. Oh . . . the band! They've come to play to you. And just as you're going!

JOSÉ MARÍA. Never mind! Have 'em in. Come in, Señor Julián. What's all this about?

[SEÑOR JULIÁN *comes in, followed by the band and a number of neighbours . . . men and women. The laundresses move about placing the tables and chairs against the wall, except one on the left.*]

SEÑOR JULIÁN. Oh nothing . . . nothing much. But we've come, neighbours and friends, you know, to congratulate you. And we've brought the band to make it livelier, and so that the young people can dance. But they tell me that you're off . . . that you've been asked to the Palace. . . .

JOSÉ MARÍA. [*Without attempting to undeceive them about the Palace.*] What does that matter? Come in,

all of you. Yes, I've got to go, but the family's all here.
Go on and enjoy yourselves. Mariana will look after you,
won't you, my dear?

[*The horn of a motor car sounds in the street.*]

ANDREA. There's a motor car!

CARMEN. It's stopping at the door.

JOSÉ MARÍA. Ah . . . that's for me. [*To his father-in-law.*] Go out and say I'll be there directly. Well . . .
good-bye, all.

ANDREA. Good-bye, my boy!

JOSÉ MARÍA. Good-night. Dance all you want to . . .
Have a good time.

ALL. Viva! Viva! Viva!

[*He goes out . . . they all see him off from the
door.*]

MARIANA. He's gone!

[*She sits down in a corner with the baby in her arms,
and the other two children in front of her.*]

SEÑOR JULIÁN. Come along now. Start up the band!

RAMÓN. Come along, child. Take a turn with me.

MARIANA. No, thank you. I don't feel like it.

RAMÓN. Why, what's the matter, with you? Aren't
you proud of your husband being the hero of the day?

MARIANA. Yes, of course, but . . . well, you see . . .
it's just because he is . . . that I've got to do without
him.

RAMÓN. Get along with you, woman . . . and don't
be a goose. That's what it means to be married to a famous
man!

[*The band begins a two-step, and everyone begins to
dance. They dance it like a schottische. But* MARIANA
rather sadly caresses her children.]

CURTAIN.

ACT II

SCENE I.

A very modest dining-room in JOSÉ MARÍA'S *house.* At *the back there is a door communicating with the ironing-room which was the scene of the First Act.*

Right and left there are doors to inner rooms. JOSÉ MARÍA *is seated at the table before a dish of codfish stew.* MARIANA *and his mother are waiting on him.*

During the scene RAMÓN *comes and goes from the ironing-room, smoking a cigar, in high good humour.*

MARIANA. [*With solicitude.*] But you're not eating. Don't you feel hungry?

ANDREA. Aren't you well?

JOSÉ MARÍA. [*Loftily.*] The fact is, you know, that this sort of food makes me sick! [*With disdain.*] Codfish stew!

MARIANA. But it used to be your favourite dish!

JOSÉ MARÍA. [*Still loftily.*] Used to be isn't is, is it?

MARIANA. But . . . good heavens . . . !

ANDREA. Have some salad then. Lettuce and olives. . . .

JOSÉ MARÍA. [*Getting up.*] No . . . thanks.

MARIANA. [*Irritated.*] That doesn't do either, doesn't it! You haven't made much of a meal, have you? Well . . . you know best. And the less you weigh, I suppose the better you can fly.

JOSÉ MARÍA. This is a nice way of looking after a man, isn't it?

MARIANA. Well, it's the same I've always had, and you've never complained till now.

ANDREA. But, my darling boy, why aren't you eating anything?

MARIANA. Because codfish stew isn't good enough for him . . . that's why! [*To* SEÑORA ANDREA.] Well, you can clear away then. [*To* JOSÉ MARÍA.] Next time you'd better write out a menu on a piece of paper beforehand, then we can send it from a restaurant.

> [SEÑORA ANDREA *hobbles out sighing and carrying some dishes.*]

JOSÉ MARÍA. Are you trying to start a row, or what is the matter with you?

MARIANA. Nothing's the matter with me.

JOSÉ MARÍA. Well, try and be a little better tempered. [*He goes out.*]

MARIANA. Thank you . . . the same to you.

RAMÓN. Woman, woman . . . do remember who you're talking to!

MARIANA. [*Ill-humoured.*] I'm talking to my husband, I believe.

RAMÓN. But now he's such a famous man. . . .

MARIANA. Oh, no doubt he is to everyone else . . . but as far as I'm concerned, he's my husband . . . and that's all about it.

RAMÓN. All right . . . all right! Don't get excited! I can't help it, can I?

> [*He turns to go out.*]

MARIANA. [*Angrily.*] That's right . . . off with you . . . run away from anything unpleasant. [*Desperately, half to herself.*] Holy Mother . . . it's a lonely world!

RAMÓN. [*Returning.*] Now, now . . . what's the matter?

MARIANA. [*Pointing to the plate left on the table.*] What's the matter? Oh, nothing! That's nothing, I suppose!

RAMÓN. Well, there's no need to get in such a state just because a man's lost his taste for codfish!

MARIANA. [*Nearly crying.*] It's not the codfish, it's not the codfish, it's everything that's put before him! First the house is small, and then the wine is bad . . . and the soap isn't scented . . . even the sheets on the bed are too coarse . . . [*With hurt pride.*] The sheets! We've slept in them well enough for these ten years, haven't we?

RAMÓN. Oh, nonsense, nonsense, child.

MARIANA. And my hands are coarse too, aren't they? Well, as I've been slaving ten years at an ironing board to support him . . . may the Blessed Virgin forgive me! Our bed common, indeed! You see how we'll all end if what I think is true! . . . You'll see!

RAMÓN. If what you think is . . . ? What *do* you think, then . . . Have you found out anything?

MARIANA. [*With concentrated wrath.*] If I'd found out anything d'you think I'd be sitting here quietly?

RAMÓN. Quietly! Did you say quietly?

MARIANA. And if I want to make a noise I will!

RAMÓN. No doubt . . . till you've driven *me* out of the house to escape hearing you . . .

MARIANA. [*Without looking at him, finishing clearing the table.*] Perhaps you'll find another one as cheap to live in . . . I'd try.

RAMÓN. [*Taking no offence.*] Well . . . I'm off now anyway. When you've come to your senses just let me know.

MARIANA. And God go with you!

[SEÑOR RAMÓN *goes out. As soon as she is alone,* MARIANA *takes an illustrated periodical out of a drawer and, sitting down at the table, turns over the leaves. Leaning on her elbows as she looks, attentively, at the photographs.*]

MARIANA. [*Reading.*] "The Aerodrome of Guidad Lineal. The famous Madrid aviator, José María López, surrounded by his friends and admirers. A group of ladies and gentlemen congratulating the aviator." [*With contempt and anger.*] *Ladies* indeed!

[José María *comes in and stands looking at the
paper over her shoulder.*]

José María.   What are you looking at?

Mariana.   [*Without looking around.*]   I'm looking to
see how indecently fashionable ladies dress themselves nowadays.

José María.   A bit saucy, aren't they?   Necks for sale
back and front . . . and one leg going cheap!

Mariana.   [*Still angry and contemptuous.*]   Disgusting!   How some of them have the impudence! !   Look at
that one!

José María.   [*Elaborately ignorant.*]   Which one?

Mariana.   That one on the right . . . that's glued herself close to you . . .

José María.   [*Who dissimulates very badly.*]   Oh . . .
with the small hat?

Mariana.   No . . . with the large hat!

José María.   [*With extreme indifference.*]   Oh . . .
yes . . . !

Mariana.   [*Looking at him slyly.*]   Handsome . . .
isn't she?

José María.   Showy . . . I shouldn't call her handsome!

Mariana.   [*Getting up.*]   What's her name?

José María.   How can I tell?   I don't know her.

Mariana.   Don't you?   Well . . . I do!

José María.   What d'you mean . . . ?

Mariana.   She's the one that you go about with a photograph of in your pocket-book. . . .

José María.   Oh . . . I've got a photograph of her in
my pocket-book, have I?

Mariana.   Well, you haven't . . . because I took it out
this morning.   And here it is!   [*She takes the picture from
her pocket and throws it on the table.*]   There you are
. . . the very same . . . except that she's managed to undress herself even a bit more in the photograph.   [*Empha-*

sizing her words.] Well, now, do you know her . . . or not?

JOSÉ MARÍA. [*Stammering a little.*] Know her? . . . yes, certainly I know her . . .

MARIANA. [*Ironically.*] By sight . . . I suppose? Well?

JOSÉ MARÍA. [*Asserting himself like a man.*] Well . . . I'm not called on to give an account of myself to you or to anyone . . . and you may think what you damned well please!

MARIANA. May I?

JOSÉ MARÍA. [*Wanting to get out of the difficulty by putting her in the wrong.*] And if it comes to that, I'd like to know what the devil you mean by searching my pocketbook!

MARIANA. If I smell burning I go through the house to see what's on fire, don't I? Do you suppose . . . suspecting what I do . . . that I'm going to sit still with my hands folded. Just you wait, my friend.

JOSÉ MARÍA. And might I ask what you suspect?

MARIANA. I suspect that it was in that lady's house that you learned to tell whether the sheets were coarse or not. So there!

JOSÉ MARÍA. [*Taking a high stand.*] Oh dear me . . . jealous, are we! The same old tale!

MARIANA. "The same old tale." I like your conceit. And when have I ever been jealous, I'd like to know?

JOSÉ MARÍA. Once a month for the last five years.

MARIANA. Once a week for the last ten years . . . if you could have had your wish . . . but you never got further than wishing for all your efforts!

JOSÉ MARÍA. [*Wounded in his pride as a lady-killer.*] Oh indeed . . . Oh, I like that! You don't know what you are talking about . . . you don't seem to know the sort of man I am!

MARIANA. I know you better than I know my two

babies. And I know this, conceited as you are . . . that if there was nothing in it this time, as there never has been before . . . then you'd be pretending there was . . . as you always have. When you keep quiet there's something wrong.

JOSÉ MARÍA. But what on earth do you expect, I should like to know? When a fellow's the hero of the day, and there's a something about him besides . . . though I say it that shouldn't . . . ! Well, when women take a fancy for a man . . . and especially these ladies from the theatre . . . why he looks a perfect fool if he turns his back at the least little attention. Never mind whether he wants it to go further or not . . . he can't snub her or give her a box on the ears, can he, as a woman can a man . . . as cool as you please.

MARIANA. [*Ironically.*] Go on! Anything else?

JOSÉ MARÍA. Nothing else! This lady (who is a quite celebrated singer, if you want to know) was kind enough to present me with her photograph. Now I couldn't throw it away, could I? And you've seen for yourself the effort I made to hide it. Why . . . d'you suppose I thought for a moment that you'd think . . . ? And nothing more has happened. Oh, . . . don't you know what you are to me? And the mother of my children as well. How could I deceive you? Never . . . never in this world. Do you want me to swear it.

MARIANA. [*Half won over all the same.*] I want you to stop talking humbug. As you always lie like a newspaper it doesn't matter much what sort of tale you tell, for no one's going to believe you. But . . . just you look out. Your luck's in for the minute, isn't it . . . and you think you're no end of a fellow, just because a few pesetas have fallen on you out of the sky. Make the most of them while they last. But I'm used to earning what I need for myself and my children. It's little enough and it's hard to come by . . . but it makes me a queen in this kingdom anyhow. My kingdom's my home. And don't forget this. There's never been any man let come in it but you . . . I love you a long sight more than you deserve to be loved. But let's have this clear . . . there aren't going to be any women in the case but me either. And if you're not agreeable to that . . . well, there's lots of room in the world for us both, and it's as easy to take the train as to buzz through the air. Off you go then . . . and we'll meet again on Judgment Day.

JOSÉ MARÍA. [*Coaxingly.*]   And leave you behind me?

MARIANA. [*Tenderly.*]   That wouldn't worry you!

JOSÉ MARÍA. [*Kissing her.*]   Come here . . . you dragon . . . you little wretch . . . ugly little devil that you are!   Who loves you . . . eh . . . eh . . . eh?

> [*The two smile, in each other's arms.* RAMÓN *enters and sees them.*]

RAMÓN. Ah, God be praised!   Then everything's all right again!   The devil's not so black as he's painted, is he? [*To* MARIANA, *who has broken away from her husband.*]   So we do love him just a little!   He gets his ration of kisses . . . does he?

MARIANA. [*Masking her confusion in asperity.*]   Oh . . . let me be!

> [*And she flings out, blushing furiously.*]

JOSÉ MARÍA. [*Watching her go, with pride and satisfaction.*]   Blushing like a girl . . . such a simple soul!

RAMÓN. [*Confidentially.*]   No doubt . . . but I'd sooner not be in her black books for all that. Look out for yourself, if she ever does lose her temper.

JOSÉ MARÍA. Oh, don't worry!   I know how to manage women, I should hope!

> [*A motor car is heard in the street.*]

RAMÓN. A motor car . . . stopping here.

JOSÉ MARÍA. Someone from the Club, I daresay . . . coming to take me to the Aerodrome. It's just about time . . .

> [JULIETA'S *voice is heard outside.*]

JULIETA. Señor José María López?

José María. [*With terror, recognising the voice.*] Who's that?

Julieta [*Appearing at the door.*] May I come in?

[Señor Ramón *politely rushes forward to receive her.*]

José María. Good Lord . . . to think of her turning up here!

Ramón. [*As sweet as honey.*] Come in, Señora, come in!

Julieta. [*Who hasn't seen* José María *yet.*] Is Señor José . . . ? [*Seeing him.*] Ah . . . good afternoon!

José María. [*Disconcerted.*] Good afternoon!

Julieta. Oh, don't be vexed with me . . . because I've come to fetch you. Yes, my car's outside. We can be at the Aerodrome in ten minutes. Will the weather be right for flying today?

[*There is a little most expressive by-play.* Ramón *is greatly struck by the lady, and quite alive to the situation.* José María *doesn't know what on earth he's about.* Julieta *alone commands the situation.*]

José María. Oh yes, Señora, certainly . . . the weather's magnificent.

Julieta. I warn you . . . I'm very nervous . . .

José María. Not more than I am . . . no, I assure you . . . but as you say, the weather . . . oh yes, magnificent! [*He is looking very uneasily at the door by which his wife left the room.*] Señor Ramón, will you be good enough to see if the passage door is shut? . . . because . . . because there's a draught.

Ramón. [*With a smile of complicity.*] Certainly, my dear boy, certainly . . . I'll see to it. [*Then to himself as he goes.*] Now the cat's coming out of the bag! That girl of mine . . . she has a sharp eye . . . !

[*He goes out, shutting the door.*]

José María. [*Who, not knowing what to do or say,*

gets out of the difficulty as best he can.] So . . . you've come to fetch me?

JULIETA. [*With coquetry.*] Yes, Señor . . . if the wind will be kind enough to let us fly away together!

JOSÉ MARÍA. [*Wishing to go.*] Well . . . let's be off then . . . the sooner the better . . .

JULIETA. [*Who is in no hurry, and is looking, curiously around the room.*] Is this where you live?

JOSÉ MARÍA. Yes, Señora . . . for a few days. I am . . . so to speak . . . staying as a sort of a guest.

JULIETA. Ah! You don't live with your family?

JOSÉ MARÍA. Oh certainly . . . I live with my family. But . . . well, you see, this little place is only a sort of a workshop. It did well enough before . . . but now . . . [*He is giving himself airs.*]

JULIETA. [*Romantically.*] Only a workshop! My father's home was his workshop!

[*She, with quite a coming on disposition, gets nearer to him as she talks, while he, who is half dead with fright lest his wife should appear, tries to edge away from her without seeming to do so.*]

JULIETA. Yes . . . I come from the people, just as you do. I've gone hungry to bed, often and often . . . just as you have.

JOSÉ MARÍA. [*A little annoyed.*] I never went hungry to bed in my life!

JULIETA. Well, never mind how hungry! But as long as you've been poor and down-trodden . . . as long as you've known what it is to hate the people that have got everything and despise you for having got nothing at all. . . . That's why I took to you so, I do believe. For we know what it is, don't we, to have people cringing to us . . . in the old days they wouldn't even have known we were there. And now *we* can do something, can't we . . . we've got inferiors too. Birth and breeding . . . there's nothing in it. I've scrubbed a Marquis's floors, I have . . .

but my hands are soft enough, aren't they? And I tell you
if a Duke wanted to kiss me, I'd have him down on his
knees to ask.

[JOSÉ MARÍA *doesn't know how to reply to this
discourse, and even if he had known he wouldn't be
able to do so, because the voice of his wife can be heard,
disputing with* SEÑOR RAMÓN, *while she is trying to
open the door.*]

RAMÓN. [*Outside.*] But I tell you you can't . . .
he's talking to some gentlemen . . .

MARIANA. And I tell you I will if I want to . . . so
there!

JOSÉ MARÍA. [*Crossing himself as if he heard thunder.*]
Blessed Saint Barbara! . . . My wife!

JULIETA. Who is making that dreadful noise?

JOSÉ MARÍA. Oh, I'm sure I don't know . . . it's
nothing. We'd better start.

[*He tries to make her leave.*]

JULIETA. No, wait . . . they're having a great row
about something.

JOSÉ MARÍA. We shall be late . . .

RAMÓN. [*Outside.*] I say you shan't go in. . . .

MARIANA. I say I will . . . and nothing's going to
stop me! [*The door bursts open violently.*] Can't walk
about my own house, can't I . . . well, that is the last
straw! [*She comes in and sees* JULIETA.] Aha! . . .
well, now you see! . . . And didn't I feel it in my
bones . . . ?

[*She goes towards* JULIETA, *who looks at her with
a little alarm.*]

RAMÓN. [*To* JOSÉ MARÍA.] And couldn't you have
taken yourself off, you prize fool!

MARIANA. Good afternoon, Señora. [*Looking her up
and down.*] Charmed to meet you! [*Turning to* JOSÉ
MARÍA.] Well now . . . what about it? Who's this
lady? Some actress . . . or what? You've got pretty cool
cheek, haven't you . . . the pair of you!

Julieta. [*Loftily.*] Señora!

Ramón. Now, my dear child . . . take care!

Mariana. And what have *I* to take care about?

José María. This lady has come . . .

Mariana. This lady has come . . . to the wrong shop . . . as she'll find out now!

José María. Mariana! . . .

Mariana. Let me alone! [*To* Julieta.] You've taken a fancy to my husband . . . have you? Well . . . nothing wrong in that, of course! If only you weren't a little late . . . for ten years ago you see he took a fancy to me. . . .

Julieta. Your husband . . . ?

Mariana. Yes, Señora, there he is . . . as large as life!

Julieta. [*Indignantly* . . . to José María.] And you never told me . . . !

Mariana. [*Interrupting her.*] Never told you he was married? Just fancy! But then he always was forgetful! But he is . . . married to me by Holy Church . . . and me with three babies . . . and another one coming . . . so now what have you to say?

Julieta. I came to call for this gentleman. We had arranged to go flying.

José María. That's all.

[*The two women look at each other with some disdain.*]

Mariana. [*Ironically.*] Flying!

Julieta. There's no harm in flying that I know of.

Mariana. Well, he won't be flying this afternoon.

José María. [*Feeling his importance.*] I . . . shan't be flying . . . !

Mariana. No, Señora . . . he has rather a cold, and the draughts up there would be bad for him. So if flying's all you're after . . .

Julieta. [*Serious.*] I'm sorry. Of course that would never do. Good afternoon.

MARIANA. [*Without moving.*] Good afternoon to you.

JOSÉ MARÍA. [*Feeling that he has been made cut a pretty poor figure.*] Julieta . . . I . . .

JULIETA. [*With a grimace of distaste.*] Oh, please don't trouble to explain!

MARIANA. You hear what she says. She's quite right. Don't!

[JOSÉ MARÍA *slinks into a corner.* JULIETA *starts to go out, but being somewhat perturbed goes toward the wrong door.*]

MARIANA. No, Señora, this way . . . [*Generously, and repenting a little.*] I'm sorry if I've hurt your feelings. But you just go away and forget all about it, won't you? For though, of course, it's worse for me, it's not very pleasant for you either . . . and I know it wasn't your fault. But that's the way with a man. He runs up the bill . . . and we have to pay it between us, don't we? But don't you worry.

[JULIETA *goes out.* RAMÓN, *very gallant, opens the door for her,· and* JOSÉ MARÍA *tries to follow her, but* MARIANA *puts herself in his way, and stops him.*]

MARIANA. And where are you going?

JOSÉ MARÍA. Wherever I choose . . .

MARIANA. What . . . going after her again, are you . . . going to take her flying! Yes, a nice safe place for you both to sit laughing at me . . . where I can't get at you. Wasn't it bad enough to bring her to my very house . . . playing your tricks on me under my very nose.

JOSÉ MARÍA. [*Furious.*] I didn't bring her. I didn't know she was coming. And we weren't playing any tricks on you either. That's the truth . . . and if you don't want to believe it, so much the worse for you. But I tell you this. I'm not going to be treated like the dirt under your feet. I've a business appointment with a lady, and I'm going to keep it . . . as any man would who calls himself a man. There now . . . is that clear?

MARIANA.   Well . . . I give you fair warning. . . .

JOSÉ MARÍA.   Let's have it!

MARIANA.   If you go out of that door, you don't come back again!

JOSÉ MARÍA.   What d'you mean?

MARIANA.   Not back to this house.

JOSÉ MARÍA.   Who's the master here . . . I'd like to know? You or I?

MARIANA.   Neither. The one that's in the right is the master.

JOSÉ MARÍA.   Am I your husband . . . or not?

MARIANA.   [*Turning about.*]   It would be all the same to me if you were Garibaldi!

JOSÉ MARÍA.   [*To his father-in-law.*]   What do you think of this? Isn't it enough to make a man hit her over the head? I tell you I'm going to fly with the lady . . . I'm going to take her flying . . . and that's all!

RAMÓN.   Now, my dear child, do remember that he's got to keep his engagements. The public is expecting him . . . he's a famous man!

MARIANA.   A famous man, is he! She thinks so the first time she sees him flying through the air. But I've seen him do it once before . . . when the bull tossed him there . . . the last time he tried to be a famous man. I knew all about his fame, thank you . . . and just how long it lasts . . . till his first tumble!

JOSÉ MARÍA.   Very well then . . . have it your own way!

MARIANA.   You're going?

JOSÉ MARÍA.   I'm going.

MARIANA.   Listen to me now . . .

JOSÉ MARÍA.   Thank you, I've heard all I want to . . . till next time.

[*He goes out, very dignified.*]

MARIANA.   There won't be any next time! Yes . . . you've done it now!

[ANDREA *comes in, carrying a dish of fried ham and
doesn't see that* JOSÉ MARÍA *isn't there.*]

ANDREA. Now, my dearest boy, you'll be seasick if you
try to fly without eating anything first. Try these two
slices of fried ham . . .

[*She looks around with amazement at not finding
him.*]

MARIANA. [*Laughing bitterly.*] Ham! . . . So that's
what you've been busy with! A lot of use, isn't it?

ANDREA. Why?

MARIANA. Now that your son's going to take his meals
out in future . . . for ever and ever . . . amen!

[*She sits down in a corner and cries, drying her eyes
with her apron.*]

SCENE II.

*The same scene as in the first act. At the rising of the
curtain* MARIANA *and the three laundresses are seen ironing.*

MARIANA. Put everything tidy now, and be off to your
dinner; it's one o'clock.

[*She takes off her white apron and sleeves and folds
them up, putting them on one side. The girls do the
same. The postman appears at the street-door and
takes a letter out of his bag.*]

POSTMAN. [*Presenting   the   letter.*] José   María
López.

MARIANA. [*Curtly.*] It's the wrong address . . .

[*The girls look at her with amazement.*]

POSTMAN. Wrong address? [*Looking at the letter.*]
28 Madera Alta. Laundry.

MARIANA. Yes, Señor. 28 Madera Alta. Laundry.
What's that got to do with it?

POSTMAN.   [*A little baffled.*]   But he always did live here.

MARIANA.   No one lives here but me!

POSTMAN.   You mean that Señor José María López has moved?

MARIANA.   That's it.

POSTMAN.   And can you inform me . . . ?

MARIANA.   [*Turning her back on him.*]   He didn't leave his address.

POSTMAN.   Oh, very well.   [*Making a note on the letter.*]   José María López . . . wrongly addressed . . . Good afternoon.   Sorry, I'm sure.

MARIANA.   Good afternoon.   Don't mention it!   [*To the girls, who are still looking at her, astonished.*]   Here . . . what are you all standing around for?   Off with you . . . and be back again at a quarter to, sharp.   It's Saturday and I can't have things left half-done!

[*The girls put on their shawls and go out to the street.   SEÑOR RAMÓN appears from the family rooms. He is smoking a cigar.*]

RAMÓN.   Who was that you were talking to?

MARIANA.   [*Taking up the linen from the table, and folding it.   She doesn't look her father in the face.*]   The postman.

RAMÓN.   Who was the letter for?

MARIANA.   For nobody here, that's clear, as he took it away again.

RAMÓN.   But . . . who was it for?

MARIANA.   I think the name was José María López.

RAMÓN.   [*Who can't believe his ears.*]   And you didn't take it?

MARIANA.   No, I didn't!

RAMÓN.   Have you taken leave of your senses?

MARIANA.   Perhaps!

RAMÓN.   [*Putting on the manner of a tyrannical father.*]   Answer me now.   How long is this nonsense going to last?

MARIANA. [*As if she hadn't heard him.*] Have you all finished dinner?

RAMÓN. Did you hear what I said?

MARIANA. I asked if you'd had your dinner?

RAMÓN. [*Ill-humouredly.*] Yes . . . we've had our dinner.

MARIANA. Well then, go out and take a little walk, . . . it'll help you to digest it!

RAMÓN. [*Now really angry.*] I want to know how long you mean to keep this up?

MARIANA. Who means?

RAMÓN. You and your husband.

MARIANA. I haven't got a husband!

RAMÓN. I never saw such a pig-headed . . . !

MARIANA. Well, I didn't make myself!

RAMÓN. Look here . . . do you think that any woman born has a right to throw a man out of the house in this way?

MARIANA. He went away because he wanted to, didn't he?

RAMÓN. Well, he's been wanting to come back for a long time now.

MARIANA. He didn't hurry back that night, I noticed!

RAMÓN. What did you expect him to hurry back for? To give you a shaking . . . which is what you deserved?

MARIANA. To give *me* a shaking . . . after everything else he'd done to me! You men make me laugh!

RAMÓN. He didn't do anything to you! And even if he did . . . that's all over now. Look, I'll tell you . . . that woman went off to Paris three days ago . . .

MARIANA. Oh! so that's why he wants to come home, is it? And do you think I'm going to take anyone else's leavings! Get that out of your head. Let him spend the summer where he spent the winter!

RAMÓN. [*Philosophic.*] Now this would be all very well, you know, if you were the same sort that she is. But you are his wife . . . and that's a very different thing.

I'm not standing up for him, but what sort of a state would this world get into, if every time a man started to amuse himself a little his wife went on like this? Here you are in your own house, and no one can take that away from you. . . .

MARIANA. [*Interrupting.*] No . . . I pay the rent!

RAMÓN. [*With great dignity.*] I was not referring to that! This is your home . . . and no matter what happens you must remember that you're his wife . . . and that he's your husband . . . and above all, that he's the father of your children!

MARIANA. Yes . . . a lot of trouble that's put him to!

RAMÓN. [*Sincerely indignant.*] I don't know how I have the patience to listen to such talk! . . . The man has gone too far already . . . he has begged your pardon for something that he's never done. And I go too far when I come on such an errand. Why should I bother to make you friends again? What is it to do with me?

MARIANA. You're pretty well paid for it, aren't you?

RAMÓN. [*Dignified.*] And pray what do you mean to insinuate by that?

MARIANA. Well, I've noticed that for the last few days you've been smoking some very good cigars.

RAMÓN. [*Trying to hide the cigar which he's smoking at that moment.*] I?

MARIANA. And cigarettes . . . and you go to the café every afternoon . . . and have a glass of something. And every evening to the Cinema, and you've got a ticket for the bull-fight tomorrow. That'll have cost you seven pesetas. And you've got the five I gave you last Sunday besides . . . and today is Saturday. . . .

RAMÓN. And what then . . . ?

MARIANA. [*Beginning to cry.*] Oh, I wouldn't have believed you'd sell your own daughter for a packet of cigars and a bull-fight!

RAMÓN. [*Walking wrathfully up and down.*] I

wouldn't have believed that any man in the world could be such a nincompoop as to sit waiting his wife's permission to come back to his own house. If my Candelas . . . now in glory . . . had tried anything of the sort on me . . . ! However, she was always a perfect fool!

[ANDREA *appears in the door, hears the last words, and stands looking at him scornfully.*]

ANDREA. *I see!* And so yours is all the sense we've got left in the house!

RAMÓN. [*Rounding on her.*] I was not addressing my remarks to you, Señora!

ANDREA. A "perfect fool" was she? No doubt . . . beside such a very wide awake old man as you are!

[MARIANA *goes into the sitting-room, leaving them to their quarrel.*]

RAMÓN. And may I ask why you want to pick a quarrel with me?

ANDREA. I shouldn't be surprised if the answer was that what has happened here is more your fault than anyone's.

RAMÓN. My fault that your son went flying and got the little sense he ever had blown out of him!

ANDREA. If the poor boy hadn't been set a bad example by the one person who ought to have set him a good one! Yes . . . that's what I mean.

RAMÓN. Señora, I am a widower, and I am free to behave as I please.

ANDREA. I am a widow . . . but I don't know that that's a reason for not behaving myself!

RAMÓN. Señora, you are a woman, and with a woman it's very different!

ANDREA. You're quite right. It is . . . very different indeed!

[MARIANA *comes back with the baby in her arms, one child by the hand, and another clinging to her skirts.*]

MARIANA. Quarrelling as usual, are you? . . . Do drop it . . . it's nobody's business but mine. . . . [*She sits down on a low chair, and looks at the biggest child.*]

Dirty nose! Come here! [*Takes out a handkerchief and wipes it furiously.*] Blow now! Harder! . . . harder!

RAMÓN. He *can't* blow any harder, my dear!

MARIANA. That's right! Take his part against me . . . so that he'll be well brought up from the beginning! [*To the little girl, who is biting her nails.*] Very well, bite your nails, if you want to! [*Gives her a slap.*]

RAMÓN. But my good girl. . . .

MARIANA. [*Getting up.*] In this house everybody's got to sit up and behave themselves!

[SEÑOR RAMÓN *goes towards the door.*]

MARIANA. Are you going out? Take the children and leave them at the school as you go by.

> [*The children take their grandfather's hands, without saying a word, looking terrified at their mother.*]

MARIANA. Tie up that shoe-lace!

> [*The little boy lets go his grandfather's hand, and ties the shoe-string with trepidation.*]

RAMÓN. [*While he waits for the tying to be finished.*] All right . . . and if I happen to see . . . *him* . . . what am I to say?

MARIANA. [*To the little boy, as if she hadn't heard her father.*] Don't fidget, child!

RAMÓN. But suppose I do see the man, what *am* I to say to him!

> [*He goes out with the children.* MARIANA, *with the smallest one in her arms, watches him from the door.* SEÑORA ANDREA *sighs.*]

ANDREA. Oh, Lord!

MARIANA. [*Affectionately, her harshness quite gone.*] Oh, come now . . . what's the trouble?

ANDREA. What should be?

MARIANA. Of course you take his part.

ANDREA. Ah, I'm too old now, my dear, to take anybody's part.

MARIANA. D'you think I'm a beast?

ANDREA. No. He's my son . . . and I'm fond of him

. . . that's only natural. But you're a woman . . . and I've been a woman too, and I've known what it was to go through what you're going through . . . that's all.

MARIANA. [*To hide her feelings.*] Would you like to have me do your hair for you?

ANDREA. [*Hiding hers too.*] Much you know about hair-dressing! Anyway you're in no state for it now! Let it go till another day . . . [*She's on the point of going into the inner room, but stops on the threshold.*] You haven't had any dinner . . . don't you want me to make you a cup of chocolate?

MARIANA. I'm not hungry. Make some soup for the baby, he hasn't had anything.

ANDREA. Well . . . it'll all be as God wills! . . . [*She sighs and goes out.*]

MARIANA. [*Looking around with the child in her arms.*] The house does seem so empty! [*Sits down on the low chair; a street-organ begins to play outside.*] A street-organ now! [*Sighs and looks at the child almost with tears in her eyes.*] You've got your father's face! [*Kisses him passionately.*] Little angel! [*A pause.*] And to think that if God spares you to me you'll grow up to be a man . . . and as great a villain as any of them! [*She kisses him again, tenderly, as if to beg his forgiveness for her evil thought.*] Oh . . . if I could only keep you as you are . . . even if I had to bottle you!

[SEÑOR JULIÁN *appears at the door. The organ goes on playing for a moment still.*]

SEÑOR JULIÁN. [*Insinuatingly.*] Alone as usual, neighbour!

MARIANA. [*Raising her eyes, and still smiling at the child.*] Alone with my worries!

SEÑOR JULIÁN. [*Approaching and making a grimace at the child.*] I say! How fat the little rascal's getting!

MARIANA. [*With the pride of a mother.*] Isn't he?

SEÑOR JULIÁN. [*Enthusiastically.*] Whatever you put your hand to you do well!

MARIANA. [*A little dryly.*] Oh, sometimes well, and sometimes badly.

SEÑOR JULIÁN. [*Sighing.*] Some men have luck!

MARIANA. Do they?

SEÑOR JULIÁN. [*Insinuatingly.*] And mostly don't value it when they have it, worse luck!

MARIANA. Worse luck for them!

SEÑOR JULIÁN. Do you want to know why I never married?

MARIANA. No . . . why should I?

SEÑOR JULIÁN. Not out of curiosity?

MARIANA. [*Despondently.*] Thank you! I know all I want to know about this wretched world!

SEÑOR JULIÁN. [*A little impudently.*] You've had lessons from your husband, haven't you?

MARIANA. [*Head high.*] And who else should I get them from?

SEÑOR JULIÁN. [*Approaching again.*] Well . . . you've had a very poor teacher!

MARIANA. [*Angrily.*] Now you be careful!

SEÑOR JULIÁN. There . . . there . . . I didn't mean anything. [*Smiling.*] God bless me! . . . how you do fly out!

MARIANA. Then you'd better keep clear of me, hadn't you?

SEÑOR JULIÁN. All I did mean was . . . what a shame that a woman like you shouldn't be better appreciated. Why, any man ought to be on his knees to you. . . .

MARIANA. That's for me to say!

SEÑOR JULIÁN. [*Not disconcerted.*] What . . . with a face like yours, and a figure like yours, and those eyes and that hair, not to mention that you're the best house-keeper in all the quarter . . . and to think that you spend your life slaving to support a man who's not worth a snap of your fingers!

MARIANA. [*Wrathfully.*] Will you be quiet!

SEÑOR JULIÁN. [*More and more agitated.*] And if

ever he does earn a few pesetas, off he goes to spend them,
with whoever. . . .

MARIANA. [*Trying not to cry.*] Well, they're his
own, aren't they? He has nobody's leave to ask.

SEÑOR JULIÁN. [*Very close.*] But do you know who
it is that's been helping him spend them lately?

MARIANA. [*Beside herself with suffering jealousy and
anger.*] Get out of my sight!

SEÑOR JULIÁN. Now don't be angry . . . I tell you
these things because I . . . I care for you . . . Yes, indeed! More than you think.

MARIANA. Care for *me* . . . you!

SEÑOR JULIÁN. And that's why I'm so sorry, Señora
. . . terribly, terribly sorry, to see you caring so much for a
man who is as unworthy of you. . . .

MARIANA. [*Greatly excited.*] Oh ho . . . unworthy
is he! But you're not, I dare say. For all you do is to
take advantage of being his friend and come like this when
you think there's no one else in the house to protect
me . . . ! But there is! This child in my arms, and two
others, and another yet, please God. And the man's not
born that could make me forget the joy of the pain of bringing them into the world to be . . . to be their father's children! So now!

SEÑOR JULIÁN. [*Hiding his chagrin with a slight
laugh.*] Well, don't scratch my eyes out, just because I
can't help being in love with you. . . .

[*Voices and steps are heard in the street.*]

MARIANA. What's that? What has happened?

[*She dashes towards the door at the same time that
SEÑOR RAMÓN and another man enter supporting JOSÉ
MARÍA, who has his head bandaged.*]

MARIANA. José María . . . an accident!

[*She leaves the baby in the arms of the APPRENTICE
who has come in with the other two work-women and
some neighbours, and throws herself upon her husband.*]

RAMÓN. [*Consequently.*] Carefully . . . this way now!
All right, don't be frightened!

MARIANA. This is what comes of flying! I might have
known!

ANDREA. [*Appearing in the door.*] Oh . . . my precious boy! . . . Is he hurt?

RAMÓN. [*Trying to keep* MARIANA *away from* JOSÉ
MARÍA, *who has fallen, as if fainting, in a chair.*] Keep
calm, child, keep calm . . . !

MARIANA. Let me alone!

> [*They all move a little aside, and she goes up to her
> husband.*]

MARIANA. What is it? What happened?

ANDREA. But isn't anybody going for the doctor?

JOSÉ MARÍA. [*In a dying voice.*] Can you forgive me?

MARIANA. Oh, yes, my darling, yes! . . . But what
happened? . . . Where are you hurt?

> [*She tries to take off the bandage.*]

JOSÉ MARIA. [*Resisting.*] No! . . . No!

MARIANA. Yes! . . . Yes! . . . I   must   see. . . .
[*She begins, feverishly, to take off the bandage.*] There's
no blood! [*She finishes taking off the bandage, and sees
that there is nothing wrong at all.*] There's nothing wrong
at all! Oh . . . you miserable fraud!

ANDREA. He isn't hurt? . . . Praise be to God!

MARIANA. How dare you come here and give me such
a fright?

JOSÉ MARÍA. [*Going up to her and taking her in his
arms.*] How else was I to get into the house? I had to
do something.

MARIANA. [*Wishing to appear implacable.*] Let me
alone!

JOSÉ MARÍA. Do you want me to go off again? Well
. . . I've kept the cab waiting. Look! Shall I go, or
shall I stay? . . . Come now . . . which is it to be?

MARIANA. Well, if you do stay, you're going to belong

to me . . . and I don't go shares with anyone. So I warn you.

JOSÉ MARÍA. Get along with you! . . . I'm much too much of a man for one woman to get in her pocket. [*She makes a half angry gesture.*] Why . . . one woman would bore me to death! But you're about six women rolled into one . . . !

MARIANA. [*Lovingly.*] You're a funny fellow, aren't you?

JOSÉ MARÍA. Am I? . . . Well . . . as long as I can make *you* laugh . . . !
        [*He kisses her.*]

MARIANA. [*Accepting the kiss.*] Oh, anyone can take me in!

JOSÉ MARÍA. I like that! Here's a famous man for you to order about . . . and still you're not satisfied! What more do you want, pray?

MARIANA. Oh dear me! If you're not to be trusted when you're only men, God help us all when you're famous as well!!

JOSÉ MARÍA. You hold your tongue! As if you didn't know that every woman looking at you now isn't green with envy! [*He kisses her again.*] But then, of course, the men looking at me are even greener. Aren't they . . . aren't they? Well, then . . . all's fair!

MARIANA. Don't you be so conceited! It might be far better for both of us if no one could see us at all! [*Then stepping forward to address the audience.*] But here's an end to our little play, dear Public. And this is its moral. When a woman truly loves a man . . . whether he's a hero or whether he's a scoundrel, she's bound to suffer for it. Because it's like this with love, ladies and gentlemen, whoever can give the most has got the most to lose. It has been a simple story and quite unimportant. But perhaps . . . just because you've heard it so often . . . you may find more to think about in it than you would in many a high-toned tragedy.

And the author asks me to say how much he wishes that the simple words he has used, the simple speech of the common people, will help you to feel as he felt—while he wrote this little song of praise (that's what it is)—the honesty and good sense, the sturdy charm, the self-forget-fulness, the generous heart, the just mind, that go to make that admirable thing, unspoiled, sound as a ripe nut, sweet but not too sweet, Manola, as we call her, the working woman of our Madrid. Such good sense she has! Her heart's in its place, and her head's not too far from it. She walks through the muddy streets keeping her shoes so spotless. How on earth does she do it? Well, her soul is as bright! That's all. Good night!

THE ROMANTIC YOUNG LADY

(SUEÑO DE UNA NOCHE DE AGOSTO)

COMEDY IN THREE ACTS

TEATRO ESLAVA, MADRID
1918

ROYALTY THEATRE, LONDON
1920

CHARACTERS

ROSARIO.

DOÑA BARBARITA.

MARÍA PEPA.

IRENE.

AMALIA.

THE APPARITION.

EMILIO.

MARIO.

PEPE.

DON JUAN.

GUILLERMO.

The action passes—at the present time, more or less, and in Madrid—between one August evening and the next, at Doña Barbarita's house and at the abode of the Apparition.

ACT I

The scene is in a room in Doña Barbarita's *house. It is a study furnished modestly but in good taste. There is a table with books, papers, periodicals: a large bookcase full of books; an easy chair; a chaise-longue or a large sofa placed against the table; other chairs of course; some prints and engravings on the walls, of small value but well chosen. There are doors at the back and on the right. The one on the right leads to a bedroom. The one at the back communicates with the rest of the house. At the left is a large window; it must be obvious that it is not a very great height above the street. An electric light fixture hangs from the ceiling; another, movable, with a blue shade is on the table, in such a way that its light is useful to anyone seated, or lying, on the sofa, and that it can be turned out from there without moving.*

At the rising of the curtain, Pepe, *who is about 21, in evening dress but without having yet put on his dinner-coat, is standing before the mirror over the mantelpiece, trying to tie his tie, but not succeeding very well.* Emilio, *his brother, eight or nine years older, at the table is writing a letter and showing signs of impatience because the pen and ink are not working as well as he would like, and hunting among the papers on the table to find a sheet which he can substitute for the one he has just blotted.*

Pepe. Oh, this tie, Rosario!

Rosario. [*From the bedroom.*] I'm coming.

Emilio. What a pen! What ink! Another blot . . . that sheet's done for now. Where on earth is the writing paper? Rosario!

Rosario. I'm coming! I'm coming! [Rosario *comes in. She is a very pretty girl of 23.*]

ROSARIO.   What *is* the matter?

PEPE.   Tie my tie for me.

EMILIO.   Where *is* the writing paper?

ROSARIO.   [*Affectionately.*]   Come   here . . . clumsy!
What useless creatures men are!   [*She ties his tie.*]

EMILIO.   And why, may I ask, is the baby of the family
to be attended to first?

ROSARIO.   Because he howled first.   Don't mix up those
papers, or Mario will be angry.   [*Finishing the tie.*]
There!   [*To* PEPE.]

EMILIO.   And suppose Mario is . . . Does Mario own
the whole house?

ROSARIO.   Not the house—but the table.

EMILIO.   And may I ask why that dearly beloved brother
of ours is to keep to himself the only place in the house
where one can write?

ROSARIO.   Because he's the only one in the house who
does any writing.   If anyone else had a claim, what about
mine, to the table and the room, too?

EMILIO.   And am I not writing . . . or trying to—
Heaven help me!

ROSARIO.   Writing a love letter is not writing.   [*She
searches the table quickly and methodically.*]   Here you
are . . . paper, envelope, blotting paper . . . stamp.
Now, shall I dictate the letter as well?

EMILIO.   No, thank you.

ROSARIO.   That's something.

PEPE.   The clothes brush?

ROSARIO.   I'll lend you one.

> [*She goes into the bedroom and comes out almost
> immediately with a clothes brush in her hand.*]

PEPE.   One never can find anything in this house.

ROSARIO.   Because you never look in the right place.
And haven't you a bedroom to dress in?

PEPE.   [*Looking at himself in the glass.*]   I can't see
myself in the bedroom.

ROSARIO. You're very smart tonight. Where are you off to?

PEPE. The theatre.

ROSARIO. Bent on conquest?

PEPE. Yes, indeed.

ROSARIO. Of the leading lady?

PEPE. Of someone far more important . . . of the leading lady's backer.

ROSARIO. Really!

PEPE. He's an American and a millionaire. And he's looking for a private secretary, and I'm to be introduced to him tonight. If he takes a fancy to me, isn't my fortune made? Off to America, I shall work for him like a nigger, and, in a year or two's time, when he can't do without me, he'll give me a share of his business . . . Say a prayer for me, my child . . . my foot's on the ladder. And when I'm rich, think of all the chocolates I'll buy you.

EMILIO. Could you stop talking just for one minute? I've made three mistakes already.

ROSARIO. [As she leans over the writing table.] Passion spelt with one "s" again. Give her my love. Oh, but I wish you'd get married.

EMILIO. Not more than she does.

ROSARIO. Not more than you do, I hope.

EMILIO. Well, you know, personally, now that we've waited five years . . .

ROSARIO. Yes . . . and why have you waited five years? She has to wait till you're rich enough to get married. If I'll kindly wait till you're rich I shall have chocolates.

[DOÑA BARBARITA and MARIO have come in. She is a very old lady and leans on her grandson's arm. He is 27 or so.]

MARIO. No, my dear, not till then . . . not all that time! Wait till I'm editor of my paper . . . till I've had

a few plays produced. . . . Then you shall see. As you
go along the street you'll hear them whispering: "That's
Mario Castellanos' sister, Castellanos, the dramatist!

[*While he is talking, he has crossed the room and
helped his grandmother to sit down on the sofa near
the window.*]

ROSARIO. It's quite like a fairy tale. Once on a time
there were three brothers—famous, rich and happy. And
they had a sister. Well, what about her?

MARIO. You?

EMILIO. How do you mean? . . . what about you?

ROSARIO. What happens to me when you're all such
thrilling successes?

PEPE. I suppose you'll marry.

MARIO. Won't you?

ROSARIO. Suppose I don't?

EMILIO. But why shouldn't you? You're very pretty.

MARIO. And clever enough . . . to be anybody's wife.

ROSARIO. Thank you. [*She curtseys ironically to all
three.*]

MARIO. How old are you now, Rosario?

ROSARIO. Can't you remember? Twenty-three last
birthday.

EMILIO. Well . . . it *is* time you were looking around.

ROSARIO. [*Very much offended.*] What do you mean?

PEPE. Don't worry, my child. I'll find you a husband.

ROSARIO. Thanks. I'm not sure I'd trust to your
taste.

PEPE. Why not?

ROSARIO. Well . . . if I'm to judge by the cigarette
girl I saw you out walking with yesterday . . .

PEPE. Oh, did you? I must be off or I shall miss my
millionaire. Good-night, Grandmamma. [*He kisses her
hand.*] You were married three times, weren't you? Tell
this silly girl how to catch a husband before she's past
praying for. [*As he goes he tries to kiss* ROSARIO.]
Good-night, ugly duckling.

ROSARIO. Run away, idiot!

DOÑA BARBARITA. Don't come walking in at half past nothing o'clock now . . . for I'm awake and I hear you.

PEPE. [*At the door.*] But, my dear Grandmamma, if I'm going to conquer America you must expect me to be late home.

> [*He goes off gaily, and outside is heard singing some popular song.*]

DOÑA BARBARITA. That young gentleman is riding for a fall!

EMILIO. Good-night, Grandmamma. [*Kisses her hand.*]

DOÑA BARBARITA. Are you off too?

EMILIO. To post my letter.

ROSARIO. And then to find consolation till the answer comes. That's what you call being in love.

EMILIO. My good child, what do you know about being in love? I shall be a model husband.

DOÑA BARBARITA. Are you taking lessons in the art?

EMILIO. Well . . . anything to forget one's troubles, you know. Good-night.

> [*He goes out, embracing* ROSARIO *as he passes her, while she shakes her fist at him affectionately.* RO- SARIO *then picks up the torn papers which have been left on the table. She then sets all the table in order, picks up the clothes brush which* PEPE *has left on a chair and goes into the bedroom, and comes back again.* DOÑA BARBARITA *remains seated on the sofa.* MARÍO *walks about idly, looks out of the window at the street, takes another turn and sits down in a chair.*]

ROSARIO. Aren't you off, too?

MARIO. I wish I weren't! But what would my re- spected editor say if he had to go to press without my column of spiteful gossip about the great ones of the earth? Wait till I'm one of them! Patience . . . patience. [*To* ROSARIO.] Good-night, my precious. Ten years hence, on such a night as this—the poor wretch doing the comic

chippings in my stead will be racking his brains to think—
"What can I say this time about Mario Castellanos?"—
which is precisely my trouble at the moment over my
favourite dramatist. Good-night, Grandmother.

[*He kisses her hand and goes out.*]

ROSARIO. [*Looking out of the window.*] What a divine night! How the jasmine smells. [*Waving her
hand.*] Good luck!

DOÑA BARBARITA. Whom are you waving to?

ROSARIO. Mario. [*To the unseen* MARIO.] What?
Wait, I'll see. [*As she goes to the table she says to* DOÑA
BARBARITA.] His fountain pen! Here!

[*She leans over out of the window to hand it to
MARIO who is down below.*]

DOÑA BARBARITA. Take care, you'll fall.

ROSARIO. I shouldn't kill myself . . . tumbling six feet
into the street.

[*She waves to the disappearing* MARIO; *then sits
on the window seat with a sigh.*]

DOÑA BARBARITA. Why are you sighing?

ROSARIO. Envy, I suppose. Off he goes . . . so happily!

DOÑA BARBARITA. To his work.

ROSARIO. Well . . . one to his work, another to amuse
himself . . . another to look for his lucky chance. But
the thing is that they go . . . and here we stay. [*There
is a short pause, then quickly.*] Have you ever noticed,
Grandmamma . . . ?

DOÑA BARBARITA. What?

ROSARIO. How quickly men walk off once they reach
the door? While we stand buttoning our gloves, and
look up the street and down and hesitate . . . as if we
feared someone might stop us. It's as if they went off by
right but we were stealing out of jail. [*She looks out into
the street and takes a deep breath of the perfumed air.*]
Oh, what a wonderful night! [*She leaves the window and
takes her grandmother's hand sitting close by her.*] Grand-

mother, suppose I should say to you . . . I'm a free woman. I can make a will, run a business, commit suicide, go off to America, go on the stage. Therefore I want a latchkey, just as my brothers have. And I want to come and go as I like just as they do . . . by day or night without questions asked. What would you think of that?

Doña Barbarita. I should think it quite a natural caprice.

Rosario. [*A little astonished.*] Would you give it to me?

Doña Barbarita. Why not? The cook's key will be hanging behind the back door. Go and get it, and go out by all means if you want to. [Rosario *jumps up.*] Now, I wonder where you'll go.

Rosario. [*Perplexed . . . brought to a standstill.*] I know . . . that's just it. Where can a girl go alone at this time of night without fear of being thought something she isn't? Fear! That's a woman's curse.

Doña Barbarita. Perhaps it's her blessing. [*Smiling.*] If we feared as little as men do what the world would think of us we should soon be as shameless as they. And that would be a pity, for if we lost *our* sense of decency where else in the world would you find it?

Rosario. [*Sitting down by her grandmother again.*] Do you believe, grandmamma, that all men who go off at night so gaily . . . behave wickedly?

Doña Barbarita. No doubt some of them do . . . and some try to. But most of them only want to pretend that they are being wicked. And I expect that oftenest they all get cheated out of their money and their wickedness both. And that's why they come back so depressed. [*Stroking her hair.*] I shouldn't envy them, my dear, if I were you.

Rosario. [*With a great deal of feeling which, little by little, changes into a pretty anger.*] Oh no, not their wickedness, or even their fun, as they call it. But their

courage and their confidence. They're so ready to fight
and so sure that they'll win. "I mean to get on—you
must get married . . ." to some other bold gentleman
who has got on, who can afford to buy me and keep me.
"And when we're all rich what a good time we'll give
you." Suppose I don't want to be given a good time.
[*Imitating* MARIO.] "That's Mario Castellanos' sister"
[*With much dignity.*] I don't want to be anyone's sister,
or anyone's wife . . . I don't want to reflect someone
else's fame. I want to hear them say: "That's Rosario
Castellanos." Why can't I be myself? Are you laughing at me?

DOÑA BARBARITA. I seem to remember that while the
sun is masculine the moon that reflects him is a lady.

ROSARIO. Yes, in Spanish, but in German the sun's a
woman and the moon's a man, and in English, which is a
most commonsensical language, sun is sun and moon is
moon and each is itself and no one thinks of being masculine or feminine until . . . well, until that particular
question arises. [*Sits down yet again by her grandmother.*]
You're laughing again. You don't understand—you belong
to the past—you all liked being slaves.

DOÑA BARBARITA. No, my dear, only masters like *having* slaves . . . but while you want to be free of the
tyranny we were satisfied by being revenged on the tyrants
now and then.

ROSARIO. How?

DOÑA BARBARITA. We just made their lives unbear-
able. [*She takes from her neck a sort of triple
locket which she opens. Smiling tenderly.*] My three
masters! Ernesto my first, Enrique my second and your
grandfather, my dear . . . the third. How they loved
me . . . and how I loved them!

ROSARIO. [*Somewhat scandalised.*] All three?

DOÑA BARBARITA. Yes . . . each in turn. And how
I plagued them!

ROSARIO. Did you?

Doña Barbarita. [*Very pleased with her conjugal re-collections.*] I was jealous of every woman my first husband looked in the face . . . and he was a portrait painter, do you remember? My second husband suffered tortures from his own jealousy . . . of your grandfather. That was premature, but prophetic, for your dear grandfather was our neighbour in those days and he used to stand and look at me from his balcony. And then he in his turn tortured himself, poor man, with jealousy of my second husband, who was dead by that time to be sure . . . but that only seemed to make it worse. When I think of the times I've walked into my first husband's studio, shaking all over, to see what sort of a woman he was painting this time . . . and how much of her, and of the times when I'd glance up at your grandfather on his balcony and let my dear second husband imagine . . . God forgive me . . . that I was smiling at him; and then when your grandfather would catch me looking at my poor second husband's portrait . . . my first husband had painted it while they were both alive . . . and if I wanted to drive him to fury I'd only to give one sigh. Well, now they're in Heaven all three and I'm almost sorry I worried them so. [*And she kisses the three pictures.*]

Rosario. Oh, Grandmother!

Doña Barbarita. But never forget that I was an obedient wife, gentle and loving, an angel of the fireside, an angel in crinoline. No doubt it's far nobler to "live your own life" (isn't that what you call it?) but I fear you'll never find it so amusing.

[María Pepa, *a maid—a family servant, nearly as old as* Doña Barbarita *herself, appears. She remains planted in the doorway with folded arms and doesn't speak.*]

Doña Barbarita. [*Rather ill-humouredly; she knows the footstep so well.*] And what do you want?

María Pepa. It's past eleven.

Doña Barbarita. What of it?

MARÍA PEPA. You've to put in your curl papers and say your prayers—a special one tonight, too, for tomorrow was Señor Emilio's birthday—and if you stop here talking much longer you won't be in bed before midnight.

DOÑA BARBARITA. What of it?

MARÍA PEPA. You have to be up early tomorrow for Mass, and if you don't get your eight hours and a half you'll have another of your attacks.

DOÑA BARBARITA. [*Slyly.*] What sort of an attack is it *you* get when you try to sit still for five minutes without coming to hear what we're talking about?

MARÍA PEPA. [*Very offended.*] Little I care what you're talking about!

DOÑA BARBARITA. How long have you been listening at the door?

MARÍA PEPA. Listening? Holy saints!

DOÑA BARBARITA. I heard you tiptoeing up the passage like a ghost.

MARÍA PEPA. And if one walks like a human being you say the noise upsets your nerves.

[*She turns to go with extreme dignity.*]

DOÑA BARBARITA. Where are you going?

MARÍA PEPA. To the kitchen . . . my proper place. Where else?

DOÑA BARBARITA. Sit down.

MARÍA PEPA. Thank you. I'm not tired.

DOÑA BARBARITA. Sit down!

[MARÍA PEPA *sits stiffly and haughtily on the edge of a chair.*]

DOÑA BARBARITA. And don't start a grievance when no one has done a thing to you. We're not talking secrets. I was just telling my granddaughter—

MARÍA PEPA. What an angel you were to your three husbands—I heard you.

ROSARIO. [*Bursting into a hearty laugh.*] Oh, María Pepa!

DOÑA BARBARITA. [*Ironically.*] Don't laugh, my

dear, please. She'll take offence and then what shall I do! Has the cook gone to bed yet?

MARÍA PEPA. What on earth would the woman be doing sitting up to this hour?

DOÑA BARBARITA. Good heavens, you talk as if it were three in the morning. Why can't you say at once that you're dead with sleep yourself?

MARÍA PEPA. [*As if she had been accused of a crime.*] I . . . dead with sleep!

DOÑA BARBARITA. Oh, come along, come along. [*Getting up.*] When my maid is tired of course I must go to bed. Good-night, my child.

MARÍA PEPA. Sit up till daybreak if you like. You suffer for it, not I!

ROSARIO. [*Kissing her.*] Good-night, Grandmamma.

DOÑA BARBARITA. [*Patting her cheek.*] But don't sit up till all hours reading.

ROSARIO. No, Grandmamma.

MARÍA PEPA. She will, she will! If food failed I believe the women of this family could eat books. It's an unnatural appetite.

DOÑA BARBARITA. Well, you're no glutton. Sixty-five years I've been trying to teach you your letters.

MARÍA PEPA. Thank you. I hear enough lies as it is without splitting my skull getting more out of books.

DOÑA BARBARITA. Get back to your tub, Diogenes, and don't talk so much.

[*The two go out, arm in arm without its being quite clear which one is supporting the other.* ROSARIO, *with her characteristic instinct of order, puts the furniture in place almost unconsciously, afterwards she sighs, stretches herself lazily, yawns, sighs again, yields to the little clock which is on the mantelpiece, begins to unhook her dress. When she has it nearly unhooked, she goes into the bedroom, and comes out after a minute with a kimono half put on and some slippers in her hand. She finishes putting on the kimono, sits down*

*on the sofa, takes off her shoes, and puts on the slip-
pers, puts the shoes carefully under the sofa, takes her
hair down serenely, lights the lamp which is near the
sofa, puts out the other light; throws herself comfort-
ably on the sofa and begins to read.* MARÍA PEPA
comes back and goes towards the window.]

ROSARIO. [*Without looking up from her book.*] What
are you doing?

MARÍA PEPA. I must shut the window. There's going
to be a storm. There's a big wind blowing up.

ROSARIO. I'll shut it when I go to bed. [*Goes on reading.*]

MARÍA PEPA. [*Hovering near the writing table for
a chance of conversation.*] Your brother's verses mustn't
be blown about, or there'll be trouble.

ROSARIO. Put a paper weight on them.

MARÍA PEPA. I'll put the sheep dog on them. That's
heavy.

ROSARIO. It's not a sheep dog; it's a lion.

MARÍA PEPA. [*Placing the paper-weight which is, indeed, a bronze lion.*] When first I saw it I thought it was
a sheep dog. I've always called it a sheep dog and I always shall. [ROSARIO *goes on reading, but* MARÍA PEPA
goes on talking nevertheless.] It was a present from
Señor Enrique—that was your dear grandmother's second
husband, but before he was her husband, to Señor Ernesto
—that was her first husband—given on her birthday. She
was twenty-three and she wore a Scotch plaid poplin with
a green velvet coat hemmed with gold acorns which was
a sight for sore eyes and I have it still put away and not
at all moth-eaten. Your poor grandfather . . . God rest
his soul . . . hated the sight of it.

ROSARIO. [*Interested in spite of herself.*] The green
velvet?

MARÍA PEPA. No, the sheep dog. Because your grandmother whenever she went into the room where it stood on
the table, always stroked it . . . so. [*Stroking the bronze*

lion.] And one day when he would have her go to the
theatre with him on the very anniversary as it was of
her second husband's death which, of course, she couldn't,
he changed into a basilisk as soon as she had left the
room crying like a Magdalen, and he took the sheep dog
and threw it at Señor Ernesto's—no, at Señor Enrique's
portrait which hung over the mantelpiece and, as it is a
bronze dog, of course the glass was broken so he had to
have a new frame made carved with a crown of laurel and
bevelled glass and that cost him a lot of money.

[*All this* MARÍA PEPA *says without taking breath.*]

ROSARIO. Grandmamma liked her second husband,
didn't she, the best of the three?

MARÍA PEPA. [*With disdainful and Olympian superiority.*] I can tell you this much . . . that your poor dear
grandfather was the worst.

ROSARIO. Oh, María!

MARÍA PEPA. [*With resentful calm.*] God forgive him
. . . a jealous, obstinate, stingy tyrant; and the only way to
manage him at all was just to keep on reminding him
what a perfect angel the one before him had been. Though
he had given us trouble enough, heaven knows, for he was
a gambler. And when he lost—which was always—the
way we had to pinch and screw! And that didn't come
easily at all because Señor Ernesto—he was her first—
though he wasn't a practical man being an artist and he
told lies worse than the newspapers—still he was generous
and while he was alive your dear grandmamma never put
her foot to the ground. "Angels mustn't tread on the
dust of the earth," he'd say, and not a yard did we go without our own carriage. Though for all that we might go
to bed without supper sometimes because, if he didn't paint
why he didn't earn anything, and there'd be times when he
lacked inspiration—so he said, and he'd lie on the sofa for
weeks at a stretch in a state of artistic torpor—smoking,
just smoking. But a kinder, refineder, more considerate
and gentlemanly man . . .

Rosario. There's grandmamma's bell.

María Pepa. That means she has finished her beads. Will you turn out the lights?

Rosario. Yes, I'll put out the lights. And I'll close the window. Take away those shoes, please.

María Pepa. [*Picking up the shoes with a sigh.*] Well, pray God you may never know the troubles of a married life.

Rosario. Thank you! [*She is very offended.*]

María Pepa. Ah! . . . you mean to get married, do you? And to half a dozen, I daresay, just to outdo your grandmother. . . . Well, if you make your bed you must lie on it. [*With compassionate superiority.*] We shan't be able to help you. We shall be snugly in Heaven. Though what's going to happen there when they all three come out to meet us, each one expecting to have us all to himself for eternity . . . ! They'll fight it out, I suppose.

Rosario. María, that's the third time the bell has rung.

María Pepa. [*Calmly.*] I hear it. No doubt St. Peter will settle things somehow. I'll shut the door, there's a draught.

> [*She goes out slowly, having closed the bedroom door.* Rosario *tries to return to her reading, but she can't do it because* María Pepa's *reminiscences have distracted her attention from her book. She meditates incoherently.*]

Rosario. Half a dozen! [*She starts reading her book aloud, though in a low voice, so that she may enjoy the poetry of it more.*] "Love is a solitary flower of an exquisite evanescent fragrance." How true—a *solitary* flower. "It blooms but once in the life of the soul and then the soul which this triumphant lily has enriched. . . ." This triumphant lily? What a wonderful phrase . . . "dies when it dies, but ony for love's single service can it wish to live." Ah yes! But then how could grandmamma have

been really in love with all three of them? "But into a
life may come visions and phantoms, envoys and heralds of
the true love that still delays . . ." [*Meditating.*]   That
might explain it.   Grandpapa came last, so her first and her
second were heralds and phantoms perhaps.   "But on that
divine night, when the love of Carlos and Esperanza . . ."
[*She goes on reading in an undertone for a minute, but
interrupts herself almost immediately turning over and supporting herself on an elbow.*]   Or was grandpapa a herald and a phantom, too, and did grandmamma only think
she loved all three because she really never loved anyone
at all?   I wonder!   [*Reads.*]   "But on that divine night
. . ."   [*Impatiently.*]   Oh, I can't read.

　　　[*The wind can be heard blowing.*]
What a wind!   I'd better go to bed.   But then I shall
only dream of all three of them fighting over grandmamma
at the gate of Heaven.   I'll lie still for ten minutes and
think.

　　　[*She switches off the light without moving from the
　　　sofa and lies down again.   The room remains in the
　　　dark, lighted only at intervals by the light, not very
　　　brilliant, which comes in by the window.   The wind
　　　goes on howling.*]

Rosario.   I do believe there will be a storm.   What a
dust!   I'd   better   shut   the   window. . . . Too   much
bother.

　　　[*By this time she is half asleep.   Suddenly a straw
　　　hat, carried on the violent wind, blows in the window,
　　　and falls beside the sofa.*]

Rosario.   [*Opening her eyes.*]   What's that?   Something flew in at the window?   [*Looking round her to see,
but not getting up.*]   A bird?   A hat!   A man's hat . . .
what has happened?

　　　[*She looks alternately on the floor, where the hat
　　　is and at the window.   She gets up with a certain
　　　timidity and goes slowly towards the window.   At this
　　　moment there is a tremendous lightning flash, fol-*

[*lowed immediately by a terrifying burst of thunder,
and in the really infernal resplendence of the lightning flash there appears at the window the figure of
a well-dressed, but hatless man, who looks around
the room a second, and then jumps.* ROSARIO, *terrified
and bewildered by the thunder and lightning, sees the
man, and not knowing whether he is reality or a vision, remains frozen with horror and gasps in a low
voice.*]

ROSARIO. Jesu! Ave Maria! Virgén del Carmen!
Blessed souls in Purgatory! Blessed Saint Barbara who
art enrolled in Heaven . . .

THE APPARITION. [*Observing that there is a woman
in the room, and going toward her uncertainly, because an
almost total obscurity has succeeded to the lightning flash.*]
Don't be alarmed . . . please don't be alarmed.

[*There is another flash, then thunder and then a perfect downpour of rain begins.* ROSARIO *sees by the
light of the lightning flash that the man is directing
himself toward her, and, horrified, stretches out her
arms to keep him off.*]

ROSARIO. Keep off! Keep away! Help!

THE APPARITION. [*Going up to her.*] Don't shout
. . for Heaven's sake, don't shout. I'm not a thief. I
am an entirely respectable person.

ROSARIO. Yes, yes . . . but go away!

THE APPARITION. I am going, Señora, this very
minute.

[*But in the darkness he has accidentally come quite
close to her and when he moves he finds that a piece
of her hair is entangled in his sleeve link.*]

THE APPARITION. No . . . I can't!

ROSARIO. Why not?

THE APPARITION. Your hair has got twisted in my
sleeve links.

ROSARIO. [*Impatiently.*] Then untwist it at once.

THE APPARITION. That's not so easy . . . in the

dark. Could you turn on some light perhaps . . . where is it?

ROSARIO. On the table. [*She starts to move, and he follows her, but in spite of his precautions, he pulls her hair.*] Aah! . . . You're pulling my hair. It hurts.

THE APPARITION. Ten thousand apologies! [*He stops, and as she is going on, he pulls it a second time.*]

ROSARIO. [*Angrily.*] But come with me . . . then it won't.

THE APPARITION. I'm coming . . . I'm coming.

[*But as they go towards the table in the pitch dark he stumbles; and to save himself—and her—puts his arms round her. They fall on the sofa together.*]

ROSARIO. How dare you? This is outrageous. How dare you put your arms round me?

[*Another lightning flash discloses the situation.*]

THE APPARITION. [*Very calmly.*] I assure you I did not put my arms round you. I fell . . . and you fell in them. And I have bruised my shin most confoundedly. This is quite as unpleasant for me as for you.

[*She makes a gesture of protesting amazement . . . whether at the supposition that any man could find it disagreeable to have his arms around her or not.*]

ROSARIO. Then if you realise that please move away . . . as far as you can . . . till I've turned on the light.

THE APPARITION. [*Calmly.*] But now your hair has caught in my studs and if I move at all I shall hurt you extremely. Until you can turn on the light I'm very much afraid there's no real alternative . . . to this.

ROSARIO. [*Impatiently.*] Very well then, don't move. I mean . . . do move . . . when I move. Now.

[*She tries to find the light, but her hair is badly pulled in spite of precautions.*]

ROSARIO. Oh—oh—oh!

THE APPARITION. I told you so.

ROSARIO. [*As she manages at last to turn on the light.*] Thank heaven!

[*The two then look at each other for a moment in silence and with not a little curiosity. Then he speaks, very much at his ease.*]

THE APPARITION. Now perhaps we can undo the tangle. If you'll try the stud I'll do the sleeve-links.

[*They devote themselves to the job in silence. After a moment he says quite casually.*]

THE APPARITION. You really have most infernal hair.

ROSARIO. [*Offended.*] I beg your pardon?

THE APPARITION. I meant for present purposes. Does it often get caught up like this. And do you always wear it floating in the breeze?

ROSARIO. [*Offended.*] I wear it as I choose.

THE APPARITION. Quite so . . . and of course it's not very long. I beg your pardon. That again is not criticism. If I had to criticise I should say only that you must find it most inconveniently fine. But a charming colour.

ROSARIO. [*Furious.*] Thank you.

THE APPARITION. And it smells of . . . what is it, violets? Violets.

ROSARIO. How dare you?

THE APPARITION. Don't move please . . . it'll hurt you horribly. But it does smell of violets surely.

ROSARIO. [*Now at the height of her indignation.*] Does that concern you?

THE APPARITION. I never said it concerned me. I said it smelt of violets. I'm sorry that offended you—but it does.

ROSARIO. As you please. Have you finished? [*She has by this time got the studs free.*]

THE APPARITION. Not nearly.

ROSARIO. [*Reaching to the table for some scissors.*] Take them! Cut it!

THE APPARITION. Cut it! But what a pity!

ROSARIO. Cut it! Give them to me, then. [*She cuts*

herself free.] There! [*She rises with dignity and turns to him.*] And now.

THE APPARITION. [*Who rises too and bows to her most formally.*] Señora . . . or Señorita . . .

ROSARIO. [*Without noticing either the bow or the interruption.*] Would you please explain why a thoroughly respectable person—as you say you are—[*She looks at him up and down and observes that he is, indeed, very well dressed in informal evening clothes,*] has presumed to enter a stranger's house like this? [*The beginning of the sentence is said with great violence but at the end it has been modified to something like suavity.*]

THE APPARITION. Certainly. This high wind which preceded this storm blew my hat off my head, but thoughtfully blew it in here. I came in to find it. Having found it I will, with your kind permission, take my leave.

ROSARIO. [*Angry again, because his calm manner makes her so nervous.*] And so, for the sake of a miserable straw hat, you jump in at a window like a burglar at this time of night.

THE APPARITION. Señora—or Señorita . . . ?

ROSARIO. [*Shortly.*] Señorita.

THE APPARITION. [*Bowing and smiling.*] Señorita . . . so much depends upon one's point of view. To you my hat—[*He picks it up.*] and I grant you aviation is not a suitable career for it—is naturally a thing of no consequence. But to me it was . . . and on this occasion particularly so, for I was on my way to keep a most important appointment.

ROSARIO. Indeed!

THE APPARITION. And I prefer not to walk through the streets in this weather bareheaded and arrive looking like a pursued pickpocket. Sooner than take the liberty of ringing the bell of a strange house and waking everyone up I climbed in at the window. The room was dark, I thought no one was here. I meant to get my hat and go on my way and, if you had not made such a needless noise . . .

ROSARIO. Do you expect—

THE APPARITION. . . . I should have gone as I came, quite quietly, quite discreetly.

ROSARIO. [*Convinced, but a little annoyed with herself for having let herself be convinced.*] Very well, I accept the explanation. And now, having recovered the priceless object will you be good enough to show your discretion—by going as you came—and at once.

[*She makes a magnificent gesture towards the window and then sits down with her back to it. He goes and looks out, then turns.*]

THE APPARITION. Señorita!

ROSARIO. [*Without moving.*] What is it?

THE APPARITION. It's pouring in torrents.

ROSARIO. And what of that?

THE APPARITION. Well, I haven't an umbrella; it was quite fine when I started. If I launch myself into this flood in two minutes I shall look like a drowned rat.

ROSARIO. [*With completely unreasonable but entirely feminine animosity.*] And quite unfit to be seen by the lady you are going to visit.

[*He is startled for a moment. Then he smiles and sits by her on the sofa.*]

THE APPARITION. And who told you it was a lady?

ROSARIO. [*Rising indignantly.*] Go away at once. The rain is stopping.

THE APPARITION. The rain is not stopping.

[*And indeed it is pouring harder than ever. ROSARIO makes a gesture of despair.*]

THE APPARITION. Besides, look at the concierge standing at the door of the house opposite. If he sees me jump out of the window he'd either think I'm a thief and arrest me . . . or he will not arrest me thinking . . . that I'm leaving by the window for reasons best known to both of us. And then you will be horribly compromised.

Rosario. [*Dismayed.*] So I shall be!

The Apparition. [*Most respectfully.*] Therefore, with your approval, I'll wait till he has gone in, and that will prevent any possible scandal.

Rosario. [*In a voice of anguish.*] Please sit down.

The Apparition. Thanks. [*He sits at a most respectful distance.*]

Rosario. We must certainly prevent any possible scandal. [*There is a pause. Then* Rosario's *anguish develops into anger again and she speaks, half to him, half to herself.*]

Rosario. When is one allowed to forget one's misfortune in being a woman!

The Apparition. Do you find that a misfortune?

Rosario. Isn't this a good sample of it? You jump out of my window, with my connivance, so people think, and my reputation is gone. Mine . . . but not yours . . . oh no! Do you call that fair?

The Apparition. [*Humbly.*] No, Señora.

Rosario. [*Aggressively.*] Does it seem to you just that men should have all the rights and women none?

The Apparition. You feel you should be free to jump in and out of windows if you want to?

Rosario. Not at all . . . But I think the man who jumps out of windows should be as much dishonoured as the woman who remains within.

The Apparition. Yes, there's something in that.

Rosario. There is everything in it. Equal rights . . . equal obligations.

The Apparition. [*With a slight twinkle, with the least touch of irony in his voice—she is so very young.*] I see that you are very advanced in your ideas.

Rosario. [*Getting up with great dignity.*] I hope so. [*He smiles.*] Do you doubt it?

The Apparition. Forgive me for questioning it just a little, when I see that you waste your time reading . . .

this sort of stuff. [*He points to the book that she has left on the sofa.*]

ROSARIO. [*Bridling.*] Really! Do you happen to know what that book is?

THE APPARITION. Yes, it is a sentimental novel called "A Spring Romance."

ROSARIO. [*Challenging.*] Have you read it?

THE APPARITION. Yes, I have read it.

ROSARIO. [*Sarcastically.*] But it doesn't please you?

THE APPARITION. [*With a slight grimace of contempt.*] Well . . . it isn't so badly written.

ROSARIO. [*Indignant.*] It is beautifully written.

THE APPARITION. But the writer's conception of life—

ROSARIO. What's wrong with that, pray?

THE APPARITION. The fellow hasn't any sense.

ROSARIO. Señor!

THE APPARITION. His heroine's a fool of a girl with not an idea in her head except love; all she wants is to be lied to in the moonlight by a young man who is, if possible, a bigger fool than she. Every half dozen pages or so they are swearing their love will endure for eternity . . . which is absurd; and that they'll be faithful to death . . . which is almost as unlikely.

ROSARIO. Good heavens!

THE APPARITION. The situations are ridiculous. Now, that "divine night of love" in a gondola . . .

ROSARIO. . . . When they float through the narrow canals of Venice.

THE APPARITION. Well, now, have you ever floated at night through the narrow canals of Venice? They smell most abominably, and anything may be thrown out of windows on your head . . . I assure you, anything.

ROSARIO. [*Scandalised.*] You are very vulgar.

THE APPARITION. [*Politely.*] I am a man of ordinary common sense. I like the realities of life. And, if you were what you like to think yourself—a "modern" woman instead of being—forgive me—a girl trying to bal-

ance herself between new ideas and traditional senti-
ments . . .

ROSARIO. [*Interrupting him.*] Señor, doesn't it occur
to you that one needs now and then a dream and a little
poetry to compensate, perhaps, for those more real things
which will never come one's way? This man can probe
the depths—the very depths—of a woman's heart. [*She
tries to make these speeches sound imposing . . . but she
is very young.*]

THE APPARITION. Do you really think so?

ROSARIO. Do you deny it?

THE APPARITION. I think that the poor wretch writes
his stories as well as he knows how and stuffs them full
of all the pretty lies he can invent in the hope of selling
as many as possible to that vast crowd of old-fashioned,
romantically minded women who . . .

ROSARIO. Please don't talk such libellous nonsense. He
is a genius. And womanhood—all that is best in it—owes
him a deep debt of gratitude. And I wish I could tell
him so . . . old fashioned and romantic though I may be.

THE APPARITION. Well . . . I think that could be
managed.

ROSARIO. [*Marvelling.*] Do you mean that you know
him?

THE APPARITION. Oh yes, I know him!

ROSARIO. You're not friends?

THE APPARITION. Well, I could introduce you both to
each other. I'll write him a letter.

ROSARIO. [*Enthusiastically.*] Oh, will you? It isn't
asking too much?

THE APPARITION. Not a bit. [*He sits at the table
and starts to write.*] Now then . . . "I very much want
you to know Señorita . . ." By the way, what's your
name?

ROSARIO. Rosario Castellanos. [*But her face has
fallen; and he notices it.*]

THE APPARITION. What's troubling you?

Rosario. Nothing . . . that is . . . no, nothing. [*Distressed but still determined.*] Please go on with the letter. What are you laughing at?

The Apparition. You, a strong-minded, up-to-date woman sitting quaking at the mere thought of going to call on a distinguished author . . . just to tell him how much you admire his work. Come, come, now . . . equal rights, equal responsibilities, you know.

Rosario. [*Angry.*] I am not quaking. I don't in the least mind going. It's only for fear he should misunderstand.

The Apparition. What . . . that expert in women's hearts misunderstand?

Rosario. [*Exceedingly angry.*] Please go on writing the letter.

The Apparition. Still—he's a lucky fellow!

Rosario. [*Flashing resentment at his mischievous tone.*] Please do not write that letter.

The Apparition. But why disappoint yourself—?

Rosario. That is my business.

The Apparition. Well, let's think of some other plan. Ah!

Rosario. What?

The Apparition. Have you this morning's newspaper?

Rosario *takes it from a heap of papers, gives it to him and he starts searching among the advertisements.*]

The Apparition. Because I rather think that . . . yes. Read that.

Rosario. [*Reading.*] "Wanted, well-educated and responsible lady as secretary to a literary man. Typing, not shorthand." [*Without taking breath.*] Do you think that is . . .

The Apparition. I know it is. . . . That's his address. A fortnight ago I heard him say he'd be wanting a secretary—and this morning I saw this. What luck! You can take him the letter. I'll change it a little—on the pretext of applying for the place. [*He sets himself to finish his letter.*]

ROSARIO. Thank you . . . I think that I will apply for the place.

THE APPARITION. [*Astonished.*] What did you say? Apply for the . . . seriously?

ROSARIO. Why not? I'm quite responsible and fairly well educated. I know French, German, English—besides Spanish.

THE APPARITION. Splendid!

ROSARIO. Well, what is astonishing you then?

THE APPARITION. [*Looking round the room.*] It is only that I fancied—to judge by the way you live—that you had no need to—

ROSARIO. Earn my living? I needn't. I have brothers quite ready to earn it for me. [*Pathetically.*] There again . . . that's the bitter humiliation of being a woman. One must rise above that. I want to work—to earn the bread that I eat. I am tired of being a parasite.

THE APPARITION. [*As he writes.*] Talk like that to him and, as a literary man, he will engage you at once. [*He gives her the letter while he writes an envelope.*]

ROSARIO. [*Reading it with great delight.*] Oh, how kind you are. [*When she reaches the signature she makes a slight grimace.*] Your name is Obdulio . . . ?

THE APPARITION. [*Resigned and meek.*] Yes, Señorita, Obdulio Gomez. Commonplace, isn't it? But we're not all lucky enough to be called, as your hero is, Luis Felipe de Córdoba. Ah, well!

[*He sighs, puts the letter in the envelope and hands it to her.*]

ROSARIO. Thank you a thousand times. [*She puts the letter in her dress and gives him her hand.*]

THE APPARITION. [*Holding her hand and bowing.*] Not at all. I shall be proud to have helped a little towards raising you from the humiliation of being merely a most attractive young lady.

[*They shake hands smilingly. At that moment* PEPE *and* EMILIO *can be heard letting themselves into the house and rather noisily.* PEPE *is singing.*]

EMILIO'S VOICE. Shut up man, for heaven's sake. You'll rouse the house.

ROSARIO. Good heavens . . . there are my brothers.

[*She starts to run.* THE APPARITION *catches for a minute at her wrap.*]

THE APPARITION. But . . . please . . .

ROSARIO. Let me go . . . let me go.

[*She bolts into her bedroom, losing a slipper as she goes.* THE APPARITION *picks it up and stands for a moment holding it. The two boys are in the passage now, so he moves to the window. But before he can reach it, they are in the room.* PEPE *is still singing sotto voce.*]

EMILIO. Oh, do be quiet.

PEPE. [*Seeing* THE APPARITION.] What's that? A man!

EMILIO. Catch him!

[*They proceed to try. But* THE APPARITION *is too much for them. He throws them both off and to the floor. Then he jumps out of the window.*]

PEPE. Thief!

EMILIO. Stop thief.

[*The noise brings in* DOÑA BARBARITA *and* MARÍA PEPA *in their dressing gowns. They may look a little odd, but* DOÑA BARBARITA *is as dignified as ever.*]

DOÑA BARBARITA. Whatever is happening?

MARÍA PEPA. What is all this?

[ROSITA *appears from her bedroom, limping because she has only one slipper but with the most innocent air in the world.*]

ROSARIO. What on earth are you shouting about?

EMILIO. [*Who has succeeded in getting up.*] A man.

PEPE. In the room.

MARÍA PEPA. A man!

ROSARIO.   [*With the greatest innocence.*]   Nonsense.

EMILIO.   Was it indeed?

ROSARIO.   How could he have got in?

PEPE.   By the way he went out . . . The window.

ROSARIO.   Impossible!

MARÍA PEPA.   This comes of getting too merry.   You see things.

EMILIO.   Well, I like that!

PEPE.   The rain has gone to our heads, I suppose.

EMILIO.   [*To* PEPE.]   Didn't you see him as plainly as . . .

PEPE.   [*Rubbing his arm.*]   I felt him.

DOÑA BARBARITA.   Well, I daresay, I daresay—

[*But suddenly* EMILIO *sees on a chair . . . the straw hat.*]

EMILIO.   And here is his hat.

DOÑA BARBARITA, ROSARIO, and MARÍA PEPA.   [*Together.*]   His hat!

EMILIO and PEPE.   [*Together.*]   So now, what do you say?

ROSARIO.   Let me see it.

[*She takes it and then . . . deliberately throws it out of the window.*]

PEPE and EMILIO.   What are you doing?

ROSARIO.   Sending it after its owner.

[*And now, as if in exchange for the hat, there sails in* ROSARIO'S *slipper, which falls at her feet.*]

MARÍA PEPA.   What's that?

PEPE and EMILIO.   A slipper!

ROSARIO.   [*Completely off her guard.*]   My slipper!!

DOÑA BARBARITA.   [*Who has been watching her keenly.*]   My dear child . . . think what you're saying.

EMILIO.   Your *slipper.*

PEPE.   *Your* slipper.

ROSARIO.   [*Losing her head completely.*]   Yes . . . it is—but . . . that's to say.

EMILIO and PEPE.   How did he get your slipper?

Rosario. I don't know.

Pepe. You must know.

Emilio. Explain.

Pepe. Tell us at once.

Rosario. But I . . . it is my slipper . . . but—[*She gasps.*]

Emilio and Pepe. Go on.

Emilio. Will you go on, please.

[Rosario *finding no way out, falls flat on the sofa.*]

María Pepa. [*Running to her.*] She has fainted.

Doña Barbarita. [*To herself.*] Thank God . . . I was afraid that it wouldn't occur to her.

Emilio. Don't faint!

Pepe. Don't be a fool.

Emilio. Tell us what has happened.

Doña Barbarita. Keep away from her—let her be. When a woman sees fit to faint . . . there's no more to be said.

ACT II

The Scene is the working-room of the novelist, Luis Felipe de Córdoba. It is a room with bright walls, and a great deal of light which comes in by two large windows with balconies; it is furnished with much comfort, but without any pretensions to fashion. A big writing table—not a desk—is placed near one of the two balconies, on it the disorder of a table where anyone works; sheets of papers, books, periodicals, and reviews—among them three or four foreign ones—of fashions and women's affairs. Near the other balcony is a typist's table, with its typewriter and sufficient work ready on it, shorthand tablets, papers ready for the machine. Nearly all the left wall (except the space where a door opens on the inside rooms) is occupied by a wide and comfortable divan. Near it there is another small table, also full of books and papers; but in perfect order. Over the divan are some small pictures and a little mirror of porcelain or carving; the only one there is in the room. On the right wall there is another door which is supposed to lead to the vestibule, and by which people coming in from the street enter. The rest of the wall is occupied by a low bookcase, full of books; on the top of the bookcase some well-chosen china. On the walls some few good modern pictures and old engravings. On the big writing-table a gold fish bowl with gold fish swimming in it. On the floor, before the divan the working-table and the typist's table are bright coloured rush mats. There are some very comfortable English chairs and armchairs.

On the rising of the curtain IRENE *and* DON JUAN *are discovered.* IRENE, *the secretary, is an attractive girl of twenty-two. She is wearing a simple tailor suit and a black apron.* DON JUAN *is a gentleman of 50, well-dressed and rather foolish. The secretary is at her table, putting her notes and papers in perfect order.* DON JUAN *walks up and down while he is talking. Although he is paying a visit, he has neither hat nor stick, because he has left both of them in the hall.*

DON JUAN. Our distinguished novelist is a long time.

IRENE. [*Very occupied.*] Yes.

DON JUAN. Do you know where he has gone?

IRENE. [*Still very occupied.*] No.

DON JUAN. Doesn't usually go out in the morning, does he?

IRENE. [*Even more occupied.*] No. [*With a gleam of hope.*] If you'd like to leave a message—

DON JUAN. I'd rather wait if it doesn't disturb you.

IRENE. Not in the least.

DON JUAN. [*Who is one of those people who cannot keep quiet even though they know that they are annoying other people by talking.*] Is that work you are doing?

IRENE. No. [*She has finished, and is now putting her papers in order.*] Work is over.

DON JUAN. For today?

IRENE. For ever and a day. That was my last "official" job. [*Rises.*]

DON JUAN. "Official"?

IRENE. Well, I must look in unofficially for a few days to put the new secretary in the way of things.

DON JUAN. Oho! A new secretary?

IRENE. [*Laughing.*] Don't rejoice too soon . . . she's not engaged yet. He put aside a whole lot of applications this morning, too.

> [*She goes up to the table and puts the books and papers in order.*]

DON JUAN. Am I likely to rejoice at the thought of losing you. Irene, Irene . . . how dare you desert us!

IRENE. [*Smiling.*] How dare I get married?

DON JUAN. Is he *very* fond of you?

IRENE. [*Laughing.*] Scandalously.

DON JUAN. In the army, isn't he? And twenty-four?

IRENE. [*Very well content and enumerating prettily.*]
He's an engineer, he's very good-looking and he's an only
son. Anything else you'd like to know?

DON JUAN. [*Going close to her.*] Why wouldn't you
marry me?

IRENE. [*Moving away from him and looking at him
with mocking seriousness.*] It would have seemed so . . .
disrespectful.

DON JUAN. What a delicate reminder that I'm too old.

IRENE. [*Very modestly.*] Not at all . . . but there's
a limit even to my daring.

DON JUAN. [*Going close to her again.*] But tell me—

IRENE. [*Moving away from him again and profoundly
respectful.*] Well?

DON JUAN. [*Mischievously, pointing to the chair which
undoubtedly is that of the novelist, and as if he were present.*] Why haven't you married the "great man?"

IRENE. [*Laughing.*] How many more?

DON JUAN. [*Impudently.*] Didn't you ever find yourselves falling the least little bit in love?

IRENE. [*A little drily, because the conversation is beginning to annoy her, but forcing herself to keep up her
jesting tone.*] It never occurred to us.

DON JUAN.   Not to him?

IRENE. Not to my knowledge.

DON JUAN. I can't believe it. For three years you've
been typing out these love scenes for him.

IRENE. Just three years.

DON JUAN. Why, if it was only to get a fresh idea
or two for them.

IRENE. [*Very serious and annoyed.*]   Do you mind my
telling you that the "great man" as you call him, is not
only a distinguished novelist but a distinguished gentleman
as well . . . who knows the difference between a secretary
and an . . .

Don Juan. I beg your pardon.

Irene. Not at all.

[*She gets to the typewriter again.*]

Don Juan. [*Incorrigible.*] You said you'd finished work.

Irene. [*Very drily.*] I've some letters of my own to write.

[*She writes violently.*]

Don Juan. You want me to go?

Irene. [*Without looking at him.*] I don't think Señor de Córdoba will be in before lunch.

[*She continues writing violently and making a great deal of noise with the machine.*]

Don Juan. Well, if that's so . . . good morning.

Irene. [*Without changing her attitude.*] Good morning.

Don Juan. [*Hoping even yet to renew the conversation.*] You will excuse me?

Irene. Certainly.

Don Juan. I hope you will be very happy.

Irene. Thank you.

[Don Juan *prepares to leave, but at the door stumbles on* Guillermo, *who is the novelist's servant.* Guillermo *is a man of more than 50, of a type, half servant, half professor. He is completely bald, and is scrupulously well-dressed, not in livery, but in a suit of good material, and well cut, though evidently not made for him; he is in fact dressed in his master's cast off clothes. He is amiable, smiling, discreet.* Don Juan *pauses on seeing him come in, because he likes to know everything that is going on, and wants to find out who has come.*]

Guillermo. Señorita Irene, there's a young lady come in answer to the advertisement.

Don Juan. [*Pleasantly excited.*] Aha! . . . a recruit to replace a deserter.—[*To* Guillermo.] Is she pretty?

[GUILLERMO *does not answer and looks imperturbably at* IRENE.]

IRENE.   Show her in.   [*To* DON JUAN *who, as a pretext for awaiting the candidate's entrance, looks from one side to another as if in search of something.*]   If you are looking for your hat it is in the hall.

DON JUAN.   [*Ironically.*]   Thank you!

[*He is preparing to leave, seeing there is nothing else for it, when* GUILLERMO *shows in* ROSARIO, *who is shy and a little inclined to take* DON JUAN *for the novelist. He'd be willing enough, but* IRENE *interrupts with:*]

IRENE.   Guillermo, please give Señor Don Juan Medina his hat.

GUILLERMO.   Sí, Señorita.   [*He holds the door for* DON JUAN *who goes out, furious with* IRENE.]

ROSARIO.   Oh, I thought—

IRENE.   [*Amiably.*]   That he was Señor de Córdoba . . . not he, indeed.   Señor de Córdoba won't be long . . . if you don't mind waiting.   Do sit down.

ROSARIO.   [*Without sitting down.*]   Are you . . . Señora de—

IRENE.   [*Smiling.*]   I'm his secretary.

ROSARIO.   [*Nervously.*]   Oh . . . then it's no use my waiting.   I came . . .

IRENE.   No, no . . . do sit down please.   I should have said "I was."   I'm only staying on till my successor can take possession.   [*She evidently takes to* ROSARIO *in a flash, as a young girl may.*]   I hope he'll engage you.   I would.

ROSARIO.   Thank you *so* much.

IRENE.   [*Looking about the room almost maternally.*]   Well—I should hate to leave all this . . . that I've grown so fond of . . . to anyone who wouldn't appreciate it.

ROSARIO.   Why are you giving it up?

IRENE.   Change of profession.   I'm getting married.

ROSARIO.   To . . . him?

IRENE.   Oh no.   You've never met him?

ROSARIO. Señor de Córdoba?

IRENE. Yes.

ROSARIO. No . . . is he married?

IRENE. No.

ROSARIO. [*Wishing to show how casual she is about it.*] I admire his work immensely. [*She emphasises the "work."*] I've tried so often to get a picture of him, but they're not to be had.

IRENE. No, he won't be photographed. He prefers, he says, to have his woman readers picture him each for herself, and he doesn't want to spoil any one of their illusions.

ROSARIO. Is he so ugly?

IRENE. [*With all the indifference of a young lady who is going to be married.*] Oh no, I shouldn't call him ugly —not bad looking—for a civilian.

ROSARIO. He's not young?

IRENE. Thirty-eight.

ROSARIO. Is this where he works? What a charming room—and so beautifully kept!

IRENE. [*Drily.*] Yes . . . he's the untidiest man in the world, and the one thing he won't stand is untidiness. That's where his secretary comes in. He'll go out leaving his writing strewn all over the place, pages unnumbered, books on the floor, torn up paper in the drawers and his notes in the waste paper basket. But when he comes back, he likes to find everything just so. Have you ever done this sort of work before?

ROSARIO. Not just this sort.

IRENE. You've been in an office?

ROSARIO. I—I saw the advertisement. I came with a letter.

IRENE. [*Interested.*] Oh!

ROSARIO. Here.

> [*She takes the letter which* THE APPARITION *gave her out of her bag and offers it to* IRENE.]

IRENE. Better leave it on the table.

[*She takes it and puts it there, then, at the sight
of the handwriting, gives a jump.*]

IRENE. Well!

ROSARIO. [*Alarmed.*] What is it?

IRENE. [*Puzzled, looking at the letter and at* ROSARIO.]
Wh gave you this letter?

ROSARIO. [*A little curtly.*] A friend.

IRENE. [*Still watching her.*] Gave it to you . . . personally?

ROSARIO. Yes. Why?

IRENE. I thought I knew the handwriting.

[*She leaves the letter on the table.*]

ROSARIO. It's from Don Obdulio Gomez.

IRENE. [*Full of amazement.*] Then you know . . .
Señor Gomez.

ROSARIO. Why not? Is it any disgrace?

IRENE. [*Smiling.*] No, of course not.

ROSARIO. [*Doubtfully.*] He told me he was a friend
of Señor de Córdoba's. Isn't he?

IRENE. His best. [ROSARIO *gives a sigh of relief.*]
By the way, talking of friends, [*She sits by* ROSARIO *confidentially.*] If you get this place . . .

ROSARIO. D'you think I shall?

IRENE. With that letter . . . yes, I think you're sure
to.

ROSARIO. Oh!

IRENE. Well then . . . look out for that fat gentleman
I was getting rid of when you arrived.

ROSARIO. [*Opening her eyes wide.*] Did I hear you
calling him Don Juan?

IRENE. Yes, his name is Don Juan and he's always
trying to live up to his name. He'll make love to you
without ceasing. He'll bring you sweets, he'll interrupt
your work to tell you stupid little jokes . . . But that
doesn't matter . . .

ROSARIO. [*Opening her eyes wide.*] Doesn't it?

IRENE. But what does is that he has a horrible influence

over Señor de Córdoba. It's a secret, but you'll soon find it out. The man's mad enough about women in real life . . . but when it comes to literature he loathes us all . . .

ROSARIO. Does he?

IRENE. And he plots against us.

ROSARIO. How?

IRENE. You've read "A Spring Romance"?

ROSARIO. Of course.

IRENE. You remember the girl with fair hair who sells carnations and oranges on the banks of the Arno at Florence?

ROSARIO. [As if she were speaking of her dearest friend.] Bettina?

IRENE. [As if BETTINA were her dearest friend too.] Yes, Bettina Floriana, who falls in love with the handsome English painter—

ROSARIO. And then throws herself into the river . . .

IRENE. Because she finds out that he doesn't love her . . . that's to say he does love her . . .

ROSARIO. But he's married already.

IRENE. Well . . . he was to blame for that.

ROSARIO. Who?

IRENE. Don Juan!

ROSARIO. That nasty fat man?

IRENE. [Much excited.] Yes. The Englishman wasn't married at all to begin with. But he insisted, if you please, that it was much more artistic for a rich painter to deceive a poor flower girl than that they should get married and live happily ever after.

ROSARIO. [Indignantly.] And Señor de Córdoba let himself be persuaded?

IRENE. Yes . . . and why? Because Don Juan's a critic and writes for the newspapers! A critic! [Contemptuously.] Why he can't even spell. He sent me a love-letter one day—hid it under the typewriter . . . said my pretty hands as I worked looked like Carrara marble

. . . and spelt it with one *r*. Well, and now—not content with that—he's trying to have Juanita Llerena—are you reading "The Budding Pomegranate"?

ROSARIO. In the *"Revista Gráfica"* . . . yes of course.

IRENE. The dunderhead has made up his mind that Juanita . . . you remember she's studying chemistry—such a good idea—because she means to be independent, to earn her own living and marry Mariano Ochoa—

ROSARIO. Such a nice boy!

IRENE. But he is determined that she shall fail in her examination and then marry that rich old man who has been making love to her for years.

ROSARIO. [*Horrified.*] Don Indalecio!!

IRENE. [*With fatal affirmation.*] Don Indalecio!

ROSARIO. [*On fire with indignation.*] But it must be stopped.

IRENE. I'd like to know, he says, how a girl with her head full of poetry and stuff is ever to remember a dozen chemical formulae correctly.

ROSARIO. [*Combative.*] That's the sort of silly thing they all say.

IRENE. And besides, he asks, what girl nowadays will take a poor young man when she can get an old rich one?

ROSARIO. Disgusting!

IRENE. And, to crown all, won't it be time enough for her to be in love with the young man once she's married to the old one.

ROSARIO. The man is a shameless cynic.

IRENE. So now you see. And next week the chapter in which Juanita decides has to go to press.

ROSARIO. [*Terribly anxious.*] Is she going to marry the old man?

IRENE. It's still unsettled. Yesterday Señor de Córdoba gave me two sheets to copy in which she said yes . . . but when he saw the expression of my face he told me not to go on with them.

Rosario. [*With great relief.*] Ah!

Irene. And I simply hate to go away in this uncertainty. Over poor Bettina—well, after all, death's a poetic end, one could make up one's mind to it. But this about Juanita is horrible.

Rosario. Revolting.

Irene. [*Suddenly seeing the clock.*] Oh, good heavens—half past eleven! Paco has been waiting half an hour.

Rosario. Perhaps I'd better go, too.

Irene. No, no—Señor de Córdoba will be in directly. He told me to wait till eleven, but he knew I had to go then. Would you tell him that I'll be here by nine in the morning.

[*She takes off her apron and puts it away; takes out a clothes brush and generally puts herself to rights.*]

Guillermo, I'm going now! You don't know what a nuisance a wedding is, especially for me. I've no mother. I have to do everything myself. Paco is an angel and helps all he can, but like all men, he loathes shopping. To-day we're going to buy saucepans.

[Guillermo *brings in her outdoor things.*]

Thanks, Guillermo. This young lady will wait.

Guillermo. Yes, Señorita Irene.

Irene. If Don Juan comes back before Señor de Córdoba does, don't let him in.

Guillermo. No, Señorita Irene.

Irene. If the printer sends . . . the proofs are on the table.

Guillermo. Yes, Señorita Irene.

Irene. Don't forget to change the water for the gold fish.

[Guillermo *through this has waited on* Irene *like a perfect valet, handing her hat, veil, gloves, parasol, bag, etc. She goes to the gold fish.*]

Irene. [*Putting her hand on the glass globe.*] Poor little things! I hate to leave you, too. [*To Rosario.*]

But you'll take good care of them, won't you? They
only eat flies. We'll meet tomorrow.

ROSARIO. Thank you so much.

IRENE. And I trust you about Juanita. I think you
can save her.

ROSARIO. [*Fired with excitement.*] Do you?

IRENE. Yes, I do. [*Mysteriously.*] Tomorrow I
will tell you why. Good morning, Guillermo.

[*She departs.*]

GUILLERMO. Good morning, Señorita Irene. [*He
notices that* ROSARIO *is standing by the gold fish.*] Are
you wondering what the gold fish are for, Señorita?
Señor de Córdoba always has them on his table while he
works; he says that their twisting and turning helps him
to think out the plots of his novels . . . especially the
love episodes. [*Philosophically.*] Art must find inspiration somehow . . . and he drinks nothing but water as a
rule. I bring them their flies every morning . . . a bag-
ful—the boy at the grocer's catches them for me. [*A bell
buzzes in the distance.*] The telephone! Excuse me a
minute, Señorita.

[*He goes out.* ROSARIO *left alone looks curiously
about and studies the typewriter with some apprehen-
sion. Then she returns to the gold fish and says half
unconsciously.*]

ROSARIO. They do twist and turn—especially in the
love episodes.

[*Without her hearing him* THE APPARITION *of the
night before comes in. Seen in the full light he is an
attractive man, close on 40. He puts down his hat
and stick, closes the door softly and comes over to her
and says with the most perfect suavity.*]

THE APPARITION. Do you like gold fish?

[ROSARIO *turns and sees him, and is quite as surprised and almost as alarmed as when he came through
the window.*]

ROSARIO. Oh!

The Apparition. [*Reassuredly.*] Señorita.

Rosario. [*Backing away.*] Don't come near me.

The Apparition. [*Smiling.*] Do you still take me for a ghost?

Rosario. [*Passing from fright to indignation.*] Don't add mockery to persecution, sir.

The Apparition. [*Bowing with even greater amiability.*] I do most honestly protest . . .

Rosario. Isn't it enough to compromise me?

The Apparition. I . . . !

Rosario. What on earth made you throw my slipper in at the window?

The Apparition. You threw my hat out of it.

Rosario. Because I was sorry you should be going through the streets in the rain with nothing on your head.

The Apparition. [*Bowing, very pleased.*] Thank you . . . and I could not bear to think of the little foot, companion to that merciful hand, unshod.

Rosario. I had to pretend, and tell lies . . . and even to faint.

The Apparition. Was that very difficult?

Rosario. [*Much offended.*] I am accustomed to speaking the truth.

The Apparition. I have heard that women sometimes do.

Rosario. [*With immense dignity and emphasising the name with a certain contempt.*] Señor Don Obdulio Gomez . . . [*He starts at the name, then recollects and recovers himself.*] I think that you have some very mistaken ideas about women.

The Apparition. [*Meekly.*] Possibly.

Rosario. [*Very much the superior person.*] You seem to imagine that it flatters a woman to persecute her . . .

The Apparition. [*Interrupting her, with a certain seriousness.*] Forgive me . . . you have used that word twice in two minutes. As far as I am concerned it is quite uncalled for . . .

ROSARIO.   !!!

THE APPARITION.   Even at the risk of accusing you of
. . . I am sure the most pardonable vanity . . . I protest
that I have never had the least intention of persecuting
you.

ROSARIO.   [*In a challenging tone.*]   Do you mean to
tell me that you didn't come today knowing that I should
be here?

THE APPARITION.   [*Meekly.*]   Yes, I can't deny that.

> [ROSARIO *makes a gesture equivalent to "There, you
> see!"*]

THE APPARITION.   I expected . . . if you insist upon
greater exactness, I hoped that you would be.   Are you
offended?   You have a most offended air, but somehow
I don't believe you are.   [*She starts to protest, but his
mischievous, insinuating voice checks her.*]   But what
would you have thought of me if, when I'd met you so
romantically, I had by the next day forgotten all about
it?

ROSARIO.   [*With intense scorn.*]   Romantically!

THE APPARITION.   [*Good-humouredly.*]   Now don't be
a hypocrite.

ROSARIO.   Sir!

THE APPARITION.   [*Going up to her with an agreeable
"calinerie" as if her indignation was nothing at all.*]   Can't
you imagine how easily in a tangle of hair black as a
black cat's . . .

ROSARIO.   [*Unable to resist it.*]   Such an "infernal
tangle" of hair!

THE APPARITION.   [*Continuing, as if he had not noted
the aggressive tone of the interruption.*]   . . . one's heart
may be caught, for all that one twists and turns.

ROSARIO.   [*Her eyes straying to the gold fish.*]   Twists
and turns . . .

THE APPARITION.   . . . trying to escape from the
snare.   Not that one really wants to, perhaps.

ROSARIO.   [*Who, as soon as she scents the merest whiff*

*of a declaration in the air, feels apparently that she is be-
having like an idiot.*]   Please don't talk like this . . .

THE APPARITION.   [*Going a little closer and speaking
in an insinuating tone, half tender, half mocking.*]   Not
that you really want me to either.

ROSARIO.   It is most insulting.

THE APPARITION.   You know you really are a terrible
dragon.   How is a man to guess that you'll take a few
casual compliments in the course of a friendly conversation so seriously as this?   What would happen if anyone started making love to you?

ROSARIO.   [*Desperately disillusioned at this and at heart
disappointed.*]   In the course of—

THE APPARITION.   But you don't take them seriously
. . . or did you?   Oh come now, you don't think I'm
so simple as to fall in love with a woman just from seeing
her with her hair down.   Hardly!

ROSARIO.   [*Now really on the point of throwing something at him.*]   You dare say that to me . . . you dare remind me of that!

THE APPARITION.   I, also, am accustomed to speaking
the truth.

ROSARIO.   [*With immense dignity.*]   Leave this house
immediately.

THE APPARITION.   [*With mock resignation.*]   Good
heavens!   Last night by the window . . . this morning
at least it's by the door.   But do you mean to spend your
life in ordering me out of the house?

ROSARIO.   Certainly, if you spend yours coming in when
you are not asked!

    [*He goes towards the door, then as if he could not
    bring himself to leave without a humble protest.*]
THE APPARITION.   Women are so ungrateful.

ROSARIO.   [*Falling into the trap.*]   What have I to be
grateful to you for?

THE APPARITION.   The first real thrill of your life.

Rosario. [*Contemptuously.*]   Seeing you jump through that window.   You flatter yourself.

The Apparition. [*With affected modesty.*]   Not because it was me you saw . . .

Rosario. [*Childishly.*]   I wasn't in the least thrilled.

The Apparition. [*Trapped in his turn.*]   Then, what in Heaven's name would thrill you I'd like to know.

Rosario. [*Pleased to have exasperated him, even a little.*]   When I know I'll tell you.   Perhaps it does take more than one has imagined.

The Apparition. [*Sarcastically appealing to the Heavens.*]   Save me from the innocence of young ladies who read books like "A Spring Romance!"

Rosario. [*She shows the first signs of a serious attack of nerves.*]   Oh do be quiet . . . and go away. [*He grows a little alarmed, puts down the hat which he had taken up and goes towards her.   This makes matters worse.*] Don't come near me!

   [*But he fears she is going to faint and goes nearer still.*]

Rosario.   If you touch me . . . I shall scream.

   [*More alarmed still he puts out his arms to support her, and at this she does scream.*]

Rosario.   Guillermo!   Guillermo!   Guillermo!

   [Guillermo *appears, calm and smiling.*]

Guillermo.   Did the Señorita call? [*He looks alternatively at the "Señor" and the "Señorita" and smiles.*]

The Apparition.   Bring a glass of water.

Rosario. [*Recovering her school-girl dignity.*]   And please show this gentleman out.

   [Guillermo *quite dumbfounded can only look at "this gentleman."*]

Don't you hear me?

   [Guillermo *remains speechless.*]

Then will you be good enough to do as I tell you?

The Apparition. [*Coming to the rescue.*]   He hears,

but is in rather a difficulty. For, if he shows me the door, I shall certainly kick him down the steps.

ROSARIO. [*Half comprehending.*] You'll kick him down—

THE APPARITION. [*Smiling.*] And we'd be sorry to part with each other, Guillermo and I.

ROSARIO. [*With alarm.*] So that you are—?

THE APPARITION. [*Bowing meekly.*] . . . and your favourite author.

ROSARIO. [*Amazed.*] You? [*Then with more wrath and astonishment.*] You! [*In the anguish of disillusion.*] You!

> [*She throws herself in a heap on the sofa. This time* DE CÓRDOBA *is really frightened.*]

THE APPARITION. Guillermo, get that glass of water —and put some orange flower in it.

> [GUILLERMO *goes.* DE CÓRDOBA *sits by her on the sofa and soothes her as if she were a child.*]

THE APPARITION. Forgive me. There, there! And don't cry, please. It's not worth it.

> [*She goes on crying, without answering but is growing quieter, little by little, lulled by his caressing voice.*]

THE APPARITION. Is it really such a shock? Are you so disappointed that the Apparition has materialised into . . . me? Do look at me, please, and answer. Come now, little Rosario.

ROSARIO. [*Like an angry child, but taking out her handkerchief, to dry her tears, nevertheless.*] Don't call me Rosario.

THE APPARITION. I'm sorry, it came so naturally.

> [GUILLERMO *brings in the glass of water and goes out again, discreet and silent.*]

THE APPARITION. Drink a little water . . . there's some orange flower in it.

ROSARIO. Thanks; I don't need it.

> [*She gets up.*]

THE APPARITION. Where are you going?

ROSARIO. [*Like a lost child.*] Home.

DE CÓRDOBA. [*Getting up still holding the glass of water.*] No, no, no! Not till you are quite yourself again.

> [*She has her parasol. He takes it from her. She glares at him.*]

DE CÓRDOBA. *Please.* [*She faces him aggressively.*] What will the concierge think if he sees you looking like this?

ROSARIO. Yes. . . . I suppose I'm a perfect fright.

> [*Furiously she proceeds to put her hair tidy, and has to fling off her hat to start with.* DE CÓRDOBA *still clings to the glass of water.*]

DE CÓRDOBA. You really don't need the water . . . with a little orange flower?

ROSARIO. No!

> [*He drinks it off—she sees him in the mirror.*]

ROSARIO. You do!

DE CÓRDOBA. [*Putting down the glass on the table.*] I tell you you gave me a scare.

ROSARIO. [*Sarcastically.*] Forgive me.

DE CÓRDOBA. [*Recovering his slightly mocking courtesy.*] I will exchange forgiveness with you . . . and I need yours rather more.

ROSARIO. Why did you tell me last night your name was—

> [ROSARIO *turns on him and they stand face to face.*]

DE CÓRDOBA. Obdulio? Alas, it *is!*

ROSARIO. [*Who wishes, at all costs, to go on being angry and can't because* THE APPARITION, *in spite of everything, is extraordinarily attractive.*] Then Luis Felipe de Córdoba is a fraud you practice on the public?

DE CÓRDOBA. It's called a pseudonym usually. I ask you . . . how could a man named Obdulio set out to write romantic novels? Obdulio! With Gomez to follow! What woman of really refined taste would ever open a

book with that on the cover? Think how it shocked you
last night!

ROSARIO. You could at least have told me who you
were.

DE CÓRDOBA. [*Lowering his eyes.*] I didn't dare.

ROSARIO. [*Sarcastically.*] You were too shy? You
are very shy!

DE CÓRDOBA. I was ashamed to. What! After you'd
lauded my wretched books to the skies to say, "I wrote
them?" What an anticlimax! I am only human. I
really could not bear to have you disillusioned under my
very eyes.

ROSARIO. But then . . . why did you give me the letter?

DE CÓRDOBA. Once again, I'm very human. And I
was tempted.

ROSARIO. [*Looking at him askance.*] By what?

DE CÓRDOBA. Promise you won't fly out again.

ROSARIO. Don't be afraid.

DE CÓRDOBA. Well then . . . [*While he speaks he is
stepping backwards and away from her as if he was afraid
of her.*] I gave you the letter because I wanted so much
to see you once more. And if last night—the moment we
had cut ourselves loose . . . I'd asked might I call on
you, you'd probably have said no.

[ROSARIO *looks at him cryptically, but says nothing.*]

DE CÓRDOBA. And if . . . advertisement for a secretary
or no . . . I had asked you to call on me . . .

[ROSARIO *gives an indignant exclamation.*]

DE CÓRDOBA. You see! You'd certainly have said no
—so what else could I do?

ROSARIO. [*With a certain soft bitterness.*] Having
got me here though, you don't seem to mind how disillusioned I am.

DE CÓRDOBA. I mind very much. But . . . the fact
is . . . I thought the horrid business would have been got
over . . . I wasn't at home, you know, when you came.

ROSARIO.   Did you think that I'd not have the courage to come?

DE CÓRDOBA.   I was sure that you would.   I went to the café at the corner and waited till I saw you pass. . . . Didn't you find my secretary here?

ROSARIO.   Yes.

DE CÓRDOBA.   Didn't you tell her why you came?

ROSARIO.   [Beginning to see the point.]   Yes!

DE CÓRDOBA.   Didn't you give her my letter?

ROSARIO.   Yes!

DE CÓRDOBA.   But what did she say when she saw the handwriting?

ROSARIO.   Nothing . . . the little wretch!

DE CÓRDOBA.   Nothing!   Good God!   [Quite overcome by the revelation he lifts his hands to his head.]   I have found a discreet woman.

ROSARIO.   [Tartly.]   A pity to lose her.

DE CÓRDOBA.   [Smiling.]   I must make a note of this.

ROSARIO.   Well, I am glad I have helped you discover that there was something about women you didn't know. May I go now?   Am I calm enough not to scandalise the concierge?

DE CÓRDOBA.   Quite.   And, therefore, there is now no need for your going at all.   Please [With caressing insistence] be generous . . . say you forgive me.

ROSARIO.   [With some bitterness.]   For your practical joke?

DE CÓRDOBA.   For a harmless bit of fun.   I am older than you . . . but there are times when I do badly want to behave like a child.   Do sit down.

[Now she obediently does so and he takes her hat from her.]

DE CÓRDOBA.   Thank you.   Do you think you could smile?

[She can't help smiling.]

DE CÓRDOBA.   Thank you so much.   Besides, it was a bit your fault, you know.   You did seem such a little girl

. . . with your hair down . . . and those slippers which wouldn't stay on.

[*She frowns.*]

DE CÓRDOBA.   Don't frown.   I know how you dislike being treated like a child . . . a plaything—an inferior being; that—though you may not always look it—you are a very serious-minded person, an advanced thinker.   Well, let's make a fresh start on that basis.

[*He sits at his table in a most business like way. She is on the other side of it.*]

DE CÓRDOBA.   You have most kindly come in answer to my advertisement, and we have been more or less introduced.   Or shall we leave that intruding busybody, Obdulio Gomez, and his confounded letter right out of it? Anyhow Luis Felipe de Córdoba has great pleasure in asking Señorita Rosario Castellanos this important question . . . Will you be my secretary?

[*At this moment* AMALIA *and* GUILLERMO *are heard in the hall and a moment later* AMALIA *comes in.*]

GUILLERMO.   But he's at work!

AMALIA.   Then he can stop for a minute.

[*She is a woman of thirty, dressed with aggressive elegance. Although it is morning she is wearing an exaggerated hat, and an afternoon dress. She is handsome, although one immediately feels that the square shawl and the high comb would suit her better than the hat and frock of a fashionable dressmaker. She walks in a little as if the room were her own.*]

AMALIA.   Well, what happened to you last night? [*Then seeing* ROSARIO.]   Oh sorry, sorry, sorry!   Am I in the way?

[ROSARIO *on seeing her, jumps up.* DE CÓRDOBA *who has received a rude shock, gets up also, but dominates the situation almost immediately.*]

DE CÓRDOBA.   Didn't Guillermo tell you I was at work?

AMALIA.   [*Divided between confusion and impertinence.*]   Yes, but not with . . .

De Córdoba.   [*Without making any introduction.*] My secretary.

Amalia.   [*Quite indifferent to secretaries.*]   Oh . . . is she?   I want a word with you.

De Córdoba.   [*To* Rosario.]   Excuse me.

Amalia.   Come here!

[*They go towards the window.*]

Amalia.   [*Quite good-temperedly.*]   D'you think it the right thing to keep a good woman waiting supper for you till daybreak and never even write her one of the usual lies to say you can't come?   Why didn't you?

De Córdoba.   I was caught in the storm and lost my hat.

Amalia.   Well, as long as you'd turned up with your head on—but don't lose that, will you?   I shall so miss it . . . it's a handsome head.

[*She taps it with her fan.* De Córdoba *steals a horrified glance at* Rosario *who is studying the gold fish.*]

Amalia.   Oh, how cross we are when we're interrupted in the middle of a chapter!

[Rosario *makes a movement to go.*]

De Córdoba.   [*To* Rosario.]   Please don't go yet . . . I hadn't finished.

[Rosario *snatches the hat and parasol wrathfully and takes up a position where she can look out of the balcony.*]

Amalia.   But as for me . . . please do.

De Córdoba.   If you don't mind.

Amalia.   I don't mind . . . I'll go one better and take you with me.   Ain't I forgiving?   You cut me for supper and I ask you to lunch.   Hurry up . . . the car's waiting.

De Córdoba.   I can't!

Amalia.   Why not?

De Córdoba.   You know I work all the morning.

Amalia.   Very bad for you.

De Córdoba.   [*Very seriously.*]   I must finish what I'm doing.

Amalia.   Well, finish, my lad . . . [*She drops suddenly in a chair.*]   I'll wait.

De Córdoba.   How much work shall I do with you sitting there? I'll come along in half an hour.

Amalia.   Word of honour?

De Córdoba.   [*Rather nervous.*]   On the word of— a novelist.

Amalia.   [*Getting up.*]   Ain't I an angel? With my best halo on too! 200 pesetas, straight from Paris . . . what do you think of it? I don't believe a word you say and I'm going to pretend I do and leave you to finish your chapter. Half an hour? I'll give you three quarters . . . and if I have to come back and fetch you, it's not your hat you'll lose this time but your hair . . . I'll pull it out bit by bit.

De Córdoba.   You shall do anything you like. Goodbye. [*He gets her to the door.*]

Amalia.   [*To* Rosario *who does not respond.*]   Good morning. [*In the doorway.*]   Nice manners, hasn't she? Why do you have a woman for a secretary?

De Córdoba.   Why do you have a man?

Amalia.   Because I can't spell. But at least he's my brother.

    [*She goes out.*]

De Córdoba.   [*To* Rosario.]   One moment.

    [*He follows to see her safely away.* Rosario *furiously jams on her hat and pulls on her gloves, seizes her parasol and, when he returns, is on her way to the door, too.*]

De Córdoba.   [*Feigning a scandalised surprise.*]   You're going?

Rosario.   [*Drily.*]   Good morning.

De Córdoba.   [*Putting himself between her and the door.*]   But you've given me no answer.

Rosario. [*Wishing to pass.*] My answer is good morning.

De Córdoba. [*With comic despair.*] But I've no secretary.

Rosario. Let me go . . . *please.*

De Córdoba. But who is to type my first chapter of a brand new story—such a good story, seething in my head —and I'm going to call it *"The Romantic Young Lady."*

Rosario. [*Unable to conceal her jealous anger any longer.*] That . . . "lady!"

De Córdoba. Now I ask you—!

Rosario. Then try her brother . . . since he can spell.

De Córdoba. Little Rosario . . .

Rosario. Don't dare call me by that name again!

De Córdoba. [*With humorous inflection.*] It's such a pretty name.

[*They might really be two children playing "tag" or "bull-fighting" because she is always turning about trying to get out, and he is always putting himself in her path, with slow, but mathematical movements. He does not lose his self-possession, but she grows more and more upset.*]

Rosario. Let me go!

[*Here she is on the point of getting out; but he detains her with a question.*]

De Córdoba. Do you know who that was?

Rosario. [*Pausing for a moment, which he takes advantage of to obtain a desirable position.*] The person, I presume you were on your way to last night when you unfortunately lost your hat.

De Córdoba. And when I'd so fortunately found my hat I did not go on my way. Well, who is to be blamed— or shan't we say thanked . . . for that?

Rosario. [*Sarcastic and aggressive.*] *Me?*

De Córdoba. Not precisely the indignant lady that I see now before me but—if I may disobey just once . . .

little Rosario. But you prefer to be treated as an up-to-date woman! Then cultivate some common sense.

[*She however taps the ground with her foot and looks at him with a dangerous expression.*]

De Córdoba. That's the first qualification, believe me. My quite friendly relations with Señorita Amalia Torralba . . . professionally known as La Malagueña—

Rosario. [*Furiously.*]—don't concern me in the slightest.

De Córdoba. [*Serenely.*] Then why are you so angry? Even a fairy princess, you know, straight out of a story book and worthy of any man's most loyal love, cannot expect a poor novelist, no matter how bewitching the curls are, to be faithful and true *before* he has had even a chance of rescuing his hat and losing his heart in the tangle. Last night, when I set out to supper, I didn't even know you existed. Now—I want you to be jealous . . . I love you to be jealous.

Rosario. [*Flaming with wrath.*] Jealous!!!

De Córdoba. [*Wishing to calm her.*] Señorita!

Rosario. [*Wishing to slay him.*] Did you say jealous?

De Córdoba. [*Defending himself.*] *Not that you* were—but that I *wished* you were.

Rosario. [*Stammering and trying hard to control herself.*] Why should I be?

De Córdoba. Quite so—you've no cause.

Rosario. I'm not talking of that woman!

De Córdoba. Ah, but I am—for the moment.

Rosario. And I think you're going to lunch with her.

De Córdoba. One should keep one's promise. I made it to get her to go.

Rosario. I did not want her to go.

De Córdoba. You only wish that she hadn't come.

Rosario. Not at all. I am glad that she came! And now, if you please, for the last time, before I call for help, will you let me go?

De Córdoba. But listen to reason. Pretend, just pretend, for a moment that you are a strong-minded, cynical, up-to-date woman—

ROSARIO. [*Approaching hysterics again.*] I won't. Very well then, I can't—can't if you like . . . and don't want to be.

> [*She flings out. He calls after her, "*ROSARIO! *Little* ROSARIO." *But the street door slams violently. Then he sighs and smiles, first with resignation, then with mischief, then tenderly; goes towards the balcony and remains looking out on the street, along which it may be supposed she is going away from him—all with the absorption of the true lover—until she may be thought to have turned the corner. Then he again sighs and smiles and after ringing the bell seats himself at his writing table.* GUILLERMO *enters.*]

DE CÓRDOBA. Guillermo, I want you to go yourself to Señorita Amalia's and explain why I can't lunch with her. I've been suddenly called out of town—I've gone already—and you might add that, as far as you know, I shan't be back for a fortnight.

GUILLERMO. Very good, sir.

> [*He goes.*]

DE CÓRDOBA. A new story . . . "The Romantic Young Lady."—No, no—too good to write—too good to spoil by writing it.

ACT III

We are at Doña Barbarita's *house again.* It is evening. *The window stands open.* Rosario, *her three
brothers, and* Doña Barbarita *are present.* Doña Barbarita *is seated in an armchair near the table, smiling as
always. She is looking at an illustrated weekly.* Rosario,
*buried in the sofa, wears an expression of profound ill-
humour, which she tries neither to conquer nor conceal.
The three brothers once more are all about to go out, but
this time they are all in morning clothes.* Emilio, *standing
near the table, has just finished sealing a letter to his
absent fiancée.* Pepe *is carefully smartening himself.*
Mario *is by the window, looking out.*

Pepe. [*To* Mario.] Is it going to rain again tonight?

Mario. I don't think so . . . not a cloud.

Doña Barbarita. Nor a breath of air.

Emilio. If there is a storm it'll get cooler.

Mario. There won't be.

Doña Barbarita. [*Fanning herself with her newspaper.*] One can't breathe!

Rosario. [*Aggressively.*] Dear grandmamma . . . if
there's no air at least there's lots of cigarette smoke . . .
and the boys enjoy that even if we don't. [*And she beats
the air with her handkerchief.*]

Mario. Hullo, how long have you disliked tobacco?

Rosario. Ever since I first smelt it.

Emilio. You might have mentioned it earlier.

Rosario. Who am I to interfere with your pleasures?
[Mario *throws his cigarette out of the window.*] Oh,
please don't start being unselfish—*now!*

276

[MARIO *looks at her with amazement, but says nothing.* MARÍA PEPA *comes in with a letter.*]

MARÍA PEPA. A letter.

ROSARIO. [*Rousing suddenly.*] Give it me.

MARÍA PEPA. It's for Señor Pepe.

[ROSARIO *flings back on the sofa again.*]

PEPE. [*Slyly.*] Were you expecting one?

ROSARIO. I? Who ever writes to me?

MARIO. [*Astonished.*] My dear Rosario, what's the matter with you?

ROSARIO. Nothing. What should be?

EMILIO. [*To* MARÍA.] Nothing for me?

MARÍA PEPA. Nothing.

EMILIO. Nor by the afternoon post. Sure?

MARIA PEPA. Nothing.

EMILIO. It's very odd. Two days running . . . no letter!

ROSARIO. [*Unpleasantly.*] Perhaps she has heard how well you amuse yourself without her . . . so why not without your letters as well? If I were she I'd throw you over tomorrow.

EMILIO. My dear girl!

[MARIO *goes to* ROSARIO; *takes her wrist with one hand—feels her forehead with the other.*

ROSARIO. What are you doing?

MARIO. Pulse rapid . . . head hot. I thought this bad temper wasn't natural.

ROSARIO. [*Rises and goes from settee.*] So now, I'm bad tempered, am I?

MARIO. No, my dear, with all your faults you are not . . . that is why this exhibition of it alarms me.

MARÍA PEPA. It's the heat.

ROSARIO. [*Yielding a little.*] I'm not ill nor cross . . . really I'm not . . . but bored, bored, bored!

PEPE. Then let's go out somewhere. Come along. What about the Winter Garden? La Malagueña is doing some new dances.

Rosario. Is she?

Emilio. Ever seen her?

Doña Barbarita. Here's a picture of her. [*In the paper she is reading.*]

Three Men. Graceful creature, isn't she?

Pepe. I love her. I love her!

Mario. Yes . . . she has got that spice of something . . .

[Rosario *rages but nobody notices.*]

Emilio. But they say she's getting quite spoiled. All these painters and writers that crowd round her only make her do things that don't suit her at all.

Mario. Nonsense . . . she dances better than ever she did.

Emilio. She's a Spanish gypsy, and while she's content to remain one she's perfect. But look at her dressed up as Madame Pompadour—absurd!

Pepe. Let her dress in a blanket with a rope round her waist—let some one introduce me to her—that's all. Now do you know why one wants millions of money? I love her . . . I adore her . . . I worship her! When she steps on the stage I feel funny all over. Come along, my child—hurry—we shall be late.

Rosario. [*Drily.*] Thank you—I think not.

Pepe. *Not!*

Rosario. If you're going to swoon with ecstasy when you see her I should have to carry you out.

Emilio. I'll help. What a tribute to the lady!

Rosario. Oh . . . you're going, too.

Emilio. Good! [*Then to* Mario.] Aren't you?

Mario. Worse luck . . . no. I've got work to do.

Rosario. Why don't I fall in love with a lion comique of the music halls?

Three Men. [*Highly scandalised.*] Really, Rosario!

Doña Barbarita. Well, why shouldn't she? Bull-fighters, singers, actors, dancers have always had great success with the ladies.

MARIO. With a certain sort of lady, no doubt.

EMILIO. A rather foolish, hysterical sort of lady.

ROSARIO. I see. If I lose my head over Nijinsky that's hysterics . . . but when you go stark mad about Pavlova you're just three normal, sensible, healthy young men.

PEPE. Oh, it's quite different.

MARIO. There *is* a difference.

EMILIO. Which I think I can explain.

ROSARIO. [*With a grim smile.*] Well?

EMILIO. Well—it goes rather deep . . . [*He stops, not knowing indeed how to go on.*]

PEPE. If we lose our heads . . . [*He stops too.*]

MARIO. But I don't admit that we do. We are conscious . . .

EMILIO. It's the difference of temperament.

ROSARIO. Don't get too tied up. There isn't any difference. But, for all that, you needn't be afraid . . . I shan't make that sort of a fool of myself. Still what puzzles me is how a man of real genius . . .

PEPE. [*Bowing.*] Thank you.

ROSARIO. . . . I'm not speaking of you . . . can go mad over a face that—well, look, it's nothing wonderful, and a pretty trick of kicking her heels up.

PEPE. Well—are you coming or not?

ROSARIO. [*A little more amiably.*] *Not.* Thank you all the same, but I'm tired.

EMILIO. [*Insinuatingly.*] Did you take too long a walk this morning?

MARIO. You were very late back to lunch.

ROSARIO. [*With renewed ill-humour.*] And last night I fancy you were not back at all—late or early.

PEPE. Really, my dear girl—you're impossible.

EMILIO. We'd better be off—she'll be throwing things at us. Good-night, grandmamma.

[*He bids good-night to his grandmother, kissing her hand.*]

PEPE. Shut the window tight in case the ghost comes back.

EMILIO. Yes . . . I'm afraid these nocturnal alarms upset poor Rosario rather.

PEPE. What annoys her is that the ghost didn't stay.

MARIO. Or abduct her. Remember the Rape of the Sabines. The Sabine ladies liked it.

EMILIO. Oh, some fellow came after the forks and spoons and made a mistake in the window . . .

PEPE. And got nothing but Rosario's slipper!

MARIO. And that he threw back!

PEPE. Well, it was too large for him!

[*The three young men laugh heartily.*]

ROSARIO. Oh, do go away and leave us in peace.

MARIO. I'll be home early, grandmother.

DOÑA BARBARITA. Oh yes, you're a wonderful watch dog.

MARIO. Well, you wouldn't let me tell the police.

DOÑA BARBARITA. What's the use? There's nothing missing—we've looked.

EMILIO. Very well . . . good-night.

PEPE. Till to-morrow.

[EMILIO, MARIO *and* PEPE *go out.*]

ROSARIO. [*Who has gone sulkily up to the table, and picked up the illustrated paper that contains the picture of La Malagueña almost without knowing what she is doing.* All three of them . . . cracked about that worthless creature. I detest men! [*Throws down the paper.*]

[MARÍA PEPA *has just come on again.*]

MARÍA PEPA. *That's right.*

DOÑA BARBARITA. [*Severely.*] It is very wrong.

ROSARIO. [*With the air of a little girl who is enjoying her own fit of temper.*] Why wrong?

DOÑA BARBABITA. One doesn't alter things by hating them.

ROSARIO. And is it an inevitable law of nature that some man should be able to poison one's whole life?

[*She sits down near the table, takes a lace-making pillow, which is on a chair, and begins to work furiously.*]

DoÑa Barbarita. Is "poison" quite the right word?

María Pepa. They wipe their boots on us.

DoÑa Barbarita. And you hold your tongue. You know perfectly well that I don't like to hear women abusing men. It is exceedingly vulgar.

María Pepa. They abuse us enough. You don't know half the things they say—and none of us know the other half.

DoÑa Barbarita. That makes it no better. If men and women can't share the burden of life between them—

María Pepa. With the man sneaking out from under his share whenever he can!

[*Rosario has been trying to work at the lace she has in hand. She now gives it up in despair. Throws the lace pillow violently on the table; the bobbins roll about mixing themselves up.*]

Rosario. I can't do this . . . I simply can't. The bobbins get mixed, the threads break, all the pins bend! Lace making is idiotic work!

DoÑa Barbarita. [*Severely.*] My dear, this is like a spoiled child.

Rosario. Oh . . . and who am I spoiled by I'd like to know?

DoÑa Barbarita. By everybody.

Rosario. I wish I were.

DoÑa Barbarita. By me, by your brothers, by life itself. And because in twenty-two years you have never had a pain or a sorrow you think you've the right to behave like a baby when anything annoys you.

Rosario. Nothing has annoyed me.

DoÑa Barbarita. That makes it all the worse.

Rosario. [*Sitting down on the sofa and holding her head in her two hands.*] It's only that I've got a most awful headache.

Doña Barbarita. [*Smiling.*] Keep those excuses for your husband when you're married. They don't go down with other women—you have no headache.

[Rosario *looks at her a little alarmed, a little guiltily.*]

I ask you no questions. But when a girl can't control herself she had better shut herself in her room and not make other people uncomfortable.

María Pepa. [*Firing up, as indignant and distressed as if she herself were being scolded.*] That's right . . . now scold the poor child.

Doña Barbarita. I am not scolding her. I'm trying to teach her to control her nerves—for she'll need to know how.

María Pepa. I like to hear you talk about nerves; if I had as many pennies as you've had attacks of nerves in your life—

Doña Barbarita. At the right moment. Never at the wrong.

María Pepa. The poor dear child.

Doña Barbarita. Don't make a fool of yourself . . . and what's more important—don't make one of her. There's no need for any one to pity her.

Rosario. [*Suddenly showing both good temper and good sense.*] I'm sorry grandmamma, I'm a fool . . . and unjust . . . and ill-tempered.

María Pepa. Oh, well . . . if you're going to call yourself names—!

[Rosario *smiles affectionately at* María Pepa. *Then sits down at her grandmother's feet, who strokes her hair soothingly.*]

Doña Barbarita. You'd better go to bed—you said you were tired.

Rosario. But not sleepy—[*She looks at the window.*]

Doña Barbarita. [*Following her look.*] Well, nor am I . . . so let's sit up together. [*To* María Pepa.]

You can go if you want to . . . my granddaughter will help me undress.

MARÍA PEPA. [*Touchy, as always.*] And I should like to know why I must be supposed to get sleepier than you! But, of course, if I'm in the way—

DOÑA BARBARITA. Sit down then . . . and don't talk nonsense.

[MARÍA PEPA *sits down again. There is a silence.*
MARÍA PEPA *yawns.* ROSARIO *sighs.*]

DOÑA BARBARITA. Won't you read aloud a little? That would distract our minds. What about the novel we began the other night?

MARÍA PEPA. [*With profound contempt.*] The one about the painter man who made a fool of the girl that sold oranges and she having no sense at all threw herself into the river? What's the use of a book like that? Pages and pages to tell me something that I can learn much better by sticking my own nose any day I choose into any corner of this miserable world. There was Encarna, the porter's daughter, taken in by just such another man . . . not a painter, he taught the piano, but it's the same thing. Off he went after a while and left her with something to remember him by. She didn't throw herself into the river because it's only a foot deep, but she drank half a bottle of disinfectant—and the wonder is that she and the baby were saved. Now that's true and the book was only lies!

DOÑA BARBARITA. Have you quite finished talking nonsense?

ROSARIO. No . . . I think you're right, María. Novels are lies—and then men who write them laugh in their sleeve at us—and themselves, too.

DOÑA BARBARITA. What do you know about it, my dear?

ROSARIO. [*With sentimental bitterness.*] I should if I were they . . . at such fools of women.

MARÍA PEPA. Well, if you're not going to read I'll put out the light. They keep telling us to save all we

can—and the metre ticks it up like a taxi-cab.   Moonlight's
cheap—[*She turns out the light.   There is a bright moon.*]
—and good.

> [*There is another silence.*]

ROSARIO.   Too hot to sleep!

DOÑA BARBARITA.   Shall we tell a rosary?

> [*She takes out her rosary and, at that moment in
> through the window flies a man's straw hat, falling at
> their feet.*]

ROSARIO.   Oh!—what's that?

MARÍA PEPA.   [*Picking it up.*]   A hat!

ROSARIO.   [*Very agitated, but mischievously satisfied for
all that the adventure is not over.*]   Well, now we shall
see!

DOÑA BARBARITA.   See what, my dear?

MARÍA PEPA.   But there's no wind tonight.

ROSARIO.   [*Frightened for her secret.*]   Still—oh better
shut the window, perhaps.

DOÑA BARBARITA.   Do nothing of the sort.   Let them
climb up and come in.   Then we shall know what this
is all about.

MARÍA PEPA.   Come in!   And we have our throats
cut!   There's not a man in the place.

ROSARIO.   Come in . . . no!   No!

> [*Outside is heard the noise of someone climbing.*]

DOÑA BARBARITA.   Sh!   They are climbing up.

MARÍA PEPA.   Help!   Help!

DOÑA BARBARITA.   Be quiet.

ROSARIO.   Shut the window.

DOÑA BARBARITA.   Leave the window alone.

MARÍA PEPA.   Help—thieves—police!

> [*Looking in her terror for something to protect her-
> self with she seizes the "sheep dog" paper weight from
> the table and hurls it through the window just as a
> man's head appears there.   It catches him full on the
> forehead.   An exclamation follows that sounds very
> like a curse.   Then silence.*]

Doña Barbarita. Now, what have you done?

María Pepa. [*Proudly.*] I threw it at him.

Rosario. At who?

María Pepa. How do I know . . . ? But it hit him hard!

Rosario. Oh, my God!

[*She drops on the sofa, half fainting—the two others go to her.*]

Doña Barbarita and María Pepa. What's the matter?

Rosario. Nothing . . . that is . . . [*Seizing her grandmother's hand.*] Grandmamma, there's something I'd better tell you.

Doña Barbarita. Yes, my dear, yes. [*Then, to get rid of* María Pepa.]—Now, you can shut the window. [María Pepa, *fully aware that she is being got out of the way, does so.*]

Rosario. Grandmamma . . . last night . . . .

[*At this moment there is a loud knocking on the street door.*]

María Pepa. Someone at the door?

Rosario. The door?

Doña Barbarita. Obviously.

María Pepa. It's the police.

Doña Barbarita. That's all you've done by screaming.

María Pepa. Shall I go?

Doña Barbarita. Of course—and turn on the light.

María Pepa *goes and in a moment her voice is heard distressful and alarmed; also* De Córdoba's.]

De Córdoba. There's nothing wrong, I assure you , . . nothing at all.

María Pepa. Holy Virgin!

Doña Barbarita. Whatever is the matter?

Rosario. [*Calling.*] María Pepa!

[María Pepa *appears again—her eyes starting.*]

Rosario. Who is it?

Doña Barbarita. Is it the police?

[María Pepa *shakes an agitated head.*]

Rosario. Is it—the thief?

María Pepa. [*Bursting into speech.*] I don't think he is. It's . . . a gentleman!

Doña Barbarita. Show him in.

María Pepa. Oh, he's coming in! And don't be frightened. The poor thing . . . is wounded.

Doña Barbarita and Rosario. Wounded?

[Doña Barbarita *and* Rosario *hurry impulsively to the door, much alarmed but before they can reach it,* De Córdoba *appears quite at his ease, as usual. In one hand he has a handkerchief with which he staunches the wound in his forehead; in the other the "sheep-dog."*]

De Córdoba. Nothing serious, dear ladies . . . please don't be alarmed. A slight contusion from this little "objet d'art et vertu" which came flying out of the window as I was passing by . . . and which I now have the pleasure of returning to you—intact.

Doña Barbarita. The "sheep-dog!" [*Reproachfully.*] María Pepa!

María Pepa. [*In extreme affliction.*] Don't say anything more to me. I feel dreadfully about it. It was sure to be that nasty animal, too . . . the first thing that came!

[De Córdoba *shows no sign of knowing* Rosario *who having given an exclamation, almost of triumph, on his appearance, now maintains an impersonal silence.*]

De Córdoba. I hope you will forgive my intruding on you in this rather unconventional way, but . . .

Doña Barbarita. [*Very distressed.*] But it is we must ask your forgiveness. Dear me! you are bleeding dreadfully.

De Córdoba. Well . . . if you had a bit of court plaster—

Doña Barbarita. Plaster won't do. We'll take more

care of you than that. Sit down, please. María Pepa,
bring me some hot water and some lint and a bandage.

[MARÍA PEPA *goes out.*]

DOÑA BARBARITA. Child, don't stand there like a statue
. . . come and help.

[*She says this, while through her glasses, she is ex-*
amining DE CÓRDOBA'S *wound.*]

DE CÓRDOBA. [*With a twinkle.*] I do hope I haven't
alarmed her. Is she very easily upset?

[ROSARIO *makes an angry gesture, but approaches.*]

DOÑA BARBARITA. The hair will have to be cut. I'll
get my scissors.

[*She goes out quickly. As soon as they are alone*
DE CÓRDOBA *seizes* ROSARIO'S *hand.*]

DE CÓRDOBA. Little Rosario . . . are you still angry at
me?

ROSARIO. I consider you utterly contemptible.

DE CÓRDOBA. With my head cut open!

ROSARIO. I didn't cut your head open. But what else
did you deserve?

DE CÓRDOBA. [*Half jesting and half supplicating.*]
Rosario!

[MARÍA PEPA *enters with a beautiful antique silver*
water basin and jug, and a basket with bandages, gauze,
cotton wool, etc., and puts it all on the table. DOÑA
BARBARITA *comes in after her with a pretty scissors-*
case, a little silver bowl, and a small bottle of col-
lodion. Everything is very dainty and pretty, as is
usual with old ladies who don't any more have any-
thing but details to live for, and who have always been
accustomed to an infinite number of feminine refine-
ments.]

DOÑA BARBARITA. Now—let us see! . . . Water,
María Pepa!

[MARÍA PEPA *pours some water from the silver jug*
into the basin and comes up.]

Child, you cut the hair. Your eyes are good.

[ROSARIO *seizing the scissors which her grandmother gives her, and treating* DE CÓRDOBA'S *head with no great respect, cuts off a large lock of hair.*]

DOÑA BARBARITA. [*Scandalized.*] My dear . . . not all that!

DE CÓRDOBA. [*Slyly.*] Her hand is shaking. No wonder! What a shock to you all!

ROSARIO. Not in the least, thank you . . . but your hair is so . . .

DE CÓRDOBA. Tangled . . . infernally tangled. And it never used to be.

DOÑA BARBARITA. That's all right . . . I can manage now. [*She puts* ROSARIO *aside and sponges the wound.*] Now a little collodion. [*She applies a little.*] Does it smart?

DE CÓRDOBA. [*With an eloquent gesture.*] Doesn't it!

DOÑA BARBARITA. All the better. Now the bandage, child. There—the scar will hardly show.

[ROSARIO *has watched his sufferings with great composure, ignoring completely his appealing looks.*]

MARÍA PEPA. [*With deep sympathy.*] Think if it had been on the nose!

DOÑA BARBARITA. [*Washing her hands and drying them with a towel.*] Now would you like a comb and a looking-glass?

DE CÓRDOBA. [*Rising.*] No, indeed. I've given you quite enough trouble for this evening. But if I might call on you at a more reasonable hour—

DOÑA BARBARITA. Why of course! But we must introduce ourselves. I am Señora de Castellanos.

DE CÓRDOBA. And I am Luis Felipe de Córdoba.

DOÑA BARBARITA. [*With great surprise.*] The writer?

DE CÓRDOBA. [*Bowing.*] Yes.

DOÑA BARBARITA. [*Looking at* ROSARIO.] The famous author of "A Spring Romance."

[*On hearing this* MARÍA PEPA *stares at him as if he were a prehistoric animal.*]

DE CÓRDOBA. Am I famous?

MARÍA PEPA. Wasn't it he wrote that beautiful story about the painter and the orange-girl? And you said you were dying to know him. Now I see him I don't wonder.

[ROSARIO *thus appealed to is covered with confusion. But* DE CÓRDOBA *bows his acknowledgments to* MARÍA PEPA.]

DOÑA BARBARITA. [*Scolding her good-naturedly.*] María Pepa!

MARÍA PEPA. Well, he's very handsome. I'm old enough to be able to tell him so, God knows.

DOÑA BARBARITA. Take all this away.

[MARÍA *goes off with the bowl, jug etc., smiling sweetly upon* DE CÓRDOBA *who, when she has gone puts his hand to his head and reels slightly.*]

DOÑA BARBARITA. What is the matter?

DE CÓRDOBA. Nothing—I'm a little giddy.

DOÑA BARBARITA. Of course . . . the blow and the loss of blood. Sit down—just keep quiet.

DE CÓRDOBA. Oh, Señora!

DOÑA BARBARITA. I'll get some brandy—

ROSARIO. I'll go.

DOÑA BARBARITA. No, stay where you are—I have the keys.

[*She goes out. Once more* DE CÓRDOBA *seizes* ROSARIO'S *hand.*]

DE CÓRDOBA. Let me kiss the hand that wounded me.

ROSARIO. It was María Pepa's.

DE CÓRDOBA. [*With ironical pathos.*] I'd sooner think it was yours.

ROSARIO. I mightn't have aimed so well.

[DOÑA BARBARITA *comes back with a little decanter of brandy and a glass.*]

Doña Barbarita.   Here is the brandy.

[*She gives him some.*]

De Córdoba.   So many thanks!   Excellent brandy!

Rosario.   [*Sarcastically.*]   You prefer it to water?
. . . with a little orange flower in it?

Doña Barbarita.   [*Alert, but not knowing what on earth she means.*]   My dear!

De Córdoba.   I much prefer it.   [*Smiling.*]   And, for the future, I'll keep some in my study for the benefit of nervous, highstrung visitors.

Doña Barbarita.   Ah! . . . do many ladies come to call on you?

De Córdoba.   [*Modestly.*]   Quite a number.

Rosario.   [*Aggressively.*]   Actresses . . . and people of that sort?

Doña Barbarita.   [*A little scandalised.*]   My dear child!

De Córdoba.   [*Smiling.*]   An actress will drop in sometimes.

Doña Barbarita.   Well, do you feel better?

De Córdoba.   Much better, thank you.   Well enough to take my leave.

Doña Barbarita.   No, indeed . . . I insist on your resting a little longer.

De Córdoba.   Oh, but—

Doña Barbarita.   And, my child, I think we'll all have some tea or some chocolate and cake.   María Pepa!

[María Pepa *appears so quickly that she could only have been just on the other side of the door.*]

María Pepa.   Well, which—tea or chocolate?

De Córdoba.   Oh, not for me, indeed!

Doña Barbarita.   We don't often have so distinguished a guest.   [De Córdoba *bows profoundly.*]   And it has been a most trying ten minutes for us all.   We shall be the better for a little refreshment—I shall be.

[*She seats herself in her chair.* De Córdoba *is*

standing by the writing table. Rosario *manages to
say to him sotto voce.*]

Rosario. You're caught now! Yes, it's very late . . .
but you can't get to the theatre in time to see her new
dances. Will her picture console you, perhaps?

[*She lays the illustrated paper in front of him.*]

De Córdoba. Very like her, isn't it?

[María Pepa *has now gone for the chocolate.
There is a silence.*]

Doña Barbarita. Aren't you two going to sit down?

[*They do. And now the air of a formal call super-
venes.*]

De Córdoba. What a charming house you have!

Doña Barbarita. Old fashioned, but convenient.
This is my grandson's study. He is a writer, too.

[De Córdoba *throws out a polite "Ah," although he
takes no interest in that whatever.*]

Doña Barbarita. We are all interested in literature
and great admirers of yours. So, though we're sorry you
were hurt, we can't but be pleased at the chance of meet-
ing you.

De Córdoba. Señora, the pleasure is mine.

Doña Barbarita. But you have paid rather dearly for
it.

De Córdoba. Oh, *that* wound isn't mortal. [*He gives
a glance at* Rosario.] And, even if it were—"One man
the less, one flitting ghost the more."

Doña Barbarita. Ah . . . I recognise that quotation.
I have the whole passage in the album I kept as a girl
written out in the author's hand-writing. No, I didn't
know him personally, but I imitated it from a facsimile
there was in the newspaper. It was quite the thing in
those days to keep an album and get famous men to write
and draw in it—if you could—

De Córdoba. It still is.

Doña Barbarita. What a nuisance you must find it!

DE CÓRDOBA.   A perfect plague.

DOÑA BARBARITA.   Yes, I feared you'd think so.

DE CÓRDOBA.   But for you . . . Good heavens—why nothing would give me greater pleasure.

DOÑA BARBARITA.   [*Delighted.*]   Child, get my album at once.   The last verses were written, I'm afraid, in 1865. It was still possible then to call me young and golden-haired without taxing too much poetic license.

[*The precious album is produced.*]

DOÑA BARBARITA.   Write something romantic in it. I've not lost my love for romance.

[ROSARIO *puts the album on the table.* DE CÓR-DOBA *sits down and she silently hands him a pen. They are now hidden from the old lady in her chair.*]

DE CÓRDOBA.   [*Sotto voce, pretending to write.*]   You don't look nearly so pretty when you're cross.

ROSARIO.   I'm glad to hear it.

DE CÓRDOBA.   Couldn't you relax just a little?

ROSARIO.   No.

DE CÓRDOBA.   [*Aloud to* DOÑA BARBARITA.]   Shall it be in prose or verse?

[*As soon as she stopped talking,* DOÑA BARBARITA, *overcome no doubt by fatigue, had begun to nod.   The voice rouses her, but only a little.*]

DOÑA BARBARITA.   Eh?   Prose or verse?   Prose, if you please . . . poetical prose.

[*She nods again.*]

DE CÓRDOBA.   If I were you d'you know what I'd do?

ROSARIO.   [*Quite childishly.*]   Something stupid, probably.

DE CÓRDOBA.   I'd answer yes or no to the question we left unsettled this morning . . . Will you be my—

ROSARIO.   [*Interrupting him furiously but without raising her voice.*]   I will be nothing whatever to you.   Sh! Grandmamma!

DE CÓRDOBA.   She's asleep.   [*Then with a good deal*

of feeling in the jest.] And I was just beginning to fancy that you might be so much—almost everything.

ROSARIO. [*Very inconsequently.*] Why "almost"?

DE CÓRDOBA. Do you think that any woman can completely fulfil a man's requirements . . . no matter how perfect she may be?

ROSARIO. Are you wise then to be so particular?

DE CÓRDOBA. Wise or unwise . . . I want you . . .

ROSARIO. For a secretary?

DE CÓRDOBA. I want you.

ROSARIO. [*Looking towards her grandmother in partly pretended alarm.*] Good heavens—sh!

DE CÓRDOBA. [*Coaxing.*] Won't you answer?

ROSARIO. [*Looking at him askance, but with a little smile.*] What salary do you offer?

DE CÓRDOBA. To my secretary. Four hundred pesetas a month.

ROSARIO. It's very small.

DE CÓRDOBA. Six hours a day—and quite pleasant work.

ROSARIO. But it costs so much to live in these times.

DE CÓRDOBA. If you'll marry me as well I'll add board and lodging for nothing.

ROSARIO. [*Very haughtily.*] Thank you, I want nothing for nothing.

DE CÓRDOBA. Well, I'll raise your salary. Four hundred as secretary and three hundred and fifty as wife— with board besides—separate board. You might ask me to dinner sometimes. I shall ask you regularly on Thursdays and Mondays.

ROSARIO. [*With a little quiet and rather happy laugh.*] How absurd you are!

DE CÓRDOBA. Thank God! I've heard you laugh again. Well, will you or not?

ROSARIO. [*The modern woman with a vengeance.*] What guarantee can you give?

DE CÓRDOBA. For the money?

Rosario. [*Sentimentally.*] That we shall be happy?

De Córdoba. None.

Rosario. What?

De Córdoba. Well, what guarantee can *you* give me! Happiness, believe me, is a very strange thing. You may find it by looking for it, or it may come by pure luck. And, looking back you may find you weren't happy when you thought you were . . . or unhappy, for that matter, when you thought you were either. Guarantees are no good, oh yes, I know—people always promise each other a heaven on earth. There's no such thing.

Rosario. [*Protesting.*] Isn't there?

De Córdoba. In the last chapters of novels . . .

Rosario. [*Resentfully.*] Your novels?

De Córdoba. My last chapters are shockingly bad, don't you think? I'm always too anxious to finish. But life's not a novel.

Rosario. [*Now playing at disillusion.*] Alas, no.

De Córdoba. But a far better book than the best of us ever will write . . . such a good story, full of passion and thought, full of mysteries and revelation . . . worth living, and better, far better, worth sharing. No, little Rosario, I can't promise you, or you me that love will be heaven on earth. But it will be life. No more than life —but nevertheless, I mean well—but I've lots of faults. So have you.

Rosario. [*A little peevishly.*] Of course, I know that.

De Córdoba. . . . Or you wouldn't be human. Well, shall we try the journey together? No doubt we shall stumble a bit—and one or the other may fall now and then. But that won't matter, will it? If the one that is up helps the one that is down. I don't think we'll both ever be down together . . . that would be awful luck.

Rosario. [*Whispering.*] Yes.

De Córdoba. We shall have troubles—who hasn't! but we'll laugh at them when they'll bear it. We'll work

a great deal and we'll always have faith in our work—
that's how one keeps young. We'll never think we're important people . . . so that a bit of success will always
seem a little bit more than we deserve—and we'll be as
pleased with it as a child with his new shoes . . .

ROSARIO. [*Like a vexed child.*] That would be all very
well if you loved me . . . But you don't love me.

DE CÓRDOBA. How on earth do you make that out?

ROSARIO. Because you've been mocking me all the time.
That's not like love. With the hat . . . with the letter
you wrote yourself . . . and even when you walked in
with the sheep-dog.

DE CÓRDOBA. And my head broken.

ROSARIO. [*Quite childishly.*] Yes . . . that was one
to me . . . though I didn't do it. But the only one.

DE CÓRDOBA. And how beautifully I bear it! Little
Rosario . . . I couldn't have slept tonight if I'd not
made peace with you. Would you rather I'd sent you a
letter in my best literary style. "Señorita, since first I
had the joy of looking in your face . . ." I thought you
had a little more real imagination than that!

ROSARIO. [*Falling into his trap.*] Indeed, but I have.

DE CÓRDOBA. Oh, then why is it that I . . . so old
and serious . . . must be teaching you that the way to
get the best out of even the most serious things in life is
still . . . to keep your sense of humour about them?

[*She says nothing, so now he goes very close to her.*]

DE CÓRDOBA. Well, which is it to be? Will you
take the chance of being loved all your life by a man who
gets his head broken so that he may sit here and talk a
little real common sense to you?

[ROSARIO *longs to say yes, and struggles . . . apparently just with her inability to say it. Then suddenly* DOÑA BARBARITA *looks up.*]

DOÑA BARBARITA. Oh, my dear child . . . do say yes
or no.

[*The two of them jump out of their skins as she says this. They had quite forgotten her. But* DOÑA BARBARITA *continues coolly.*]

Quite right to make difficulties up to a *point* . . . but—

ROSARIO. [*Stammering.*] Weren't you asleep?

DOÑA BARBARITA. My dear . . . do you suppose that in eighty years I've not been able to learn when to go to sleep and when to wake up again?

[*Then* ROSARIO *runs to her Grandmother like a child, kneeling, her head hidden in the old lady's lap.*]

ROSARIO. Oh, Grandmamma . . . You say it to him . . . you say it.

DOÑA BARBARITA. [*Caressing the child.*] And last night she was asking me for a latch key! She hasn't a mother, you know. I've spoiled her a little . . . and I'm so old now, perhaps I've forgotten what the things are she wants most to learn about life. I haven't been able to teach her, you see . . . even how to say yes.

[*But* DOÑA BARBARITA *gives her hand to* DE CÓRDOBA, *who kisses it and the "yes" is thus almost said. And, at the moment . . . as usual . . .* MARÍA PEPA *comes in.*]

MARÍA PEPA. Now don't you go away till she has said it . . . or she'll cry her heart out and give us a terrible time. For we all love you, all of us . . . even though it's not my place to tell you . . . that's true.

DE CÓRDOBA. Rosario!

ROSARIO. [*Getting up and facing him, smiling, still shy, but bold.*] One condition! Juanita—

DE CÓRDOBA. Who's Juanita?

ROSARIO. You haven't forgotten . . . the girl in your new book!

DE CÓRDOBA. Good heavens! . . . I had!

ROSARIO. She's not to marry Don Indalecio . . . not on any account whatever.

DE CÓRDOBA. She shall marry her Mariano on the day that you marry me.

ROSARIO. And pass her examination?

DE CÓRDOBA. With honours?

ROSARIO. [*Holding out her two hands to him.*] You promise?

DE CÓRDOBA. [*Taking her hands.*] I promise!

[*The two old people gaze at them with entire delight and* MARÍA PEPA *says, "Pretty dears"!*]